Quantitative Studies of the Renaissance Florentine Economy and Society

Quantitative Studies of the Renaissance Florentine Economy and Society

Richard T. Lindholm

ANTHEM PRESS

Anthem Press
An imprint of Wimbledon Publishing Company
www.anthempress.com

This edition first published in UK and USA 2017
by ANTHEM PRESS
75–76 Blackfriars Road, London SE1 8HA, UK
or PO Box 9779, London SW19 7ZG, UK
and
244 Madison Ave #116, New York, NY 10016, USA

British Library Cataloguing-in-Publication Data
A catalogue record for this book is available from the British Library.

Library of Congress Cataloging-in-Publication Data
A catalog record for this book has been requested.

ISBN-13: 978-1-78308-636-8 (Hbk)
ISBN-10: 1-78308-636-X (Hbk)

This title is also available as an e-book.

To my family: Richard, Marjorie and Valaya

CONTENTS

ILLUSTRATIONS

Tables

Figures

PREFACE

This book, to paraphrase Sir Isaac Newton, is built on the shoulders of giants. The Italian Renaissance was one of the most vibrant and exciting periods of world history. It is also one of the most accessible. Florence is particularly so. Its vast archival resources provide wide-ranging opportunities for quantitative research. And its extensive literature on parallel developments in arts and letters provides context. The studies in this book rest on the achievements of many previous scholars.

Beginning with Newton is apt in another way. As an inventor of the calculus he created the modern way of thinking in terms of position, change and accumulation. The studies in the present book are largely based on this framework. The calculus is the mathematics of change and accumulation, differentiation and integration, respectively. It also forms the foundation for modern statistics—from the measurement of changes that is the basis of the regression equation to the measurement of accumulation that is the basis for information theory. These studies were chosen to show how this simple framework can lead to rich answers in Renaissance Florentine history. Much of the previous work measured positions on a scale – what was the percentage of the group that did this activity and so forth? The present study, though it is not novel, looks to incorporate the concepts of rates of change and accumulation into a broad range of topics. Each chapter uses a quantitative method and a fundamental social scientific principle to examine the Renaissance Florentine economy and society. The quantitative methods tease out the underlying process.

Historians have a wide range of research methods available. The choice of which to use can have an important influence on the findings. In general, work can use either qualitative or quantitative methods or both. Much of the research on this era is qualitative. This is completely understandable, since one's introduction to the Italian Renaissance is usually through its art. Rigorous qualitative methods, such as paleography and legal history, are already research tools that fit seamlessly into these more standard historical accounts.

The studies in this book use quantitative methods to examine the economy and society of Renaissance Florence. These methods present a number of well-known advantages for historical research: they create a picture of how the society functioned with precision and comparability; their mathematical underpinnings provide rigor and transparency; and, by building on these aspects, quantitative methods can create new questions and reveal previously unsuspected connections.

The different kinds of information produced by qualitative and quantitative methods are often seen as implying a limitation in one or the other. The wide variety of mathematically rigorous approaches does not clarify this impression. However, in order to be meaningful, the qualitative and quantitative findings should be complementary, not adversarial. The quantitative methods must produce something more than a set of numbers.

The key to this complementarity is for the researcher to embrace the notion of context. It is not enough just to quantify something; each number must be understood in proper context. This context, together with the relevant social scientific body of theory, can change the interpretation of numbers significantly. Closely connecting the underlying mathematics with the underlying theory is essential. Absent this standard, the numbers often provide too dull an edge either to interest the nonexpert or even to tease out interesting results for the specialist. For example, averages alone can hide as much as they reveal. Just counting provides a number, but nothing of the qualities of that number. Too often only the average of some distribution of numbers is calculated, though its spread is just as important. The spread can highlight not just the reliability of the average but also the consistency of the behavior that underlies the creation of that average. Moreover, the methods used to calculate the average, typically the mean or median, and the spread, often some version of the range or standard deviation, are decisions that should be dictated by more than just statistical methodology. These calculations must reflect how one understands their historical context.

As part of the approach of this book technical terms taken from economics, finance, mathematics and statistics as well as Italian history are used throughout. A glossary at the end provides explanations. This book covers a range of topics that includes financial economics, industrial organization, labor economics and public finance as well as art, epidemiology, urban planning and women's history. In addition, seemingly disparate topics are often connected. One chapter links public finance and art and architectural history. Two others connect financial economics with, respectively, epidemiology and medieval law. Taken together, this work intends to demonstrate the compatibility between qualitative and quantitative methods and open avenues for future research.

ACKNOWLEDGMENTS

It is safe to say that this book would not have been written without the encouragement and help of Julius Kirshner. He was the first to encourage me to write this book, and he was always there to help me through the process. David Surdam's constant encouragement and ever-present counsel were invaluable. The early encouragement by Robert Fredona and Sophus Reinert helped get me started. This project, first as a dissertation and then as a book, received help from many more people along the way. They include Robert W. Fogel, Eric Cochrane, Donald F. Lach, David Galenson, George Racette, Richard Saller, Robert Townsend, T. W. Schultz, Ammar Siamwalla, Paul Holbo, Glenn May, Wayne Mikkelsen, Tom Calmus, Joseph Manning, Suganya Hutaserani, Machiko Ozawa, Linda Bone, Marilyn Coopersmith, Veerakarn Suebsang and Charles and Cherry Lindholm.

Many others assisted in specific aspects of this book. Preecha Anuvattanachai, Scott Kinney, Florence Bartoshesky Lathrop, Jeff Lewis and Orrin Stoddard assisted in research, and Jill Hughes and Anna Pucilowski assisted in the preparation of the book. The staff at Anthem Press, including Brian Stone, Katy Miller, Abi Pandey, Nisha Vetrivel and the anonymous referees, significantly improved the quality of this book.

Academic institutions and organizations that helped include the Harvard Business School's Baker Library, the Inter-university Consortium for Political and Social Research, the Center for Research Libraries, the Regenstein Library at the University of Chicago, the Newberry Library, the Knight Library at the University of Oregon, the University of Oregon Computing Center, the University of Chicago Department of History, the University of Chicago Department of Economics, the University of Oregon Department of Finance and the University of Oregon Department of History all provided support in one form or another.

And, of course, this book would not have been possible without the help, encouragement and forbearance of my family: Richard W. Lindholm's motivation and sage advice, Marjorie Lindholm's editorial experience and motherly support and Valaya Lindholm, who has always been there for me.

Finally, despite all this help, I am certain this book is far from perfect. All remaining mistakes are, of course, my own.

LIST OF ABBREVIATIONS

econ.: This usage is from the field of economics.
fin.: This usage is from the field of finance.
geog.: This usage is from the field of geography.
math.: This usage is from the field of mathematics.
stat.: This usage is from the field of statistics.

INTRODUCTION

This book uses quantitative methods to examine the economy and society of Renaissance Florence. An ongoing theme is the necessity to integrate these methods with the more commonly used qualitative methods such as legal history. These methods also consistently highlight the dynamism and flexibility that appear throughout the Florentine economy and society. This book is comprised of nine chapter-length studies organized into three parts based on the primary source materials, the type of analysis and the nature of the questions researched. Each study examines one aspect of Renaissance Florentine economy and society using a specific set of quantitative methods matched to the particular issues involved. The choices are meant to show the variation possible with quantitative methods. The topics were also chosen to show a breadth ranging from the Trecento to the Cinquecento, touch on the fields of economics, finance and sociology. The topics range widely, from an application of financial market data to explain plague mortality patterns to a demonstration of how a tax loophole subsidized the Renaissance Florentine architectural and artistic explosion. The quantitative approaches also vary widely and include description, estimation, hypothesis testing and measurement.

Part 1, titled "Risks and Returns," shows the value of financial markets in the study of Florentine society. The risk, in Chapter 1, is dying from the plague, and the return, in Chapter 2, is the market yield of bonds. Both chapters substantially reinterpret previously used source material.

Chapter 1, "The Costs and Benefits of Running Away: Late Medieval Florentine Plague Mortality and Behavior," uses financial market data to explore behavior during plague outbreaks in Renaissance Florence.[1] The existing research on this subject is contradictory. On the one hand, the prevailing social historical opinion relies on aggregate death data to conclude that the plague was a purely summertime phenomenon.[2] This conclusion necessarily excludes the bubonic plague as the primary cause of death.[3] On

---

1 An early version of this chapter, demonstrating the efficiency of the currency exchange market, was presented to the Department of Finance at the University of Oregon's Lundquist College of Business in May 1988.

2 David Herlihy and Christiane Klapisch-Zuber, *Les Toscans et leurs familles: Une étude du Catasto Florentine de 1427* (Paris: Fondation nationale des sciences politiques, 1978); Ann G. Carmichael, *Plague and the Poor in Renaissance Florence* (Cambridge: Cambridge University Press, 1986); Samuel K. Cohn Jr., *The Black Death Transformed: Disease and Culture in Early Renaissance Europe* (New York: Oxford University Press, 2002); Cohn, "The Black Death: End of a Paradigm," *American Historical Review* 107, no. 3 (2002): 703–38.

3 Cohn, "Black Death."

the other hand, medical historical research and some social historical research settle on the bubonic plague as the main cause of death and reject the claim that the plague was exclusively virulent in summertime.[4] The contradiction can be resolved by both conducting a closer examination of existing data and by applying a new set of data to the issue. The aggregate death data have a fundamental limitation. They count the total number of deaths within Florence, but not the total number of deaths of Florentines. Their ability to correlate with the mortality rate is critically dependent on the population's inability to flee the plague. This study shows how highly detailed financial market data and theory can be used to examine the aggregate behavior of the Florentine citizenry by linking currency exchange market microstructure data with epidemiological data. This method allows one to gauge the level of information possessed by market participants. The analysis here demonstrates that Florentines fled the plague in large numbers and provides a detailed model and description of that flight. This, first, implies that the plague was not an exclusively summertime phenomenon but also, in turn, supports medical historians' conclusions that the bubonic plague was responsible. The aggregate death data are misleading without context. This chapter's study is an example of how the meaning and interpretation of numbers gathered from historical sources can change in response to a detailed analysis of the human behavior that created those numbers. This study opens the way for future similar work that uses market microstructure data to analyze dynamic behavior.

Chapter 2, "When Economic Theory Meets Medieval Contracts: Calculating the Monte Comune Interest Rate," analyzes and corrects a widely used interest rate time series by placing the existing data into their proper context that is created by establishing a correspondence between financial theory and medieval law. Interest rates have been used by practitioners of the new institutional economics and others to evaluate confidence in a government.[5] A single data set provides most of the Florentine data used in those studies; however, it fails to meet the theoretical requirements of an interest rate.[6] This study creates an improved Quattrocento interest rate time series based on Florentine Monte Comune government loan data. The difference between the two series is substantial. The new series implies much higher and more volatile interest rates. This analysis shows that the correct application of social scientific theory requires closely

---

4   Alan S. Morrison, Julius Kirshner and Anthony Molho, "Epidemics in Renaissance Florence," *American Journal of Public Health* 75, no. 5 (1985): 528–35; S. R. Ell, "Some Evidence for the Interhuman Transmission of the Medieval Plague," *Review of Infectious Diseases* 1 (1979): 563–66; Kirsten I. Bos et al., "A Draft Genome of *Yersinia pestis* from Victims of the Black Death," *Nature* 478, no. 7370 (2011): 506–10. Chapter 1 has additional material on this point.

5   Douglass C. North and Barry R. Weingast, "Constitutions and Commitment: The Evolution of Institutional Governing Public Choice in Seventeenth-Century England," *Journal of Economic History* 49, no. 4 (1989): 803–32; Stephan R. Epstein, *Freedom and Growth: The Rise of States and Markets in Europe, 1300–1750* (London: Routledge, 2000); David Stasavage, *States of Credit: Size, Power, and the Development of European Politics* (Princeton, NJ: Princeton University Press, 2011).

6   Luciano Pezzolo, "Italian Monti: The Origins of Bonds and Government Debt," paper presented at the *Yale School of Management Conference on the History of Financial Innovation*, March, New Haven, CT, 2003. Chapter 2 has additional material on this point.

integrating the sources and historical context from the very beginning of the analysis. The definition of terms is critical to calculating meaningful historical statistics. The new time series should lead to a better understanding of the impact of the Florentine state on society. This method is widely applicable. Future work on the Florentine data can create a more definitive series. Work on other data sets can provide better answers to the questions social scientists have been asking.

Part 2, "Society," presents a set of studies that employ an approach to Florentine history and is based primarily on data from the *catasti* net wealth taxes. Chapters 3 and 6 examine the underlying characteristics of household wealth, and Chapters 4 and 5 examine the implications of economic changes for Renaissance culture and society.

Chapter 3 is titled "The Chances of Getting Rich in Renaissance Florence: The Wool Industry Occupational Wealth Hierarchy."[7] It assesses Florentine economic and social inequality using a new statistical approach. The study described in this chapter answers a call for a more detailed profile of the late medieval and early modern workforce and the economic performance of the individual guilds.[8] Much has been written about the distribution of wealth or social mobility in Renaissance Florence.[9] Guild regulations are thought to have provided greater certainty for their members, which helped guarantee income and thereby reduce wealth mobility. This study examines the taxable wealth in Florentine society conditional on the occupation using data from the 1427 *catasto*. It concludes that Florence was a two-tier society based on a clear occupational division between the *arte maggiore* and the *popolo minuto*. However, occupation was not the sole determinant of household wealth, and there was significant intraoccupational volatility. This suggests that the guild structure had an important, but not absolute, role in determining household wealth. The results should inform the long-running debate on Florentine inequality.

Chapter 4 is titled "Palaces and Workers: Neighborhood Residential Segregation in Renaissance Florence."[10] Whereas most of the other chapters are concerned with dynamism or flexibility in either space or time or both, this chapter is most concerned with space. It examines whether Florentine neighborhoods were segregated, whether this segregation increased over time and whether the palace building boom created a social division between the city's core and its periphery. These are the basic questions of Renaissance Florentine urban ecology,[11] and the answers have important implications

---

7 Previous versions of this chapter were presented to the Economic History Workshop at the University of Chicago and are part of Richard T. Lindholm, "Studies of the Renaissance Florentine Woolen Industry," PhD diss., University of Chicago, 1993.

8 Julius Kirshner, "Review of *Industry and Decline in Seventeenth-Century Venice*, by Richard Tilden Rapp," *Journal of Modern History* 49, no. 2 (1977): 321.

9 Herlihy and Klapisch-Zuber, *Les Toscans*; Richard A. Goldthwaite, "The Economy of Renaissance Italy: The Preconditions for Luxury Consumption," *I Tatti Studies* 2 (1987): 27 and 29–30. See chapter 3 for additional sources.

10 Previous versions of this chapter were presented to the University of Oregon History Department and are part of Lindholm, "Studies."

11 Cohn, *Laboring Classes*, 43–63 and 121–27.

for how one views the Renaissance. The study finds that Florentine neighborhoods were integrated and heterogeneous throughout the city during the Trecento and Quattrocento.

Chapter 5, "The 'State' Makes a Work of Art: The Impact of the *Catasto* Homeowner Tax Loophole on the Quattrocento Florentine Palazzo Building Boom," posits a new link among the histories of Florentine art, economics, politics and society. It finds that a tax loophole largely caused the Quattrocento Florentine architectural and artistic boom. The relationship between politics and art in the Italian Renaissance has been a major line of inquiry at least since Jacob Burckhardt addressed the issue in the nineteenth century.[12] The 1427 catasto is usually seen as a new revenue collection tool designed to balance the city's budget after years of overspending. It was designed to be progressive, and it exempted, and effectively subsidized, a household's home and furnishings. The homeownership tax loophole in the 1427 catasto appears to have driven both the *palazzo* building boom and an increase in homeownership among the general population.

Chapters 4 and 5 in combination provide insight into the long-running debate about the impact of Renaissance Florentine art and architecture, and its associated version of urban planning, on the living conditions of the poor. Burckhardt writes that there was a thorough reconceptualization of the state during the Renaissance, which led to greater equality.[13] Critics contend that the palace-building boom (Chapter 5) allegedly increased the distance between rich and poor (Chapter 4). The results of these two chapters support Burckhardt's original view. Chapter 5 shows that palace construction was driven by an effort by Florentine authorities to make their taxation system fairer, and Chapter 4 demonstrates that the social distance between rich and poor did not increase during the palace-building boom.

Chapter 6 is titled "Not Getting Ahead in Life: The Lack of Life-Cycle Wealth Accumulation in Quattrocento Tuscany."[14] A pattern of increasing earnings, income and wealth during the life cycle has been well documented for both modern societies[15] and historical societies going back to the nineteenth century.[16] A lack of data has largely precluded research on previous periods. The study in this chapter tests whether the modern pattern holds for Quattrocento Tuscany and points to the surprising finding that there

---

12 Jacob Burckhardt, *The Civilization of the Renaissance in Italy*, 2 vols. (New York: Harper, 1973); Julius Kirshner, "Introduction: The State Is 'Back in,'" *Journal of Modern History, Supplement: The Origins of the State in Italy, 1300–1600*, 67 (1995): S1–10.

13 Burckhardt, *Civilization of the Renaissance*; Kirshner, "Introduction."

14 An earlier version of this chapter was presented to the Oregon State University Department of Agricultural Economics Workshop in 1997.

15 Franco Modigliani and A. K. Ando, "The 'Life-Cycle' Hypothesis of Saving: Aggregate Implications and Tests," *American Economic Review* 53, no. 1 (1963): 55–84; Edward N. Wolff, "The Accumulation of Household Wealth over the Life-Cycle: A Microdata Analysis," *Review of Income and Wealth* 27, no. 1 (1981): 75–79. See chapter 6 for other material on this point.

16 David W. Galenson and Clayne L. Pope, "Precedence and Wealth: Evidence from Nineteenth-Century Utah," in *Strategic Factors in Nineteenth-Century American Economic History: A Volume to Honor Robert W. Fogel*, ed. Claudia Goldin and Hugh Rockoff (Chicago: University of Chicago Press, 1993), 225–42; J. R. Kearl, Clayne L. Pope and Larry T. Wimmer, "Household Wealth in a Settlement Community," *Journal of Economic History* 40, no. 3 (1980): 477–96. See chapter 6 for other material on this point.

was no demonstrable life-cycle wealth accumulation in Tuscany during the time examined. The data are then thoroughly validated, with highly robust results. This study then suggests three possible explanations for the surprising finding: (1) missing assets, (2) widespread societal poverty and (3) the behavior of Florentines. None of these explanations alone is completely satisfactory. Clearly this subject needs further investigation. Perhaps a new source will resolve the issue or some broader explanation will be found.

Part 3, "Work," takes a very different methodological approach from the previous two parts, offering three studies that focus on the Florentine wool-manufacturing industry. The industry was one of the two great pillars, along with banking, of the Florentine economy. In 1427 the industry employed 27 percent of household heads with an identifiable occupation, while less than 0.5 percent worked in banking or money changing.[17] As opposed to the macroanalyses in parts 1 and 2, the studies in part 3 turn to a more microhistorical approach primarily based on the Medici-Tornaquinci account books and the different kind of data they contain. The nature of the wool industry's production process permits an unusually deep examination. Usually the process is seen as a black box, where the internal operations are hidden from outside view. Here, however, the prices and quantities are clearly visible at each step in the production process. Thus, one could call this a transparent box. Additionally, the data in these studies are dynamic and therefore provide a sense of the interaction and timing of behavior. Part 3 of this book consistently emphasizes the flow of time in society, whether it is the use of time or the risk that arises from this flow.

Chapter 7 is titled "Just Doing Business: Testing Competition in the Renaissance Florentine Wool Industry."[18] Economic historians have debated the competitiveness of Florentine markets for more than a century. This chapter summarizes previous research and adds a set of new tests. Throughout, the economic theory and statistical methods used are closely matched to the historical data. First, the study presents and reanalyzes previous research. Prior evidence arrived at contradictory conclusions. This reanalysis shows that, when commonly used economic standards of monopoly power are applied, the industry clearly functioned competitively. Next, applicable static measures of monopoly power are applied and bolster this conclusion. Finally, a multivariate regression model is used to test the applicability of neoclassical production theory, which is not rejected. The evidence of a competitive wool industry, in turn, provides evidence of how Renaissance Florentine society functioned.

Chapter 8, "Time for It All: Working Women in the Renaissance Florentine Wool Industry,"[19] answers a call for a more detailed profile of the late medieval and early

---

17   David Herlihy and Christiane Klapisch-Zuber, *Census and Property Survey of Florentine Domains and the City of Verona in Fifteenth-Century Italy* [machine-readable data file]. Cambridge, MA: David Herlihy, Harvard University, Department of History and Paris, France: Christiane Klapisch-Zuber, Ecole Pratique des Hautes Etudes [producers], 1977. Madison: University of Wisconsin, Data and Program Library Service [distributor], 1981.

18   Previous versions of this chapter were presented to the University of Chicago History Department and are included in Lindholm, "Studies."

19   Previous versions of this chapter are part of Lindholm, "Studies," and were presented to the Women in History Workshop of the Department of History and the Economic History Workshop of the Department of Economics, both at the University of Chicago.

modern workforce.[20] Previous studies have found that working women in Renaissance Italy faced more limited opportunities than those for women in other areas of Europe.[21] Such an interpretation creates a paradox because Florence was wealthier than other places in Europe, and the Renaissance would seem to have opened rather than closed doors for women. This has become a challenge to the notion of modernism during the Renaissance.[22]

This study explores whether this conclusion could be because of the type of source used, which can largely determine the results of a historical investigation. Studies to date have largely been based on surveys and legal records. The study presented in this chapter uses as its primary source account book entries of men and women weavers for one wool-manufacturing firm in mid-Cinquecento Florence. Though work opportunities were limited for women, this study takes advantage of the one occupation where both men and women worked. Doing so permits the dynamic analysis that is critical to understanding the behavior of working women and provides a new perspective: it finds that working women used time differently and that women adjusted their use of time to respond to the market system. Doing so connects Florentine family law[23] and household production theory. This result reconciles a wide range of seemingly disparate observations. These include that women worked in different occupations, tended to have smaller operations, engaged in different types of contracts, did part-time work, worked less frequently and took less time to complete the production of cloths. Although the results are based on a small sample size, the value of dynamic data in the study of working women is apparent. The chapter thereby opens the door to future research.

Chapter 9 returns to two themes that were introduced in the first part of the book. These are the notion of risk that was examined in the first chapter and the new institutional economics from the second chapter. These are combined to see how the institutions of the Arte della Lana guild and the putting-out system interacted as part of the Florentine wool industry production system. Therefore, in contrast to Chapter 1, the effects of risk rather than its causes are the subject. This chapter then uses the contract-based approach of Chapter 2 to develop a theoretical structure. Chapter 9 is titled "Why Were Renaissance Florentine Wool Industry Companies So Small?" and shows that risk management was a critical factor in the Florentine manufacturing process.[24] The chapter

---

20 Kirshner, "Industry and Decline," 321.

21 Joan Kelly-Gadol, "Did Women Have a Renaissance?," in *Becoming Visible: Women in European History*, ed. Renate Bridenthal and Claudia Koonz (Boston: Houghton Mifflin, 1977), 137–64; Samuel K. Cohn Jr., *Women in the Streets: Essays on Sex and Power in Renaissance Italy* (Baltimore: Johns Hopkins University Press, 1996); P. J. P. Goldberg, *Women, Work, and Life Cycle in a Medieval Economy: Women in York and Yorkshire, ca. 1300–1520* (Oxford: Clarendon Press, 1992), 325.

22 Kelly-Gadol, "Did Women Have a Renaissance?"

23 Regarding this literature on family law, see, for instance, Julius Kirshner, *Marriage, Dowry, and Citizenship in Late Medieval and Renaissance Italy* (Toronto: University of Toronto Press, 2015); Thomas Kuehn, *Law, Family, and Women: Toward a Legal Anthropology of Renaissance Italy* (Chicago: University of Chicago Press, 1991); Thomas Kuehn, *Heirs, Kin, and Creditors in Renaissance Florence* (Cambridge, UK: Cambridge University Press, 2008).

24 An early version of this chapter was first presented to the Finance Department of the University of Oregon's Lundquist College of Business in September 1997.

answers a call for a more detailed analysis of guilds and the workforce.[25] The study presented here is motivated by a simple but puzzling observation: for centuries, the industry was very large and profitable though allegedly inefficient. The wool industry produced cloth using a putting-out system organized by the Arte della Lana guild. Modern economists generally view both this production system and guilds as inefficient anachronisms that damaged the economy. In addition, the extremely small companies increased the transaction costs. However, the debate about guilds has recently been rekindled.[26] The key question is why guilds were created in the first place and then lasted for centuries. Current economic theory argues that transaction costs limit the extent of a firm, but that approach does not explain many of the behaviors observed among wool-manufacturing companies in Renaissance Italy.[27] The Arte and the putting-out system reduced transaction costs for the company, yet its existence is insufficient to explain other behaviors.

Previous work has either emphasized the guild and its regulations[28] or the firm's manufacturing technology and organization of production.[29] This study approaches the problem from a different direction: the contractual framework within which the firm

---

25 Kirshner, "Industry and Decline," 321.

26 This debate is succinctly stated by the main protagonists in: Stephan R. Epstein, "Property Rights to Technical Knowledge in Pre-Modern Europe, 1300–1800," *American Economic Review* 94, no. 2 (2004): 382–87; Epstein and Maarten Prak, eds., Introduction to *Guilds, Innovation, and the European Economy, 1400–1800* (Cambridge: Cambridge University Press, 2008), 4–24; Sheilagh Ogilvie, *Institutions and European Trade: Merchant Guilds, 1000–1800* (Cambridge: Cambridge University Press, 2011); Ogilvie, "The Economics of the Guild," *Journal of Economic Perspectives* 28, no. 4 (2014): 170.

27 R. H. Coase, "The Nature of the Firm," in *The Firm, the Market, and the Law* (Chicago: University of Chicago Press, 1988), 33–56; Oliver E. Williamson, *Markets and Hierarchies: Analysis and Antitrust Implications* (New York: Free Press, 1975); Oliver E. Williamson, *The Economic Institutions of Capitalism* (New York: Free Press, 1985).

28 Alfred Dören, *Studien aus der Florentiner Wirtschaftgeschichte*, vol. 1: *Die Florentiner Wollentuchsindustrie vom Vierzehnten bis zum Sechzehnten Jahrhundert* (Stuttgart: J. G. Cotta'sche Buchhandlung Nachfolger, 1901); Francesco Ammannati, "Craft Guild Legislation and Woollen Production: The Florentine Arte della Lana in the Fifteenth and Sixteenth Centuries," in *Innovation and Creativity in Late Medieval and Early Modern European Cities*, ed. Karol Davids and Bert De Munck (Farnham: Ashgate 2014), 55–79.

29 Raymond de Roover, "A Florentine Firm of Cloth Manufacturers," in *Business, Banking, and Economic Thought in Late Medieval and Early Modern Europe*, ed. Julius Kirshner (1938; Chicago: University of Chicago Press, 1974), 85–118; Federigo Melis, *Aspetti della vita economica medievale: Studi nell'Archivio Datini di Prato* (Siena, Italy: Monte dei Paschi di Siena, 1962), 455–634; Richard A. Goldthwaite, "The Florentine Wool Industry in the Late Sixteenth Century: A Case Study," *Journal of European Economic History* 32, no. 3 (2003): 527–54; Francesco Ammannati, "L'Arte della Lana a Firenze nel Cinquecento: Crisi del settore e risposte degli operatori," *Storia economica: Rivista quadrimestrale* 11, no. 1 (2008): 5–39; Ammannati, "Francesco di Marco Datini's Wool Workshops," in *Francesco di Marco Datini: The Man the Merchant*, ed. Giampero Nigro (Florence: Firenze University Press, 2010). 489–514; Ammannati, "Production et productivité du travail dans les ateliers laniers florentins du XVIe siècle," in *Les temps du travail: Normes, pratiques, évolutions (XIVe–XIXe siècle)*, ed. Corine Maitte and Didier Terrier (Rennes: Presses Universitaires de Rennes 2014), 225–49.

operated. This opens up a new perspective. Market-wide risk determined the structure of the wool industry, and companies and workers both faced high risk. By minimizing the extent of each component of the production process, the associated risk was minimized. The guild and the putting-out system made possible the smaller company, which reduced the overall risk the companies and workers faced. This study emphasizes the importance of the form of the contract. It was critically important. The size of the companies offers an important clue about their environment. The chapter then uses this theoretical framework to examine the decline of the wool industry during the Seicento. The wool industry, up until then, had been extraordinarily resilient. The English joint-stock companies, however, posed a new kind of competition. They faced problems similar to those of the wool industry companies but with a key difference: their contractual form allowed, even encouraged, them to become much larger. Size became an advantage in the international wool marketplace. As the wool industry declined, the silk industry rose and was based on the same basic pattern as the wool industry.

A concluding chapter ties together broader themes from the nine chapters. The book finishes with a complete glossary of all foreign language and technical terms. The aim of the conclusion is to demonstrate how the disparate chapter topics are representative of common themes. In particular, one goal is to show how common themes underlie the mathematical approaches in the chapters. A glossary is included because, as this book straddles the boundary between economics and history, it is impossible to avoid terms unfamiliar to either side. Precise technical terms are used consistently. Terms ranging from Italian historiography to medieval law to mathematical economics are used. These terms are placed in their proper context, be it economic, financial, geographic, historical or statistical. In this regard, the use of the terms *Trecento, Quattrocento* and *Cinquecento* requires some explanation. Social scientists rarely find periods that interesting or useful. Generally, time is taken to be just another variable. The approach used here maintains that these time periods are valuable Florentine social historical divisions. The usage here is intended as a reminder that this is history, not econometrics. For example, the Black Death and its aftermath make distinguishing between the Trecento and the Quattrocento critical for many theories. The analysis in Chapter 4 makes use of this. The Quattrocento period, in turn, is qualitatively distinct from the Cinquecento, and this is brought out in Chapter 5. This particular usage is one way to demonstrate the compatibility between qualitative and quantitative methods.

Part I

RISKS AND RETURNS

.

Chapter One

THE COSTS AND BENEFITS OF RUNNING AWAY: LATE MEDIEVAL FLORENTINE PLAGUE MORTALITY AND BEHAVIOR

Introduction

The Black Death that ravaged Europe and arrived in Florence, Italy, in 1348 is one of the best-known events in the history of medieval Europe. It is widely considered a transformational event that produced fundamental changes in both the economy and the society.[1] However, there is more to the story. That plague was only the first in a long series that periodically revisited Europe for centuries. Plague outbreaks became a fundamental characteristic of the society. In the case of Florence during the following century alone the plague returned 11 times: 4 times later in the *Trecento* and 7 times during the first half of the *Quattrocento*.[2] It returned as late as the seventeenth century.[3] Despite its importance, critical aspects of the disease are unknown and have been debated for decades among medical and social historians.[4] The plague's societal impact is also unclear. For example,

---

1 David Herlihy, *The Black Death and the Transformation of the West*, ed. Samuel K. Cohn Jr. (Cambridge, MA: Harvard University Press, 1997).

2 David Herlihy and Christiane Klapisch-Zuber, *Les Toscans et leurs familles: Une étude du Catasto Florentine de 1427* (Paris: Fondation nationale des sciences politiques, 1978), 191.

3 Ann G. Carmichael, *Plague and the Poor in Renaissance Florence* (Cambridge: Cambridge University Press, 1986), 63–64.

4 This study frequently refers to plagues in the generic sense and not as a reference to any specific plague. Herlihy and Klapisch-Zuber, *Les Toscans*; Alan S. Morrison, Julius Kirshner, and Anthony Molho, "Epidemics in Renaissance Florence," *American Journal of Public Health* 75, no. 5 (1985): 528–35; Carmichael, *Plague and the Poor*; Samuel K. Cohn Jr., *The Black Death Transformed: Disease and Culture in Early Renaissance Europe* (New York: Oxford University Press, 2002); Samuel K. Cohn Jr., "The Black Death: End of a Paradigm," *American Historical Review* 107, no. 3 (2002): 703–38. Relevant work by medical historians includes S. R. Ell, "Some Evidence for the Interhuman Transmission of the Medieval Plague," *Review of Infectious Diseases* 1 (1979): 563–66; Edward A. Eckert, "Seasonality of Plague in Early Modern Europe: Swiss Epidemic of 1628–1630," *Clinical Infectious Diseases* 2, no. 6 (1980): 952–59; M. Achtman et al., "Microevolution and History of the Plague Bacillus, *Yersinia pestis*," *Proceedings of the National Academy of Sciences* 101, no. 51 (2004): 17837–42; M. Drancourt, G. Aboudharam, M. Signoli, O. Dutour and D. Raoult, "Detection of 400-Year-Old *Yersinia pestis* DNA in Human Dental Pulp: An Approach to the Diagnosis of Ancient Septicemia," *Proceedings of the National Academy of Sciences* 95 (October 1998): 12637–40; Kirsten I. Bos et al., "A Draft Genome of *Yersinia pestis* from Victims of the Black Death," *Nature* 478, no. 7370 (2011): 506–10; Michael Knapp, "The Next Generation of Genetic Investigations into the Black Death," *Proceedings of the*

its impact on certain segments of society, such as the poor or children, and whether it led to greater social controls are all open questions.[5]

These repeated outbreaks allow a researcher to assemble multiple observations of the same phenomenon and to better test his or her theories. The plague's seasonal pattern provides clues to its nature because changing temperature and humidity affect the disease's transmission vectors. Although historians using the available aggregate death data have found a summertime peak in deaths,[6] the implications of these findings would exclude bubonic plague, *Yersinia pestis*,[7] the most likely cause identified by medical researchers.[8] To date, researchers have concentrated on medical data or demographic records in trying to understand the disease. The study presented in this chapter uses a very different source of quantitative behavioral data—the Florentine currency exchange market—to analyze the seasonality of plague virulence. Although the market is an indirect source, it provides daily updates of actual behavior during a given plague and in the periods before and after that plague. The market data imply that flight from the plague was significant and that people sometimes stayed away from the city of Florence for long periods of time. This implies that the plague was not exclusively a summertime phenomenon and explains both the evolution in total deaths across plagues and the differences in the timing of deaths between major and minor plagues. The rest of this chapter works through the analysis. First, it outlines a model of behavior during a plague based on how people use information. It then reviews a range of evidence that uses this model to show the Florentines fled the plague. The White Death of 1400 provides a starting point for this analysis. The long market closure from July through September and the timing of plague deaths imply that many people fled Florence from the plague. Next, the market indicators for the remainder of 1400 indicate that many people continued to stay away for months afterward. Finally, the chapter presents a link between currency price shocks

National Academy of Sciences 108, no. 38 (2011): 15669–70; Boris V. Schmid et al., "Climate-Driven Introduction of the Black Death and Successive Plague Reintroductions into Europe." *Proceedings of the National Academy of Sciences* 112, no. 10 (2015): 3020–3025.

5   On the impact on the poor, see Cohn, *Black Death Transformed*, 205; Carmichael, *Plague and the Poor*, 67–78. For a discussion of the limitations of the sources on this and related issues, see Julius Kirshner, "Review of *Plague and the Poor in Renaissance Florence* by Ann G. Carmichael," *Journal of Modern History* 59, no. 4 (1987): 870–73. On the impact on children, see Carmichael, *Plague and the Poor*, 90–94; Morrison, Kirshner and Molho, "Epidemics," 533; Cohn, *Black Death Transformed*, 212–19. On social controls, see Carmichael, *Plague and the Poor*, 108–26; Carlo M. Cipolla, *Faith, Reason, and the Plague in Seventeenth-Century Tuscany* (New York: Norton, 1979).

6   Herlihy and Klapisch-Zuber, *Les Toscans*, see esp. 192, 193 and 465; David Herlihy and Christiane Klapisch-Zuber, *The Tuscans and Their Families* (New Haven, CT: Yale University Press, 1985), 191; Carmichael, *Plague and the Poor*, 54–57 and 62–67; Cohn, *Black Death Transformed*, 140–87.

7   Carmichael, *Plague and the Poor*, 55–69; Cohn, *Black Death Transformed*, 187, chap. 7; Cohn, "Black Death," 703–38.

8   Carmichael, *Plague and the Poor*; Achtman et al., "Microevolution"; Drancourt et al., "Dental Pulp"; Bos et al., "Draft Genome."

and the plague during the first third of the Quattrocento. Three appendices to this chapter present supplemental mathematical and statistical materials.

Florentine Plague Seasonality Research

Late medieval Florence is an important venue for plague research, which typically draws from a range of sources. Qualitative sources include chronicles that provide descriptions of the plague and general indications of behavior but little about the numbers of deaths or the mortality rates.[9] Quantitative sources provide detailed data about the plague's seasonality. Although access to population-wide mortality rates would be ideal, these data are not available for the late medieval period. In their absence either the mortality rate aspect or the characteristic of the plague's being population wide has been sacrificed.

Studies of the plague have usually used the aggregate death totals from the death registers of specific cities. These cannot compute a mortality rate, however, because the population base is unknown. The Florentine registers, the *Libri dei morti*, provide running lists of burials and causes of deaths between the 1390s and 1450s in Florence.[10] David Herlihy and Christiane Klapisch-Zuber, Ann Carmichael and Samuel Cohn base their work primarily on these documents;[11] Cohn uses notarial records to supplement the *Libri dei morti*.[12] All conclude that there was a late summer peak in plague deaths during each July, with generally high numbers in August and September and few deaths later in the year. These strong summertime plague seasonality observations present a puzzle. They clearly contradict medical research,[13] because they would exclude *Yersinia pestis*.[14] The summertime seasonality hypothesis will be closely examined in the remainder of this chapter.

Not all plagues were alike. The number of deaths varied substantially between outbreaks. Based on the estimated number of deaths registered, among the early Quattrocento plague epidemics, the 1400 plague, the *Moria dei Bianchi*, or White Death, was the most severe, and the 1417 plague was the second most severe.[15] The *Libri dei morti* data also reveal three additional patterns. First, the plague's virulence appears to have declined over time. This was noted by contemporaries,[16] and modern research confirms it.[17] Second, the seasonal peak of deaths due to the plague became progressively later

---

9 Ell, "Interhuman Transmission," 563–66.

10 Carmichael, *Plague and the Poor*, 63.

11 Herlihy and Klapisch-Zuber, *Les Toscans*, see esp. 192, 193 and 465; Herlihy and Klapisch-Zuber, *Tuscans*, 191; Carmichael, *Plague and the Poor*, 54–57 and 62–67; Cohn, *Black Death Transformed*, 140–87.

12 Cohn, *Black Death Transformed*, 149.

13 Carmichael, *Plague and the Poor*; Achtman et al., "Microevolution"; Drancourt et al., "Dental Pulp"; Bos et al., "Draft Genome."

14 Carmichael, *Plague and the Poor*, 55–69; Cohn, *Black Death Transformed*, 187, chap. 7; Cohn, "Black Death," 703–38.

15 Carmichael, *Plague and the Poor*, 63.

16 Ibid., 88; Cohn, *Black Death Transformed*, 239.

17 Carmichael, *Plague and the Poor*, 63 and 89; Morrison, Kirshner and Molho, "Epidemics," 530.

in the calendar year.[18] Third, deaths from less deadly, minor plagues began later in the calendar year than deaths from more deadly, major plagues.[19] Taken together, these three observations present a second puzzle. The declining virulence can be explained by a growing immunity. However, neither the increasingly later seasonal peak in total deaths nor the timing of deaths by plague severity is likely to be related to acquired immunity.

Alan Morrison, Julius Kirshner and Anthony Molho exploit a different source to examine mortality rates and causes of death among young women: the records of the *Monte delle doti*, a fund to provide dowries for young women that was created in 1425.[20] Morrison and his colleagues find both a less prominent summertime peak in the years 1425 through 1600 and that autumn was the second deadliest season.[21] Unlike the *Libri dei morti* work, this does not contradict the work of medical researchers.

Figure 1.1 compares the two plague mortality patterns. The summertime seasonality hypothesis is supported by the aggregate death data from the *Libri dei morti* and rejected by the *Monte delle doti* mortality rate data. These conflicting results make it clear that more data are needed to resolve the issue. Cohn suggests more work with the *Libri dei morti* data.[22]

The characteristics of the two types of sources help explain the different research results. On the one hand, the *Monte delle doti* covered only a subset of the population, but did so more accurately. Cohn questions whether the limited population covered by the *Monte delle doti* evidence can be generalized.[23] However, there was a significant financial incentive to report deaths to the *Monte delle doti*, but not in the case of the *Libri dei morti*. Such an incentive would have significantly improved reliability.[24] On the other hand, the value of the aggregate death data from the *Libri dei morti* is critically dependent on how many people fled the plague. The data include only burials at a single fixed location. Flight would have reduced, but not eliminated, recorded plague deaths. Some people who fled the plague and died outside the city would not be counted. This is an important limitation, as it is difficult to imagine many people carrying a body of a plague victim back to Florence in order for the victim to be buried and included in plague death records. (Appendix 1A provides more detail on this point.)

Carmichael recognizes this limitation. She acknowledges that there is ample evidence that some Florentines fled,[25] but argues that only a small number of Florentines were

---

18 Carmichael, *Plague and the Poor*, 59.

19 Ibid., 67.

20 Morrison, Kirshner and Molho, "Epidemics," 528–35. For information about the *Monte delle doti*, see Julius Kirshner and Anthony Molho, "The Dowry Fund and the Marriage Market in Early *Quattrocento* Florence, *Journal of Modern History* 50 (1978): 403–38; Anthony Molho, *Marriage Alliance in Late Medieval Florence* (Cambridge, MA: Harvard University Press, 1994).

21 Morrison, Kirshner and Molho, "Epidemics," 533.

22 Cohn, *Black Death Transformed*, 240n105.

23 Ibid.

24 Rebecca Jean Emigh, "What Influences Official Information? Exploring Aggregate Microhistories of the Catasto of 1427," in *Small Worlds: Method, Meaning, and Narrative in Microhistory*, ed. James F. Brooks, Christopher R. N. DeCorse, and John Walton (Santa Fe, NM: School for Advanced Research Press, 2008), 210–13.

25 Carmichael, *Plague and the Poor*, 99–101.

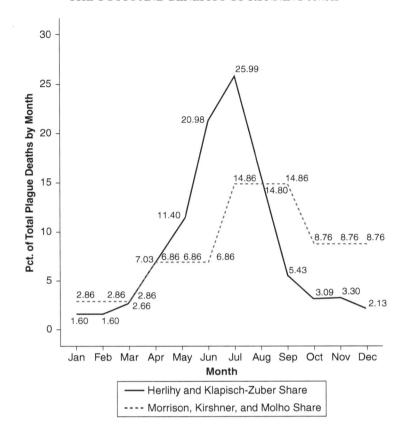

Figure 1.1 Comparison of seasonal mortality rates based on two leading theories
Sources: Herlihy and Klapisch-Zuber, *Les Toscans*, table 18; Herlihy and Klapisch-Zuber, *Tuscans*, 79; Morrison, Kirshner and Molho, "Epidemics," 533. The figure is based on the share of deaths for each month in the Herlihy and Klapisch-Zuber table and for each quarter in the Morrison, Kirshner and Molho table (divided by three for comparability). The rates were normalized. The assumption is that the absolute number of deaths remained constant over a 12-month period. The resulting values are included in the figure.

able to flee. She claims that poorer citizens were stuck in the city and, as a result, died disproportionately.[26] Kirshner demonstrates that Carmichael's evidence is based on a shaky foundation.[27] Even taking at face value the evidence that few fled, Carmichael's result is, at best, inconclusive. Disproportionate deaths among the poor do not demonstrate that large numbers stayed. Because of worse nutrition and living conditions than the rich, the poor would be expected to die in greater numbers regardless of any other factors. However, a wide range of evidence shows that flight from the plague was common. Medical and government authorities certainly acted as if it was. Contemporary medical

---

26 Ibid., 99 (on being stuck in the city), 77 and 89 (on dying disproportionately).
27 Kirshner, "Review." The results in Chapter 5 reinforce Kirshner's concerns.

theory held that corrupt vapors spread disease and recommended that people flee and then stay away as long as possible.[28] This made sense, as the countryside was generally spared the plague.[29] At the same time, cities passed laws to prevent flight, which would have been unnecessary had flight been rare, and they imposed taxes on those who fled.[30] Literature, chronicles and letters also testify to flight. Giovanni Boccaccio's *Decameron* is set among a group of people who fled Florence during the 1348 Black Death and went to the countryside.[31] And Marchionne di Coppo Stefani notes that during the 1383 plague richer citizens fled the city for the safer countryside, but the poorer *popolo minuto* did not.[32] So many rich people fled that there was a fear of revolt, and armed guards were posted in response.[33] Many people fled during the summer and returned in the autumn.[34] Coluccio Salutati, writing letters during the plagues of August 1383 and August 1390, notes the large flight from the plague,[35] and Scipione Ammirato states that people fled the 1400 plague.[36]

At this stage, before introducing new source material and data, it is important to point out that already published evidence casts doubt on the summertime peak theory. This is based on data presented by Herlihy and Klapisch-Zuber that cover the years 1424 through 1430.[37] This period includes two plagues, in 1424–25 and 1430, as well as the intervening nonplague years. The percentage of deaths due to the plague by month measures the seasonality of plague deaths compared to all other deaths among the population that remained in Florence. This percentage is an intermediate measure that has the characteristics of both the aggregate death and mortality rate measures. Flight would have reduced the total number of deaths but not the percentage of deaths in the city due to the plague. (See Appendix 1A for more information.) The percentage also indicates the plague's virulence among the population remaining in Florence at any particular time. There was no significant seasonality in aggregate deaths during nonplague years and certainly no peak during fall months.[38] This implies that the mortality rate from all other causes is approximately constant.

---

28 John Henderson, "The Black Death in Florence: Medical and Communal Responses," in *Death in Towns: Urban Responses to the Dying and the Dead, 100–1600*, ed. Stephen Bassett (London: Leicester University Press, 1992), 139 and 146–47; Cohn, *Black Death Transformed*, 118.

29 Carmichael, *Plague and the Poor*, 1–2.

30 Ibid., 99–101.

31 Giovanni Boccaccio, *The Decameron*, 2nd ed., trans. G. H. McWilliams (1995; New York: Penguin, 2003).

32 Marchionne di Coppo Stefani, *Cronaca fiorentina*, ed. Niccolò Rodolico (1913; Florence: Reggello, 2008), 426–27.

33 Carmichael, *Plague and the Poor*, 100.

34 Ronald G. Witt, *Hercules at the Crossroads: The Life, Works, and Thought of Coluccio Salutati* (Durham, NC: Duke University Press, 1983), 280.

35 Coluccio Salutati, *Epistolario di Coluccio Salutati*, ed. Francesco Novati (Rome: Istituto Storico Italiano, 1891–1911), 2: 88–89 and 222.

36 Scipione Ammirato, *Istorie fiorentine di Scipione Ammirato*, ed. Luciano Scarabelli (Torino, Italy: Cugini Pomba, 1853), 4: 317.

37 Herlihy and Klapisch-Zuber, *Les Toscans*, 465.

38 Carmichael, *Plague and the Poor*, 55, 67–69.

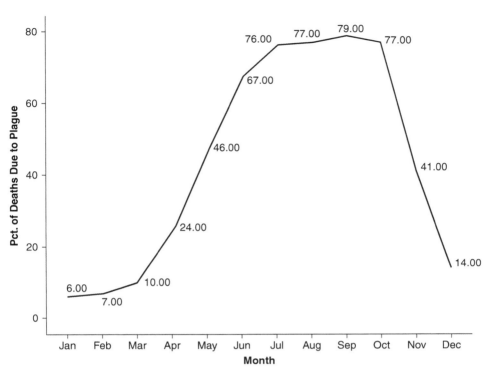

Figure 1.2 Share of deaths due to plague by month
Source: Herlihy and Klapisch-Zuber, *Les Toscans*, 465. The nonplague deaths and the share of deaths from the plague were calculated based on these data.

The plague remained virulent into the autumn months. Although the average number of deaths dropped by nearly half (46 percent) between July and October, the plague continued to account for a nearly constant 75 percent of those deaths.[39] (See Fig. 1.2.) Although these results are inconsistent with the summertime seasonality thesis, they are fully consistent with the Morrison, Kirshner and Molho results in combination with the thesis that there was significant flight from the city. The rest of the study in this chapter offers more evidence that flight was an important response to the plague.

Surviving Plagues, Information and the Currency Exchange Market

The behavioral response to epidemics can have a significant impact on mortality rates. Examples range from the ancient to the modern eras. Early Christian behavior showed that religion's superiority during a major plague in the third century. While the pagans

---

39 Herlihy and Klapisch-Zuber, *Les Toscans*, 465.

fled, the Christians stayed to care for the sick.[40] Similarly, in recent years a focus on behavior has been critical in the fight against AIDS.[41]

A model of behavior based on a person's evolving information set can be constructed to explain the Florentine observations. The decision to flee the city or stay in the face of possible death was based on the information that was available to citizens. Typically people would hear about the plague progressing through Italy but would be uncertain whether or when it would arrive in Florence. Florentines heard about the 1400 White Death nearly a year before it arrived in the city.[42] Flight was costly, so many people resisted fleeing until the danger was imminent. The medical advice to flee for as long as possible implies that people were reluctant to stay away from home for too long. A person's business virtually stopped while they were out of town. This was just as true for the *lanaiuoli*, who ran the woolen-cloth manufacturing companies, as it was for the *sottoposti* the piece-rate independent contractors who worked for them. (Appendix 1B presents a more detailed derivation of this model.)

The information model can explain the seasonal differences between major and minor plagues. People would tend to flee earlier in response to a major plague, whereas minor plagues would have been less recognizable earlier on, so fewer would flee. Therefore relatively more deaths from minor plagues would occur later in the year. Stefani writes that during the plague of 1383 many people fled the city starting in July. People had seen no indications of the coming plague in March and April of that year.[43] This model can also explain the drop in aggregate deaths over time. Though the drop might be due to declining virulence, it might also be attributed to a more effective use of information, as the avoidance of any infection in the first place would reduce deaths. Herald waves could have been another source of information. These are early episodes from the virus of a future epidemic and appear to be a common feature of seasonal diseases.[44] Such waves have been observed before major cholera and influenza epidemics.[45]

The present study brings an entirely new and quantitative source to bear on this issue: currency exchange market data. Research on people's behavior during plagues has previously relied on qualitative assessments in chronicles. To date, late medieval

---

40 Rodney Stark, *The Rise of Christianity: How the Obscure, Marginal Jesus Movement Became the Dominant Religious Force in the Western World in a Few Centuries* (San Francisco: Harper San Francisco, 1996), 73–94.

41 John L. Martin, "The Impact of AIDS on Gay Male Sexual Behavior Patterns in New York City," *American Journal of Public Health* 77 (1987): 578–81.

42 Daniel E. Bornstein, *The Bianchi of 1399: Popular Devotion in Late Medieval Italy* (Ithaca, NY: Cornell University Press, 1993), 65.

43 Stefani, *Cronaca fiorentina*, 426.

44 Joseph H. Tien, Hendrik N. Poinar, David N. Fisman and David J. D. Earn, "Herald Waves of Cholera in Nineteenth-Century London," *Journal of the Royal Society Interface* 8, no. 58 (2011): 756–60.

45 Lewi Stone, Ronen Olinky and Amit Huppert, "Seasonal Dynamics of Recurrent Epidemics," *Nature* 446 (2007): 533–36; Tien et al., "Herald Waves of Cholera"; W. Paul Glezen, Robert B. Couch and Howard R. Six, "The Influenza Herald Wave," *American Journal of Epidemiology* 116, no. 4 (1982): 589–98.

currency exchange market studies have mainly focused on economic and financial issues. However, currency exchange markets trade on information, and therefore they provide a window on information levels and behavior during plague outbreaks.[46] The Florentine economy was fully monetized. The city's currency exchange market was essential because of the large number of currencies in use.[47] The market traded a gold-backed money of account for silver-backed moneys of account,[48] and a single exchange rate was established each business day.[49] Money changers (*cambiatori*) appear to have operated as independent market makers.[50] They were members of the Arte del Cambio guild, which also included bankers. It was a small guild and in 1427 included only 22 household heads, both bankers and money changers.[51] The market functioned throughout the late medieval period. Continuous daily data exist from January 4, 1389, n.s., through February 11, 1432, n.s.;[52] the data cover the plague years of 1390, 1400, 1411, 1417–18, 1423–24 and 1430.[53]

The next three sections of this chapter examine different aspects of this larger data set that provide indirect evidence that people fled the plague. The first of these sections focuses on the 1400 plague—the White Death—and specifically examines the 1400 market closure and its timing. The following section reveals the thin markets for currency that persisted for months after the market resumed normal operations in 1400. Such thin currency markets imply that people fled the city and returned only gradually. The third section focuses on the seasonality of the currency exchange rate during the first third of the Quattrocento. The price of gold in terms of silver increased when people were expected to flee, and the size of that increase was generally correlated with the observed number of total deaths.

46 John H. Cochrane, *Asset Pricing*, rev. ed. (Princeton, NJ: Princeton University Press, 2005), 390.

47 Carlo M. Cipolla, *The Monetary Policy of Fourteenth-Century Florence* (Berkeley: University of California Press, 1966), 22–28.

48 Three types of money were traded in Florence during this period: gold (*fiorino d'oro*), white silver (*grosso*), and black silver (*quattrino*). This study focuses on the exchange rate between the fiorino d'oro and the quattrino, because that is the longer exchange rate time series.

49 Cipolla, *Monetary Policy*, 27.

50 Saverio La Sorsa, *L'organizzazione dei cambiatori fiorentini nel Medio Evo* (Cerignola: Scienza e Diletto), 1904), esp. 95–146; Giulia Camerani Marri, ed., *Statuti dell'arte del cambio di Firenze (1299–1316) con aggiunte e correzioni fino al 1320* (Florence: Olschki, 1955); Charles M. de La Roncière, *Un changeur florentin du Trecento: Lippo di Fede di Sega (1285 env–1363 env.)* (Paris: S.E.V.P.E.N., 1973).

51 Calculation by the author based on data from David Herlihy and Christiane Klapisch-Zuber, *Census and Property Survey of Florentine Domains and the City of Verona in Fifteenth Century Italy* [machine-readable data file]. Cambridge, MA: David Herlihy, Harvard University, Department of History and Paris, France: Christiane Klapisch-Zuber, Ecole Pratique des Hautes Etudes [producers], 1977. Madison: University of Wisconsin, Data and Program Library Service [distributor], 1981.

52 Mario Bernocchi, *Le monete della Repubblica fiorentina*, vol. 4: *Valute del Fiorino d'Oro 1389–1432* (Florence: Olschki, 1978).

53 Herlihy and Klapisch-Zuber, *Les Toscans*, 191.

The White Death and the Market Closure Timing

This section examines the response of the market to the 1400 Florentine plague, called the White Death. In terms of severity among Florentine plagues, it is generally ranked second only to the 1348 Black Death. It was called the White Death because of its association with a religious movement called the Bianchi, whose participants were active in northern Italy in the late summer of 1399; however, there is no evidence the Bianchi spread the plague from town to town.[54] The plague took some time to reach its full extent. It had just reached Tuscany at the time of the Bianchi's arrival in August 1399, and it would not become a major plague until nearly a year later, in the summer of 1400.[55]

The plague caused the currency exchange market to close from July 19 through September 19, 1400, except on August 30 and September 13, when it opened temporarily so that people would have money to buy necessities.[56] The extended closure was the only time in the 43 years between 1389 and 1432 that the market closed for more than two weeks for any reason. This includes holidays, Easter and Christmas, and during the other five plagues of the period.[57] Besides holidays, there were two shorter extended closures during this period. The market closed for 13 days, from August 27 through September 8, 1399, for the Bianchi and for 4 consecutive business days, on October 25–28, 1406, to celebrate the defeat of Pisa.[58]

The cost of market closures created a clear incentive to keep the market open if anyone was willing to trade. This is presumably why the market reopened twice during the plague closure. In addition, even when the market was closed, trading was apparently not completely stopped. For days when the market was closed the Florentine chamberlain established fixed exchange rates one week at a time.[59] This implies that one important value of the market was to provide information to its participants. The dates the market closed due to the White Death can be linked with a weekly time series of total burials, aggregate deaths, from the *Libri dei morti* published by Carmichael.[60] Figure 1.3 presents the resulting time series. It shows that the number of aggregate deaths dropped dramatically once the market closed. The drop in aggregate deaths could either mean that the plague suddenly became much less virulent or that large numbers of people had fled the plague. The drop in virulence is unlikely. Florentines first ceased counting the dead, then

54 Bornstein, *Bianchi*, 169.
55 Ibid., 83 and 65.
56 Bernocchi, *Monete*, 4: 73–74. "non si poté avere la valuta per il fatto della moria; e' proveditori vollono si desse a' chamarlinghi a s. 76 d. 0 il fiorino."
57 Ibid., 67–68; Anthony Molho, *Florentine Public Finances in the Early Renaissance, 1400–1433* (Cambridge, MA: Harvard University Press, 1971), 213. For the relatively short closure for the arrival of the Bianchi, see Bornstein, *Bianchi*, 91–92.
58 Bernocchi, *Monete*, 4: 67–68 and 115.
59 Ibid., 4: 73–74.
60 Carmichael, *Plague and the Poor*, 72.

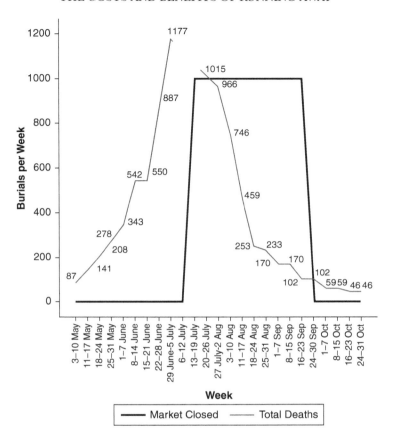

Figure 1.3 Deaths by week with currency exchange market closure dates superimposed
Sources: Weekly Deaths: Ann G. Carmichael, *Plague and the Poor*, 67; Market Closure Dates: Bernocchi, *Monete*, 4: 73–74. The market closure dates are assigned to the week in which each happened. The market closure began on July 19. The first day is grouped with the week in which it occurred. The discontinuity in July is because the number of deaths overwhelmed the grave diggers. The June 29–July 5 death total is probably well below the actual death totals for the weeks of July 6–12 and July 13–19. September and October are computed bimonthly averages and probably minimize the variation.

closed the market, and only then did the aggregate deaths start dropping dramatically. The counting cessation implies that the number of dead simply overwhelmed the available resources to bury them. The market was closed, and the deaths dropped only after counting ceased. A large flight is very likely; however, as the market closure implies, there was practically no one left to trade. The timing further makes sense if people first had to confirm the virulence of the plague and then flee. Finally, one more point should be made. The market closure came well after the seasonal peak identified by Herlihy and Klapisch-Zuber, Carmichael and Cohn. However, the timing corresponds well with the evidence from Morrison, Kirshner and Molho that the plague remained dangerous into the autumn months.

Thin Market Postclosure

Not only did people leave Florence when faced with the plague but they also stayed away. The effect can be observed in the noticeably thinner postclosure market. Research on medieval financial markets typically focuses on the exchange rate or the price of currency. The approach used here is different because it incorporates market microstructure variables. This takes advantage of research on prices during medieval times showing that the market efficiently integrated new information into prices.[61] This observation implies that the market price tends to follow a random walk and therefore is unpredictable.[62] Market microstructure analysis in financial economics takes this a step further and provides data about the underlying market characteristics. The exchange rate volatility and the bid/ask spread are used to measure the level of market information and liquidity. The volatility is the relative size of exchange rate movements over time, which can be measured in a number of ways. One simple and statistically robust measure is the median monthly absolute deviation of the daily exchange rate. The spread is the absolute value of the difference between the price buyers are bidding or offering and the price sellers are asking. It is measured here in terms of the percentage difference between the bid and ask prices. The notebooks containing the exchange rate data identify the bid price as *dassene* and the ask price as *vale*.[63]

A large flight from the city would have a significant impact on the market. It would reduce the information available to accurately value currencies, which would increase the volatility directly and the spread indirectly. The spread would increase due to the greater uncertainty and consequent need for caution by the cambiatori with their coin inventories. It would also reduce the liquidity of the market, which would further increase the spread.[64] When people fled, they would take their coins with them. Dealer inventories would therefore become smaller, reducing liquidity.

Both the volatility and the spread patterns presented here fit what one would expect if many people fled. The volatility pattern implies that market information and liquidity remained lower after the market reopened (see Fig. 1.4). The middle quintile, between the 40th and 60th percentile points, is displayed as a robust measure of dispersion. The month of September 1400, immediately after the plague hit, clearly had the greatest volatility. The increased exchange rate volatility continued through October and November,

61   G. Geoffrey Booth and Umit G. Gurun, "Volatility Clustering and the Bid-Ask Spread: Exchange Rate Behavior in Early Renaissance Florence," *Journal of Empirical Finance* 15 (2008): 131–44.

62   Richard Meese and Ken Rogoff, "Empirical Exchange Rate Models of the Seventies: Do They Fit Out of Sample?" *Journal of International Economics* 14 (1983): 3–24; Richard Meese and Ken Rogoff, "The Out-of-Sample Failure of Empirical Exchange Rate Models: Sampling Error or Misspecification?," in *Exchange Rates and International Macroeconomics*, ed. Jacob A. Frenkel (Chicago: University of Chicago Press, 1983), 67–112; Richard Meese and Ken Rogoff, "Was It Real? The Exchange Rate–Interest Rate Differential Relation over the Modern Floating-Rate Period," *Journal of Finance* 43, no. 4 (1988): 933–48; Barbara Rossi, "Exchange Rate Predictability," *Journal of Economic Literature* 53, no. 4 (2013): 1063–119.

63   Bernocchi, *Monete*, 4: 266–72, 354–60.

64   Maureen O'Hara, *Market Microstructure Theory* (Malden, MA: Blackwell, 1995), 13–88.

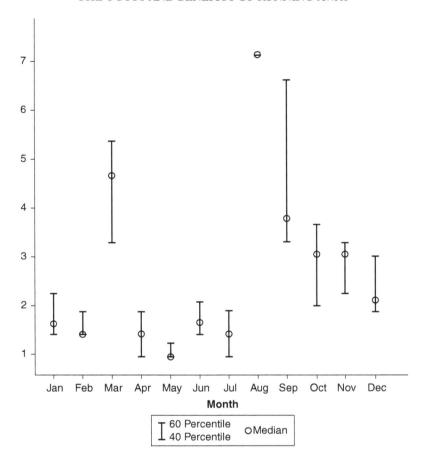

Figure 1.4 Median daily absolute exchange rate movements by month in 1400
Source: Bernocchi, *Monete*, 4: 70–75. The change in the exchange rate is measured in units of 1/100ths of 1 percent. The range of the middle quintile of the distribution of exchange rate movements is displayed for each month.

as one would expect in the case of an extended flight from the city. The spread pattern also implies that market information and liquidity remained lower after the market reopened. Again due to the market closure, September clearly had a large spread. The increased spread continued through October and November (see Fig. 1.5), and is what one would expect to see in the case of an extended flight from the city. This spread pattern is statistically robust.

The September Seasonal Gold Premium

This section looks at a long-term market inefficiency that corresponds to the timing and magnitude of the plague shocks in Florence. Inefficiencies associated with shocks occur in an otherwise efficient market because the market is incomplete and the shocks are

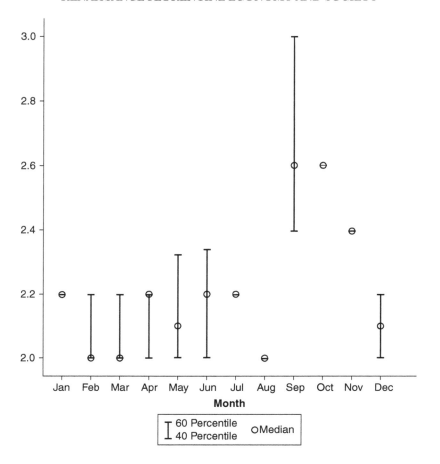

Figure 1.5 Median daily exchange rate spread by month in 1400
Source: Bernocchi, *Monete*, 4: 70–75. The spread is measured in units of 1/100ths of 1 percent. The range of the middle quintile of the distribution of spreads is displayed for each month.

not diversifiable. Nondiversifiable risk is an important characteristic of early modern economic history. The seasonality of exchange rates was driven by the seasonality of commerce.[65] However, the particular seasonality pattern at a trading center could vary significantly depending on the traded goods, location and currencies traded.[66]

The plague was certainly not a diversifiable risk in Trecento and Quattrocento Florence. Everyone was susceptible. The size of the gold premium shock over silver can indicate whether people stayed or fled. Flight from the city would increase the gold

---

65 Reinhold C. Mueller, *The Venetian Money Market: Banks, Panics, and the Public Debt, 1200–1500* (Baltimore: Johns Hopkins University Press, 1997), 306; Raymond de Roover, *The Bruges Money Market around 1400* (Brussels: Paleis der Academiën, 1968), 49–50.
66 Mueller, *Venetian Money Market*, 306; de Roover, *Bruges Money Market*, 49–50.

premium because those fleeing would want to make the coins more portable. People hiding in their homes from the plague would care only about the total value of their money, not the value by weight of the coin. The transport advantage of gold was the converse of the economic problems caused by a scarcity of small change.[67] The size of the shock would be influenced by both the plague's virulence and people's experience with previous plagues.

The anomalies in the time series were identified using a seemingly unrelated regressions model (SUR) to test for seasonality. Arnold Zellner advocates this method.[68] The shock is the coefficient to the monthly dummy variable in this regression. (See Appendix 1C for more information.) The data consist of first differences in the logarithms based on end-of-month exchange rates. Therefore, the September first difference would be associated with price changes during September. The SUR method approximates the percentage change and makes the time series stationary. The notebooks containing the exchange rate data also include monthly calculations of the mean exchange rate data. The information previously has been published in this format by Bernocchi and Molho.[69]

The positive September shock, increased gold price, was the largest and only statistically significant monthly shock at a 95 percent confidence level (see Fig. 1.6). The shock would not necessarily occur every September. There would just be more frequent and bigger spikes in September than in any other month, because the size of the relative demand for gold at that time was unanticipated. Although there are many possible causes for such a spike, it would make sense if there was flight from the city in September. That flight, in turn, would make sense only if the plague was still dangerous in September.

This observation can be explored in greater detail. The September first differences by year are presented in Figure 1.7. The size of the September shock declined over time in parallel with the declining aggregate death totals from the plague. This parallel decline could have occurred because people built up immunity over time to the plague and there was less need to flee, or they learned how to better identify the time when plagues were coming and left town earlier, or it could be explained by a combination of both.

The increasing experience theory fits the observations well. The information people had would be rough and imperfect. The irregularity of the plague's impact from city to city reduces the effectiveness of that kind of early warning system. The failure of the market shocks to exactly match the severity of the plagues could be due to false alarms. Though the 1400 plague was the most severe plague between 1389 and 1432, and though the shock is large, it is not the largest plague of the years included in that time period. It is likely that the early reaction by the Florentines together with the prolonged market closure that started in July would have reduced the size of the financial shock.

---

67 Thomas J. Sargent and François R. Velde, *The Big Problem of Small Change* (Princeton, NJ: Princeton University Press, 2002).

68 Arnold Zellner, "An Efficient Method of Estimating Seemingly Unrelated Regressions and Tests for Aggregation Bias," *Journal of the American Statistical Association* 57, no. 298 (1962): 348–68.

69 Bernocchi, *Monete*, vol. 4; Molho, *Florentine Public Finances*, 209–13.

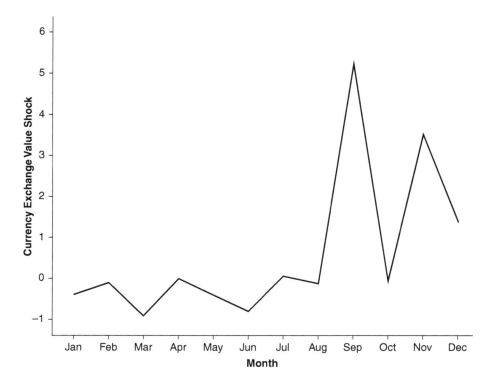

Figure 1.6 Exchange rate shock by month, 1389–1432

Source: Bernocchi, *Monete*, 4: 3–272. The shock is the coefficient to the monthly dummy variable in the SUR. See Table 1.1 for more information. See Appendix 1C for discussion of the methodology and the underlying statistical results.

Concluding Remarks

The results in this study lead to a number of conclusions regarding the importance of behavior, the relative merits of different kinds of death data and what is known about the plague. First, these results confirm research by medical historians that places the *Yersinia pestis* as the most likely cause of the plague. Second, these results imply that aggregate data on death dates should be used with caution. There are so many uncontrolled factors that in a range of circumstances these data might contain little to no value for historians. Flight from the city to avoid the plague significantly affected aggregate seasonal mortality statistics. Modern diagnoses of the medieval plague need to be more careful. Ex post diagnoses of the "true" illness based on the seasonality of aggregate deaths are likely in error. The available mortality rate data, though covering a more limited population, better match the behavioral patterns than do the aggregate death data. Aggregate deaths, with good reason, are rarely used by modern epidemiologists. The results presented here simply reaffirm that epidemiologists should use the mortality rate whenever possible and that other measures do not work nearly as well. In the case of Renaissance Florence, aggregate deaths, though appealing and easy to obtain, are no substitute for mortality rates.

Third, these results show that the behavior of Renaissance Florentines in response to the plague had a dramatic impact on survivability. Florentines appear to have learned to better anticipate the arrival of a plague over time. It is clear that because the severity of the plague varied from year to year, the Florentines could not know how severe a given plague would be before it arrived. However, each outbreak was a chance to learn and led to a gradual accumulation of information. Florentines adapted to circumstances. The steep drop in deaths at the height of the plague severity in 1400 implies that the people of Florence, far from being poor and immobile, were capable of quickly moving out of town. Modern financial market traders call buying safe assets like treasury bills and gold a flight to safety. The flight to the gold currency from the silver currency would have been part of a literal flight to safety. In one sense it could be called an "inverse quarantine," because the Florentines dispersed in order to reduce the effect of the contagion. The social controls, such as quarantines, came only later, and they alone cannot explain the significant drop in deaths on a month-to-month basis. The information model developed in this study and presented in Appendix 1B explains both the later deaths from minor plagues and the reduction in deaths over time. People had to learn about each individual plague, and each successive plague increased their aggregate information.

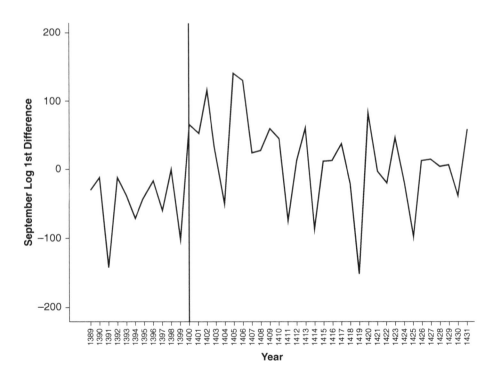

Figure 1.7 Magnitude of the September shock by year, 1389–1432
Source: Bernocchi, *Monete* 4: 3–272. The September first difference in 1400 is flagged. See Appendix 1C for more information.

Finally, these results show how data from an unexpected source can shed light on historical behavior. In this case currency exchange rate records are used to study plague mortality. The link between financial markets and plague mortality rates would appear to be remote. One would not expect a connection, but there is one.

Appendix 1A: Aggregate Deaths and Mortality Rates

This appendix first works through the algebraic relationships between the definitions of aggregate deaths and mortality rates and associated variables. It then shows how the empirical observations fit together.

The Algebra of Aggregate Deaths and Mortality Rates

The first step is to demonstrate that the share of deaths from the plague remains approximately constant in the face of flight from the city of Florence.

Definitions of variables:

D: Total deaths,
P: Total plague deaths,
N: Total population,
F: Total population fleeing due to plague,
d: Mortality rate and
p: Plague rate.

This implies: $D = dN$ and $P = pN$.
Therefore: $P/D = pN/dN = p/d$.

This model assumes that there is no selectivity bias in the population that flees. However, this is not exactly accurate. We know that the rich were more likely to flee, which implies that the mortality rate and the plague mortality rate were likely to be higher among those remaining than for the overall population.

Now define the observed (in the *Libri dei morti*) number of deaths in the face of flight (D*):

$$D^* = d(N - F) < dN = D.$$

Now define the observed (in the *Libri dei morti*) number of plague deaths in the face of flight (P*):

$$P^* = p(N - F) < pN = P.$$

This results in the following relationship between the ratios:

$$P^*/D^* = p(N - F)/d(N - F) = p/d.$$

This is exactly the same ratio one would observe if there were no migration.

These equations imply that the mortality rates remain constant; however, the total number of deaths does not.

How the Empirical Observations Fit Together

This section derives each of the models presented in the research by Herlihy and Klapisch-Zuber; Carmichael; Cohn; and Morrison, Kirshner and Molho.[70]

Definitions of variables:

N^f: Total population during the fall,
N^s: Total population during the summer,
P^f: Total plague deaths during the fall,
P^s: Total plague deaths during the summer,
D^f: Total deaths during the fall,
D^s: Total deaths during the summer and
F: Total population fleeing due to plague.

First assume that the fall population is lower than the summer population during plague years due to flight from the city: $N^f = N^s - F$.

The general findings by Herlihy and Klapisch-Zuber, Carmichael and Cohn are that there were more deaths from the plague in summer than in fall: $P^s > P^f$.

Supplemental analysis of Herlihy and Klapisch-Zuber findings implies that there was the same plague share in mortality rates in summer and fall: $P^s/D^s = P^f/D^f$.

This implies $D^s > D^f$.

And then one can combine these three results, which implies $N^s > N^f$ and $F > 0$.

The Morrison, Kirshner and Molho findings are that $P^s/N^s = P^f/N^f$.

Combining the three results reconciles the available empirical work.

Appendix 1B: Model of Information Acquisition and Flight

This appendix presents a model of the decision to flee, employing much of the notation developed in Appendix 1A. The model is a simple optimal stopping problem: one flees when the observed risk exceeds the cost of flight.

Basic Theory Underlying the Model

The total information (I) is a function of the number of traders. This implies:

---

70 Herlihy and Klapisch-Zuber, *Les Toscans*; Morrison, Kirshner and Molho, "Epidemics"; Carmichael, *Plague and the Poor*; Cohn, *Black Death Transformed*.

I(N, other variables), where $\partial I/\partial N > 0$.
$\partial \text{Volatility}/\partial I > 0$ and
$\partial \text{Spread}/\partial I > 0$.

The total liquidity (L) is a function of the number of traders. This implies:

L(N, other variables), where $\partial L/\partial N > 0$,
$\partial \text{Volatility}/\partial L > 0$ and
$\partial \text{Spread}/\partial L > 0$.

The Information-Gathering Stage

Given that flight from the city is costly and the impact of each year's plague is unknown in advance, people determine the severity of each plague by observation. This observation is costly because it increases the risk of mortality: the longer people wait and watch, the more likely they are to die. A standard search model therefore fits the data. People flee the plague if the expected mortality rate is high enough. There are two types of learning going on during the plague outbreak: (1) the observed mortality rate provides information about the plague's severity, and (2) the population over the long term learns more about the plague, how to survive it and any signals that the plague is coming.

Cost-to-Benefit Analysis

The costs of staying are summarized below. The risk of death increases based on these factors:

1. Cumulative mortality rate from current outbreak from initial to current period,
2. Estimate of the future rate, where "n" approximates the sample size, "n" increasing.

The net costs to flight may be summarized:

1. Lost wages and/or business opportunities = B,
2. Costs of travel, including maintaining security for home while away and risk of losing home = M.

Regarding security for the home, poorer households were smaller than richer households.
    The next step is to estimate the probability of death and formulate this as an estimate of probability.

If leaving, then the net cost to move = M + B

    Definitions of variables:

d: Mortality rate,
n: Number days in Florence.

The risk of death $= f(d, n)$.

The expected loss in utility from probability of death $= v(d, n)$, where v is the indirect utility.

Where $v(d, n) - (M + B) > 0$ implies the household would move out of town.

The reservation level of confirming information gives us the reservation mortality rate: d^R,

where $v(d^R, n) = (M + B)$.

Model of Increasing Volatility

1. Basic pattern

    Risk of plague death up implies number of traders down.

    Number of traders down implies market liquidity down.

    In equation form this would be:

    Liquidity $= f(N^T)$.

    Where

    N^T: Number of traders. =

    Decreasing market liquidity implies both exchange rate volatility and the spread would increase.

    Decreasing information and increasing risk of death both increase volatility.

2. Draft model of market closure: extreme case of market failure

    Define:

    t: Percentage of population that trades,

    N^{TR}: Reservation number of traders to keep market functioning.

    N^R: Reservation population to keep market functioning.

    Therefore theminimum number of traders to keep the market functioning $N^{TR} = tN^R$, where market activity $A = f(T)$

    $N - N^m < N^R$ implies there can be no market.

    Where N^m: Total population who flee (move).

    Now, define as in Appendix 1A:N^f: Total population during the fall,

    N^s: Total population during the summer,

    Together these imply that in 1400:

$N^s = N$,

$N^f = N - N^m$ and

$N^s > N^f$.

Model of Increasing Gold Premium

Assumptions:

1. Exchange rate follows a random walk.

2. Trading is based on information.
3. Traders gain information about the plague over time.
4. When the net benefit of staying drops below the net benefit of flight, then the household flees.
5. Persons who flee have higher value of gold versus silver than do those who stay.

Assume, for simplicity, that there are two representative agents: those who flee and those who stay.

Define the following variables:

g^m: Demand per person for those who move,
g^s: Demand per person for those who stay and
G: Total gold demand for Florence.

These would imply:

$$g^m > g^s$$

Total demand is therefore

$$G = N^m * g^m + (N - N^m) g^s.$$

An increase in N^m therefore increases total demand for gold:

$$\partial G / \partial N^m > 0.$$

If the supply of gold and silver is constant or varies randomly, then the gold premium over silver should increase as a result of flight from the plague.

Appendix 1C: Seemingly Unrelated Regressions Model and the September Seasonality Anomaly

A SUR approach was used to determine the month of the greatest increase in the premium of gold over silver (*quattrino*) currency. Zellner points out that the SUR approach is the best way to determine seasonal patterns in data.[71] The first differences of the logs of

---

71 Zellner, "Efficient Method of Estimating," 348–68.

Table 1.1 SUR system for monthly seasonality estimates of quattrino-to-florin exchange rates, 1389–1432

Month	Constant	Dummy
January	2.1517	−0.3902
February	2.1269	−0.0926
March	2.1948	−0.9074
April	2.1193	−0.0016
May	2.152	−0.3939
June	2.1859	−0.8007
July	2.1142	0.06
August	2.1298	−0.1279
September	1.6839	5.2228***
October	2.1242	−0.0606
November	1.8246	3.5353*
December	2.0038	1.3844

*** statistically significant at the 99 percent level.
* statistically significant at the 90 percent level.

Source: Bernocchi, *Monete*, vol. 4. See Arnold Zellner, "An Efficient Method of Estimating Seemingly Unrelated Regressions and Tests for Aggregation Bias," *Journal of the American Statistical Association* 57, no. 298 (1962): 348–68, for a discussion of the method.

the currency exchange rates were taken; these are approximately the percentage changes. Taking the differences has the effect of making the time series stationary as in the context of the Box-Jenkins formulation of an autoregressive integrated moving average (ARIMA).[72]

---

72 James D. Hamilton, *Time Series Analysis* (Princeton, NJ: Princeton University Press, 1994), 43–68.

Chapter Two

WHEN ECONOMIC THEORY MEETS MEDIEVAL CONTRACTS: CALCULATING THE MONTE COMUNE INTEREST RATE

Introduction

The development of the state was one of the first topics in Renaissance Italian historiography.[1] Though interest in the subject waned and became unfashionable for a time, it is returning. The ambition of one recent work is "to raise once again the theme of the Italian Renaissance with a declared emphasis on politics."[2] The latest research on state formation has proceeded in directions hardly imaginable to earlier generations of Renaissance historians, with the development of the modern public debt system often placed at the center of the debate.[3] The research employs the large-scale theoretical apparatus of the new institutional economics and related methods, which use a relatively straightforward approach.[4] The structure of the public debt indicates the government's

---

1 Jacob Burckhardt, *The Civilization of the Renaissance in Italy*, 2 vols. (New York: Harper, 1973). For more information, see Julius Kirshner, "Introduction: The State Is 'Back in,'" *Journal of Modern History, Supplement: The Origins of the State in Italy, 1300–1600*, 67 (1995): S1–10.

2 Andrea Gamberini and Isabella Lazzarini, Introduction to *The Italian Renaissance State*, ed. Andrea Gamberini and Isabella Lazzarini (Cambridge: Cambridge University Press, 2012), 1.

3 Anthony Molho, "The State and Public Finance: A Hypothesis Based on the History of Late Medieval Florence," *Journal of Modern History, Supplement: The Origins of the State in Italy, 1300–1600*, 67 (1995): S97–135. Reprinted as Anthony Molho, "The State and Public Finance: A Hypothesis Based on the History of Late Medieval Florence," in *Firenze nel Quattrocento*, vol. 1: *Politica e Fiscalità* (Rome: Edizioni di Storia Letteratura, 2006): 165–202.

4 This topic already has a large literature. Douglass North produced the seminal work. Key works include Douglass C. North and Barry R. Weingast, "Constitutions and Commitment: The Evolution of Institutional Governing Public Choice in Seventeenth-Century England," *Journal of Economic History* 49, no. 4 (1989): 803–32; Douglass C. North, *Institutions, Institutional Change, and Economic Performance* (Cambridge: Cambridge University Press, 1990); Philip T. Hoffman and Kathryn Norberg, eds., *Fiscal Crises, Liberty, and Representative Government 1450–1789* (Stanford, CA: Stanford University Press, 1993); James MacDonald, *A Free Nation Deep in Debt: The Financial Roots of Democracy* (Princeton, NJ: Princeton University Press, 2003); David Stasavage, *States of Credit: Size, Power, and the Development of European Politics* (Princeton, NJ: Princeton University Press, 2011); Gary W. Cox, "Was the Glorious Revolution a Constitutional Watershed?", *Journal of Economic History* 72, no. 3 (2012): 567–600. Luciano Pezzolo has created the time series used for Florence: Luciano Pezzolo, "Italian Monti: The Origins of Bonds and Government Debt," paper presented at the *Yale School of Management Conference on the History of Financial Innovation*, March, New Haven, CT, 2003; Luciano Pezzolo, "The Venetian Government

ability to credibly commit to obligations. In turn, the interest rate on government debt measures this level of confidence. The time series of interest rates gauges the progress of the government toward becoming a modern state.

The study in this chapter provides a cautionary tale for this new line of research. It shows what can go wrong when two independent methodologies collide. It estimates interest rates on Quattrocento Florentine *Monte Comune* credits as a case study. Previous estimates were in error because they failed to closely link the medieval legal contracts to modern financial economic theory. Such a linkage permits a more accurate interest rate calculation. The analysis first describes the Monte Comune in terms of modern bond theory, which permits a formal analysis using financial economics. It then uses this formal analysis to create a new time series of Quattrocento interest rates.

Interest Rates and Institutions

Interest rates are an important measure in studies of long-term economic growth and institutional development. In both senses they measure confidence in the future. Physical capital and human capital have important roles in economic growth.[5] Interest rates place a price on the cost of physical and human capital accumulation.[6] People are also more likely to hold on to their money if interest rates are lower.[7] The interest rate's institutional

---

Debt, 1350–1650," in *Urban Public Debts: Urban Government and the Market for Annuities in Western Europe (14th–18th Centuries), Studies in European Urban History* (1100–1800), vol. 3 (Tourhout, Belgium: Brepols, 2003), 61–74; Luciano Pezzolo, "Bonds and Government Debt in Italian City-States, 1250–1650," in *The Origins of Value: The Financial Innovations That Created Modern Capital Markets*, International Center for Finance at the Yale School of Management, ed. William N. Goetzman and K. Geert Rouwenhorst (Oxford: Oxford University Press, 2005), 145–63; Luciano Pezzolo, "Government Debts and Credit Markets in Renaissance Italy," in *Government Debts and Financial Markets in Europe*, ed. Fausto Piola Caselli (London: Pickering and Chatto, 2008), 17–32; Luciano Pezzolo, "Republics and Principalities in Italy," in *The Rise of Fiscal States: A Global History, 1500–1914*, ed. Bartolomé Yun-Casalilla and Patrick K. O'Brien (Cambridge: Cambridge University Press, 2012), 267–84 (An earlier version is Luciano Pezzolo, "Fiscal System and Finance in Northern Italy in the Early Modern Age," [2003]); Luciano Pezzolo, *Il fisco dei veneziani: Finanza pubblica ed economia tra XV e XVII secolo*, Cierre Edizioni, Verona, 2003; Luciano Pezzolo, *Una Finanza d'Ancien Régime La Repubblica Veneta tra XV e XVIII Secolo*, Storia Finanziara. Collana di Studi, Atti e Documenti, vol. 8 (Naples: Edizioni Scientifiche Italiane, 2006); Luciano Pezzolo, *Una finanza d'Ancien Régime. La Repubblica veneta tra XV e XVIII secolo* (Naples: Edizioni Scientifiche Italiane, 2009).

5   On physical capital, seminal work includes Robert M. Solow, "A Contribution to the Theory of Economic Growth," *Quarterly Journal of Economics* 70, no. 1 (1956): 65–94. Extensive subsequent literature exists. On human capital, see Gary S. Becker, Kevin M. Murphy and Robert Tamura, "Human Capital, Fertility, and Economic Growth," *Journal of Political Economy* 98, no. 5, pt. 2 (1990): S12–37; Robert E. Lucas Jr., *Lectures on Economic Growth* (Cambridge, MA: Harvard University Press, 2006).

6   James J. Heckman, "A Life Cycle Model of Earnings, Learning, and Consumption," *Journal of Political Economy* 84, no. 4, pt. 2 (1976): S11–44.

7   Seminal work includes William J. Baumol, "The Transactions Demand for Cash: An Inventory Theoretic Approach," *Quarterly Journal of Economics* 66, no. 4 (1951): 545–56; James Tobin,

role is also important, because it is the price of a government's debt. Therefore an interest rate that is free to move according to market sentiments, and not government sentiments, measures the confidence the market has in a particular government's debt.

The development of public debt began in twelfth-century Italy; however, Italian public debt still did not yet look modern by the fifteenth century.[8] Molho argues that the political history of the time, the "internal politics of regimes in power," drove decisions on taxation and public finance.[9] Following this line of inquiry, Francesco Franceschi and Luca Mola point out that the "economic policies [of the Italian city states] were conditioned by an increasing fiscal burden."[10] The modern form of public debt originated in seventeenth-century Holland and eighteenth-century Britain.[11] John Munro distinguishes modern public debt from its predecessors by six characteristics: (1) the earlier debt was permanent; (2) it was national, or at least provincial, as opposed to being municipal or personal; (3) there were annual payments authorized by legislative action; (4) there was no state coercion; (5) the public had "complete confidence" in the government to meet its obligations; and (6) the instruments were freely negotiable.[12] The term "complete confidence" is unfortunate and is, in a literal sense, an impossible standard. It does not exist, nor could it, even in today's advanced financial markets. "A high level of confidence" would probably be a better term.

Social scientists often link the evolution of public debt to state formation. Charles Tilly's governmental "capitalized coercion" theory asserts that well-financed and centralized power was the single biggest stimulant of European state formation.[13] However, Molho points out that Tilly's theory does not adequately account for Florentine history.[14] Economic historians have used public debt data to examine late medieval and early modern state formation in greater detail. Michael Veseth examines the history of public debt from a macroeconomic perspective as opposed to an institutional perspective.[15] He applies macroeconomic "crowding out" theory, which implicitly assumes a modern institutional framework where the markets operate smoothly and governments have high credibility.

"The Interest-Elasticity of Transactions Demand for Cash," *Review of Economics and Statistics* 38, no. 3 (1956): 241–47. Extensive subsequent literature exists.

8   Pezzolo, "Venetian Government Debt," 67; Julius Kirshner, "States of Debt" (paper, *Mellon Sawyer Seminar on Debt, Sovereignty, and Power*, University of Cambridge, 2006).

9   Molho, "State and Public Finance," S103 and S135.

10 Francesco Franceschi and Luca Mola, "Regional States and Economic Development," in *The Italian Renaissance State*, ed. Andrea Gamberini and Isabella Lazzarini (Cambridge: Cambridge University Press, 2012), 464.

11 John Munro, "The Medieval Origins of the Financial Revolution: Usury, *Rentes*, and Negotiability," *International History Review* 25, no. 3 (2003): 505.

12 Ibid.

13 Charles Tilly, *Coercion, Capital, and European States, A. D. 990–1992* (Cambridge, MA: Blackwell, 1992).

14 Molho, "State and Public Finance."

15 Michael Veseth, *Mountains of Debt: Crisis and Change in Renaissance Florence, Victorian Britain, and Postwar America* (New York: Oxford University Press, 1990).

The new institutional economics offers a different approach to the history of state formation in that it examines the evolution of institutions over time. R. H. Coase's work on legal theory established the fundamental importance of transaction costs: an institution expands to the point where the transaction costs are balanced by the benefits.[16] Douglass North extends Coase's theory and points out that transaction costs can measure the efficiency of institutions. Interest rate levels are associated with the public's patience and confidence levels in those institutions.[17] North points out that transaction costs are difficult to measure, but interest rates are quite straightforward and provide the most visible quantitative measure of the efficiency of the institutional framework.[18] This implies that interest rates are closely associated with institutional development, including state creation and market formation.

Interest rates have been used in several recent large-scale studies designed to examine the evolution of state institutions in late medieval and early modern Europe. The rest of this section reviews this work. North and Barry Weingast introduce the use of public debt interest rates with their study of the English Glorious Revolution of 1688. They see it as a watershed event in the development of government credibility and argue that it caused a structural change in the credibility of the English government.[19] Their article on the subject, however, has led to considerable debate, and the currently accepted view is more nuanced.[20]

The body of research on the evolution of institutions has expanded both chronologically and geographically. Stephan Epstein, James MacDonald, David Stasavage and Luciano Pezzolo use Florentine interest rates to understand late medieval and early modern European institutional development. Epstein's early work on Sicily is widely considered a breakthrough because it links North's approach to Italian history.[21] Epstein continues to follow North's approach in later work.[22] He looks at the interplay of economic growth and institutional development through the joint evolution of interest rates and market integration and finds that property rights are the key to the long-term development of the European economy from 1300 to 1750.[23] As the government structure evolves over time, public debt interest rates decline.[24] Epstein concludes that interest rates were lower in the Italian city-states and lowest of all in Florence due to the Florentines' superior financial skills.[25] MacDonald's long-term theory of European history is based on the development of public debt.[26] He concludes that the role of public debt goes back

16 R. H. Coase, "The Problem of Social Cost," in *The Firm, the Market, and the Law* (Chicago: University of Chicago Press, 1988), 95–156.
17 North, *Institutions*, 69.
18 Ibid., 68–69.
19 North and Weingast, "Constitutions and Commitment."
20 Hoffman and Norberg, *Fiscal Crises*, 567–600.
21 Franceschi and Mola, "Regional States and Economic Development," 444.
22 Stephan R. Epstein, *Freedom and Growth: The Rise of States and Markets in Europe, 1300–1750* (London: Routledge, 2000).
23 Ibid., 16–17.
24 Ibid., 19.
25 Ibid.
26 MacDonald, *Free Nation Deep in Debt*.

millennia and that its expansion is intimately associated with democracy.[27] He links its development in Italy to the creation of direct taxation systems such as the *catasto*.[28]

Stasavage examines the joint development of representative assemblies and public borrowing in Europe during the medieval and modern eras. One of his earlier books focuses on France and England, paralleling North and Weingast, but without a central role for public debt.[29] Stasavage's most recent work uses interest rates as an indicator of state formation throughout Western Europe and engages in three debates: the relationship between war and state formation, the sources of early modern growth and the development of institutions and credible commitment.[30] The ability of institutions to credibly commit to repaying debt is a key determinant of behavior in Stasavage's theory. Finally, Pezzolo analyzes public debt and institutional structure in the northern Italian city-states.[31] His later work focuses on the debt burden, particularly in Venice.[32] He confirms that Italian interest rates were lower than those of the northern European monarchies.[33]

The Monte Comune of Florence

This and the next three sections describe the Monte Comune. This section provides a brief description and a broad outline of its history. The following three sections, in turn, review bond contract theory in the context of the Monte Comune; then offer an analysis of who was holding credits and why; and, finally, present a synthesis of how all of these features are used to calculate an interest time series.[34] The Monte Comune was the consolidated government loan (bond) market of the Comune of Florence. It was established on December 29, 1343, when the Comune consolidated all of its outstanding obligations.[35] The Comune gave the Monte full funding and declared its bonds assignable in February 1345.[36] This secondary market increased liquidity and reduced the Comune debt by 30 to 40 percent.[37] The ability to assign holdings also created a dynamic quality

---

27   Ibid., 6 and 5.
28   Ibid., 100–101 and 104.
29   David Stasavage, *Public Debt and the Birth of the Democratic State: France and Great Britain, 1688–1789* (Cambridge: Cambridge University Press, 2003).
30   Stasavage, *States of Credit*, 3–5.
31   Among this body of work are Pezzolo, "Italian Monti"; Pezzolo, "Venetian Government Debt"; and Pezzolo, "Bonds and Government Debt." Pezzolo, "Government Debts"; Pezzolo, "Republics and Principalities"; Luciano Pezzolo, *Il fisco dei veneziani: Finanza pubblica ed economia tra XV e XVII secolo* (Verona: Cierre Edizioni, 2003); Pezzolo, *Finanza d'Ancien Régime*, 2006; Pezzolo, *Finanza d'Ancien Régime*, 2009.
32   Pezzolo, "Republics and Principalities."
33   Pezzolo, "Bonds and Government Debt," 163.
34   Frederic S. Mishkin, *The Economics of Money, Banking, and Financial Markets*, 4th ed. (New York: Harper Collins, 1995), 217–23.
35   De Roover, *Medici Bank*, 22; Becker, *Florence in Transition*, 2: 156.
36   Bernardino Barbadoro, *Le finanze della Repubblica fiorentina: Imposta diretta e debito pubblico fino all'istituzione del Monte, Biblioteca storica toscana*, no. 5 (Florence: Olschki, 1929), 629–87.
37   Becker, *Florence in Transition*, 2: 157.

to the market.[38] Nevertheless, the Monte holdings were steeply discounted on the open market during the *Trecento* and *Quattrocento*.

The Monte was a vital part of Florentine communal finances for centuries. The 1470 budget of the Florentine republic noted, "The Monte is the heart of this body which we call city […] every limb, large and small, must contribute to preserving this heart as the guardian fortress, unmovable rock and enduring certainty of the salvation of the whole body and government of your State."[39] The Monte used an improved government management system. Bodies of magistrates, which had no equivalent in other Italian cities, were established to run the consolidated Monte.[40] These "technical-administrative" effects spread throughout the Florentine government and reduced potential venality by government officials.[41] The Monte holdings by the public originated as forced loans in lieu of direct taxes. At different times these forced loans were called both *prestanze* and *catasti*. The subjectively assessed *Trecento estimi*, or estimated direct taxes, were replaced by the impersonal and progressive wealth taxation of the catasto in 1427. Its progressivity increased when a graduated wealth tax rate scale began in 1442.[42] The Monte holders at issuance were therefore not willing participants in a competitive market. This implies that the credibility of the Comune government had little role at the time of issuance.[43]

The Monte possessed some of the characteristics of a public debt bond market. One can refer to Monte holdings either as credits or as bonds. Each term emphasizes a different aspect of the financial instrument. They are credits in the sense that they match the debits of the Comune. This is a more historical legal and accounting usage. They are bonds in the sense of modern financial economic theory. The Monte holdings are sometimes called loans; however, that term is less precise. Loans typically have individual features in each contract, which makes transfer difficult. The Monte contract terms were uniform and holdings were easily assignable.

The Monte Comune and Bond Contract Theory

This section examines the Monte contract in detail. The contract structure is critical to the valuation of financial assets. A bond contract has a number of necessary elements, including the issuer, face value, coupon, payment schedule and maturity. The bond issuer receives the money up front from the bondholder and then contracts to pay a predetermined cash flow to the bondholder. In this particular case the issuer was the Comune

---

38 Julius Kirshner, "Papa Eugenio IV e il Monte Comune. Documenti su investimento e speculazione nel debito pubblico di Firenze," *Archivio storico italiano*, 127 (1969): 341.

39 L. Marks, "The Financial Oligarchy under Lorenzo," in *Italian Renaissance Studies*, ed. Ernest Fraser Jacob (London: Faber and Faber, 1960), 127. Marks cites *Registri delle provvisioni*, 161, fo. 168, Archivio di Stato, Florence.

40 Castelnuovo, "Offices and Officials," 376.

41 Ibid.

42 Elio Conti, *L'imposta diretta a Firenze nel Quattrocento (1427–1494)* (Rome: Palazzo Borromini, 1984), 199.

43 Pezzolo, "Government Debts and Credit Markets," 30.

of Florence. The bondholder was an individual citizen of the Comune of Florence or a foreigner who had petitioned to hold bonds.

The face value, also called the par value, is the value of the bond specified at issuance. In the case of the Monte the face value was usually the amount paid in the initial forced loan. The face value of the Monte credit was not necessarily equal to the amount lent to the Comune. The de facto coupon rate could change significantly. The face value would have influenced the initial depositor's willingness to accept the Monte credit, because the return per florin deposited was changed but not the willingness to sell on the secondary market. The face value was measured in the Florentine gold money of account. In the late medieval world, where the gold and silver content of coins was often suspect, the money of account offered a constant and credible standard. Each government authorized its own money of account. The money of account was the *fiorino d'oro* (gold florin) or *fiorino suggello* (sealed florin), depending on the date. Since inflation during this period was nearly zero, the nominal and the real interest rates were virtually equivalent.

The coupon is the periodic cash payment to the bondholder. Each Monte coupon (payment) was called a *paga* (plural: *paghe*). The coupon multiplied by the annual frequency of payments divided by the face value equals the coupon rate, also called the coupon interest rate. The coupon rate changes during the Quattrocento were usually applied to the entire consolidated debt.[44] A variety of Monte accounts were traded at any one time, each with a different contract and trading price.[45] The number of coupon payments per year varied by account and over time. They were made five times per year on the Monte Comune during the late Trecento and three times per year for the Monte delle doti 7 percent fund during the late Quattrocento.[46] This implies that there were multiple market interest rates and that the interest rate was sensitive to the specific contract. Multiple accounts allowed the Comune to increase the quantity of bonds held and to discriminate among categories and holders of Monte credits.

The Comune made changes to correct problems with the Monte. Financial problems early in the 1340s led to the creation of a market for Monte holdings in 1345.[47] The Monte proved very successful until the plague of 1348 struck the city and disrupted the prestanze that supported the system. The paghe payments were suspended in 1349.

44 Conti, *L'imposta diretta*, 31 and 34.
45 Giuseppe Canestrini, *La scienza e l'arte di stato desunta dagli atti ufficiali della Repubblica fiorentina e dei Medici* (Florence: Le Monnier, 1862), 427–31; Ciappelli, "Il mercato dei titoli," 627 ff.
46 *Monte Comune* 1939, Archivio di Stato, Florence; Julius Kirshner and Jacob Klerman, "The Seven Percent Fund of Renaissance Florence," app. 5.
47 Barbadoro, *Le finanze della Repubblica fiorentina*, 629–87; Roberto Barducci, "Politica e speculazione finanziaria a Firenze dopo la crisi del primo Trecento (1343–1358)," *Archivio storico Italiano* 137, no. 2 (1979): 177–219; Roberto Barducci. "… Cum parva difficultate civium predictorum …: Spunti introduttivi per un regesto della legislazione finanziaria fiorentina del Trecento (1345–1358)," in *Renaissance Studies in Honor of Craig Hugh Smyth*, ed. Andrew Morrogh, Fiorella Superbi Gioffredi, Piero Morselli and Eve Borsook, 2 vols. (Florence: Giunta Barbèra, 1985), 1: 3–15.

In 1351 the Comune made the changes necessary to pay the paghe more securely.[48] Subsequently, the commune would occasionally create new categories of debt with higher coupon rates.[49]

By 1380 the Monte was offering different coupon rates for money deposited into three kinds of Monte accounts: *Monte vecchio* (*vecchio*), *Monte dell'uno due* (*due*) and *Monte dell'uno tre* (*tre*). The tre was created in 1358[50] and the due in 1362.[51] The coupon rate on the face value was the same 5 percent for all three. The vecchio face value equaled the deposit. However, the due face value was double the deposit, and the tre face value was triple the deposit. Therefore the de facto coupon rate on the due was 10 percent and on the tre 15 percent. The reason for this increased coupon rate is disputed. Molho argues that it was caused by market conditions, while Marvin Becker and Gene Brucker argue that the increase was a way of paying off the patricians.[52]

The coupon rate on the face value was reduced to 5 percent in 1380.[53] This rate was artificially low in response to political, not market, pressures.[54] Later in the Trecento the Comune created special funds with coupon rates of 8 percent and 10 percent.[55] The 5 percent general coupon rate was reduced to 3.75 percent in August 1425.[56] The coupon rate was again reduced to 3.375 percent in May 1444 and to 3.25 percent in January 1471.[57]

A forced loan is simultaneously a loan and a tax. The relative importance of each of these two aspects could change over time. The higher coupon rates early in the history of the Monte indicate that it was intended more as a loan initially. Subsequently, the declining coupon rates made it appear more as a tax. The relationship between these two aspects also changed over time in other Italian cities. Pezzolo notes that over time "it is likely that Venetian citizens were increasingly regarding themselves more as taxpayers rather than investors."[58]

---

48   Becker, *Florence in Transition*, 2: 168; Roberto Barducci, "Le riforme finanziarie nel tumulto dei *Ciompi*," in *Il Tumulto dei Ciompi: Un momento di storia fiorentina ed europea* (Florence: Olschki, 1981), 95–103; Barducci, "Politica e speculazione"; Barducci. "Cum parva difficultate civium predictorum."

49   Canestrini, *L'arte di stato*, 427–31; Giovanni Ciappelli, "Il mercato dei titoli del debito pubblico a Firenze nel Tre-Quattrocento," in *Actes: Colloqui corona, municipis i fiscalitat a la Baixa Edat Mitjana*, ed. Manuel Sánchez and Antonio Furió (Lleida: Institut d'Estudis Ilerdencs, 1997), 627 ff.

50   Kirshner, "Papa Eugenio IV," 346; Julius Kirshner, "'Ubi est ille?' Franco Sacchetti and the Monte Comune of Florence," *Speculum* 59, no. 3 (1984): 572; Julius Kirshner, "Angelo degli Ubaldi and Bartolomeo Saliceto," *Rivista Internazionale di Diritto Comune* 14 (2003): 84.

51   Kirshner, "Papa Eugenio IV," 346; Kirshner, "Franco Sacchetti," 572; Kirshner, "Angelo degli Ubaldi," 84.

52   Molho, *Florentine Public Finances*, 65; Becker, *Florence in Transition*, 2: 173–74; Brucker, *Florentine Politics and Society*, 93–95.

53   Kirshner, "Papa Eugenio IV," 346; Molho, *Florentine Public Finances*, 69.

54   Kirshner, "Angelo degli Ubaldi," 84.

55   Molho, *Florentine Public Finances*, 70.

56   Conti, *L'imposta diretta*, 34.

57   Ibid.

58   Pezzolo, "Venetian Government Debt," 67.

The Comune prioritized coupon payments in times of fiscal stress. For example, with the Monte delle doti, a dowry insurance fund established in 1425, coupon payments were given preference when the Monte was suffering from a deficit in 1470.[59] Considering the importance of dowries in the society, this was probably a political decision. The prioritization reduced the risk of the Monte delle doti. It also likely made it easier for the less wealthy to buy and hold the Monte delle doti. Though the coupon was imposed and not determined by the market, it was not completely arbitrary. It provided the government's price of its own debt. However, it was, at best, an imperfect measure of the Florentine cost of borrowing. The Comune had an incentive not to raise the coupon rate over time. To begin with, an increased coupon rate was a de facto tax decrease.

The enforcement of usury laws provided another check on interest rates.[60] They kept the coupon rate low and the initial offering price high.[61] It seems that 5 percent was generally the acceptable maximum rate. Legal authorities were aware of and discussed market interest rates as well.[62] Epstein argues that the coupon rate was like the market rate, since the elites did not object; however, it is not clear why elite citizens in particular would object in the first place.[63] The choice was not between a forced loan and a market rate. Since forced loans were usually collected in lieu of taxes, the choice was between paying taxes with no payment or paying taxes and receiving a small payment.

Monte credits were perpetuities and had no maturity date. They paid only interest and no principal.[64] The credits therefore resemble the later British consols (consolidated stocks), although the credits did have coupons.

The Secondary Market

This section examines the secondary market where the Monte contract was traded. The secondary market was established in 1345, only two years after the creation of the Monte. The issuance of bonds as forced loans meant the secondary market added significant value. Both Monte credits and individual paghe were traded.[65] The reasons to hold

---

59 Marks, "Financial Oligarchy," 130; Anthony Molho, *Marriage Alliance in Late Medieval Florence* (Cambridge, MA: Harvard University Press, 1994), 156.

60 Munro, "Medieval Origins," 506ff; Julius Kirshner, "Authority, Reason, and Conscience in Gregory of Rimini's *Questio prestitorum communis Venetiarum*," in *Reichtum im späten Mittelalter: Politische Theorie, ethische Norm und soziale Akzeptanz (voraussichtlich: Vierteljahrschrift für Sozial- und Wirtschaftsgeschichte. Beihefte)*, ed. Petra Schulte and Peter Hesse (Stuttgart: Franz Steiner, 2015): 115–43.

61 Pezzolo, "Italian Monti," 542.

62 Kirshner, "Franco Sacchetti," 558. For more general discussions, see: Lester Little, *Religious Poverty and the Profit Economy in Medieval Europe* (Ithaca, NY: Cornell University Press, 1978); John T. Noonan Jr., *The Scholastic Analysis of Usury* (Cambridge, MA: Harvard University Press, 1957).

63 Epstein, *Freedom and Growth*, 18–19n18.

64 Kirshner, "Franco Sacchetti," 557–58.

65 Canestrini, *L'arte di stato*, 430–31.

on to Monte credits included regular paghe payments, assignment as collateral,[66] portfolio diversification, a hedge against silver coinage debasement and potential redemption to pay fines and taxes.

The Monte credits were typically discounted steeply. Careful historians report both the discount rate, the price as a percentage of the face value and the coupon rate.[67] The large discount was not because the paghe were late. Payment delays were, in fact, infrequent. The paghe were paid regularly and reasonably on time.[68]

Monte credits were assignable, not negotiable. The assignment was only a derivative title. Claims against the original holder could count against the future holder. In this case the lack of an ownership trail could cause serious problems. Paghe, like the credits, were also assignable and could be the object of a loan.[69] Paghe were redeemable, and any encumbrances expired at a particular point in time.

Monte credits were not bearer bonds. The Comune recorded the original owner of the bond and any subsequent assignments at the central registry. Paghe assignments and all encumbrances were also recorded in communal account books.[70] Recording the assignments in a central location had several additional benefits. It prevented forgery, guaranteed tax payments on transactions and reduced the costs of tracking the creditworthiness for the original bondholder. It also benefits modern historians. Accurate recordings were important to the Florentines. For the first few years, monks recorded the contracts, presumably because of their incorruptibility. The Comune became dissatisfied with them due to their lack of competence, however, so they assigned government officials, the *ufficiali di Monte* (Monte officials), to oversee the Monte in 1353. They were brought in to "correct the errors and wrongful acts found in the registers."[71] This kind of diligence on the part of the Comune shows that the public information contained in the registers was of real value to them. The Venetians also recorded contracts, but this appears to have been primarily for taxation purposes.[72]

The Florentines followed standard accounting practices; transactions were entered into a journal and then summarized in a ledger. The journal was the typical account book of the period with its stout cover. The journal entries included all relevant information such as the date of assignment, the assignee and assignor and their places of residence, the amount, the type of contract, the tax on the contract and any paghe assigned. The journal also tracks contracts recorded into the ledger by using the familiar diagonal

66 Julius Kirshner, "Encumbering Private Claims to Public Debt in Renaissance Florence," in *The Growth of the Bank as Institution and the Development of Money-Business Laws*, ed. V. Piergiovanni (Berlin: Duncker & Humblot, 1993), 58.

67 Conti, *L'imposta diretta*, 34; Giovanni Ciappelli, *Fisco e Società a Firenze nel Rinascimento* (Rome: Istituto Nazionale di Studi e Letteratura, 2009), 266.

68 Kirshner and Klerman, "Seven Percent Fund," app. 5.

69 Kirshner, "Encumbering Private Claims," 30, 31 and 34.

70 Ibid., 32.

71 Kirshner, "Encumbering Private Claims," 32n41.

72 Mueller, *Venetian Money Market*, 519.

stroke from lower left to upper right used to indicate a closed or transferred account.[73] Following is an example of a typical entry:

> 1371 day 18 of March [At top of sheet]
> [First entry of day] Monte dell' un due account: Stefano del Migliore, Pursemaker, Quarter Santo Spirito, [assigned] to Tommaso Dugolino di Vieri, Quarter Santo Spirito, Florins 11, Soldi 5, with the paghe. [Tax] ½ a florin.[74]

The entry shows a clear mix of medieval and modern. The script was small, as was common in medieval documents, but was in the italic characteristic of the Renaissance. The year and day of the month were generally written in Roman numerals, while the currency amounts were nearly always in Arabic numerals. There was a clear fondness for abbreviation. The "Monte dell' un due account" was indicated by an Arabic numeral two to the left side. Letters were abbreviated.

Tax rates on the Monte varied over time. Two different kinds of taxes were assessed during the Trecento and the Quattrocento. The first was a transaction tax of 0.5 percent on most trades of Monte holdings. This was part of a general tax on contracts, and it reduced liquidity. The second kind of tax, the city's wealth taxes, was levied irregularly. The initial wealth tax was the *estimo*, which was based on estimated wealth, including Monte credits. The 1427 catasto was the first tax that assessed actual wealth. Florence taxed Monte holdings until the 1480 *Decima Scalata* tax assessment.[75] The irregular catasto impositions added a risk to taxation that does not exist with modern taxation. These assessments were procyclical with wars, which further increased the risk of holding Monte credits.

The Florentine authorities also created implicit surcharges on the Monte credits. For example, they arbitrarily set the discount rate of Monte credits for assessment purposes at 50 percent of face value for the 1427 catasto.[76] The market discount rates at that time were closer to 30 percent.[77] This surcharge amounted to about two-thirds of the total value on Monte credits.

In practice both the Comune and the bondholder had options to initiate redemption of Monte credits. The Comune had a de facto call option that would have reduced the bond's value.[78] There were periodic reductions in the Monte principal.[79] There was no

---

73 For an example of its use in the Monte journal, see: Monte Comune, Vol. 1939, 2r ff.

74 Ibid., 10r.

75 Elio Conti, ed., *Matteo Palmieri Ricordi Fiscali (1427–1474) con due Appendici relative al 1474–1495* (Rome: Palazzo Borromini, 1983), 176 and 198; Conti, *L'imposta diretta*, 282.

76 Herlihy and Klapisch-Zuber, *Les Toscans*, 68.

77 Anthony Molho, *Florentine Public Finances in the Early Renaissance, 1400–1433* (Cambridge, MA: Harvard University Press, 1971), 161–62.

78 A call option is the right, but not the obligation, to buy something. A put option is the right, but not the obligation, to sell something. In modern terminology, the writer sells the option to the buyer. In general, an option transfers risk from the buyer to the writer.

79 Richard A. Goldthwaite, *The Economy of Renaissance Florence* (Baltimore: Johns Hopkins University Press, 2009), 494.

set redemption schedule, but only a portion would be called at any one time. A discount rate, this time much below the market rate, would sometimes be established for redemption purposes. As a match to the call option held by the Comune, the bondholder had a de facto put option to redeem at face value that would have increased the bond's value. As it evolved over time, the put option encouraged certain people to hold the bonds, including those who were more likely to owe fines, pay more taxes or who were brokers. Monte credits could be redeemed in lieu of taxes by the 1360s (*composizione*) and to pay fines from 1371.[80] Richard Goldthwaite argues that the ability to redeem Monte credits in order to pay taxes converted the forced loan into a direct tax,[81] but that is incorrect. The option increased the value of Monte credits.

The Comune government could combine these policies. It gave people incentive to retire vecchio credits instead of either the due or the tre, so by 1372 the contract tax was not being applied to transactions in vecchio credits.[82] This implies that the expected return on the vecchio was higher than it was for either the due or the tre.

The Monte holdings were distributed widely among the Florentine population during both the Trecento[83] and the Quattrocento.[84] The breadth of the market implies that there was broad public confidence. This confidence, however, varied over time and by the type of financial instrument. The Monte delle doti was more widely held than the Monte Comune during the Quattrocento.[85] The breadth of ownership in Florence appears unique compared to other Italian cities. In other places, only the ruling elite appear to have held bonds.[86] This lack of breadth could have led to problems.[87]

Florentine Monte ownership was skewed toward the wealthier members of society in 1427.[88] This was initially caused by the portfolio effects that influenced the secondary market and later on by the progressivity of the forced loan issuance.[89] Wealthier citizens

---

80 Goldthwaite, *Economy of Renaissance Florence*, 496; *Monte Comune* 1939, Archivio di Stato, Florence.

81 Goldthwaite, *Economy of Renaissance Florence*, 497.

82 De Roover, *Medici Bank*, 22. This date may not be exact. A vecchio transaction on December 12, 1373, among others, appears with a contract tax assessment (*Monte Comune* 1939, 138v. Archivio di Stato, Florence).

83 Anthony Molho, "Créditeurs de Florence en 1347: Un aperçu statistique du quartier de Santo Spirito," in *Firenze nel Quattrocento*, vol. 1: *Politica e Fiscalità* (Rome: Edizioni di Storia Letteratura, 2006), 97–112.

84 Analysis using data from David Herlihy and Christiane Klapisch-Zuber, *Census and Property Survey of Florentine Domains and the City of Verona in Fifteenth-Century Italy* [machine-readable data file]. Cambridge, MA: David Herlihy, Harvard University, Department of History and Paris, France: Christiane Klapisch-Zuber, Ecole Pratique des Hautes Etudes [producers], 1977. Madison: University of Wisconsin, Data and Program Library Service [distributor], 1981.

85 Marks, "Financial Oligarchy," 131.

86 Pezzolo, "Government Debts and Credit Markets," 31.

87 MacDonald, *Free Nation Deep in Debt*, 104.

88 Analysis using data from Herlihy and Klapisch-Zuber, *Census and Property Survey*.

89 Lorenzo Tanzini, "Tuscan States: Florence and Siena," in *The Italian Renaissance State*, ed. Andrea Gamberini and Isabella Lazzarini (Cambridge: Cambridge University Press, 2012), 91.

thus had a greater role in running the Monte, at the expense of others.[90] Leaders of the 1378 Ciompi Revolt complained that the Monte gave the wealthy an unfair advantage in that they made money at the expense of the poor.[91] Foreigners, particularly landed nobles, occasionally attempted to buy Monte credits. However, certain laws restricted foreign ownership. This foreign interest implies that either the risk-return profile for the Monte credits was superior to what was possible with land or that they were a useful diversification for portfolios that were overly weighted in land. The Florentine restriction on foreign investors suggests that there was an economic rent accruing to the holders of the Monte credits. An increased investor pool would be expected to increase the price of the Monte. The restriction against foreigners holding debt limited liquidity. However, foreigners could get special permission to invest in Monte credits, and there were cases of this happening in the Trecento and in the 1420s.[92] Foreign investors in the Monte could expect the face value to be at a premium.[93]

Speculation was an important part of the market. Speculators helped the market find the true price of the bonds and thereby assess the credibility of a government. There was significant speculation in Monte bonds.[94] Speculation was also important in Genoa and in Venice.[95] There were potentially large arbitrage opportunities as well. For example, the multiple Monte accounts would have increased the possibility of arbitrage and provided incentives for speculators to make markets. The speculators' role was particularly important because the initial offerings were forced loans. Citizens turned to professional brokers to pay prestanze assessments. This process was different from the redemption provision put option. These brokers paid the tax at a discount and then collected the interest.[96] Such brokerage arrangements converted the prestanze into a discounted direct tax for many investors,[97] a process that could have a significant impact. For example, in April 1378 approximately 5,000 of 13,074 households paid speculators to take their assessment of the prestanze at a reduced rate.[98] The 1378

---

90 Castelnuovo, "Offices and Officials," 377.
91 Barducci, "Le riforme finanziarie nel tumulto dei Ciompi," 101. The *Ciompi* were wool workers.
92 Molho, *Florentine Public Finances*, 142; Munro, "Medieval Origins," 546; Kirshner, "Angelo degli Ubaldi," 101.
93 Molho, *Florentine Public Finances*, 147; Kirshner, "Papa Eugenio IV," 346.
94 For a detailed and specific example, see Becker, *Florence in Transition*, 2: 175.
95 Pezzolo, "Government Debts and Credit Markets," 30–31; Jean-Claude Hocquet, "À Venise, dette publique et speculations privées," in *L'impôt dans les villes de l'Occident méditerranéen XIIIe–XVe siècle, Colloque tenu à Bercy les 3, 4, et 5 octobre 2001*, ed. Denis Menjot, Albert Rigaudière and Manuel Sánchez Martínez (Paris: Comité pour l'Histoire économique et Financière de la France, 2005), 15–37.
96 Kirshner, "Franco Sacchetti," 564.
97 Ibid.
98 Number of households: Ildefonso il San Luigi, *Delizie degli Eruditi Toscani: Stefani. Marchionne di Coppo*, vol. 16. *Istoria florentina* (Florence: Gaetano Cambiagi, 1783), 123–24. Number selling: Stefani, *Cronaca fiorentina*, Rubrica 883, 385. The number here differs from Goldthwaite, *Economy of Renaissance Florence*, 497.

assignment was a clear profit opportunity. It gave the speculators the state obligation at a reduced price.[99]

Conflicts of interest in the relatively small Italian city-states were real. Florence had no law against insider trading;[100] thus, traders could act on any information they acquired, and a Florentine official could be an investment adviser.[101] In today's market such acts would be both a clear conflict of interest and illegal. It is likely that the most powerful families had an information advantage. However, the small size of Quattrocento Florence would have reduced the advantage of inside information.

The Florentine record-keeping approach resembles the modern financial market requirements that insiders report transactions. It provided some level of public disclosure and reduced the potential return from insider trading; therefore, there was less need to make insider trading illegal. Venice, in contrast, did outlaw insider trading,[102] which could account for the city's less active secondary market. The reduced information would increase uncertainty and reduce the value of the bonds. It would also diminish or eliminate the role of speculators.

The Monte Comune and Interest Rate Theory

This section combines the analyses from the previous three sections to show how the Monte contract's characteristics described above lead to a new time series for the interest rate. At any given time, in any given market, many versions of the interest rate are observed. The yield to maturity is the standard definition and most accurate measure of the observed interest rate.[103] The bond contract is the starting point to determine the interest rate. Other factors could include, but are not limited to, wars and fiscal pressures, manipulation, overissuance of bonds, the Monte delle doti, the relative tax rate on bonds compared to other assets and portfolio factors. This long list can be simplified to "wealth, expected returns on bonds relative to alternative assets, risk of bonds relative to alternative assets, and liquidity of bonds relative to alternative assets."[104]

The real interest rate equals the sum of the long-term risk-free rate, the risk premium, liquidity premium and tax rate. The risk-free interest rate can be associated with the underlying price of buying the contract and deferring consumption. Risk-free interest rates in the post-World War II United States have historically been about 1 percent.[105] The risk premium puts a price on the contract's risk. This can be a significant portion

99   Goldthwaite, *Economy of Renaissance Florence*, 497.

100 Gene A. Brucker, "Un documento fiorentino sulla guerra, sulla finanza e sull'amministrazione pubblica," *Archivio storico Italiano* 115, no. 2 (1957): 165–87.

101 MacDonald, *Free Nation Deep in Debt*, 83.

102 Mueller, *Venetian Money Market*, 519.

103 There are many sources on this point. For example, see Hirshleifer, *Investment, Interest, and Capital*, 35; Mishkin, *Money, Banking, and Financial Markets*, 69.

104 Mishkin, *Money, Banking, and Financial Markets*, 113–14.

105 John H. Cochrane, *Asset Pricing*, rev. ed. (Princeton, NJ: Princeton University Press, 2005), xiii.

of the price of bonds. For example, in the United States, the risk premium's mean and volatility have been much larger than the underlying interest rate's mean and volatility in recent years.[106] The prices of many of today's long-term assets are "driven by the possibility of extraordinarily bad news."[107]

The Monte price provides information about default likelihood. The new institutional economics literature implies that the default risk is a key to evaluating government credibility. The Florentine authorities clearly recognized the need for a credible commitment. For example, the committee governing Monte operations made adjustments to the coupon rates periodically during the Quattrocento. These *riforme* (reforms) became more frequent as the century progressed.[108]

The liquidity premium measures how easy it is to trade the contract. Increased liquidity increases the price of a bond while lowering the interest rate. The liquidity of a market decreases as transaction costs increase. The creation of the Monte secondary market in 1345 increased liquidity in the Florentine market,[109] and it also made the interest rate observable and increased the price. The steep interest rate drop in 1345 implies that liquidity was an important factor in the price. The approximately 40 percent participation rate in the secondary market in 1378 noted above confirms its importance.

Finally, higher tax rates decrease the bond price and increase the yield. This was particularly important during the repeated financial crises facing Florence during the Trecento and the Quattrocento.

The above discussion implies that there was a significant difference between the Florentine market interest rate and the coupon rate. The Florentine Monte secondary market provides a true market price that can be used to calculate the interest rate. Directly comparing loans on a primary market, such as those in northern Europe, with coupon and interest rates in places where a secondary market existed, such as Italy, is problematic. For example, when funds are tight, one would expect the coupon rate to decrease but the interest rate to increase, because the paghe default risk increases.

Late Medieval Interest Rate Measurement

The effort to measure late medieval interest rates goes back more than half a century. Sidney Homer's systematic modern compilation of interest rates is the standard and covers interest rates from Ancient Mesopotamia to the modern era.[110] That breadth, however, prevents him and his successors from making any detailed analysis of changing

---

106 Ibid., xv.

107 Ian Martin, "On the Valuation of Long-Dated Assets," *Journal of Political Economy* 120, no. 2 (2012): 46–358.

108 Marks, "Financial Oligarchy," 124n2.

109 Carlo M. Cipolla, *The Monetary Policy of Fourteenth-Century Florence* (Berkeley: University of California Press, 1982), 12.

110 Sidney Homer, *A History of Interest Rates* (New Brunswick, NJ: Rutgers University Press, 1963); Sidney Homer and Richard Sylla, *A History of Interest Rates*, 4th ed. (Hoboken, NJ: Wiley, 2005).

Table 2.1 Pezzolo's time series of
Florentine Monte Comune rates

Years	Rate
1276–1300	10.00
1301–1325	8.00
1326–1350	12.00
1351–1375	5.00
1376–1400	5.00
1401–1425	3.75
1426–1450	3.37
1451–1475	3.25
1476–1500	2.50

Source: Pezzolo, "Bonds and
Government Debt," 157.

contractual forms. Homer, of necessity, used coupon rates for medieval Europe. Today's scholars, when refining his work, do not need to be so limited.

Several authors calculate isolated examples of late medieval and early modern Italian market yields. Reinhold Mueller calculates yields in Venice between 1285 and 1500 and finds a long-term decline in the market value of government credits.[111] He further notes that government and commercial interest rates were linked.[112] For Florence, Roberto Barducci distinguishes between Monte coupons of between 5 and 15 percent and interest rates of between 20 and 30 percent.[113] MacDonald calculated a yield of 17.86 percent on the Monte dell'uno tre.[114] However, he does not distinguish between the yield on the initial offering and the market yield. Kirshner and Klerman find the Monte delle doti paid between 15 and 21 percent in 1433 depending on the term to maturity,[115] whereas Pezzolo cites a 17 percent figure for the Monte delle doti.[116]

Pezzolo's is the most complete and widely used time series of Italian city-state interest rates for Florence, Genoa and Venice.[117] He reports (1) the discount as a percentage of the face value and (2) the coupon rate.[118] Table 2.1 presents Pezzolo's quarter-century averages

---

111 Mueller, *Venetian Money Market*; Reinhold C. Mueller, *The Venetian Money Market: Banks, Panics, and the Public Debt, 1200–1500* (Baltimore: Johns Hopkins University Press, 1997), 462, 474–75 and 557.
112 Ibid., 473.
113 Barducci, "Le riforme finanziarie nel tumulto dei *Ciompi*," 97.
114 MacDonald, *Free Nation Deep in Debt*, 83.
115 Julius Kirshner and Jacob Klerman, "The Seven Percent Fund of Renaissance Florence," in *Banchi pubblici, banchi private e monti di pieta nell'Europa preindustriale: Amministrazione, tecniche operative e ruoli economici: atti del convegno–Genova* (1–6 ottobre 1990) (Genova: Società Ligure di Storia Patria, 1991), 1: 367–98.
116 Pezzolo, "Italian Monti," 3.
117 Pezzolo, "Bonds and Government Debt," 145–63; Pezzolo, "Government Debts and Credit Markets," 25 and 29.
118 Pezzolo, "Bonds and Government Debt," 154–55; Pezzolo, "Venetian Government Debt," 65; Pezzolo, "Republics and Principalities in Italy," 280.

of Monte Comune interest rates. They show a low, nearly flat and slowly declining interest rate. The Quattrocento interest rates range from 2.5 to 5.0 percent. This sharply contrasts with the calculations by Mueller, Barducci, MacDonald, and Kirshner and Klerman. Pezzolo's time series has serious problems, however. To begin with, he uses coupon rates instead of market interest rates. He refers to the interest rate he calculates as a nominal interest rate.[119] However, his nominal interest rate is actually the coupon rate.[120] The error could have arisen because the nominal interest rate also means the "named" interest rate and could be confused with the coupon rate, which would be the only explicit, or named, rate. If, instead, Pezzolo is using the coupon rate to proxy for the debt service costs, he does so incorrectly. He ignores the differences between the Florentine vecchio, due and tre accounts and calculates the rate based on the face value of the bond and not the amount deposited. Therefore, although the due paid 10 percent and the tre paid 15 percent on the amount deposited, both are only credited with the 5 percent paid on the face value.[121]

Both Epstein and Stasavage use secondary sources, including Pezzolo, for their interest rate data.[122] Epstein employs coupon rates on public debt in a wide range of European governments including 18 cities and urban republics and 12 monarchies.[123] He focuses more on market integration, which is less problematic than examining state formation. Epstein's use of the rates is reasonably accurate when considering market integration. There are, however, still some problems. The contracts underlying coupon rates in Italy were very different from those issued by the English king.

Stasavage examines annual interest rate observations from a sample of 31 polities, including 19 city-state and 12 territorial state debts.[124] His focus on institutional development leads him to examine the direct costs to the institution from borrowing.[125] In his model, debt service costs are used as a proxy for interest rates. However, he also claims that the ratio of debt service to stock of debt is not an interest rate.[126] His inclusion of forced loans is likely to increase the disparity between the debt service and the interest rate. Stasavage is aware that he mixes and matches different types of interest rates and acknowledges comparability issues.[127] He uses data from life annuities, perpetual annuities, nominal interest rates and the ratio of debt service to stock of debt.[128] He does not mention coupon rates and does not distinguish them from interest rates.[129] The variability in institutional practice across Europe further reduces the comparability. First, some

---

119   Pezzolo, "Fiscal System and Finance," 13; Pezzolo, "Bonds and Government Debt," 157; Pezzolo, *Monti*, 8.
120   Based on a comparison of Pezzolo, "Bonds and Government Debt," 157; Conti, *L'imposta diretta*, 34.
121   Becker, *Florence in Transition*, 2: 173–80.
122   Epstein, *Freedom and Growth*, 19–23; Stasavage, *States of Credit*, 30–31.
123   Epstein, *Freedom and Growth*, 19–23.
124   Stasavage, *States of Credit*, 39.
125   Ibid., 38–43.
126   Ibid., 38–39.
127   Ibid., 38 and 42–43.
128   Ibid., 38–39.
129   Ibid., 30–31.

governments, such as France, sold debt below par level.[130] Florence also did this during the second half of the Trecento. This tactic implies that the government set the price above the market level and the coupon rate below. Second, the rates do not necessarily reflect interest rates on the open market.[131] Third, some cities, such as those in the Low Countries, sometimes borrowed on behalf of princely overlords.[132] Stasavage treats the resulting measures as market rates when he compares the costs of borrowing with land rents.[133] Whereas the rate of return on land is derived from the market, the interest rates he uses often are not from market rates.[134]

The use of problematic data compromises their results to some extent. Stasavage looks at credible commitment but limits the value of his approach by mixing interest rates, coupon rates and borrowing costs. Epstein consistently uses the coupon rates in all cases.[135] This economic rigor makes his analysis more valid.

A New Time Series of Quattrocento Interest Rates

This section computes a new time series of market interest rates for Quattrocento Florence based on the yield to market. Pezzolo's coupon rate time series is shown by the circle points, the lower set, in Figure 2.1. It slowly and steadily declines over the entire period. As noted earlier, the Comune had an incentive not to increase the coupon rate.

After examining the trend of the coupon rates, the next step is to calculate a yield to market over the same time period. All the underlying data for these calculations come from Elio Conti.[136] Since the Monte credits were perpetuities, only the coupon rate and the price are needed to calculate the yield to maturity. It is a straightforward net present value problem. (See Appendix 2A.) The calculation is simplified in two ways due to lack of data: (1) it is not adjusted for the frequency of coupon payments and (2) it is not adjusted for the call and put option features, because data are not available to make such a calculation. In general, the Comune call option implies that the calculation would be an underestimate, and the bondholder put option implies that it would be an overestimate. On net, none of these would change the calculation significantly. Regardless, this new series is meant to demonstrate a method and is not intended to be comprehensive.

The upper set of diamond-shaped points in Figure 2.1 shows the time series of yields to market. The yield to market is significantly different from the coupon rate. This difference makes clear the forced loan nature of the Monte. Whereas the coupon rate is smoothly and constantly decreasing, the interest rate is first increasing and then decreasing in an inverted-U shape. The following section examines this relationship in greater detail.

---

130 Ibid., 42.
131 Ibid.
132 Ibid., 43.
133 Ibid., 40.
134 Ibid., 41.
135 Epstein, *Freedom and Growth*, 18–19n18.
136 Conti, *L'imposta diretta*, 34.

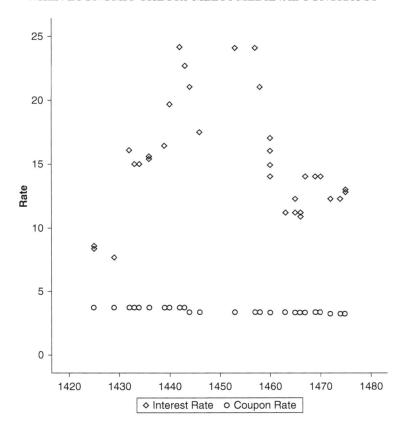

Figure 2.1 Examples of Monte Comune coupon and interest rates by year, 1420–80
Source: Elio Conti, *L'imposta diretta a Firenze nel Quattrocento (1427–1494)* (Rome: Palazzo Borromini, 1984), 34. Coupon rate as reported. Interest rate calculated by author.

Some Implications of the New Interest Rate Time Series

Figure 2.2 is a more analytical version of the data in Figure 2.1. It adds trend lines for both time series. The coupon rate and yield-to-market time series are fundamentally different. The trend dominates any variation in the case of the coupon rate time series. The coupon rate time series has a high linear R^2 fit. The R^2 is 0.836. This implies that nearly 84 percent of the variation is explained by the trend line. However, in the case of the yield-to-market time series, the variation dominates the trend. It has a low linear R^2 fit. The R^2 is 0.009, which suggests that the trend line explains less than 1 percent of the variation. Together, these two observations would imply that the two time series have a very low correlation. This is correct, as the correlation is only 0.072 (see Table 2.2), meaning that only 7.2 percent of the variation of one is explained by the variation of the other.[137]

---

137 The fit and the correlation estimates differ slightly because the fit is calculated allowing for the possibility of a nonzero intercept term.

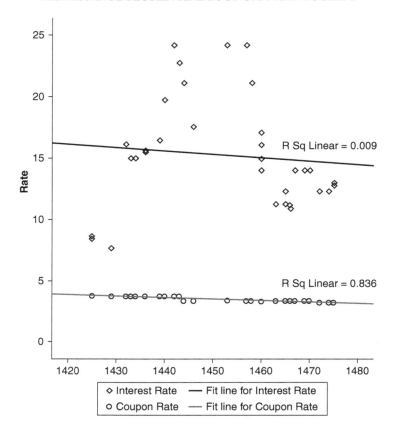

Figure 2.2 Examples of Monte Comune coupon and interest rates by year, 1420–80, with overlay of trend lines. Coupon rate as reported. Interest rate calculated by author.
Source: Conti, *L'imposta diretta*, 34.

Table 2.2 Correlation between coupon rate and estimated interest rate

Sample Size	35
Pearson Correlation	0.072
Significance (Two-Tailed)	0.679

Sources: Coupon rates: Pezzolo, "Bonds and Government Debt," 157; Discount rates: Conti, *L'imposta diretta*, 34. Estimation by author. See text and Appendix 2A for details.

Figure 2.2 shows that the Monte credit yield-to-market time series followed an inverted-U shape beginning in the early 1430s and ending in the 1460s, though it remained high through the 1480s. This pattern demonstrates that no long-term constant trend dominated Florentine interest rates during the Quattrocento, the credibility of the

Comune could be subject to significant change over time, any bad fiscal problems were recoverable and the economy was resilient.

Historians of the Monte have highlighted several important events. These include the war with Milan during the 1420s, the fiscal crisis of 1431–33,[138] the Reform of 1458 and the subsequent series of constitutional reforms through 1475 that shifted control of the Monte.[139] Turning points in the interest rate time series appear associated with the fiscal crisis of 1431–33 and the Reform of 1458. However, this assessment is necessarily tentative given the incomplete nature of the time series. For example, the relatively more mundane aspect of spikes in revenue collection could have had an impact.[140] In addition, there are statistical problems linking events and turning points ex post without applying rigorous decision criteria. At this point the only thing one can be sure of is that more analysis of the time series of interest rates is warranted.

Conclusion

The study in this chapter finds that the most commonly used Florentine interest rate time series is incorrect because it uses coupon rates rather than yields to market. Further, there is little in common theoretically or empirically between the coupon rate and the yield to market. Coupon rates are significantly lower, less volatile and uncorrelated with the estimated interest rates. The coupon rate is a poor indicator of credibility, because the Florentine authorities had the ability and incentive to manipulate it.

This result has implications regarding the historiography of state formation and interest rates. First, the results in this study lend support to Molho's argument that the "internal politics of regimes in power" drove the decisions on taxation and public finance.[141] Close examination of both the relationship among the legal requirements of the Florentine Monte Comune and the differences between the coupon rate and the interest rate certainly supports this position. The timing of the inverted-U shape of the Florentine market yields clearly merits further investigation. Second, there are broader implications of the interest rate time series. These results restore economic risk as an important factor in the late medieval and early modern economy. Finally, the results have implications for a larger body of theoretical work that is beginning to emerge from the new institutional economics and associated perspectives. Recent work has often relied on the differences between coupon rates in various polities to deduce differences in constitutional effectiveness.[142] Such an approach should be reconsidered.

This study provides more evidence that the historical context and the economic theory have to be merged appropriately. In the case of this study, the definition of the interest rate had to match that from economic theory. Local historical details form an essential part of

---

138   For more information, see Molho, *Florentine Public Finances*, 153–82.
139   Marks, "Financial Oligarchy," 123–47.
140   Conti, *L'imposta diretta*, 365–69.
141   Molho, "State and Public Finance," S103.
142   Epstein, *Freedom and Growth*; Stasavage, *States of Credit*.

the underlying bond contracts. The Florentine forced loan system makes the coupon rate an unreliable measure of the true interest rate. The nature of the sources is important.[143] The research results from this study emphasize the importance of developing a fundamental and reliable understanding of the underlying legal and institutional framework such as that provided by Kirshner's work.[144]

The study presented in this chapter provides another example of the importance of historical circumstances and the dangers of oversimplification that can result from ignoring the historical context. From this perspective, these results touch on the use of big data approaches. Big data is more familiar as a tool used by business and government to extract usable information from very large data sets. The range of applications expands daily.[145] Big data has recently been used to study the rate of occurrence of words in books.[146] For example, in an exercise in American history, Erez Aiden and Jean-Baptiste Michel analyzed when the phrase "United States" switched from being used as a plural noun to being used as a singular.[147] Here, the results point to a cautionary note. Although the interest rates across cities appear comparable, and coupon rates that appear to have a common definition were chosen as the root for the analysis, this chapter seriously questions the viability of this approach to examine state formation. The conclusion is that big data applications must make sure the qualitative characteristics, not just the quantitative diagnostics, demonstrate the data are relevant and consistent.

Appendix 2A: Calculating the Monte Comune Interest Rates from the Coupon and Discount Rates

Since the Monte Comune bonds were perpetuities, the formula for the interest rate is relatively simple.[148] This calculation does not factor in the coupon payment schedule, because that was not reported by Conti. The assumption was made that the full coupon payment was made at the end of the year. The impact is minimal because the individual coupon payments are small and the bond is a perpetuity.

143 Rebecca Jean Emigh, "What Influences Official Information? Exploring Aggregate Microhistories of the Catasto of 1427," in *Small Worlds: Method, Meaning, and Narrative in Microhistory*, ed. James F. Brooks, Christopher R. N. DeCorse and John Walton (Santa Fe: School for Advanced Research Press, 2008), 199–223.

144 Kirshner, "States of Debt"; Kirshner, "Encumbering Private Claims"; Kirshner, "Authority, Reason, and Conscience."

145 For a readable history of the use of big data techniques in American politics, see: Sasha Isenberg, *The Victory Lab: The Secret Science of Winning Campaigns* (New York: Crown Publishers, 2012). For a discussion of big data applications in business, see: Bill Schmarzo, *Big Data MBA: Driving Business Success with Data Science* (Indianapolis: Wiley, 2015).

146 Erez Aiden and Jean-Baptiste Michel, *Uncharted: Big Data as a Lens on Human Culture* (New York: Riverhead Books, 2013).

147 Aiden and Michel, *Uncharted*, 3–4.

148 Richard A. Brealey and Stewart C. Myers, *Principles of Corporate Finance*, 7th ed. (Boston: McGraw Hill Irwin, 2003), 37.

The standard formula for a convergent series issues:

$$S = \sum_{t=1} \frac{a}{r^t},$$

where
S: Sum,
r: A value less than one (interest rate),
t: Time period and
a: A constant.

This leads to

$$S = \sum_{t=1} \frac{a}{r^t} = \frac{a}{1-r}.$$

Now, making the following substitutions into the formula

$$r = \frac{1}{1+i}$$

$$S = P = dF$$

$$a = cF,$$

where
P: Price,
c: Coupon rate,
F: Face value,
i: Interest rate,
t: Date,
d: Discount,

this gives

$$P = dF = \sum_{t=1} \frac{cF}{(1+i)^t} = \frac{cF}{i}$$

$$d = \frac{c}{i},$$

Which implies

$$i = \frac{c}{d}.$$

So if the coupon rate is 5 percent and the discount is 50 percent, the interest rate is 10 percent.

$$i = \frac{0.05}{0.50} = 0.10$$

There is no need to assume that Florentines were able to calculate the exact mathematical solution. The formula $i = \frac{c}{d}$ is simple enough to find by trial and error.

Part II

SOCIETY

Chapter Three

THE CHANCES OF GETTING RICH IN RENAISSANCE FLORENCE: THE WOOL INDUSTRY OCCUPATIONAL WEALTH HIERARCHY

Introduction

It is difficult to study the Italian Renaissance without studying its wealth. In a highly visible way, wealth financed the creation of the renowned art and architecture of Renaissance culture.[1] In a less visible way, it largely determined an individual's social standing in the commercial Renaissance society.[2] The importance of wealth in the cultural and social worlds inextricably links both to the economic world that produced that wealth. This chapter shows how the creation of wealth at the household level was highly volatile and explores the implications of that observation for Renaissance society.

The Renaissance Florentines made efforts to organize their economy. As part of this effort, production was organized around guilds. Each guild was associated with a level of social status. The *arte maggiore* structure divided Florence into a hierarchy of major and minor guilds. Guilds were fundamentally economic entities, and many of their regulations were designed to reduce uncertainty for members.[3] Regulating production prices and quality helped guarantee income and reduce wealth volatility within each

---

1   Examples of work based on this perspective includes: Richard A. Goldthwaite, *The Building of Renaissance Florence* (Baltimore: Johns Hopkins University Press, 1980); Richard A. Goldthwaite, *Wealth and the Demand for Art in Italy, 1300–1600* (Baltimore: Johns Hopkins University Press, 1993); Lisa Jardine, *Worldly Goods: A New History of the Renaissance* (New York: W. W. Norton, 1996).

2   Lauro Martines, *Social World of the Florentine Humanists, 1390–1460* (Princeton, NJ: Princeton University Press, 1963), app. 2; Richard A. Goldthwaite, *Private Wealth in Renaissance Florence: A Study of Four Families* (Princeton, NJ: Princeton University Press, 1968); Francis William Kent, *Household and Lineage in Renaissance Florence* (Princeton, NJ: Princeton University Press, 1977); Samuel K. Cohn Jr., *The Laboring Classes in Renaissance Florence* (New York: Academic Press, 1978); Dale V. Kent and Francis William Kent, *Neighbours and Neighbourhood in Renaissance Florence: The District of the Red Lion in the Fifteenth Century* (Locust Valley, NY: J. J. Augustin, 1982), 9; Ronald F. E. Weissman, *Ritual Brotherhood in Renaissance Florence* (New York: Academic Press, 1982), 3; Francis W Kent, *Bartolomeo Cederni and His Friends: Letters to an Obscure Florentine* (Florence: Olschki, 1991).

3   Karl Gunnar Persson, *Pre-Industrial Economic Growth. Social Organization and Technological Progress in Europe* (Oxford: Blackwell, 1988), 75–76.

occupation. This could, in turn, lead to a correlation between occupation and income and create a hierarchy that generated significant inequality and a lack of mobility.

Historians' opinions are mixed about the implications of the guild system for Florentine social status.[4] Armando Sapori points out the importance and role of this hierarchy,[5] and Epstein sees prestige as the key difference between the arte maggiore and the *popolo minuto*.[6] Brucker, though, argues that guilds did not demarcate classes,[7] and Goldthwaite contends that guild membership was not the critical determinant for social position: "in Florence guild membership did not necessarily define a man's economic activity, let alone his economic status."[8]

The key question, therefore, is the extent of the influence of guilds, through the occupational structure, on household wealth. In other words, it asks how much of a household's wealth was determined by the household head's occupation. The core of this study analyzes wealth volatility conditional on the household head's occupation for the set of occupations in the wool industry during the mid-Quattrocento. The size of the wool industry as well as its diversity of occupations makes an ideal focus for this type of analysis. The 1427 catasto makes it the perfect sample for this kind of study.

Wealth volatility in a modern society is typically measured using only one dimension. The role of guilds in Florence noted above, however, requires analyzing wealth volatility using two dimensions: the wealth volatility for the overall society, which is an unconditional volatility, and the wealth volatility due to the economic system of medieval guilds, a conditional volatility. The rest of this study develops the analysis outlined above. It shows that there was a difference in wealth between arte maggiore and popolo minuto occupations and then examines the variation conditional on the occupation in the wool industry.

Economic Growth and Inequality

Economic historians have spent much effort examining the changing levels of wealth and their implications for society. Measures of wealth, at a more basic level, are closely associated with measures of welfare. This concept can be broadened. Robert Fogel has shown that health is a viable alternative to wealth as a measure of welfare, but his innovative approach is beyond the scope of this study.[9] The link between wealth and welfare is complex. Evaluating the aggregate welfare associated with a specific level

---

4   See chapter 9 for a broader discussion of guilds and European economy and society.
5   Armando Sapori, *The Italian Merchant in the Middle Ages*, trans. Patricia Ann Kennen (New York, Norton, 1970), 94.
6   Steven A. Epstein, *Wage Labor and Guilds in Medieval Europe* (Chapel Hill, NC: University of North Carolina Press, 1991), 140–54.
7   Gene Brucker, *Renaissance Florence* (1959; Huntington, NY: Krieger, 1975), 59.
8   Richard A. Goldthwaite, *The Economy of Renaissance Florence* (Baltimore, MD: Johns Hopkins University Press, 2009), 547.
9   Roderick Floud, Robert W. Fogel, Bernard Harris, and Sok Chul Hong, *The Changing Body: Health, Nutrition, and Human Development in the Western World since 1700* (Cambridge, UK: Cambridge University Press, 2011).

of wealth leads to multiple approaches. There are three distinct approaches to this link, each using a specific quantitative dimension of the distribution of wealth to infer societal welfare. Therefore, each is mathematically independent of the other two. The first, and probably most common, measure of an area's living standard or material well-being is the mean wealth per household. The second is the distribution of wealth across households, which provides information about economic and social inequality unconditional on other variables. There are a wide variety of ways to measure the wealth distribution.[10] It is conceptually equivalent to the unconditional volatility of wealth. In this case high volatility could either be associated with greater relative suffering among the poor or greater opportunities for the best prepared. Though the former view occupies the economic debates today, the latter can be seen a kind of Schumpeterian entrepreneurial dynamism.[11] The third measure is the level of wealth conditional on occupation, which provides information on social mobility and is a form of conditional volatility.[12] In this case high volatility implies a fluid social structure, where families have both the opportunity of increasing social standing and the risk of decreasing social standing. The conditional volatility is therefore dependent on the mean and the unconditional volatilities.

A variety of theoretical explanations have been proposed to describe or explain the historical evolution of income inequality. The Kuznets Curve is motivated by observations of historical and developing economies. It theorizes that as a nation's economy develops. income inequality first rises and then declines in a kind of inverted-U shape.[13] This is driven by the shift of production from the primary sector (natural resources) to the secondary sector (manufacturing) and then to the tertiary (service) sector. This framework is applied widely to examine short- and long-term changes in income inequality. Shocks can produce inequality, and this pattern can resemble a Kuznets Curve.[14] Though the theory once had wide acceptance, recently doubts have arisen. The increasing inequality in the United States and other developed countries since 1980 contradicts the empirical expectations based on the Kuznets Curve.[15]

---

10 See Lee Soltow and Jan Luiten Van Zanden, *Income and Wealth Inequality in the Netherlands 16th–20th Century* (Amsterdam: Het Spinhuis, 1998), chap. 2. These methods continue to evolve. For example, see: Branko Milanovic, Peter H. Lindert and Jeffrey G. Williamson, "Pre-Industrial Inequality," *Economic Journal* 121, no. 551 (2011): 255–72.

11 Joseph A. Schumpeter, *The Theory of Economic Development: An Inquiry into Profits, Capital, Credit, Interest, and the Business Cycle*, trans. Redvers Opie (1934; New Brunswick, NJ: Transaction, 1983).

12 Peter M. Blau and Otis Dudley Duncan, *The American Occupational Structure* (New York: The Free Press, 1967); Otis Dudley Duncan, "A Socioeconomic Index for All Occupations," in *Class: Critical Concepts*, 1, ed. John Scott (London: Routledge, 1996), 388–426.

13 Simon Kuznets, "Economic Growth and Income Inequality," *American Economic Review* 45, no. 1 (1955): 1–28.

14 Yujiro Hayami, "Induced Innovation, Green Revolution, and Income Distribution: Comment," *Economic Development and Cultural Change* 30, no. 1 (1981): 169–76.

15 Finis Welch, ed., *The Causes and Consequences of Increasing Inequality* (Chicago: University of Chicago Press, 2001); Peter H. Lindert and Jeffrey G. Wiliamson. *Unequal Gains: American Growth and Inequality Since 1700* (Princeton, NJ: Princeton University Press, 2016)a.

Economic theory suggests that human capital, or skill formation, is an important driver of economic growth[16] along with physical capital[17] and technology in the modern world. This theory has been extended to cover preindustrial Europe.[18] One important theory of premodern economic history is the Great Divergence. This refers to the divergence in economic growth rates between Europe and the rest of the world, and the Small Divergence refers to that between northwestern Europe and Italy. The size of the skill premium after the Black Death has often been seen as a driver of these divergences.[19] Theoretically, the population decline and subsequent growth would affect real wages and the skill premium. However, these two variables are distinct. While real wages are an economy-wide phenomenon, the skill premium is a difference between portions of that economy. Empirical work is divided over whether human capital formation drove early modern economic growth.[20] Research using literacy growth as a proxy for human capital formation has found that the timing does not fit well,[21] but research using the skill premium as a proxy has found mixed results.[22] The relationship between human capital

---

16 Theodore W. Schultz, "Nobel Lecture: The Economics of Being Poor," *Journal of Political Economy* 88, no. 4 (1980): 639–51. Gary S. Becker, *Human Capital: A Theoretical and Empirical Analysis, with Special Reference to Education*, 3rd ed. (Chicago: University of Chicago Press, 1993).

17 Robert M. Solow, "A Contribution to the Theory of Economic Growth," *Quarterly Journal of Economics* 70, no. 1 (1956): 65–94.

18 Gary S. Becker, Kevin M. Murphy and Robert Tamura, "Human Capital, Fertility, and Economic Growth," *Journal of Political Economy* 98, no. 5, pt. 2 (1990): S12–37; Robert E. Lucas Jr., *Lectures on Economic Growth* (Cambridge, MA: Harvard University Press, 2006).

19 The skill premium in this literature has been measured in a wide variety of ways. Studies examining medieval and early modern Europe typically use something similar to the following formula:

$$\text{Skill Premium} = 100 * \left(\frac{\text{Wage rate for skilled construction workers}}{\text{Wage rate for unskilled construction workers}} - 1 \right)$$

20 For studies that support the human capital and growth thesis, see Stephan R. Epstein, "The Late Medieval Crisis as an 'Integration Crisis,'" in *Early Modern Capitalism: Economic and Social Change in Europe, 1400–1800*, ed. Maarten Prak (London: Routledge, 2001), 25–50; Stephan R. Epstein, "Property Rights to Technical Knowledge in Pre-Modern Europe, 1300–1800," *American Economic Review* 94, no. 2 (2004): 382–87. For studies that see this thesis as problematic, see Robert C. Allen, "Progress and Poverty in Early Modern Europe," *Economic History Review* new ser., 56, no. 3 (2003): 403–43; Gregory Clark, "Human Capital, Fertility, and the Industrial Revolution," *Journal of the European Economic Association* 3, nos. 2/3 (2005): 505–15; Gregory Clark, "The Condition of the Working-Class in England, 1209–2004," *Journal of Political Economy* 113, no. 6 (2005): 1307–40; Gregory Clark, *A Farewell to Alms: A Brief Economic History of the World* (Princeton, NJ: Princeton University Press, 2007).

21 Clark, "Working-Class"; Jan Luiten Van Zanden, *The Long Road to the Industrial Revolution: The European Economy in a Global Perspective, 1000–1800* (Leiden: Brill, Leiden, 2009), chap. 6.

22 Studies that use skill premium in this context include: Sevket Pamuk, "The Black Death and the Origins of the 'Great Divergence' across Europe, 1300–1600," *European Review of Economic History* 11 (2007): 289–317; Jan Luiten Van Zanden, "The Skill Premium and the 'Great Divergence'," *European Review of Economic History* 13 (2009): 121–153; Van Zanden, *The Long Road*, 173; Nico Voigtländer and Hans-Joachim Voth, "Malthusian Dynamism and the Rise of Europe: Make War, Not Love, Urbanization, Mortality, and Fertility in Malthusian England,

and economic growth implies that both are related to inequality, though not necessarily in any simple way.[23] Claudia Goldin and Lawrence Katz[24] argue that a human capital premium,[25] specifically from a college education, has driven increasing income inequality in the United States since 1980. They see technological growth requiring educational growth by people in order to maintain their relative income. This is associated with a much older approach. A human capital premium has been used by economists to explain income inequality changes for nearly a century.[26] Changes in the premium create fluctuations in the level of inequality and the resulting time series would appear as a series of Kuznets Curves resembling waves in an ocean. The relationship between physical capital and economic growth is another connection seen by some researchers as a cause of income inequality. Thomas Piketty argues that wealth inequality naturally increases under capitalism.[27] His work would imply that both the Kuznets Curve[28] and human capital premium theories are in error.[29]

The effort to confirm or reject a very long-term Kuznets Curve that would span the premodern era, motivates a wide-ranging research agenda. This work generally finds that inequality in Europe was increasing prior to 1800 and, consequently, rejects the original version of the Kuznets Curve.[30] The results, though, are far from simple. Local studies are

Disease and Development: Historical and Contemporary Perspectives," *American Economic Review: Papers and Proceedings* 99, no. 2 (2009): 248–54. "Urbanization, Mortality, and Fertility in Malthusian England, Disease and Development: Historical and Contemporary Perspectives," *American Economic Review: Papers and Proceedings* 99, no. 2 (2009): 248–254.

23 Kevin M. Murphy, and Robert H. Topel, "Human Capital Investment, Inequality, and Economic Growth." *Journal of Labor Economics* 34, no. 2, pt. 2 (2016): S1–29.

24 Claudia Goldin and Lawrence Katz, *The Race Between Education and Technology*, (Cambridge, MA: Harvard University Press, 2008).

25 Conceptually, the

$$\text{Human capital premium} = 100*\left(\frac{\text{Wage rate for persons with a college degree}}{\text{Wage rate for persons without a college degree}} - 1 \right).$$

This measure can be made much more precise. For example, estimated wage rates that adjust for gender and age differences could be used in the equation.

26 Paul H. Douglas, *Real Wages in the United States: 1890 to 1926* (Boston: Houghton Mifflin Co., 1930); Jan Tinbergen, "Substitution of Graduate by Other Labour," *Kyklos* 27, no. 2 (1974): 217–26

27 Thomas Piketty, *Capital in the Twenty-First Century*, trans. Arthur Goldhammer (Cambridge, MA: Harvard University Press, 2014), 20–24.

28 Ibid., 11–15.

29 Ibid., 314–15.

30 For broad reviews, see: Jan Luiten Van Zanden, "Tracing the Beginning of the Kuznets Curve: Western Europe during the Early Modern Period," *Economic History Review* 48, no. 4 (1995): 643–64; Guido Alfani, "Prima della curva di Kuznets: Stabilità e mutamento nella concentrazione di ricchezza e proprietà in età moderna," in *Ricchezza, valore, proprietà in età preindustriale 1400–1850*, ed. Guido Alfani and Michela Barbot (Venice: Marsilio, 2009), 143–67. For specific regional studies, see: Soltow and Van Zanden, *Inequality in the Netherlands*; Guido Alfani and Francesco Ammannati, "Economic Inequality and Poverty in the Very Long Run: The Case of the Florentine State (Late Thirteenth–Early Nineteenth Centuries)." No. 70. Dondena Working Paper (2014). ftp://ftp.dondena.unibocconi.it/WorkingPapers/Dondena_WP070.pdf;

an important part of this research agenda.[31] Nuanced explanations appear to be needed to explain inequality during the period.[32] Other work expands the number of databases and evaluates their quality.[33] The limitations of the available data are important. Time series measurements of inequality based on tax data can be affected by changes in the underlying tax law. Perhaps the best-known case was caused by the 1986 Tax Reform Act, which substantially changed the US income tax structure. This change induced a measured increase in income inequality in some time series based on income tax returns.[34] In the case of Florence, the shift from the estimi, which was based on all wealth, and the catasto, which exempted the home and furnishings, for example, would have affected the measured income inequality independent of any actual change. These effects could be large in Florence. Chapter 5 presents a study of the extensive and intensive homeownership increases due to the catasto. This admonition of care about wide-ranging studies of inequality in time parallels a similar admonition against ignoring local differences in space presented in chapter 2.

Wealth Distribution and Social Mobility in Renaissance Florence

The economic and social trends during the *Trecento* and the *Quattrocento* have been closely studied. As elsewhere, in the wake of the 1348 Black Death, real wages increased and living standards were high.[35] The population loss would have also decreased the skill premium, which, in turn, could have reduced the economic inequality. However, both real and nominal causes have been put forward to argue that inequality increased during this

Guido Alfani, "Economic Inequality in Northwestern Italy: A Long-Term View (Fourteenth to Eighteenth centuries)," *Journal of Economic History* 75, no. 4 (2015): 1058–96.

31 Guido Alfani and Michela Barbot, eds. *Ricchezza, valore, proprietà in Età preindustriale: 1400–1850* (Venice: Marsilio, 2009); Guido Alfani, "Proprietà, ricchezza e disgualianza economica," in *Ricchezza, valore, proprietà in età preindustriale 1400–1850*, ed. Guido Alfani and Michela Barbot (Venice: Marsilio, 2009), 11–22; Guido Alfani, "Wealth Inequalities and Population Dynamics in Early Modern Northern Italy," *Journal of Interdisciplinary History* 40, no. 4 (2010): 513–49; Matthieu Scherman, "La distribuzione della ricchezza in una città: Treviso e I suoi estimi (1434–1499)," in *Ricchezza, valore, proprietà in età preindustriale 1400–1850*, ed. Guido Alfani and Michela Barbot (Venice: Marsilio, 2009), 169–84.

32 Guido Alfani and Wouter Ryckbosch. "Was There a 'Little Convergence' in Inequality? Italy and the Low Countries Compared, ca. 1500–1800," No. 557. CEPR Working Paper (2015). http://www.igier.unibocconi.it/files/557.pdf.

33 Michela Barbot, "Gli estimi, una fonte di valore," in *Ricchezza, valore, proprietà in età preindustriale 1400–1850*, ed. Guido Alfani and Michela Barbot (Venice: Marsilio, 2009), 23–27; Francesco Ammannati, Davide De Franco and Matteo Di Tullio. "Misurare la diseguaglianza economica nell'età preindustriale: Un confronto fra realtà dell'Italia centro-settentrionale." No. 65. Dondena Working Paper (2014). ftp://ftp.dondena.unibocconi.it/WorkingPapers/Dondena_WP065.pdf.

34 Thomas Piketty and Emmanuel Saez, "Income Inequality in the United States, 1913–1998," *Quarterly Journal of Economics* 118, no. 1 (2003): 1–39; Piketty, *Capital*; Anthony B. Atkinson, Thomas Piketty and Emmanuel Saez, "Top Incomes in the Long Run of History," *Journal of Economic Literature* 49, no. 1 (2011): 3–71.

35 Charles M. de La Roncière, *Prix et salaires à Florence au XIVᵉ Siècle, 1280–1380* (Rome: Palàis Farnese, 1982).

period. A lengthy literature argues that the Florentine government's assertion of greater control over the surrounding countryside led to significant expropriation through such institutions as *mezzadria* (sharecropping).[36] Others argue that the Florentine authorities' devaluation of the silver currency was expropriated from the poor, who were largely restricted to the use of silver currency with its smaller denominations.[37] Brucker finds a clear sense of vulnerability among late Quattrocento Florentines.[38]

Cohn finds increasing inequality between the Trecento and the Quattrocento. He uses dowry sizes as a proxy for wealth to calculate Gini coefficients.[39] However, his method is problematic, as dowries are only a rough approximation for wealth. There are several reasons for this. At a fundamental level, one would expect that the supply of dowries was wealth elastic. As a household's wealth increased, dowries would increase disproportionately, leading to a greater "inequality" in the distribution of dowries than in the corresponding distribution of household wealth. In addition, two historical circumstances would act to exacerbate this effect. To begin with, Northern Italian cities experienced a dowry inflation during the period. Legislation was enacted to restrict dowry sizes because of the perception that they had reached irrationally high levels.[40] The mismatch between wealth and dowries would have been compounded by the creation of the Florentine Monte delle doti in 1425, which reduced the cost of dowries, thus bringing larger dowries within the reach of the typical Florentine.[41] This is an example of a mismatch that results by creating a time series of measurements using data historical created by different underlying processes, in this case dowries and taxation.

Herlihy and Klapisch-Zuber seem to confirm that mid-Quattrocento inequality was high, with the Gini coefficient of wealth distribution equaling 0.79.[42] However, Florentine society was not quite as inegalitarian as they suppose. First, Gini coefficients based on

---

36 Seminal works include Enrico Fiumi, "Fioritura e decadenza dell'economia fiorentina," *Archivio storico italiano*, 115 (1957): 385–439; 116 (1958): 443–510g; 117 (1959): 427–502; Philip J. Jones, "From Manor to Mezzadria: A Tuscan Case-Study in the Medieval Origins of Modern Agrarian Society," in *Florentine Studies, Politics and Society in Renaissance Florence*, ed. Nicolai Rubinstein (London: Faber and Faber, 1968), 193–241; Anthony Molho, *Florentine Public Finances in the Early Renaissance, 1400–1433* (Cambridge, MA: Harvard University Press, 1971), 23–45.

37 Niccolò Rodolico, "Il sistema monetario e le classi sociali nel Medio Evo," *Rivista Italiana di sociologia*, 8 (1904), 462–69; Carlo M. Cipolla, *The Monetary Policy of Fourteenth-Century Florence* (Berkeley: University of California Press, 1982).

38 Gene Brucker, *Living on the Edge in Leonardo's Florence: Selected Essays* (Berkeley: University of California Press, 2005), 116.

39 Cohn, *Laboring Classes*, 124–27.

40 Cf. Diane Owen Hughes, "Urban Growth and Family Structure in Medieval Genoa," *Past and Present* no. 66 (1975): 3–28; Julius Kirshner and Anthony Molho, "The Dowry Fund and the Marriage Market in Early *Quattrocento* Florence, *Journal of Modern History* 50 (1978): 403–38.

41 Kirshner and Molho, "Dowry Fund," 403–38.

42 David Herlihy and Christiane Klapisch-Zuber, *Les Toscans et leurs familles: Une étude du Catasto Florentine de 1427* (Paris: Fondation nationale des sciences politiques, 1978); David Herlihy and Christiane Klapisch-Zuber, *The Tuscans and Their Families: A Study of the Florentine Catasto of 1427* (New Haven, CT: Yale University Press, 1985).

wealth tend to be higher than those based on income.[43] As most contemporary Gini coefficient comparisons are based on income, a relatively high Gini coefficient would be normal for wealth distribution. Second, Goldthwaite finds technical problems with Herlihy's and Klapisch-Zuber's wealth-distribution measurement. He argues that they sacrificed economic criteria for demographic ones and therefore cannot place the values into a proper context.[44] Third, as Goldthwaite notes, the Florentine wealth concentration is not as high as that in late medieval England, eighteenth-century Europe and the contemporary United States.[45] This list can be extended.[46]

Goldthwaite's critique goes even further. He asserts that the Florentine wealth distribution was, in fact, relatively egalitarian, and he sees this as an important characteristic of the Renaissance.[47] He points out that the wealth distribution in the United States in 1995 was very similar to that of Florence in 1427.[48] Though his specific comparison is incomplete because inequality began to rise from 1980, Goldthwaite's observation holds. Florentine wealth inequality in 1427 fits well in the range of developed countries during the late twentieth century.

Recent work by Guido Alfani and Francesco Ammannati finds a general decline in wealth inequality in the Distretto surrounding Florence during the century after the Black Death.[49] Their analysis links data from the Trecento and early Quattrocento estimi to the mid and late Quattrocento catasti. Though the data in these sources were created through different processes, the differences are not as great as the divide in Cohn's time series.

Analyses of Florentine intergenerational social mobility have also come to divergent conclusions. Those arguing for little mobility include Molho, who concludes that the Florentine elite were generally closed to others joining their ranks.[50] Alessandro Stella shows that family wealth for many important families changed dramatically between 1352 and 1404.[51] Marvin Becker compiles studies of guild matriculation lists to show that the ratio of new members to hereditary members was high in 1350, declined significantly by the late Trecento and early Quattrocento and then

---

43 Bureau of the Census, *Household Wealth and Asset Ownership: 1984* (Washington, DC: US Government Printing Office, 1986); Richard A. Goldthwaite, "The Economy of Renaissance Italy: The Preconditions for Luxury Consumption," *I Tatti Studies* 2 (1987): 29–30; Alice Hanson Jones, *Wealth of a Nation to Be: The American Colonies on the Eve of the Revolution* (New York: Columbia University Press, 1980).

44 Goldthwaite, "Preconditions for Luxury Consumption," 27 and 29–30.

45 Ibid., 29.

46 Lee Soltow, *Men and Wealth in the United States, 1850–1870* (New Haven, CT: Yale University Press, 1973); Jones, *Wealth of a Nation to Be.*

47 Goldthwaite, "Preconditions for Luxury Consumption," 29.

48 Goldthwaite, *Economy of Renaissance Florence*, 562.

49 Alfani and Ammannati. "The Case of the Florentine State."

50 Anthony Molho, *Marriage Alliance in Late Medieval Florence* (Cambridge, MA: Harvard University Press, 1994), 332–34.

51 Alessandro Stella, *La révolte des Ciompi: Les hommes, les lieux, le travail* (Paris: Editions de l'École des Hautes Études en Sciences Sociales, 1993), 198–99.

held roughly constant until 1550.[52] Those arguing for greater mobility include Sergio Tognetti, who finds that Florence had the potential for dramatic upward mobility.[53] John Padgett concludes that Florence had significant social mobility for most of the period from 1282 to 1494.[54] Brucker also argues that Florence had a flexible social structure,[55] and Goldthwaite prominently identifies Florentine wealth mobility as a foundation of the Renaissance.[56]

It is important to be cautious about seeing estimates of changes between the 1350s and the early Quattrocento as emblematic of some deeper change in structure that persisted for decades later. The relative income equality during the early 1350s is probably due to the Black Death. It is unlikely that anyone would seriously argue that the Black Death was a good thing, yet it decreased inequality and opened opportunities among the survivors. The large number of deaths would have increased the returns to labor as opposed to capital. As the population recovered, the relative wages of workers declined and inequality would have returned.[57] It would stop once the economy had reached a new long-term equilibrium condition. In addition, the data from the years just after the Black Death could cause a kind of "endpoint" problem. Because taxes were often collected in response to a significant fiscal emergency, Florentine tax records usually have some form of endpoint problem.[58] In this case, the 1378 estimo data can help reduce that problem.

A final approach to evaluating inequality in wealth distributions is less commonly used. It examines the distribution of taxable wealth conditional on occupation or industry at a particular point in time. Herlihy and Klapisch-Zuber rank Florentine occupations based on mean wealth in their large-scale analysis of Tuscan households. Broadly, the arte maggiore guild members were at the top; most other industries and traders were in the middle; and menial textile, government and service occupations were at the bottom.

---

52 Marvin B. Becker, *Florence in Transition*, vol. 2: *Studies in the Rise of the Territorial State* (Baltimore: Johns Hopkins University Press, 1968), 226.

53 Sergio Tognetti, *Il Banco Cambini: Affari e mercati di una compagnia mercantile-bancaria nella Firenze del XV secolo* (Florence: Olschki, 1999), 325–31.

54 John F. Padgett, "Open Elite? Social Mobility, Marriage, and Family in Florence, 1282–1494," *Renaissance Quarterly* 63 (2010): 357–411.

55 Gene Brucker, *Florentine Politics and Society, 1343–1378* (Princeton, NJ: Princeton University Press, 1962), 27.

56 Goldthwaite, *Economy of Renaissance Florence*, 547; Goldthwaite, "Preconditions for Luxury Consumption," 24–25.

57 Charles M. de La Roncière, *Florence centre économique regional au XIVe siècle, I, Le marché des denrées de première nécessité à Florence et dans sa champagne et les conditions de vie des salariés (1320–1380)* (Aix-en-Provence: S.O.D.E.B., 1976), 417–54; Charles M. de La Roncière, *Florence centre économique regional au XIVe siècle, IV, Notes et documents* (Aix-en-Provence: S.O.D.E.B., 1976), 451–500; M. de La Roncière, *Prix et salaires à Florence au 14e siècles: 1280–1380* (Rome: École Française de Rome, 1982).

58 For an impact of the plague on the Cinquecento Venetian economy, see Anna Bellavitis, "Apprendiste e maestre a Venezia tra Cinque e Seicento," Special issue, "*Donne, lavoro, economia a Venezia e in Terraferma tra medioevo ed età moderna*," ed. Anna Bellavitis and Linda Guzzetti, *Archivio veneto* 143 (2012): 144.

Herlihy and Klapisch-Zuber show that this hierarchy held in all Tuscan towns; however, their approach is limited.[59] By using only means and not standard deviations, or any other measure of spread, they ignore the level of wealth variation within occupations. Further, there is a problem with their definition of occupations. Florence Edler's detailed study provided Herlihy and Klapisch-Zuber with clear descriptions of the occupations,[60] but they did not always include all of Edler's detail, and the occupational categories are therefore inexact.[61] Most of the occupations they list are actually industries. There is also no distinction between managers and workers.[62]

Testing the Relationship between Occupations and Household Wealth

Analyzing the distribution of wealth can be refined by examining the distribution of household wealth conditional on occupation and by focusing on the occupations in a single industry. The wool industry is ideal for this kind of analysis because it permits a detailed examination of social standing within a well-defined working population and because each of the many steps in the wool-manufacturing process involved a separate occupation. The social position of workers in these occupations varied.

This section examines the wealth difference between arte maggiore and popolo minuto wool industry occupations. The next section refines this analysis and specifically examines intraoccupational wealth volatility. The data come from a complete set of fiscal households for Florentine wool industry workers from the 1427 catasto, whether headed by an active worker or a retired one and regardless of age or gender of the household head. The analysis is based on taxable wealth instead of net wealth. Since the catasto was designed to measure taxable wealth, the accuracy should be high. (See appendix 3A.) However, taxable wealth has two undesirable characteristics: (1) the value of a household's home is not included in the total asset value, and (2) taxable wealth imposes a floor on net wealth at zero florins.[63] There was therefore no incentive to collect information about debts that would drive the taxable wealth into negative numbers. All

---

59 Herlihy and Klapisch-Zuber, *Les Toscans*, 298–300; Herlihy and Klapisch-Zuber, *Tuscans*, 129–30.

60 Florence Edler, *Glossary of Medieval Terms of Business, Italian Series, 1200–1600* (Cambridge, MA: Medieval Academy of America, 1934), 324–29. Sometimes the Herlihy and Klapisch-Zuber coding does not match Edler's descriptions.

61 David Herlihy and Christiane Klapisch-Zuber, *Census and Property Survey of Florentine Domains and the City of Verona in Fifteenth-Century Italy*, University of Wisconsin, Madison, WI, Data and Program Library Service, 1977, app. B. For a more detailed analysis of wool industry occupational data, see Bruno Dini, *Manifattura, commercio e banca nella Firenze medievali* (Florence: Nardini, 2001), 162.

62 The catasto data set includes some distinctions among occupations in the cotton and silk industries. However, the detail is not as great as that for the wool industry.

63 Home values are available for Pisa but are not available in Herlihy and Klapisch-Zuber, *Census and Property Survey*. It is not clear how to quantitatively correct for this omission in the case of Florence, since little direct evidence on housing values is available.

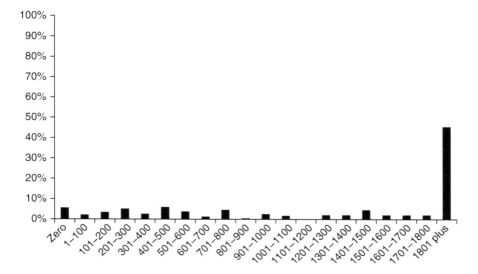

Figure 3.1 Distribution of taxable wealth among arte maggiore
Source: Herlihy and Klapisch-Zuber, *Census and Property Survey*. Calculation by author.

information about this range of wealth is lost. Net wealth does not impose this floor, and some Florentine households recorded a negative net wealth.[64]

Wool industry workers were among both the arte maggiore and the popolo minuto groups. The arte maggiore were probably the richest and most powerful group of Florentines and included the woolen-cloth merchants (*lanaiuoli*) and the woolen-cloth exporters (*Calimala* members). Dyers were divided between the two groups, but for the purposes of the analysis in this study are grouped with the popolo minuto. The popolo minuto included all other occupations. Among these, the sottoposti, subordinates,[65] included the skilled wool industry occupations: the carders, dyers, fullers, menders, spinners, stretchers and weavers.[66]

Comparing figures 3.1 and 3.2 shows that the wealth distributions of the arte maggiore and of the popolo minuto are mirror images of each other. The arte maggiore taxable wealth distribution was highly skewed to the right (see fig. 3.1). Despite the high mean and strong skew of the distribution, some of the arte maggiore were still impoverished. This parallels Stella's findings for 1352 and 1404.[67] In contrast, the popolo minuto taxable wealth distribution was highly skewed to the left (see fig. 3.2). Despite the large skew of the distribution, some of the popolo minuto were among the wealthiest in Florence.

---

64 This implies that the credit markets for individual Florentine artisans were highly developed.
65 Brucker, *Renaissance Florence*, 63.
66 Ibid., 65–68; Brucker, *Florentine Politics and Society*, 48; Weissman, *Ritual Brotherhood*, 3–5.
67 Stella, *La révolte des Ciompi*, 198–99.

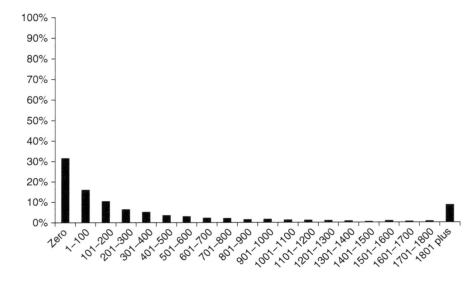

Figure 3.2 Distribution of taxable wealth among popolo minuto
Source: Herlihy and Klapisch-Zuber, *Census and Property Survey*. Calculation by author.

Table 3.1 Results of arte maggiore versus popolo minuto wealth differences test

t	7.65
degrees of freedom	237.47
Significance (2-tailed)	0
Mean Difference	2442.54
Std. Error Difference	319.35

Source: Herlihy and Klapisch-Zuber, *Census and Property Survey*.
The test is based on taxable wealth data. Calculation by author.

The difference in mean taxable wealth between the arte maggiore and popolo minuto is statistically significant. (See table 3.1 for the results.) This difference is robust to changes in specification. Neither removing household heads under age 21 from the sample nor distinguishing between married and unmarried household heads affects the results.

Measures of Occupational Wealth Volatility

This section looks at the distribution of wealth for individual wool industry occupations. Table 3.2 uses the standard measures of the center and spread of a distribution, mean and variance, respectively. This method assumes that wealth was normally distributed conditional on occupation. The ranking of occupations resembles the Herlihy and Klapisch-Zuber ranking of industries and occupations; however, there is considerable overlap. The means, on their own, would imply a simple hierarchy, but the standard deviations and

Table 3.2 Wool industry occupational taxable wealth, 1427

Name	Total	Mean	Median	S. Dev.	Coeff. Var.
Arte Maggiore					
Lanaiuolo	229	3132	1593	4886	156%
Calimala Mbr.	6	4070	1705	4873	120%
Popolo Minuto					
Wool Washer	98	43	0	129	296%
Beater	111	38	0	76	201%
Comber	209	49	0	135	276%
Stamaiuolo	54	193	33	406	211%
Lanino	21	137	0	376	275%
Weaver	276	48	0	156	325%
Carder	194	22	0	87	387%
Stretcher	19	104	0	379	363%
Shearer	41	160	0	320	199%
Mender	33	198	127	298	150%
Burler	53	97	3	194	200%
Dyer	117	475	2	2220	468%

Source: Herlihy and Klapisch-Zuber, *Census and Property Survey*. Calculation by author.
Coeff. Var.: Coefficient of Variation = Mean/Standard Deviation.

coefficients of variation show that there was significant variation. Table 3.2 shows that being a member of one of the arte maggiore guilds was no guarantee of great wealth.

Table 3.3 approaches the data from a different, more robust, direction. It examines the percentage chance that members of each occupation had of being counted among the top decile or quartile. This is less dependent on an assumption of normally distributed data. It makes clear that only a few were able to rise to the richest group. The arte maggiore formed the upper group of woolen industry occupations; a middle group was composed of dyers; and the bottom group included all the other occupations. However, even among this group, a few workers still had wealth to equal the arte maggiore. These included sewers (*rimendatori*), stretchers (*tiratori*), supervisors of spinning (*stamaiuoli* and *lanini*) and shearers (*cimatori*).

The top 10 percent of fiscal households were, precisely, those with 1,737 florins or more in taxable wealth. For simplicity, here the cutoff is taken as 1,800 and the top category is thus households with 1,801 florins or greater in taxable wealth. Table 3.4 demonstrates that most occupations among the non–arte maggiore guilds included members among the top 10 percent in wealth as well as those without wealth, the *miserabili*. Nevertheless, overall there is a clear separation in the distributions for arte maggiore and popolo minuto occupations.

Figures 3.3 through 3.8 clarify this combination of wealth differences between occupation and high volatility within occupations. They are presented in a parallel manner to better convey the relationships across occupations. Although 14 occupations were examined, only six figures are presented, as many of the results are virtually identical. These

Table 3.3 Number and percentage of workers in wool industry in top ten and *miserabili*, 1427

		Number		Percentage	
Occupation	Total	Miserabili	Top 10%	Miserabili	Top 10%
Arte Maggiore					
Lanaiuolo	229	12	105	5%	46%
Calimala Mbr.	6	1	2	17%	33%
Popolo Minuto					
Wool Washer	98	73	0	74%	0%
Beater	111	65	0	59%	0%
Comber	209	143	0	68%	0%
Stamaiuolo	54	23	0	43%	0%
Lanino	21	12	0	57%	0%
Weaver	276	193	1	70%	0%
Carder	194	154	0	79%	0%
Stretcher	19	16	0	84%	0%
Shearer	41	21	0	51%	0%
Mender	33	11	0	33%	0%
Burler	53	26	0	49%	0%
Dyer	117	58	6	50%	5%

Source: Herlihy and Klapisch-Zuber, *Census and Property Survey*. Calculation by author.

figures present distributions of taxable wealth among the lanaiuoli, a selection of the purely popolo minuto occupations. One occupation from each of the five major production steps is taken as an example.

By contrast, the distribution of taxable wealth among the lanaiuoli (fig. 3.3) was highly skewed toward the right. Although nearly half of these were among the top 10 percent of wealthiest households, more than 5 percent were miserabili. In fact, lanaiuoli were distributed more evenly from 0 to 1,800 florins than any other wool industry occupation. The distribution of wealth confirms the high level of volatility noted in table 3.3.

The distribution among combers (fig. 3.4) was highly skewed toward the left. Though nearly three-quarters of combers were among the miserabili, taxable wealth for some of them did reach more than 1,100 florins, confirming the high volatility seen in table 3.3.

Figures 3.5 through 3.7 show the distribution among three of the less wealthy occupations: the stamaiuoli, the weavers and the carders, respectively. The distributions are highly skewed toward the left. Nearly half of the stamaiuoli and three-quarters of the weavers and carders were among the miserabili. However, the taxable wealth for many was well above that level, confirming the high volatility seen in table 3.1.

Figure 3.8 presents the distribution of taxable wealth for dyers. Dyers were divided among the arte maggiore and the popolo minuto classes. This split is clearly visible. The distribution among dyers was the most even of all 14 wool industry occupations examined. Most dyers were significantly below the mean. Ten percent, the citywide average, were among the wealthiest Florentines, whereas 50 percent were miserabili, as indicated in table 3.3 and figure 3.8.

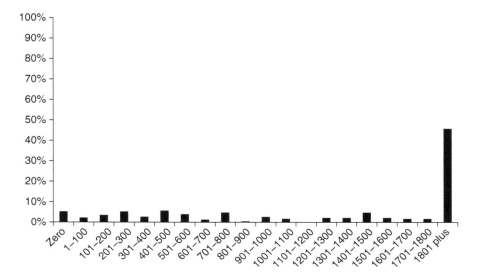

Figure 3.3 Distribution of taxable wealth among lanaiuoli
Source: Herlihy and Klapisch-Zuber, *Census and Property Survey*. Calculation by author.

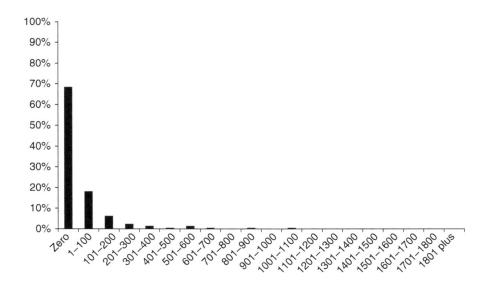

Figure 3.4 Distribution of taxable wealth among combers
Source: Herlihy and Klapisch-Zuber, *Census and Property Survey*. Calculation by author.

The difference between the arte maggiore and the popolo minuto largely determined wealth. The specific occupations had less of an impact within these two larger categories. Though some workers in popolo minuto occupations could be very wealthy, in practice this possibility was remote.

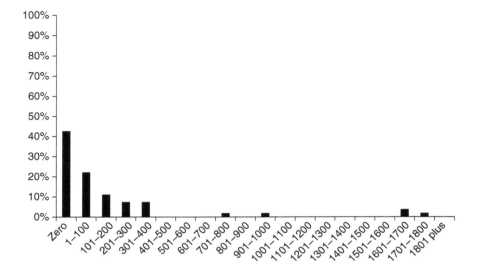

Figure 3.5 Distribution of taxable wealth among stamaiuoli
Source: Herlihy and Klapisch-Zuber, *Census and Property Survey*. Calculation by author.

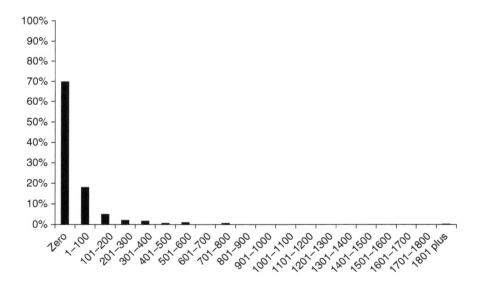

Figure 3.6 Distribution of taxable wealth among weavers
Source: Herlihy and Klapisch-Zuber, *Census and Property Survey*. Calculation by author.

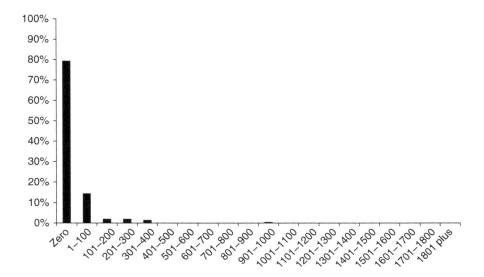

Figure 3.7 Distribution of taxable wealth among carders
Source: Herlihy and Klapisch-Zuber, *Census and Property Survey*. Calculation by author.

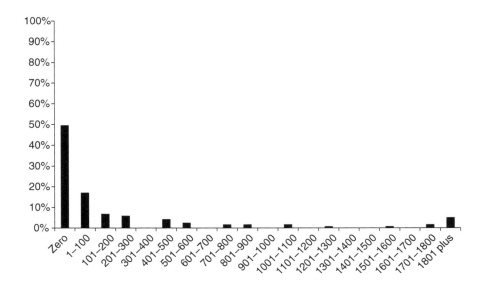

Figure 3.8 Distribution of taxable wealth among dyers
Source: Herlihy and Klapisch-Zuber, *Census and Property Survey*. Calculation by author.

Conclusions

This study has three primary findings. First, wool industry occupations can be categorized by taxable wealth into two groups based on membership in the arte maggiore. This is much as the Florentines themselves pictured the situation. Those households that did not belong to the arte maggiore could (however unlikely the chance) join the wealthiest families in Florentine society. This possibility indicates that Renaissance Florence was a city of opportunity. Second, although social status was highly correlated with wealth in a broad sense, there was significant volatility and unpredictability within specific occupations. There was no rigid segregation of occupations by taxable wealth. Although certain wool industry occupations maintained a significant advantage over others, there was substantial wealth volatility across and within occupations. A wide variety of occupations included workers who were among the top 10 percent in taxable wealth. The third result of this study stems from the method of analysis used. It is important that these results came about through an analysis of the distribution of wealth, not the mean of wealth. This method undoubtedly has fruitful applications in similar studies.

Appendix 3A: A Brief Introduction to the Catasto as a Source of Quantitative Data

The catasto was a net wealth tax collected in Quattrocento Florence and its territories. It was first assessed in 1427, and subsequent assessments continued until 1494.[68] Data are available in electronic format for all of Florentine Tuscany in 1427 and as 10 percent samples for Florence in 1458 and in 1480.[69] The data are purely cross-sectional, so they are limited compared to modern data. The assessment in 1427 was a flat rate on the total value of assets, exempting the home and its furnishings, minus the total value of debts. The tax burden was further reduced by deductions for each member of the fiscal household. Starting in 1442, the rate was made progressive.[70]

An extensive record was created to facilitate its collection. The 1427 data are subdivided by region, as defined by the Florentine authorities. The catasto data are generally reliable and consistent.[71] Historians have thoroughly checked the data during the past half-century.[72] A series of major long-term projects by a wide range of historians

---

68 Elio Conti, *L'imposta diretta a Firenze nel Quattrocento (1427–1494)* (Rome: Palazzo Borromini, 1984).
69 Herlihy and Klapisch-Zuber, *Les Toscans*; Herlihy and Klapisch-Zuber, *Tuscans*; David Herlihy and Christiane Klapisch-Zuber, "Census and Property Survey of Florence, Italy, 1427" (Madison, WI: Data and Program Library Service, 1981).
70 Conti, *L'imposta diretta*, 199.
71 Elio Conti, *I Catasti Agrari della Repubblica Fiorentina e il Catasto particellare Toscano (Secoli XIV–XIX)* (Rome: Palazzo Borromini, 1966), 50–58; Rebecca Jean Emigh, "Loans and Livestock: Comparing Landlords and Tenants Declarations from the Catasto of 1427," *Journal of European Economic History* 25, no. 2 (1996): 705–23.
72 Raymond de Roover, *The Rise and Decline of the Medici Bank, 1397–1494* (Cambridge, MA: Harvard University Press, 1963), 24; Molho, *Marriage Alliance*, 361–62; Weissman, *Ritual Brotherhood*, 10.

and social scientists since World War II have used catasto data, which have been cross-checked with other sources.[73]

The Florentine officials worked hard to ensure accuracy. The catasto process involved several steps. The final data for Florence in 1427 are contained in 16 large volumes, one for each *gonfalone*, each written in the standard small script of the time. The records in these volumes are standardized and, as such, reflect the multiple levels of processing each had undergone.[74] The tax returns were thoroughly checked and were made public; thus, neighbors were able to comment on their accuracy. There were financial incentives to report fraud as well; a whistleblower could receive half of the fraudulently taken amount.[75] The catasto was considered reliable enough by contemporaries to be presented as evidence in legal proceedings.[76]

The purpose of the catasto and its rules affect the reliability of data.[77] The system led to some predictable weaknesses. Choosing variables that required only a minimal effort by both the taxpayer and tax collector to get the correct value minimizes potential problems. Financial and economic variables were more important than demographic variables to the assessing officials because the catasto was, after all, a tax. Assets that were difficult to track, such as liquid assets, profits and livestock, were underreported.[78] Errors and evasion occurred, as they do for every tax document, but errors here appear to be minimal. Both the original submissions and final returns are available to scholars. Rebecca Emigh has compared these and found few errors.[79] There was evasion, but it appears manageable. Edler recounts an example of tax evasion.[80] Social customs and values also affected reporting. This makes the meaning and implications of the data sometimes very different from and difficult to compare with modern data.[81] However, the fiscal and legal contexts

---

73 Goldthwaite, *Economy of Renaissance Florence*, 560.

74 For examples in English translation, see: Gene Brucker, ed., *The Society of Renaissance Florence: A Documentary Study* (New York: Harper & Row, 1971), 6–13.

75 Herlihy and Klapisch-Zuber, *Les Toscans*, 71–72.

76 Julius Kirshner, "Custom, Customary law, and Ius Commune in Francesco Guicciardini," *Bologna nell'età di Carlo V e Guicciardini* (2002): 163–76.

77 Rebecca Jean Emigh "What Influences Official Information? Exploring Aggregate Microhistories of the Catasto of 1427," in *Small Worlds: Method, Meaning, and Narrative in Microhistory*, ed. James F. Brooks, Christopher R. N. DeCorse and John Walton (Santa Fe: School for Advanced Research Press, 2008), 207–10.

78 Raymond De Roover, *The Rise and Decline of the Medici Bank 1397–1494* (Cambridge, MA: Harvard University Press, 1963), 72; Conti, *L'imposta diretta*, 148–49; Florence Edler de Roover, "Andrea Banchi Florentine Silk Merchant of the Fifteenth Century," *Studies in Medieval and Renaissance History* 3 (1966): 281–82.

79 Emigh, "What Influences Official Information?," 210–15.

80 Edler de Roover, "Andrea Banchi," 281–82.

81 Christiane Klapisch-Zuber, "Le Catasto florentin et le modele europeen du marriage et de la famille," in *Les cadastres anciens des villes et leur traitement par l'informatique*, ed. J. L. Biget, J. C. Herve and Y. Tachert (Rome: Collection de Ecole Francaise de Romes, 1989), 21–31; Anthony Molho, "Deception and Marriage Strategy in Renaissance Florence: The Case of Women's Ages," *Renaissance Quarterly* 41 (1988): 193–217. Emigh, "What Influences Official Information?," 207–10; Kirshner, "Guicciardini," 163.

within which the catasto was collected relieved some of this burden. The notion of a household head was well defined in law.[82] The assessment was based on the fiscal household defined by Roman law to include unmarried children under the *pater familias*. Again, this uses legally binding financial relationships rather than kinship relationships.

Herlihy and Klapisch-Zuber have compiled 10 percent samples from the 1458 and 1480 catasti. These samples are probably less reliable than the 1427 data set for two reasons. First, the quality of the original data from 1458 and 1480 is below the standards set in 1427.[83] The 1427 data are considered to be the highest quality, as the 1427 catasto was rigorously collected.[84] It was collected with less care in 1458 and 1480; the poor and destitute, less likely to pay taxes, were more likely to be ignored. This is a problem, to a greater or lesser extent, with all catasti. Second, because the 1458 and 1480 data are samples, rather than complete sets of households, they are less able to detect subtle differences and changes. The smaller samples also tend to bias the statistical measures toward greater differences than actually existed. These samples appear representative. First, the Florentine population that was subject to taxation and represented in the documents is either not much larger (in 1480) or not much smaller (in 1458) than in 1427.[85] Second, the arte maggiore percentages for the 1458 and 1480 samples are not significantly different from the 1427 percentage.[86] Other sources similarly do not report radical drops in the percentage of arte maggiore households. Finally, the value of immovable goods assessed was not significantly different between 1427, 1458 and 1480. In parallel, the mean reported property wealth per household did not change significantly.[87] These reports correspond to observations that the economy did not grow dramatically during the Quattrocento.

Finally, tax avoidance affected the post-1427 catasti more than it did the 1427 catasto. As Florentines could adjust to the new exemptions, they would shift their assets. The magnitude of this portfolio shift would tend to increase over time. Chapter 4 shows that this had a significant impact on the homeownership rate.

Appendix 3B: A Brief Description and History of the Renaissance Florentine Wool Industry

This appendix provides a brief introduction to the Renaissance Florentine wool industry. This appendix reviews the manufacturing process, examines the industry's changing cost structure and then concludes with a brief history.

---

82 Emigh, "What Influences Official Information?," 208.
83 De Roover, *Medici Bank*, 24; Molho, *Marriage Alliance*, 361–62; Weissman, *Ritual Brotherhood*, 10; Sergio Tognetti, *Il Banco Cambini: Affari e mercati di una compagnia mercantile-bancaria nella Firenze del XV secolo* (Florence: Olschki, 1999), 70 and 80.
84 Conti, *L'imposta diretta*, 148–49.
85 Molho, *Marriage Alliance*, 362–63.
86 The percentages of arte maggiore households in this data set were 9.05% in 1427, 8.33% in 1458 and 11.31% in 1480.
87 The household mean immovable wealth by year was 490 florins in 1427; 820 florins in 1458; and 488 florins in 1480. The coefficients of variation were all at least 1.2. Molho suggests that the drop in 1480 was due to a recent war. Molho, *Marriage Alliance*, 363.

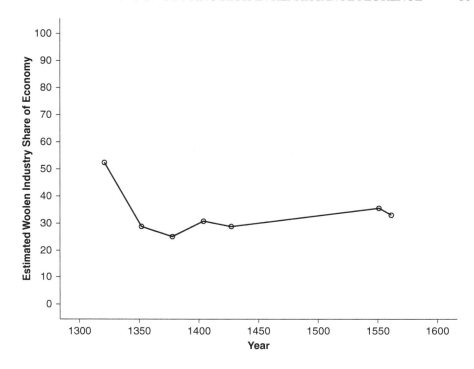

Figure 3.9 Florentine wool industry share of Florentine economy

Sources: For 1321: The share of taxes paid by the Arte della Lana from Edgcumbe Staley, *The Guilds of Florence: Illustrated after Miniatures in Illuminated Manuscripts and Florentine Woodcuts* (1906; New York, Benjamin Blom, 1967), 53.
For years 1352, 1378 and 1404: The share of household heads engaged in wool industry occupations from Alessandro Stella, *La révolte des Ciompi: Les hommes, les lieux, le travail* (Paris: Editions de l'Ecole des Hautes Etudes en Sciences Sociales, 1993), 317–50.
For 1427: The share of household heads with occupations engaged in wool industry occupations from Herlihy and Klapisch-Zuber, *Census and Property Survey*.
For 1551: The share of household heads engaged in wool industry occupations from Pietro Battara, *La popolazione di Firenza alla metà del '500* (Florence: Rinascimento del Libro, 1935), 55–56; R. Burr Litchfield, *Florence ducal capital, 1530–1630* (New York: ACLS Humanities E-Book, 2008), paragraph 275.
For 1561: The share of household heads with occupations engaged in wool industry occupations from Litchfield, *Florence ducal capital*, paragraphs 275, 282–89.

It is important to note that the wool industry is not chosen for study at random. It had a fundamental economic role. One could say it was one of the most important ways the Florentines paid the bills for the Renaissance. The wool industry was critical to the economic well-being of the city through the late medieval and early modern periods. From the early Trecento until the Cinquecento, the wool industry was responsible for a quarter or more of the Florentine economy (see fig. 3.9).

The Manufacturing Process

The wool industry was international in scope; both the raw wool and finished cloth were traded internationally. Florentines purchased wool from a variety of European regions, including England, northern Italy, Provence, Castile and Catalonia. The region where Florence received most of its supply varied over time.[88] The Medici companies studied in part 3 of the present text bought primarily high-quality wool, usually Spanish, from local importers. The use of Italian wool was prohibited within the city of Florence at that time because of its low quality.[89] Earlier the Florentines had relied primarily on English wool. A century later, the Florentines were compelled to rely almost entirely on that same low-quality Italian wool due to changing market conditions.[90] The various types of wool taken in and the cloth produced by the Medici entrepreneurs were often named for places and regions throughout their world that were associated with the product.[91] For example, the Medici produced *perpignano* cloth, which was named after the Catalan (now French) town of Perpignan because it imitated their style of cloth.[92]

The wool manufacturers' guild, the *Arte della Lana*, coordinated the production inside the city and region. The Arte was an umbrella guild and helped companies coordinate production from a wide range of occupations as opposed to representing only a single occupation.[93] It operated using a reasonably fixed structure for centuries. Records ranging from Trecento through the Seicento reveal only minimal changes in the production system.[94] The manufacturing technology remained constant from the development of carded wool, not later than 1331,[95] up to the eighteenth century.[96]

Each Florentine wool manufacturer, *lanaiuolo*, who actively produced cloth, drew up a partnership contract to set up a company, or *compagnia*.[97] These companies were extremely small and usually directly involved less than half a dozen people. The small

---

88 Munro, "Italian Wool-Based Cloth Industries."
89 De Roover, "Florentine Firm of Cloth Manufacturers," 101.
90 Munro, "Italian Wool-Based Cloth Industries," 178.
91 Medici-Tornaquinci, Ms. 600(5).
92 Ibid.
93 R. Epstein, "Craft Guilds, Apprenticeship and Technological Change in Pre-Modern Europe," *Journal of Economic History* 53, no. 3 (1998): 690; Francesco Ammannati, "Craft Guild Legislation and Woollen Production: the Florentine Arte della Lana in the Fifteenth and Sixteenth Centuries," in *Innovation and Creativity in Late Medieval and Early Modern European Cities*, ed. Karol Davids and Bert De Munck (Farnham: Ashgate 2014), 59.
94 Anna Maria E. Agnoletti, ed., *Statuto dell'Arte della Lana in Firenze (1317–1319)*, Fonti e Studi sulle Corporazioni Artigiane del Medio Evo, vol. 1 (Florence: Felice Le Monnier, 1940); Raymond de Roover, "Florentine Firm of Cloth Manufacturers," in *Business, Banking, and Economic Thought in Late Medieval and Early Modern Europe*, ed. Julius Kirshner (Chicago: University of Chicago Press, 1974), 102; Dören, *Studien aus der Florentiner Wirtschaftgeschichte*, 249–54; Richard A. Goldthwaite, "The Florentine Wool Industry in the Late Sixteenth Century: A Case Study," *Journal of European Economic History* 32, no. 3 (2003): 527–54.
95 Patrick Chorley, "The Evolution of the Woollen, 1300–1700," in *The New Draperies in the Low Countries and England, 1300–1800*, ed. N. B. Harte (Oxford: Oxford University Press, 1997), 9–12.
96 Ibid., 11; John H. Munro, "The Rise, Expansion, and Decline of the Italian Wool-Based Cloth Industries, 1100–1730: A Study in International Competition, Transaction Costs, and Comparative Advantage," *Studies in Medieval and Renaissance History* 9 (2012): 178.
97 Edler, *Glossary*, 335–47.

size meant that much of the work was done outside the direct supervision of the company. There were always a large number of companies in the industry, but over time the number of companies declined.[98] Some modern observers view craft guilds as labor organizations rather than trade organizations that aided the manufacturers. However, the Arte was clearly designed to facilitate woolen-cloth manufacture rather than labor rights. It increased the liquidity of the labor market by providing a way to match skilled labor to firms. The Arte set itself up as the only organization to establish and implement production rules. The guild statutes outlawed "conventicles" and "congregations" formed by workers.[99]

Typically a company bought wool in quantities of hundreds of pounds at a time and in a three-year period might use several thousand pounds of wool in one full production run of cloth.[100] Most of the wool was purchased at the beginning of the production run, and relatively little was purchased again until work on the first purchase was almost finished.[101] Types of purchases varied widely. One company purchased quantities ranging between one and sixteen bales per purchase with an approximately uniform distribution among the number of bales per purchase.[102]

The small-scale, highly competitive nature of the wool industry dictated the behavior of the companies. The companies were so small that most steps in the production process were completed consecutively rather than simultaneously.[103] Only occasionally would consecutive, or nearly consecutive, production steps overlap. None of the Medici companies ever worked on all of the steps simultaneously. Therefore one can examine production techniques inside a black box, which the researcher of contemporary firms is unable to do. In the Florentine case, one could say that the black box is translucent, if not transparent.

The companies produced cloth using the putting-out system, which did not take advantage of centralized production and created its own transportation costs. The production process was highly specialized, and there was an extensive division of labor. (Chapter 9 has more about this.) Table 3.4 shows the many types of subcontractors working in the woolen-cloth production process.[104]

---

98 For 1308, 1338, 1495, 1537, 1586, 1596, 1604 and 1627: Gene Brucker, *Florence: The Golden Age, 1138–1737* (Berkeley: University of California Press, 1998), 105. For 1382, 1427, 1458 and 1469: Hidetoshi Hoshino, *L'arte della lana nel basso medioevo in commercio della lana e il mercato dei panni fiorentini nei secoli XIII–XV* (Florence: Olschki, 1980), 227, 229 and 283. For 1561: R. Burr Litchfield, *Florence ducal capital, 1530–1630* (New York: ACLS Humanities E-Book, 2008), table 5.2.

99 Agnoletti, *Statuto dell'Arte della Lana*, 203.

100 Medici-Tornaquinci, Ms. 600(5).

101 Ibid.

102 This was Francesco di Giuliano di Raffaello de' Medici and Co. in 1556 and 1557. The work was done by Francesco di Giovanni di Giunta and Co., Wool-Washers at the Canal. Medici-Tornaquinci, Ms. 567 (7).

103 This can be seen clearly through the entries in any one of the general ledgers kept by the Medici firms.

104 Edler, *Glossary*, 324–30.

Table 3.4 Wool industry occupations in order of production

Preparing	Washing
	Beating/Cleaning
	Combing
	Carding
Spinning	Lanini
	Stamaiuoli
Weaving	Warping
	Weaving
Finishing	Burling
	Scouring
	Fulling
	Stretching
	Napping/ Shearing
	Mending
Dyeing	Dyeing

Sources: De Roover, "Florentine Firm of Cloth Manufacturers," 103; Edler, *Glossary*, 329–30; Franco Franceschi, *Oltre il "Tumulto": I lavoratori fiorentini dell' Arte della Lana fra Tre e Quattrocento* (Florence: Olschki, 1993), 33–37. Occupations listed in order of steps to completion.

The production of woolen cloth required a rigid organization of skilled craftsmen with apparently few substitution possibilities between steps. The precise order differs by source. The order of wool industry production steps used throughout this book is based on that from Raymond de Roover, Florence Edler and Francesco Franceschi. De Roover usefully summarizes the many woolen-cloth production steps under the following headings: preparing, spinning, weaving, finishing and dyeing.[105] (See table 3.4.) Following the order of steps noted above, the work went from preparing to spinning to weaving to finishing to dyeing.[106] Other sources report the steps in slightly different orders. These differences appear to depend on the date and type of source. The *Trattato dell' arte della lana* from the Trecento has a different order.[107] Brucker and Stella each have dyeing in a different place among the major steps. Brucker's order is preparing, spinning, weaving, dyeing and finishing.[108] Stella's order divides the preparation steps into two sets. His order is first preparing set, dyeing, second preparing set, spinning,

105 De Roover, "Florentine Firm of Cloth Manufacturers," 103; Edler, *Glossary*, 324–30, 409–26; Franco Franceschi, *Oltre il "Tumulto": I lavoratori fiorentini dell'Arte della Lana fra Tre e Quattrocento* (Florence: Olschki, 1993), 33–37.

106 Medici Ms. 600(5); De Roover, "Florentine Firm of Cloth Manufacturers," 102; Edler, *Glossary*, 329–30.

107 Alfred Dören, *Studien aus der Florentiner Wirtschaftgeschichte*, vol. 1: *Die Florentiner Wollentuchsindustrie vom Vierzehnten bis zum Sechzehnten Jahrhundert* (Stuttgart: J. G. Cotta'sche Buchhandlung Nachfolger, 1901), 485–93.

108 Gene Brucker, *Florence: The Golden Age, 1138–1737* (Berkeley: University of California Press, 1998), 104.

weaving and finishing.[109] Ammannati's description indicates that dyeing could be done at either major step in the production process.[110] Unlike what other researchers find, this order has the Florentines dyeing the wool rather than the finished cloth. These differences make it clear that the wool industry could respond to market changes. The process was constantly subject to slight changes.[111]

Preparing the raw wool for the spinners was the first major step in the cloth production process. Only men were involved in this work. First, the wool washers (*lavatori*) received the raw wool and performed the preliminary cleaning. This cleaning was considered a very dirty and unpleasant job. The wool washers worked in a *purgo*, an establishment owned by the guild.[112] Next, the beaters and cleaners (*scamatini* and *divettini*, respectively)[113] performed more detailed cleaning of the wool.[114] They worked in teams headed by a supervisor called a *capodieci*, in central workshops run by lanaiuoli.[115] Typically they worked with quantities the size of a *faldella*, approximately seven to ten pounds.[116] Two more steps readied the wool to be spun. The comber factors (*fattori di pettine*) organized the combing of both long staple and short staple wool. The carder factors (*fattori di cardo*) then organized the carding of the short staple wool, but they did not do anything with the long staple wool. They worked in central workshops run by lanaiuoli.[117] The capodieci, fattori di pettine and fattori di cardo were strictly intermediaries between the lanaiuoli and the workers.[118]

Spinning was the second major step in the woolen-cloth production process. Here, the wool was turned into threads before it would be made into the cloth. Spinning was not tiring work, although it was time consuming and required significant skills.[119] The lanini and the stamaiuoli provided essential intermediary and oversight services between the lanaiuoli and the spinners.[120] The lanini bought carded, short staple wool from the lanaiuoli to have it spun. In the Medici-Tornaquinci account books, the lanini identified the women spinners (*filatrice*) who worked for them. The stamaiuoli bought combed, long

---

109   Stella, *La révolte des Ciompi*, 102.

110   Francesco Ammannati, "Production et productivité du travail dans les ateliers laniers florentins du XVIe siècle," in *Les temps du travail. Normes, pratiques, évolutions (XIVe–XIXe siècle)*, ed. Corine Maitte and Didier Terrier (Rennes: Presses Universitaires de Rennes 2014), 225–49.

111   De Roover, "Florentine Firm of Cloth Manufacturers," 99.

112   Edler, *Glossary*, 229, 409. In some cities the purgo was privately owned, as is noted in Edler, *Glossary*, 409.

113   Other names used in the Medici-Tornaquinci account books for beaters were *battilano, vergheggiatore* and *vergheggino*.

114   Edler, *Glossary*, 325.

115   Ibid., 329. However, De Roover notes that there is no clear evidence for this practice. De Roover, "Florentine Firm of Cloth Manufacturers," 93.

116   Edler, *Glossary*, 325. The weight of the faldella differed over the course of time.

117   Ibid., 329.

118   De Roover, "Florentine Firm of Cloth Manufacturers," 95.

119   Ibid., 96.

120   Edler, *Glossary*, 413–15; De Roover, "Florentine Firm of Cloth Manufacturers," 94.

staple wool from the lanaiuoli to have it spun. The stamaiuoli were more carefully regulated by the Florentine government than the lanini.[121]

Weaving was the third major step in the woolen cloth production process. This step included both warping and weaving, which was the actual making of the cloth. The work was under the direct supervision of the lanaiuoli and involved no intermediaries.[122] The warpers (*orditrici*) set the spun threads in warps prior to weaving.[123] The male warpers worked in central workshops run by lanaiuoli; the female warpers worked in their own homes.[124] Warpers were paid on a piece-rate basis without regard for cloth type or quality of workmanship.[125] Most rates paid to warpers were regulated by ordinance.[126] The weavers (*tessitori*) then wove the cloth.[127] Both men and women worked as weavers, and both worked at home.[128] Weavers were paid on a piece-rate basis, which, unlike that of the warpers, did vary by type of cloth and by quality of workmanship.

Finishing was the fourth major step in the woolen-cloth production process. Finishing prepared the cloth to be dyed and made the cloth more presentable to customers. Burlers, scourers, fullers and stretchers first completed any necessary repairs on the cloth. The burlers (*riveditori* or *dizzeccolatori*) removed knots in the cloth after it had been woven. They usually worked for day wages in the central workshop of a lanaiuoli. The scourers (*purgatori* or *pulcatori*) washed the cloth. They were usually small-scale masters who rented space in a large washing establishment operated by the entire industry. The fullers (*calcatori, gualchierai* or *gualcatori*), who cleaned the cloth, were usually small-scale masters who rented space in the fulling mills operated by the entire industry just outside Florence. At one time, fullers worked in family-owned establishments. The stretchers, also called tenterers (tiratori), placed the cloth on large frames in order to dry it. They were small-scale masters initially working in family businesses, but over time moved into larger, industry-owned establishments.[129] The nappers, shearers and menders then improved the appearance of the cloth. The nappers and shearers (*cardatori* and cimatori, respectively) set up the nap of the cloth. The nappers raised up the loose fibers of the yarn into a nap by scratching it with teasels. The shearers then shaved the surface into a level nap. Nappers and shearers were small-scale masters working in private workshops. The menders (rimendatori or *mendatori*) corrected defects in the cloth, such as holes and missing yarn. Generally the menders were also small-scale masters who worked in private workshops, although they sometimes worked directly for the lanaiuoli.[130]

---

121   Edler, *Glossary*, 413–15.
122   De Roover, "Florentine Firm of Cloth Manufacturers," 97.
123   Edler, *Glossary*, 419–22.
124   Ibid., 330.
125   Ibid., 329–30.
126   De Roover, "Florentine Firm of Cloth Manufacturers," 98.
127   Edler, *Glossary*, 419–22.
128   Ibid., 330.
129   Ibid., 327–30.
130   Ibid., 328–30.

Dyeing was the final step in the woolen-cloth production process. It involved only one step, but there were two types of dyers, each classified by the materials they used for dyeing.[131] The *tintori di guado* used woad and indigo, and the *tintori dell'arte maggiore* used madder. Both dyes were plant products. Woad was a blue dye, and madder was a red dye. Dyers created other colors from these bases. The lanaiuoli often provided the dyes for their cloth, apparently to ensure quality.[132] The dyers worked in private workshops owned by master dyers and were paid fixed rates set by statute.[133]

The dyed cloth was then ready to be added to inventory and sold by the lanaiuolo. Florentine woolen cloth was sold in many markets, each with its own requirements and tastes. These markets ranged from local Florentine retail to international trading throughout Europe and the Near East.

Changing Cost Structure

While the Florentine wool industry's manufacturing technology and organization of production remained constant between the Trecento and the *Seicento*, the internal cost structure of the industry changed significantly.

Figure 3.10 presents the cost structure for four major firms ranging over the nearly two centuries from 1396 to 1581. Figure 3.10A shows the constancy of the industry: that wool costs hovered between 30 and 40 percent of the total costs as a percent of manufacturing (excluding raw wool and central office expense costs from total costs) throughout the period.[134] Figure 3.10B, however, shows how the industry could adapt. The costs are summarized by each of the five major steps. While the share of costs for dyeing remained relatively constant for two centuries, the shares for preparing and finishing decreased sharply, and those for spinning and weaving increased sharply.[135] It seems reasonable to conclude that these adjustments were responses to changes in market conditions and, as such, they highlight the flexibility of the industry.

A Brief History of the Wool Industry

The story of the Renaissance Florentine wool industry is not one of a simple one-time rise and decline. The industry faced significant obstacles and demonstrated the resilience to adapt and succeed multiple times. These obstacles included demographic changes, plagues, taxation, changing transportation technologies and wars. This resilience demonstrates that, though the manufacturing technology and production organization remained

---

131 Ibid., 328.
132 De Roover, "Florentine Firm of Cloth Manufacturers," 93–101. De Roover notes that the dyer could use lower quality dyes, undetectable by the producer.
133 Edler, *Glossary*, 328.
134 This conclusion differs somewhat from that of Goldthwaite, who used essentially the same data (Richard A. Goldthwaite, "Florentine Wool Industry in the Late Sixteenth Century," 539 and 548.).
135 Ibid., 539.

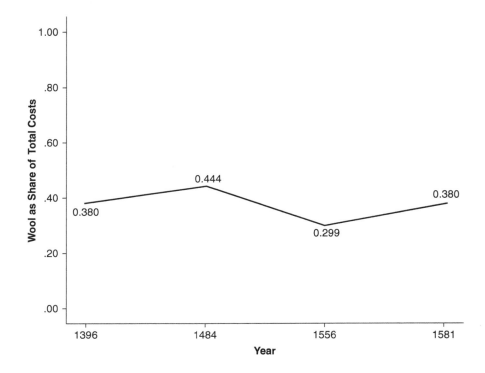

Figure 3.10A Raw wool as a share of total costs by year of firm operation, 1389–1581 (dates are first year of firm operation)

Sources: For 1396: Federigo Melis, *Aspetti della vita economica medievale: Studi nell'Archivio Datini di Prato* (Siena: Monte dei Paschi di Siena, 1962), prospetto XVII (between pp. 554 and 555); Francesco Ammannati, "Francesco di Marco Datini's Wool Workshops," in *Francesco di Marco Datini. The Man the Merchant*, ed. Giampero Nigro (Florence: Firenze University Press, 2010), 506.

For 1484: Hideotoshi Hoshino, *Industria tessile e commercio internazionale nella Firenze del tardo medioevo* (Florence: Leo S. Olschki, 2001), 120.

For 1556: Raymond De Roover, "A Florentine Firm of Cloth Manufacturers," in *Business, Banking, and Economic Thought in Late Medieval and Early Modern Europe*, ed. Julius Kirshner (Chicago: University of Chicago Press, 1974 [1938]), 118; De Roover, "A Florentine Firm of Cloth Manufacturers," *Speculum* 16, no. 1 (1941): 33.

For 1581: Richard A. Goldthwaite, "The Florentine Wool Industry in the Late Sixteenth Century: A Case Study," *Journal of European Economic History* 32, no. 3 (2003): 553.

largely unchanged, the industry was able to adapt to dramatically changing economic circumstances. Besides having a flexible cost structure as noted above, the wool industry also proved adaptable in its ability to adjust its sources of wool and its consumers.

There were three major periods of wool industry expansion between the 1330s and the mid-Seicento.[136] The first period began in the mid-Trecento and accelerated after

---

136 Patrick Chorley, "*Rascie* and the Florentine Cloth Industry during the Sixteenth Century: A Case Study," *Journal of European Economic History* 32, no. 3 (2003): 514; John H. Munro, "The Rise, Expansion, and Decline of the Italian Wool-Based Cloth Industries, 1100–1730: A Study in International Competition, Transaction Costs, and Comparative Advantage," *Studies in Medieval and Renaissance History* 9 (2012): 178–81.

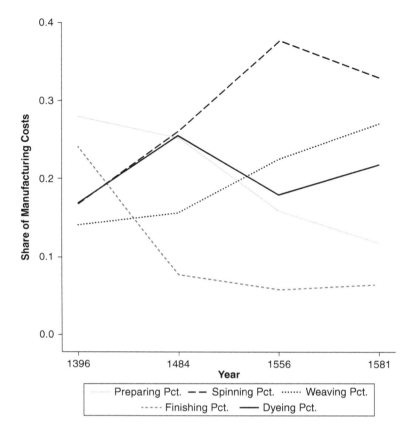

Figure 3.10B Major steps as a share of total costs by year of firm operation, 1389–1581 (dates are first year of firm operation)
Sources: For 1396: Melis, *Aspetti*, prospetto XVII (between pp. 554 and 555); Ammannati, "Datini's Wool Workshops," 506.
For 1484: Hoshino, *Industria tessile*, 120.
For 1556: De Roover, "Florentine Firm of Cloth Manufacturers," 118. De Roover, "Florentine Firm of Cloth Manufacturers," *Speculum*, 33.
For 1581: Goldthwaite, "Late Sixteenth Century," 553.

the 1348 Black Death.[137] The industry recovered from the Black Death with superfine cloth that outcompeted the Low Countries in the Mediterranean.[138] The Florentine wool industry boomed in the years after the Black Death.[139] Florentines produced luxury cloths

---

137 Munro, "Italian Wool-Based Cloth Industries," 73–82 and 93–114; Franceschi, *Oltre il "Tumulto,"* 6–28; Hoshino, *L'arte della lana*, 153–229.
138 Chorley, "Florentine Cloth Industry during the Sixteenth Century," 514.
139 Munro, "Italian Wool-Based Cloth Industries," 73–114; Munro, "The Dual Crises of the Late-Medieval Florentine Cloth Industry, c. 1320–c. 1420," in *Textiles and the Medieval Economy: Production, Trade and Consumption of Textiles 8th–16th Centuries*, eds. Angela Ling Huang and Carsten Jahnke (Oxford, UK: Oxbow Books, 2015), 131–42.

for European markets using high-equality English wool. Production gradually declined during the second half of the Trecento.[140] This growth came with troubles. The Revolt of the Ciompi (1378–82) was centered in the wool industry.[141] This often motivates studies of wealth inequality in Florence during the Trecento and the Quattrocento. This expansion had largely ended by the 1420s with the decline of the luxury market[142] and the decreased availability of English wool.[143]

The second period began in the mid-Quattrocento, after the Fall of Constantinople in 1453.[144] There was steady growth and improvement during these years. New products were introduced.[145] The industry recovered from the depression of the early Quattrocento by developing middling cloth that enabled it to exploit new Levantine markets.[146] The introduction of cheaper Garbo cloth from Italian wool for these markets began in the 1430s.[147] English wool continued to be used.[148] However, in another change from the Trecento boom, the Florentines used Spanish wool during this Quattrocento boom.[149] Transportation routes were developed. There was considerable expansion from the 1460s onward.[150] Hoshino finds that by 1488 the output had equalled that of 1338 and was of higher quality.[151] The apogee of this cycle occurred in 1520.

Turmoil in the Levant caused problems for Florentines and gave the advantage to the Venetians. As a result, the Florentine wool industry declined from the 1520s until around 1550.[152] However, the Venetians continued to increase for the next half-century. The year 1600 conveniently marks the date of the wool industry's maximum extent in Venice and the beginning of its eventual decline.[153]

The third Florentine wool industry expansion began in the mid-Cinquecento after the Peace of Cateau Cambresis in 1559.[154] The industry recovered from the loss of

---

140 Franceschi, *Oltre il "Tumulto"*, 13.
141 For the more about the economic and social history behind this event, see: Stella, *La Révolte des Ciompi*; Franceschi, *Oltre il "Tumulto."*
142 Munro, "Italian Wool-Based Cloth Industries," 99.
143 Munro, "Dual Crises," 131–42.
144 Munro, "Italian Wool-Based Cloth Industries," 122–41; Hoshino, *L'arte della lana*, 231–303.
145 Munro, "Italian Wool-Based Cloth Industries," 131–39.
146 Chorley, "Florentine Cloth Industry during the Sixteenth Century," 514.
147 Munro, "Italian Wool-Based Cloth Industries," 126–31
148 Ibid., 125–26.
149 Munro, "Dual Crises."
150 Munro, "Italian Wool-Based Cloth Industries," 123–24.
151 Hoshino, *L'arte della lana*, 35, 206, 211, 231, 281, 287 and 299–301.
152 Munro, "Italian Wool-Based Cloth Industries," 140–41.
153 Venice: Domenico Sella, "Les Mouvements longs: l'industrie lainière à Venise aux XVIe et XVIIe siècles," *Annales: économies, sociétes, civilisations* 12 (1957): 29–45. Domenico Sella, "The Rise and Fall of the Venetian Woollen Industry," in *Crisis and Change in the Venetian Economy in the Sixteenth and Seventeenth Centuries*, ed. Brian Pullan (London: Methuen, 1965), 106–26; Domenico Sella, "Industrial Production in Seventeenth-Century Italy: A Reappraisal," *Explorations in Entrepreneurial History*, Ser. 2, 6 (1969): 235–53.
154 Munro, "Italian Wool-Based Cloth Industries," 173–81.

Levantine trade by developing *rascia fiorentina*—a high-quality product—allowing it to win major markets north of the Alps.[155]

The industry began its ultimate decline in the 1570s. Though the rate of decline is still an issue, whether it was rapid[156] or gradual and not traumatic,[157] economic historians have identified a wide range of factors that could explain it. These include, first, a 1570s financial crisis caused by a tight monetary policy[158] that affected the industry.[159] The importance of this financial crisis, in turn, points to the importance of capital and investment as key ingredients in the decline of the industry. On the European stage, the network of key markets disappeared.[160] Second, the increasing cost of Spanish wool forced the Arte to shift to a lower-quality product in order to survive.[161] Next, changes in northern Europe caused problems. These include the closure of northern European markets with the Wars of Religion in France and the Troubles in the Netherlands[162] as well as the new competition from northern European production.[163] The local supplies for the English wool industry gave them a critical comparative advantage.[164] Finally, changes in the Levant caused problems. The Florentine access to the Levant market definitively ended.[165] The English Levant Company gained dominance in the Mediterranean textile trade.[166] The Italians could not compete with its novel financial organization that allowed a concentration of capital, which allowed greater coordination of production and naval power.[167]

---

155   Chorley, "Florentine Cloth Industry during the Sixteenth Century," 514.

156   Ibid.," 487–526, esp. 505; Chorley, "Volume of Cloth Production in Florence," 551–71, esp. 569.

157   Francesco Ammannati, "L'Arte della Lana a Firenze nel Cinquecento: crisi del settore e risposte degli operatori," *Storia economica: Rivista quadrimestrale*, 11, no. 1 (2008): 5–39, esp. 34; Francesco Ammannati, "Florentine Woolen Manufacture in the Sixteenth Century: Crisis and New Entrepreneurial Strategies," *Business and Economic History On-Line*, 7 (2009): 1–9; Francesco Ammannati, " 'Se non piace loro l'arte, mutinla in una altra': I 'lavoranti' dell'Arte della lana fiorentina tra XIV e XVI secolo," *Annali di Storia di Firenze* 7 (2012): 5–33.

158   Carlo M. Cipolla, *Money in Sixteenth-Century Florence* (Berkeley, CA: University of California Press, 1989), 101–13

159   Chorley, "Florentine Cloth Industry during the Sixteenth Century," 511; Chorley, "Volume of Cloth Production in Florence," 569; Ammannati, "Crisi del settore e risposte degli operatori," 37; Ammannati, "Crisis and New Entrepreneurial Strategies," 9.

160   Chorley, "Florentine Cloth Industry during the Sixteenth Century," 505; Ammannati, "Crisi del settore e risposte degli operatori," 35; Ammannati, "Crisis and New Entrepreneurial Strategies," 9.

161   Chorley, "Florentine Cloth Industry during the Sixteenth Century," 509; Ammannati, "Crisi del settore e risposte degli operatori," 38; Ammannati, "Crisis and New Entrepreneurial Strategies," 9.

162   Chorley, "Volume of Cloth Production in Florence," 569; Ammannati, "Crisi del settore e risposte degli operatori," 35.

163   Ammannati, "Crisi del settore e risposte degli operatori," 36–7; Ammannati, "Crisis and New Entrepreneurial Strategies," 9.

164   Munro, "Italian Wool-Based Cloth Industries," 153–73 and 179.

165   Ammannati, "Crisi del settore e risposte degli operatori," 35.

166   Munro, "Italian Wool-Based Cloth Industries," 153–54.

167   Ibid., 154–56 and 179.

Goldthwaite summarizes the problem well: "In short, a less flexible industry and more fluid markets."[168]

The industry declined from its late Cinquecento high and steadily contracted during the Seicento.[169] It was reduced to serving local markets by the end of the century.[170] The silk industry rose in its place.[171] The decline of the wool industry in favor of the silk industry was clear to the manufacturers in the early Seicento, who changed their investment patterns,[172] as well as to urban workers, who changed industries.[173] Urban jobs were also replaced by rural jobs.[174] Malanima argues the silk industry so precisely replaced the woolen industry that Tuscany maintained its existing woolen-industry economic organization.[175] Florence became less important relative to its surrounding rural areas and smaller towns.[176] Carmona notes that the shift in woolen-industry production out of the city and into the countryside softened the blow to the Florentine regional economy.[177] This rural production was not protoindustrialization. The goal during the seventeenth century became containing costs, which favored rural industry. The English model of protoindustrialization was not feasible.[178] In the end, historians find that the wool industry "had no answer to the adverse conjuncture of the late sixteenth and early seventeenth centuries."[179]

John Munro's synthesis of late medieval and early modern Italian textile history is written from the perspective of its decline.[180] He sees these cycles in the fortune of the wool industry driven by changing transaction costs.[181] In the end, the unchanging

---

168   Goldthwaite, "Florentine Wool Industry in the Late Sixteenth Century," 550.

169   Paolo Malanima, *La decadenza di un'economia cittadina: L'industria di Firenze nei secoli XVI–XVIII* (Bologna: Il Mulino, 1982), 289–305, esp. 304; Ruggiero Romano, "A Florence au XVIIe siècle: Industries textiles et conjuncture," *Annales. Histoire, Sciences Sociales* 7, no. 4 (1952): 508–12.

170   Chorley, "Florentine Cloth Industry during the Sixteenth Century," 514.

171   Paolo Malanima, *La decadenza di un'economia cittadina: L'industria di Firenze nei secoli XVI–XVIII* (Bologna: Il Mulino, 1982), 305–21; Jordan Goodman, "Financing Pre-modern European Industry: An Example from Florence 1580–1660," *Journal of European Economic History* 10, no. 2 (1981): 415–36.

172   Goldthwaite, "Florentine Wool Industry in the Late Sixteenth Century," 548.

173   Ammannati, "'Se non piace loro l'arte," 24.

174   Paolo Malanima, "An Example of Industrial Reconversion: Tuscany in the Sixteenth and Seventeenth Centuries," in *The Rise and Decline of Urban Industries in Italy and in the Low Countries*, ed. Herman Van der Wee (Louvain, Belgium: Leuven University Press, 1988), 63–72; Paolo Malanima, "L'industria fiorentina in declino fra Cinque e Seicento: Linee per un'analisi comparata," in *Firenze e la Toscana dei Medici nell'Europa del'500, Vol. 1, Strumenti e veicoli della cultura relazioni politiche ed economiche* (Florence: Leo S. Olschki, 1983), 295–308.

175   Malanima, "Industrial Reconversion," 68–70.

176   Ibid., 68–72.

177   Mario Carmona, "La Toscane face à la crise de l'industrie lainière: techniques et mentalités economiques aux XVIe et XVIIe siècles," in *Produzione, Commercio, e Consumo dei Panni di Lana (Nei Secoli XII–XVIII)*, ed. Marco Spallanzani (Florence: Leo S. Olschki, 1976), 151.

178   Malanima, "Industrial Reconversion," 66 and 68.

179   Chorley, "Florentine Cloth Industry during the Sixteenth Century," 514.

180   Munro, "Italian Wool-Based Cloth Industries."

181   Ibid.

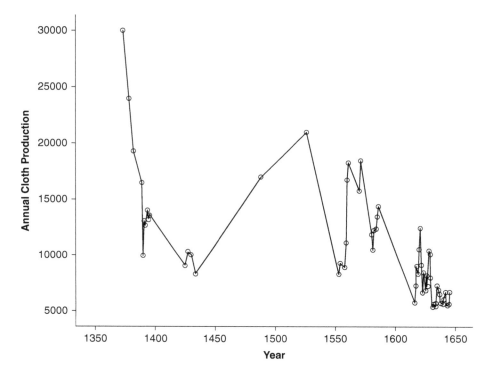

Figure 3.11 Florentine annual wool cloth production, 1373–1645

Sources: 1373–78, 1389–1433: Franceschi, *Oltre il "Tumulto"*, 13.
1382: Hoshino, *L'arte della lana*, 227.
1488–1526: Richard A. Goldthwaite, *The Economy of Renaissance Florence* (Baltimore: Johns Hopkins University Press, 2009), 278.
1553–71: Arithmetic mean of Chorley and Ammannati estimates based on: Patrick Chorley, "Florentine Cloth Industry during the Sixteenth Century," 516; Patrick Chorley, "The Volume of Cloth Production in Florence, 1500–1650: An Assessment of the Evidence," in *Wool Products and Markets (13th–20th Century)*, ed. Giovanni Luigi Fontana and Gérard Gayot (Padua: Coop. Libraria Editrice Università di Padova, 2004), 551–71; Francesco Ammannati, "L'Arte della Lana a Firenze nel Cinquecento: crisi del settore e risposte degli operatori," *Storia economica: Rivista quadrimestrale*, 11, 1 (2008): 30–31; Ammannati, "Florentine Woolen Manufacture in the Sixteenth Century: Crisis and New Entrepreneurial Strategies," *Business and Economic History On-Line*, 7 (2009): 8.
1581–86: Chorley, "Volume of Cloth Production," 563.
1616–45: Ruggiero Romano, "A Florence au XVIIe siècle: Industries textiles et conjuncture," *Annales. Histoire, Sciences Sociales* 7, no. 4 (1952): 511–12.

manufacturing technology used in Florence prevented any gains in comparative advantage in production.[182]

Munro's approach is natural. Much of the focus of economic historians has been on the final decline of the industry. There is a different way to approach wool industry history—to focus less on the decline and more on the long-term resilience of the

_____

182 Ibid., 178.

industry. It survived the Black Death in 1348, the fall of the Byzantine Empire in 1453 and the unification of Spain in 1492—all events that still resonate half a millennium later—and became stronger each time. The basic technology of European wool production did not change until the eighteenth century and the Industrial Revolution. No wool-cloth producer held a comparative advantage in technology. If the problem was transaction costs, then why did the Florentine wool industry fail to recover after the Peace of Westphalia in 1648? Florentine resilience allowed them to prevail repeatedly— until they did not.

The real question seems not why the Florentine wool industry declined, but why it did not rise again. Perhaps the answer can be found in the two major Seicento changes: that the English Levant Company took control over the Mediterranean wool trade and that the Florentine silk industry became preeminent. The silk industry's rise made the wool industry less vital. The English joint-stock companies, and their superior financial organization, however, locked tight the door that the decline had closed. Some of these issues are covered in chapter 9.

Appendix 3C: Wealth Volatility and Dowry Value

This appendix explores how wealth volatility would have affected dowries in Quattrocento Florence. The derivation is heuristic and not rigorous. Two distinct theoretical approaches provide some insight. The first views dowries as part of an altruistic marriage market.[183] Recent work shows how altruism drives large dowries.[184] The second links dowries to social structure. Marriage is widely recognized as a transmission mechanism of wealth, and social standing, across generations.[185] This approach implies that the dowry could be used as a signal in order to maintain social status.[186]

---

183   Gary S. Becker, "A Theory of Marriage," in *The Economic Approach to Human Behavior* (Chicago: University of Chicago Press, 1976), 205–50; Gary S. Becker and Kevin M. Murphy, "Sorting by Marriage," in *Social Economics: Market Behavior in a Social Environment* (Chicago: University of Chicago Press, 2000), 29–46.

184   Junsen Zhang and William Chan, "Dowry and Wife's Welfare: A Theoretical and Empirical Analysis," *Journal of Political Economy* 107, no. 4 (1999): 786–808; Siwan Anderson, "Why Dowry Payments Declined with Modernization in Europe But Are Rising in India," *Journal of Political Economy* 111, no. 2 (2003): 269–310; Maristella Botticini and Aloysius Siow, "Why Dowries?" *American Economic Review* 93, no. 4 (2003): 1385–98; Maristella Botticini and Aloysius Siow, "Why Dowries?," Boston University and University of Toronto, 2002, http://www.aeaweb.org/aer/contents.

185   Laura Bertoni, "Investire per la famiglia, investire per sé: La partecipazione delle donne ai circuiti creditizi a Pavia nella seconda metà del XIII secolo," in *Dare credito alle donne: Presenze femminili nell'economia tra medioevo ed età moderna*, ed. Giovanna Petti Balbi and Paola Guglielmott (Asti, Italy: Centro studi Renato Bordone sui Lombardi, sul credito e sulla banca, 2012), 51–73; Padgett, "Open Elite?," 357–411.

186   A. Michael Spence, *Market Signaling: Informational Transfer in Hiring and Related Screening Processes* (Cambridge, MA: Harvard University Press, 1974).

As would be expected, Tuscan dowries were a significant share of the ultimate bequests.[187] Dowries were also used to equalize wealth. For example, they were larger in the Florentine Tuscan town of Cortona when daughters married down.[188]

Two significant factors, the creation of the *Monte delle doti* and dowry inflation, increased the size of Florentine dowries during the Quattrocento. The Monte delle doti was, essentially, the dowry insurance fund of Florence.[189] It reduced the cost of dowries by creating a financial intermediary. Dowry inflation, however, was a widespread Italian phenomenon.[190] The Monte delle doti would have mitigated some of its impact on the household's budget. The economics literature offers two potential explanations for dowry inflations. Maristella Botticcini and Aloysius Siow posit that dowry inflations were due to slow urbanization.[191] Siwan Anderson, who studies modern India, finds that rapid economic growth caused dowry inflation through the link between wealth and social status.[192] He argues that castes have a critical role in causing the Indian dowry inflation. Indian castes appear more rigidly divided than the Florentine arte maggiore and popolo minuto.

The Florentine case contains additional nuances. The high wealth volatility (see chapter 3) would have increased the value of a good marriage. In this way the Monte delle doti could have helped preserve social standing by creating a kind of social-standing insurance.[193] This analysis parallels Anderson's.

The wealth elasticity of dowries also influenced dowry sizes, but this fact is not usually incorporated in the theory. The impact of wealth division on the household portfolio differed by household wealth. This is because the distribution of a dowry to a daughter divides the familial portfolio. Since the poor are more risk averse than the wealthy,[194] their dowries as a share of wealth would be smaller. The greater the financial market efficiency, the less the elasticity. Since the Florentine markets were efficient,[195] one would expect both less elasticity than in other places and a pronounced drop in dowries among

---

187 Maristella Botticini, "A Loveless Economy? Intergenerational Altruism and the Marriage Market in a Tuscan Town, 1415–1436," *Journal of Economic History* 59, no. 1 (1999): 104–21.

188 Ibid.; Botticini and Siow, "Why Dowries?," *American Economic Review*; Botticini and Siow, "Why Dowries?," Boston/Toronto.

189 For more information, see Kirshner and Molho, "Dowry Fund"; Molho, *Marriage Alliance*.

190 Cf. Hughes, "Urban Growth and Family Structure"; Kirshner and Molho, "Dowry Fund."

191 Botticini and Siow, "Why Dowries?," *American Economic Review*; Botticini and Siow, "Why Dowries?," Boston/Toronto

192 Anderson, "Why Dowry Payments Declined."

193 Richard T. Lindholm, "Studies of the Renaissance Florentine Woolen Industry," PhD diss., University of Chicago, 1993, app. 3.2; Anderson, "Why Dowry Payments Declined."

194 See John R. Hicks, "Liquidity," *Economic Journal* 72, no. 288 (1962): 787–802; John W. Pratt, "Risk Aversion in the Small and in the Large," *Econometrica* 32, no. 1/2 (1964): 122–36; Kenneth Joseph Arrow, "The Theory of Risk Aversion," in *Essays in the Theory of Risk-Bearing* (Chicago: Markham, 1971), 90–120.

195 G. Geoffrey Booth and Umit G. Gurun, "Volatility Clustering and the Bid-Ask Spread: Exchange Rate Behavior in Early Renaissance Florence," *Journal of Empirical Finance* 15 (2008): 131–44.

the miserabili. This could explain two observations. First, Kirshner and Klerman find that the bride's family often encumbered the dowry.[196] This would make sense because it would have mitigated the increased risk due to the portfolio division. Second, bequests to support dowries for poor girls were a common practice.[197] This could have been necessary because their dowries were disproportionately less due to the risk factor.

This also implies that the creation of the Monte delle doti probably resulted in a one-time increase in dowry levels for households with less wealth. The combination of these observations finds some support from Molho's work. During the years shortly after its foundation in 1425, families from a wide range of social levels participated.[198] Changes in Florentine demographic, economic and social circumstances changed people's attitudes toward the Monte.[199] During the late Quattrocento and the early Cinquecento the Monte delle doti was dominated by the most affluent and prominent families.[200] The one-time increase in dowries among the poor had at last been outstripped by the wealth elasticity effect.

---

196 Julius Kirshner and Jacob Klerman, "The Seven Percent Fund of Renaissance Florence," in *Banchi pubblici, banchi private e monti di pieta nell'Europa preindustriale: Amministrazione, tecniche operative e ruoli economici: atti del convegno–Genova (1–6 ottobre 1990)* (Genova: Società Ligure di Storia Patria, 1991), 1: 367–98.

197 Steven Epstein, "Labour in Thirteenth-Century Genoa," *Mediterranean Historical Review* 3 (1988): 133; Steven Epstein, "The Family," in *Italy in the Central Middle Ages, 1000–1300* (Oxford: Oxford University Press, 2004), 186.

198 Molho, *Marriage Alliance*, 157.

199 Ibid., 163.

200 Ibid., 164.

Chapter Four

PALACES AND WORKERS: NEIGHBORHOOD RESIDENTIAL SEGREGATION IN RENAISSANCE FLORENCE

Introduction

When Leonardo Bruni extolled the virtues of Florence at the beginning of the *Quattrocento*, he was expressing the Renaissance ideal of neighborhood equality.[1] The egalitarianism that is now widely associated with modernity was welcomed by many Renaissance writers. Jacob Burckhardt follows their lead and asserts that Florence achieved, or at least approached, this ideal.[2] Critics argue that the Renaissance was more closely associated with inegalitarian developments that eroded the rights of the lower levels of society. They claim that the emergence of the Renaissance during the period from the *Trecento* to the Quattrocento engendered increasing societal divisions in both wealth and status. They also identify a variety of forms and channels of increasing inequality in Florence and its domains, including the increasingly inegalitarian distribution of wealth, a steady advance and eventual triumph of feudal values over republican values within the city, the exploitation of the countryside and the effects of currency debasement on the poor.[3]

---

1 Hans Baron, *From Petrarch to Leonardo Bruni: Studies in Humanistic and Political Literature* (Chicago: University of Chicago Press, 1968), 237.

2 Jacob Burckhardt, *The Civilization of the Renaissance in Italy*, 2 vols. (New York: Harper, 1973).

3 For the economic inequality debate, see David Herlihy and Christiane Klapisch-Zuber, *Les Toscans et leurs familles: Une étude du Catasto Florentine de 1427* (Paris: Fondation nationale des sciences politiques, 1978), 250; David Herlihy and Christiane Klapisch-Zuber, *The Tuscans and Their Families: A Study of the Florentine Catasto of 1427* (New Haven, CT: Yale University Press, 1985), 97–105; Richard A. Goldthwaite, "The Economy of Renaissance Italy: The Preconditions for Luxury Consumption," *I Tatti Studies* 2 (1987): 29. For the movement from republican to feudal values, see Richard C. Trexler, *Public Life in Renaissance Florence* (New York: Academic Press, 1980); Anthony Molho, *Marriage Alliance in Late Medieval Florence* (Cambridge, MA: Harvard University Press, 1994), 154. For the exploitation of the countryside, see Enrico Fiumi, "Fioritura e decadenza dell'economia fiorentina," *Archivio storico Italiano*, 115 (1957): 385–439; 116 (1958): 443–510; and 117 (1959): 427–502; Philip J. Jones, "From Manor to Mezzadria: A Tuscan Case-Study in the Medieval Origins of Modern Agrarian Society," in *Florentine Studies, Politics and Society in Renaissance Florence*, ed. Nicolai Rubinstein (London: Faber and Faber, 1968), 193–241; Anthony Molho, *Florentine Public Finances in the Early Renaissance, 1400–1433* (Cambridge, MA: Harvard University Press, 1971), 23–45. For a discussion of monetary manipulations and inequality, see Niccolò Rodolico, "Il sistema monetario e

Such critics associate this growing social division with a growing physical segregation by neighborhoods created through urban renewal and palace building. The well-integrated and heterogeneous Trecento medieval neighborhoods were thereby converted into segregated and homogeneous Quattrocento Renaissance neighborhoods.[4]

This study tests the neighborhood segregation theory, which is composed of three closely linked and testable hypotheses: (1) neighborhoods were segregated, (2) core neighborhood residents had higher status during the Quattrocento and (3) segregation increased after the Trecento. A failure of any one of these three hypotheses would cast doubt on the segregation theory. The study presented here shows that none of these is supported by the evidence.

The remainder of this chapter presents the analysis of Florentine neighborhood segregation. It covers the general theories used to understand premodern urban ecology, including the Burgess Chicago School and Sjoberg models of urban ecology along with the notions of core and periphery and the segregation of neighborhoods. Next, evidence from other locations and times and the historiography of Florentine urban ecology are reviewed in order to provide some context. The key theme concerns whether Florentine neighborhoods were integrated or segregated, whether there was a general separation between core and periphery and whether the level of segregation increased. Finally, these hypotheses are tested, with the result being that all three of them are thoroughly rejected.

General Theories of Urban Ecology

This section outlines the broad social scientific theoretical work and historical empirical results that place the segregation theory and its applicability to Renaissance Florence in context. The focus here is on residential data, as these are both more easily available for Florence and more appropriate to analyze, since many Florentine workers worked at home.

The Burgess Chicago School model is the baseline for most modern models of urban ecology. It is used in urban economics, urban geography and urban sociology. The layout of this theoretical city (see Fig. 4.1) is based on that of Chicago during the early twentieth century. It envisions the city extending out in five well-defined concentric zones beginning with a central business district.[5] Housing quality improves the farther from the central

le classi sociali nel Medio Evo," *Rivista Italiana di sociologia* 8 (1904): 462–69; Carlo M. Cipolla, *The Monetary Policy of Fourteenth-Century Florence* (Berkeley: University of California Press, 1982).

4   Gene Brucker, *Renaissance Florence* (1959; Huntington, NY: Krieger, 1975), 23–25, 27 and 59; Gene Brucker, *The Civic World of Early Renaissance Florence* (Princeton, NJ: Princeton University Press, 1977), 21–30; Samuel K. Cohn Jr., *The Laboring Classes in Renaissance Florence* (New York: Academic Press, 1978), 43–63 and121–27; Dale V. Kent and Francis William Kent, *Neighbours and Neighbourhood in Renaissance Florence: The District of the Red Lion in the Fifteenth Century* (Locust Valley, NY: J. J. Augustin, 1982), 5 and 13–19; Ronald F. E. Weissman, *Ritual Brotherhood in Renaissance Florence* (New York: Academic Press, 1982), 19.

5   Ernest W. Burgess, "The Growth of the City: An Introduction to a Research Project," in *The City: Suggestions for Investigation of Human Behavior in the Urban Environment*, ed. Robert E. Park and Ernest W. Burgess (1925; Chicago: University of Chicago Press, 1966), 51.

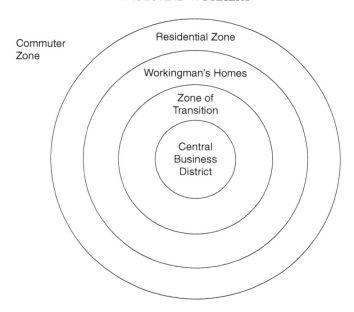

Figure 4.1 Chicago School model of neighborhood organization
Source: Ernest W. Burgess, "The Growth of the City: An Introduction to a Research Project," in *The City: Suggestions for Investigation of Human Behavior in the Urban Environment*, ed. Robert E. Park and Ernest W. Burgess (1925; Chicago: University of Chicago Press, 1966), 55.

business district a home is built.[6] The "zone of transition" includes the slum area. The "zone of workingmen's homes" includes the "Deutschland Ghetto." Apartment houses are on the inner areas of the residential zone. Residential hotels, at the time better quality than apartment houses, are in the middle areas of the residential zone. The wealthier, single-family homes are on the outskirts of the residential zone and the commuting zone. This sequence implies that the periphery is wealthier than the core region. The original model has no dynamic element; the implicit argument is that the marketplace will lead the city to converge on this pattern over time. These and other features have been added to the model gradually.[7] Factor ecology methods were developed later and provide an alternative conceptual framework for analyzing the urban ecology of modern cities. They also provide a statistically rigorous way to examine differentiation across neighborhoods, particularly residential differentiation, within a city.[8] This method results in a

6　Ibid., 55.
7　Examples include Homer Hoyt, *The Structure and Growth of Residential Neighborhoods in American Cities* (Washington, DC: Federal Housing Administration, 1939); Chauncy D. Harris and Edward L. Ullman, "The Nature of Cities," *Annals of the American Academy of Political and Social Science* 242, no. 1 (1945): 7–17.
8　Eshref Shevky and Wendell Bell, *Social Area Analysis: Theory, Illustrative Application, and Computational Procedures* (Stanford, CA: Stanford University Press, 1955); Duncan W. G. Timms, *The Urban Mosaic: Towards a Theory of Residential Differentiation* (Cambridge, UK: Cambridge University Press, 1971).

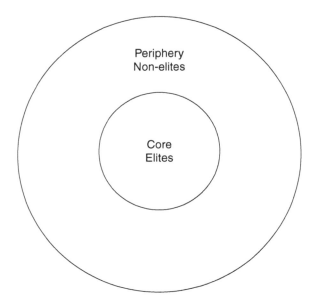

Figure 4.2 Sjoberg theory of urban ecology
Source: Based on description in Gideon Sjoberg, *The Preindustrial City: Past and Present* (New York: Free Press, 1960), 98–99.

sophisticated description rather than a deep theory. The Los Angeles School of urban sociology has recently risen to challenge the Chicago School. Its key point is the lack of any clear pattern in the layout in the emerging twenty-first-century city.[9]

In contrast to the Chicago School approach, which is meant to apply to all cities, Gideon Sjoberg's model is designed only for the preindustrial city. However, even within this narrow focus, his model has a wide range. It is intended to apply equally well to ancient and medieval cities along with cities in developing countries.[10] Sjoberg's model is less elaborate than Ernest Burgess's Chicago School model. Sjoberg's preindustrial city is segregated by class and occupation. He argues that the city was divided (see Fig. 4.2) into "well-defined neighborhoods with relatively homogeneous populations," that the homogeneity of these neighborhoods dominated all other land-use patterns and that there was little mixing. He adds that there were "certain finer spatial differences according to ethnic, occupational and family ties" and a "low incidence of functional differences in other land use patterns."[11] Further, the core predominated over the periphery, and the elite settled in the central area of the preindustrial city while the non-elite settled separately in the periphery. Sjoberg notes that this was specifically true in medieval urban neighborhoods.[12]

---

9 Michael J. Dear, ed., *From Chicago to L.A.: Making Sense of Urban Theory* (Thousand Oaks, CA: Sage, 2002).
10 Gideon Sjoberg, *The Preindustrial City: Past and Present* (New York: Free Press, 1960).
11 Ibid., 95–96 and 100.
12 Ibid., 97–102.

He provides several possible reasons why these patterns developed. First, the segregation could stem from the interaction between the limited preindustrial technology and the social classes.[13] It was simply more difficult to move around in a preindustrial city than in a modern, industrial one. Urban amenities were located in the core, and the core was religiously, socially, and, in many ways, economically, the most important part of the city. The most valuable land, therefore, was near the core. Sjoberg quotes urban sociologists who generally support this point.[14]

Second, the elite's desire to distance themselves from the non-elite was a factor in where they settled. Sjoberg argues that in order to keep their social prerogatives, the elite "must isolate themselves from the non-elite"; therefore, the elite take the better residences (which reinforces their social position), and the nonelite are restricted to the outskirts in "conformance with the rigid class structure." There were some exceptions, such as servants, but Sjoberg argues that this separation of the classes is an important characteristic of the preindustrial urban ecology.[15]

Third, urban planning restricted the work with the highest negative externalities to the outskirts. This is not strictly planning in the modern sense but is more a system of geographically organizing the city. Sjoberg argues that "low-status groups," including "workers in malodorous occupations," were "relegated to the city's outskirts."[16] His model offers little guidance about the evolution of this segregation, however. Like the Burgess model, it presents a largely static picture. Neighborhood segregation is seen as a long-term condition.

Sjoberg's theory is part of a larger debate on urban ecology. He disagrees with the Chicago School's most fundamental premise: the existence of a central business district in all cities. He maintains that these did not exist in preindustrial cities, because the central area's economic function was a secondary phenomenon.[17] Paul Wheatley, Michael Conzen and James Vance provide important criticisms of Sjoberg's theory. Wheatley considers Sjoberg a reductionist and guilty of a long series of factual and interpretive errors. Although he finds fewer problems with Sjoberg's conclusions for Europe and the Islamic world, he concludes that the theory is not useful for East, South and Southeast Asia, his areas of expertise. Wheatley strongly criticizes Sjoberg's theory for both a lack of sensitivity to historical sources and a lack of historiographical sense.[18] Conzen also argues that little supporting evidence has been found for Sjoberg's theory and adds that in fact it has proved problematic, because it has distracted research from more profitable pursuits.[19]

---

13 Ibid., 97 and 99.
14 Ibid., 98–99.
15 Ibid., 99 and 101–102. Sjoberg groups merchants as a second social group that might live alongside elites. However, this point is irrelevant in the Florentine case, since the elites themselves were merchants.
16 Ibid., 99.
17 Ibid., 97.
18 Paul Wheatley, "What the Greatness of a City Is Said to Be: Reflections on Sjoberg's 'Preindustrial City'," *Pacific Viewpoint* 4 (1963):163–88.
19 Michael P. Conzen, "Historical Geography: Changing Spatial Structure and Social Patterns of Western Cities," *Progress in Human Geography* 7 (1983): 88–107.

James Vance disagrees with Sjoberg's basic theory and adds an important refinement. He maintains that preindustrial urban ecology was dominated by "occupational districts."[20] His thesis would imply neighborhoods that are narrowly determined by occupation, not solely by class, and therefore even more homogeneous than what Sjoberg envisions. Such a strong theoretical implication is directly supportable or refutable by data on Florentine neighborhoods. There are other differences between Sjoberg's and Vance's theories as well. Sjoberg's preindustrial city was organized by the limits of technology, whereas Vance's was organized by the method of production.[21] In the Florentine case this is not a significant difference, as both imply segregation by social status. Also, Sjoberg's approach is strongly sociological, while Vance's is more geographical, although both rely substantially on historical material to support their arguments.

Vance's theory is open to criticism. For example, if transportation was costly, then one would expect basic service occupations to be located in every neighborhood of a city and relatively little organization by method of production. Sjoberg's technological emphasis more appropriately accounts for this observation. Vance also theorizes that land rent played a much less important role in the preindustrial city than in the modern city.[22] This aspect parallels Sjoberg's idea that social, rather than economic, conditions dominated the urban ecology. However, this idea directly contradicts predictions from urban economic theory. There is no obvious reason why land rents should be irrelevant, as an active rental market indeed existed in Florence (discussed more in Chapter 5).

The Burgess, Sjoberg and Vance theories have been tested across a wide set of preindustrial urban settings, and an interesting pattern emerges. Late medieval and early modern neighborhoods tend to be integrated, while nineteenth-century neighborhoods and those in developing countries tend to be segregated. Western European medieval cities and towns generally started from Roman origins.[23] After the fall of Rome, however, they needed to develop a new role.[24] Medieval cities and towns developed in a different way from their Roman predecessors.[25] Their political order was separate from the feudal system.[26] Italian cities organized economic production to a greater extent than did northern European cities.[27]

Neighborhoods in late medieval and early modern European cities appear to have been integrated. Regarding medieval Italy, Benjamin Kedar, who studies 1380s Genoese

---

20 James E. Vance, "Land Assignment in the Precapitalist, Capitalist, and Postcapitalist City," *Economic Geography* 47, no. 2 (1971): 103.

21 John Langton, "Residential Patterns in Pre-Industrial Cities: Some Case Studies from Seventeenth-Century Britain," *Transactions of the Institute of British Geographers* 65 (1975): 1–27.

22 Vance, "Land Assignment," 102.

23 Edith Ennen, *The Medieval Town* (New York: North-Holland, 1979), 17–35; Edith Ennen, *Die europäische Stadt des Mittelalters* (Göttingen: Vandenhoeck and Ruprecht, 1979), 29–48.

24 Ennen, *Medieval Town*, 37–62; Ennen, *Stadt des Mittelalters*, 49–76.

25 Ennen, *Medieval Town*, 63–93; Ennen, *Stadt des Mittelalters*, 77–109.

26 Ennen, *Medieval Town*, 95–126; Ennen, *Stadt des Mittelalters*, 110–44.

27 Ennen, *Medieval Town*, 127–36; Ennen, *Stadt des Mittelalters*, 145–54.

urban ecology, sheds light on one of Sjoberg's and Vance's conclusions: the level of occupational segregation.[28] Although Kedar does not explicitly address Sjoberg or Vance, he does address the occupational homogeneity of Genoese neighborhoods by examining the residential locations of those who were on the Council of Notaries. Kedar concludes that Genoese neighborhoods were heterogeneous in both 1380 and 1382. Notaries resided in all eight of that city's neighborhoods. In addition, he finds that important notaries were relatively evenly spread throughout the city; no neighborhood had either a preponderance of notaries or was without any whatsoever.[29] Kedar's finding contradicts both Sjoberg's and Vance's theses but is limited in its scope. One would need to know whether the upper-class notaries were accurate indicators of Genoese neighborhood heterogeneity or whether they were unique and uncorrelated with some larger Genoese occupational clustering. In addition, Paolo Montanari's study of 1395 Bolognese urban ecology finds a broad representation of occupations in both the core and the periphery of the city; most major occupations were distributed throughout the city. In addition, migrants, who were generally of lower social status, were not sorted into the periphery of the city.[30] The lack of a core-versus-periphery division among occupations and hence among social levels, the lack of occupational clustering across city neighborhoods and the lack of migrants clustering in the city's periphery all contradict Sjoberg's theory.

Regarding early modern Europe, John Langton applies Sjoberg's and Vance's models to the early modern British cities of Dublin, Exeter, Gloucester and Newcastle and finds no visible social-level zoning, either by technology or employment.[31] Spence's cartographic analysis of 1690s London reveals no clear neighborhood segregation.[32] Ackerman and Rosenfield find that early modern Paris and Rome were integrated.[33]

Nan Rothschild, in an extensive literature review, concludes that, in general, neighborhoods were integrated up to the eighteenth century and segregated after that.[34] Urban planning appears to have driven some of these changes. Riita Laitinen and Dag Lindström find that minor Swedish cities during the seventeenth century were unplanned. The planning in the capital Stockholm was evidently due to the monarchic

---

28 Benjamin Z. Kedar, "The Genoese Notaries of 1382: The Anatomy of an Urban Occupational Group," in *The Medieval City*, ed. Harry D. Miskimin, David Herlihy and A. L. Udovitch (New Haven, CT: Yale University Press, 1977), 73–94.

29 Ibid., 89–90.

30 Paolo Montanari, *Documenti su la popolazione di Bologna alla fine del Trecento* (Bologna: Istituto per la Storia di Bologna, 1966), 17, 20–22 and 30–35.

31 Langton, "Residential Patterns"; John Langton, "Late Medieval Gloucester: Some Data from a Rental of 1455," *Transactions of the Institute of British Geographers*, new ser. 2 (1977): 259–77.

32 Craig Spence, *London in the 1690s: A Social Atlas* (London: University of London, 2000), 50, 59, 82, 84 and 91.

33 James S. Ackerman and Myra Nan Rosenfield, "Social Stratification in Renaissance Urban Planning," in *Urban Life in the Renaissance*, ed. Susan Zimmerman and Ronald F. E. Weissman (Cranbury Park, NJ: Associated University Presses), 36–46.

34 Nan A. Rothschild, *New York City Neighborhoods: The 18th Century* (San Diego: Academic Press, 1990), 20.

need for and ability to impose greater control.[35] Maria Helena Barreiros finds that the 1755 Lisbon earthquake and tsunami was a catalyst that permitted transforming the city from cluttered to regulated.[36] Albane Cogné finds 1758 Milan's central area was clearly wealthier than its outskirts.[37] Walter Abbott tests the Burgess model on prerevolutionary (1897) Moscow, an example of a preindustrial city at the virtual end of Romanov rule and a feudal system of social stratification.[38] He applies a method somewhat similar to factor ecology, dividing the city into 18 sections.[39] The city clearly fits the Sjoberg model and was the inverse of the Burgess model.[40] The increased segregation is also noticeable in North American cities. Rothschild finds that the occupational concentration by street in New York City grew during the eighteenth century,[41] while Robert Lewis finds strongly segregated neighborhoods in late nineteenth-century Montreal.[42] These results also confirm the Sjoberg model.

Cities in developing countries, like other nineteenth-century and later cities, generally have homogeneous and segregated neighborhoods. T. G. McGee combines sociological and anthropological approaches to analyze contemporary developing countries. He adopts Clifford Geertz's definitions of bazaar-type and firm-type economies. A bazaar-type economy is one where the organization of the transactions is strongly decentralized. A firm-type economy is one where a variety of specialized occupations are organized toward a single productive end, as in a more developed economy or the Florentine woolen industry. Using this approach, McGee asserts that a *"bazaar-type* economy coexists with a *firm-type* economy, [which] prevents all but a few zones of homogeneous economic usage emerging."[43]

McGee's analysis concludes that the typical Southeast Asian city is composed of homogeneous neighborhoods in two distinct stages of development: the neighborhoods of the elite and those of the nonelite. Adding more support for Sjoberg's theory, he notes that "the slow development of transportation [has, among other things,] hindered the

---

35 Riita Laitinen and Dag Lindström, "Urban Order and Street Regulation in Seventeenth-Century Sweden," *Journal of Early Modern History* 12, no. 3 (2008): 257–87.

36 Maria Helena Barreiros," Urban Landscapes: Houses, Streets and Squares of 18th-Century Lisbon," *Journal of Early Modern History* 12, no. 3 (2008): 257–87.

37 Albane Cogné, "Distribuzione della proprietà a Milano a metà Settecento: La realizzazione di un GIS a partire dal catasto teresiano (1758)," in *Ricchezza, valore, proprietà in età preindustriale 1400–1850*, ed. Guido Alfani and Michela Barbot (Venice: Marsilio, 2009), 109.

38 Walter F. Abbott, "Moscow in 1897 as a Preindustrial City: A Test of the Inverse Burgess Zonal Hypothesis," in *Urban Patterns: Studies in Human Ecology*, rev. ed., ed. George A. Theodorson (University Park: Pennsylvania State University Press, 1982), 404.

39 Ibid., 400.

40 Ibid., 404 and 405.

41 Rothschild, *New York City*, 128.

42 Robert Lewis, "The Segregated City: Class Residential Patterns and the Development of Industrial Districts in Montreal, 1861 and 1901," *Journal of Urban History* 17, no. 2 (1991): 123–52.

43 T. G. McGee, *The Southeast Asian City* (New York: Praeger, 1967), 126–27 and 138; emphasis in original.

concentration of economic activity."[44] However, these cities have formed no core. McGee further notes that the colonial era and rapid post–World War II growth "has imposed certain common patterns of residence in virtually all the larger cities [of Southeast Asia]."[45]

Stella Lowder summarizes recent geographic work on developing cities. First, she distinguishes between "descriptive" and "dynamic" urban-ecology models. Descriptive models, like those of Sjoberg, Vance and McGee, simply present the actual urban morphological arrangements. Dynamic models, in contrast, make predictions about the likely direction of the evolution of the urban ecology.[46] Lowder also reviews empirical evidence on modern cities and agrees with Sjoberg's thesis that primitive transportation systems are correlated with elites living nearer the core of the city.[47]

This literature review presents a clear pattern. Late medieval and early modern cities tend to have integrated neighborhoods, while cities of the nineteenth century and developing countries tend to have segregated neighborhoods. The Chicago School model appears to fit better for more modern cities, where the costs of transportation are much less.

Theories of Renaissance Florentine Urban Ecology

This section reviews the debate over whether Florentine neighborhoods were homogeneous and segregated or heterogeneous and integrated during the Quattrocento. As noted above, the result of this debate has important implications for how one views much of the physical culture of Renaissance Florence. Each side has its proponents. Samuel Cohn, Ronald Weissman and Alessandro Stella use primarily social scientific methods and find homogeneous and segregated neighborhoods.[48] Gene Brucker and Dale and Francis Kent, in contrast, use more historical methods and find heterogeneous and integrated neighborhoods.[49]

There is a broad consensus that Trecento neighborhoods were heterogeneous, that neighborhood ties grew in importance from the post-Ciompi period onward and that the sense of neighborhood ties varied depending on a person's social standing.[50] Superficial observations are not sufficient evidence to argue one position or the other. For example,

---

44 Ibid., 138.

45 Ibid., 139.

46 Stella Lowder, *The Geography of Third World Cities* (Totowa, NJ: Barnes and Noble, 1986), 206–7.

47 Ibid., 207.

48 Cohn, *Laboring Classes*, 30, 43–63, 119–21, 124 and 127; Weissman, *Ritual Brotherhood*, 8–17, 19 and 118; Alessandro Stella, *La Révolte des Ciompi: Les hommes, les lieux, le travail* (Paris: Editions de l'Ecole des Hautes Etudes en Sciences Sociales, 1993), 263–67.

49 Brucker, *Renaissance Florence*, 23–25, 27 and 29; Brucker, *Civic World*, 21–30; Kent and Kent, *Neighbours and Neighbourhood*, 5, 13–19 and 128–36.

50 Brucker, *Renaissance Florence*, 23–25, 27 and 29; Brucker, *Civic World*, 21–30; Cohn, *Laboring Classes*, 30, 43–63, 119–21, 124 and 127; Kent and Kent, *Neighbours and Neighbourhood*, 5, 13–19 and 128–36; Weissman, *Ritual Brotherhood*, 8–17, 19 and 118; Stella, *Révolte des Ciompi*, 263–66.

the fact that Florence had the basic elements of a central business district[51] and that most Quattrocento Florentine construction projects and important institutions remained there implies neither that Florentine neighborhoods were homogeneous nor that the people living in the core were of higher status than those living on the periphery.[52] The real issue is the distribution of the overall Florentine population.

Cohn's analysis leads him to equate Florentine classes with neighborhoods.[53] He proposes that growing neighborhood homogeneity between the Trecento and the Quattrocento paralleled the growing neighborhood identity. This adds a dynamic element to a theory based on Sjoberg's work.[54] Cohn explicitly attacks the "Burckhardtian" vision of Renaissance Florence.[55] He argues that Florentine urban planning worked against ideal, integrated neighborhoods and that Florentine neighborhoods became more homogeneous and segregated over time.[56] He also argues that the large artistic building projects in central Florence replaced other, older buildings and dislocated the nonelite and poor into the city's outskirts. This led to the creation of Florentine ghettos between the period of the late Trecento Ciompi revolt and the mid-Quattrocento time of Lorenzo the Magnificent.[57] Urban planning increased social separation by literally increasing the physical separation between the classes and between rich and poor within the Florentine community.[58]

Cohn defines the central city of Florence as the area within the old Roman wall, and the inner ring and the periphery according to set distances radially outward from the Roman wall. These boundaries are arranged to follow his reconstructed parish boundaries. His functional definition is more elaborate than Sjoberg's, defining three rather than two urban regions, but the basic form remains.

Table 4.1 presents a reanalysis of Cohn's key evidence.[59] The raw percentages in his original analysis are presented in their original form and are converted into indices that show the relative share of *popolo minuto* by location. This reanalysis contradicts Cohn's basic point. There was no clear movement of popolo minuto toward the periphery. Their share decreased in the inner ring and increased in the central city and periphery. The movement Cohn observes was simply part of a general population movement toward the periphery of the city.

---

51 Guido Carocci, "Il Centro di Firenze nel 1427," in *Studi Storici sul Centro di Firenze Pubblicati di Occasione del IV Congresso Storico Italiano* (Florence: Arnaldo Forni, 1889), 17–75; Guido Carocci, "Il Centro di Firenze (Mercato Vecchio) nel 1427, Studio di Guido Carocci, Ispettore degli Scavi e dei Monumeni," in *Studi Storici sul Centro di Firenze Pubblicati di Occasione del IV Congresso Storico Italiano* (Florence: Arnaldo Forni, 1889), after 15.

52 Giovanni Fanelli, *Le città nella storia d'Italia: Firenze* (Rome: Laterza, 1981), 89–90.

53 Cohn, *Laboring Classes*; Cohn, "Corrispondenza," *Rivista storica Italiana* 98, no. 3 (1986): 919.

54 Cohn, *Laboring Classes*, 124 and 127.

55 Cohn, "Corrispondenza," 919. Cf. Samuel K. Cohn Jr., "Burckhardt Revisited from Social History," in *Language and Images of Renaissance Italy*, ed. Alison Brown (Oxford: Clarendon Press, 1995), 217–34.

56 Cohn, *Laboring Classes*, 121 and 127.

57 Ibid., 127.

58 Ibid., 124.

59 Ibid., 115–28.

Table 4.1 Percentage distribution of households by class and century, based on Cohn

	Location	Trecento	Quattrocento
Share of Population	Central City	24%	11%
	Inner Ring	33%	17%
	Periphery	43%	72%
Share of Popolo Minuto	Central City	16%	8%
	Inner Ring	39%	12%
	Periphery	44%	80%
Index	Central City	67	73
	Inner Ring	118	71
	Periphery	102	111

Source: Cohn, *Laboring Classes*, 119–21. Calculation by author.
Index statistics: The calculations are based on the city and popolo minuto data. The index equals the percentage of popolo minuto households divided by the percentage of all households by each portion of the city, multiplied by 100.

Cohn's work has a number of additional limitations. To begin with, he gathers his wealth data from two sources with very different sets of biases. The Trecento data come from the Sega of 1352, a wealth census.[60] As noted in Chapter 3, there is a likely endpoint problem using the 1352 data as a baseline to measure increasing inequality. Consequently, these data are likely to bias measures of inequality downward. The Quattrocento data are derived from marriage statistics.[61] Dowries, however, should be wealth elastic (see Appendix 3C for more discussion of this topic). This wealth elasticity should lead to a greater inequality among dowries than among wealth. These differences between the 1352 tax data and the Quattrocento dowry data should bias the change in inequality upward.

Next, Cohn uses neighborhood marriage endogamies to demonstrate class segregation, and surnames and toponymics to identify residential location. However, although an overwhelming number of Florentine families clustered in particular *gonfaloni*,[62] there was only a tenuous link between surnames and toponymics and residential location.[63] This method implicitly assumes that neighborhoods were homogeneous, which is what Cohn sets out to prove. Najemy points out that Cohn's assignment system is problematic, that his sample is skewed and that the results are not

---

60 Ibid., 119–21.
61 Ibid.
62 Kent and Kent, *Neighbours and Neighbourhood*, 18; Weissman, *Ritual Brotherhood*, 8.
63 Cohn, *Laboring Classes*, 43–63 and 121; Robert S. Lopez, "Concerning Surnames and Places of Origin," *Medievalia et Humanistica* 8 (1954): 6–16.

significant.[64] Cohn replies that his findings are statistically significant but does not directly address the broader issues that Najemy raises.[65]

Fourth, Cohn does not account for the possible effects of an increasing overall Florentine population on his estimates. He compares the Florentine population four years after the Black Death with the population three-quarters of a century later. There was substantial immigration into the city during this time, and residents were relatively free to move from one neighborhood to another.[66] All the movement among neighborhoods could be accounted for by an overall increase in population, which would have forced new families to move into the city's periphery.

Finally, Cohn applies excessive modernism to aspects of Florentine society. Florentine urban planning did not have the same comprehensive impact as modern urban planning does. Most large Florentine building projects were privately financed (see Chapter 5 for more discussion on this topic).[67] Although projects were concentrated in the core of the city, they were built throughout the city, as Bruni pointed out and as most modern travelers can clearly recognize.[68]

A number of other historians arrive at similar conclusions as Cohn. Stella finds a differentiation between the core and the periphery, based on changes in Florence between 1352 and 1404.[69] Richard Trexler generally finds that Renaissance urban planning segregated the population. His work is explicitly social scientific with his application of social action theory.[70] He argues that public life was essential to urban identity and discards the notion of Renaissance individualism. The increasing impact of planning was an important part of this process. Trexler argues that people walking around Florence saw what the city's planners wanted people to see.[71]

Weissman generally supports the homogeneous neighborhoods hypothesis.[72] Though he finds no direct evidence, he believes that the data may hide an increasing social segregation between the core and the periphery.[73] He argues that Florentine residential patterns duplicated *contado* patterns and that Florence was a fragmented city, where families continued to live in the same places, preserving preexisting friendship- or kinship-determined residences.

---

64 John M. Najemy, "Linguaggi storiografici sulla Firenze rinascimentale," *Rivista storica Italiana* 97, no. 1 (1985): 102–59; Cohn, "Corrispondenza"; Najemy, "Replica," *Rivista storica Italiana* 98, no. 3 (1986): 922–25.

65 Najemy, "Linguaggi," 127–30; Cohn, "Corrispondenza," 920.

66 Kent and Kent, *Neighbours and Neighbourhood*, 54 and 86.

67 Isabelle Hyman, *Fifteenth-Century Florentine Studies: The Palazzo Medici and a Ledger for the Church of San Lorenzo* (New York: Garland, 1977).

68 Fanelli, *Firenze*, 89–90.

69 Stella, *La Révolte des Ciompi*, 263–67.

70 Trexler, *Public Life*; Talcott Parsons, *The Structure of Social Action: A Study in Social Theory with Special Reference to a Group of Recent European Writers*, vol. 1 (1937; New York: Free Press, 1968). See also James S. Coleman, *Foundations of Social Theory* (Cambridge, MA: Harvard University Press, 1990).

71 Trexler, *Public Life*, 10.

72 Weissman, *Ritual Brotherhood*, 10 and 12.

73 Ibid., 10.

He also finds a strong tendency for surnames to cluster in 1480 Florence. Weissman reports that commercial and residential land uses were mixed. He notes that a businessman would buy all of his business properties within the same general area. Finally, he notes that a Florentine's sense of neighborhood varied by class and by social status, and by the value of using the connection of the neighborhood for personal and familial advancement.[74]

Weissman also provides evidence that contradicts the homogeneous neighborhoods hypothesis. He reports integrated neighborhoods in his analysis of the 1480 Decima Scalata and finds broad empirical evidence of interaction among different levels of Florentine society. Residents were relatively free to move about, and many families had members living throughout the city. Poorer households in 1480 did not tend to cluster any more than wealthier ones. Overall, Weissman finds a lack of economic specialization by quarter and asserts that residents were well integrated and self-sufficient.[75]

Brucker portrays Florence as a broadly mixed society with heterogeneous neighborhoods. He argues that Florence had a flexible social structure.[76] The Florentine guild system neither demarcated nor segregated classes among neighborhoods. A wide range of classes and occupations lived in all neighborhoods.[77] Commercial and residential land uses were mixed. Brucker concedes some variance among neighborhoods and some restriction of undesirable businesses.[78] It is interesting that both Brucker and Sjoberg mention laws relegating slaughterhouses and tanning establishments to the urban periphery. The similarity is especially interesting because Brucker's study was written first. However, Brucker disputes the idea that urban planning had any effect on Florentine neighborhood composition, and he clearly sees no difference between core and periphery.[79] He also does not find evidence of increasing segregation over time and makes no general distinction between Trecento and Quattrocento Florentine neighborhoods.

Whereas the above work examines the city's urban ecology from the top-down citywide perspective, it is also possible to look at the city from bottom-up individual neighborhood perspective. Although the results from citywide studies to date are mixed, the results of studies of individual neighborhood clearly suggest that Florence had integrated neighborhoods. Intensive research has been conducted on individual gonfaloni, and it emphasizes their heterogeneity. Two contrasting gonfaloni, the rich Leon Rosso and the poor Drago Verde, have received intense scrutiny from historians and provide excellent case studies to examine neighborhood integration.[80] The Florentine city center was mostly in Leon Rosso.[81] Drago Verde was on the other side of the river from the city center in the area

74 Ibid., 8, 10–11, 13–16 and 19.
75 Ibid., 9–11, 16–17 and 118.
76 Gene Brucker, *Florentine Politics and Society, 1343–1378* (Princeton, NJ: Princeton University Press, 1962), 27.
77 Brucker, *Renaissance Florence*, 23–25 and 59.
78 Ibid., 23–25, 27 and 59.
79 Ibid., 27.
80 Christopher F. Black, *Early Modern Italy: A Social History* (London: Routledge, 2001), 152.
81 Carocci, "Il Centro di Firenze nel 1427"; Carocci, "Il Centro di Firenze (Mercato Vecchio) nel 1427."

called the O ltrarno. If both of these neighborhoods were integrated, it would imply that a wide variety of Florentine neighborhoods were relatively integrated and not segregated.

Leon Rosso, in the quarter of Santa Maria Novella, is considered a core *gonfalone*. Kent and Kent note that Leon Rosso's 1427 demographics match the typical Florentine gonfalone in terms of age, distribution of wealth and occupations and household shape and structure.[82] The neighborhood was also integrated. Hundreds of Florentines, both rich and poor, were involved in the business of each gonfalone.[83] Leon Rosso meetings were no different and involved people from a wide range of occupations, with a variety of levels of wealth, power and position. For example, the *purgatori*, wool scourers, of the Brugiotti family, who engaged in an occupation supposedly segregated to the outskirts of the city, were involved in gonfalone government.[84] This could have been a result of each family's long-term connection with a particular neighborhood. Florentine families tended to cluster in one or another neighborhood.[85] According to Kent and Kent, "A man's most natural and intimate associates were 'kinsmen, neighbors, and friends [*parenti, vicini, e amici*].'"[86]

Drago Verde, in the quarter of Santo Spirito, is considered a peripheral gonfalone and among the poorest in Florence. Brucker notes that the San Frediano Parish in Drago Verde was a slum.[87] There is a belief among some historians supporting the segregated neighborhoods thesis that Santo Spirito in general was the poorest quarter. Weissman argues this,[88] as does Carmichael, who further argues that this poverty made the quarter more vulnerable to the plague.[89] However, an analysis of the catasto data prepared by Herlihy and Klapisch-Zuber shows that Santo Spirito was not poorer than other quarters.[90]

Nicholas Eckstein shows that a Florentine's neighborhood identity was very important.[91] He finds a clear neighborhood esprit de corps, where "Drago's people had a particularly powerful sense of themselves."[92] Despite the city's perceived poverty, he finds it was highly complex and diverse in 1427.[93] As in the case of Leon Rosso, Eckstein's detailed neighborhood study supports the heterogeneous and integrated neighborhoods hypothesis.

---

82 Kent and Kent, *Neighbours and Neighbourhood*, 8.

83 Ibid., 6, 8, 77 and 111–21.

84 Ibid.

85 Ibid., 18, 54 and 86; Weissman, *Ritual Brotherhood*, 8.

86 Kent and Kent, *Neighbours and Neighbourhood*, 1.

87 Brucker, *Renaissance Florence*, 24–25.

88 Weissman, *Ritual Brotherhood*, 9.

89 Ann G. Carmichael, *Plague and the Poor in Renaissance Florence* (Cambridge: Cambridge University Press, 1986), 71–87.

90 David Herlihy and Christiane Klapisch-Zuber, *Census and Property Survey of Florentine Domains and the City of Verona in Fifteenth-Century Italy* [machine-readable data file]. Cambridge, MA: David Herlihy, Harvard University, Department of History and Paris, France: Christiane Klapisch-Zuber, Ecole Pratique des Hautes Etudes [producers], 1977. Madison: University of Wisconsin, Data and Program Library Service [distributor], 1981.

91 Eckstein, "Neighborhood as Microcosm."

92 Eckstein, *District of the Green Dragon*, 226, xi.

93 Nicholas A. Eckstein, "Addressing Wealth in Renaissance Florence: Some New Soundings from the Catasto of 1427," *Journal of Urban History* 32, no. 5 (2006): 711–28.

From Trecento to Early Quattrocento Florentine Neighborhoods

The discussion in the previous section implies that the three aspects of the neighborhood segregation theory can be divided into more detailed studies of two periods. The first period is the transition from the Trecento to the early Quattrocento. This was a period of social changes, including decreasing real wages. The second period is the transition from the early to the late Quattrocento. This was the period of palace construction and would have experienced the greatest urban renewal. Finally, these two analyses are tied together, because any truly fundamental drive toward segregation during the first period would have continued into the second.

This section covers the Trecento and early Quattrocento. All three hypotheses—the segregated neighborhoods, the elite core, and the increasing segregation hypotheses—are tested using both cartographical and quantitative approaches that are consistent with similar research in urban ecology.[94] Defining the appropriate unit of analysis, the Florentine neighborhood, is the crucial first step. There are essentially three options available to the researcher: (1) to use sets of particular streets, (2) to use the parish (the smallest religious division), or (3) to use the gonfalone (the smallest Florentine civil division). This study uses the gonfalone as a household's neighborhood.[95] Figure 4.3 shows the locations of the Florentine civil divisions, the gonfaloni.[96]

Some researchers have chosen sets of streets to identify particular neighborhoods. This was one way that the Florentines themselves identified neighborhoods, and it is the method is used by R. Burr Litchfield in his study.[97] However, using sets of streets would be too subjective in a citywide project until much more research on the details of Trecento and Quattrocento Florentine neighborhoods is found and published. Litchfield looks at spatial relationships as opposed to community relationships.

---

94 E.g., Hoyt, *Structure and Growth of Residential Neighborhoods*; Shevky and Bell, *Social Area Analysis*; Timms, *Urban Mosaic*; Abbott, "Moscow in 1897."

95 Ciabani provides a pleasant historical tour through Florence's old gonfaloni. Roberto Ciabani, *Firenze di gonfalone in gonfalone* (Florence: Meridiana, 1998).

96 Guido Carocci, ed., *L'illustratore fiorentino: Calendario storico per l'anno 1909* (Florence: Tipografica Pozienicana, 1908), 81–89. Eckstein notes an error in Carocci's work that concerns Drago Verde gonfalone boundaries; however, this error is relatively minor in a citywide study. Nicholas A. Eckstein, *The District of the Green Dragon: Neighbourhood Life and Social Change in Renaissance Florence* (Florence: Olschki, 1995), xi. Maps based on Carocci can differ significantly. For example, compare Litchfield's (R. Burr Litchfield, *Florence Ducal Capital, 1530–1630* (New York: ACLS Humanities E-Book, 2008), map 1.02b, para. 162 (Permanent Link: http://quod.lib.umich.edu/cgi/t/text/text-idx?c=acls;idno=heb90034) and Weissman's (Weissman, *Ritual Brotherhood*, 8) maps. Both of these were used to construct the base map used in this chapter. Other studies used to construct the base map are Attilio Mori and Giuseppe Boffito, *Firenze nelle vedute e piante: Studio storico topografico cartografico* (Rome: Bonsignori, 1926); Consiglio comunale di Firenze, *Stradario storico e amministrativo della città e del commune di Firenze*, 2nd ed. (Florence: Enrico Ariani, 1929).

97 Litchfield, *Florence Ducal Capital*. Litchfield gets around this problem by creating a sophisticated grid system. This method would be applicable to Trecento and Quattrocento Florence if it could be implemented. Such an implementation is beyond the scope of this study.

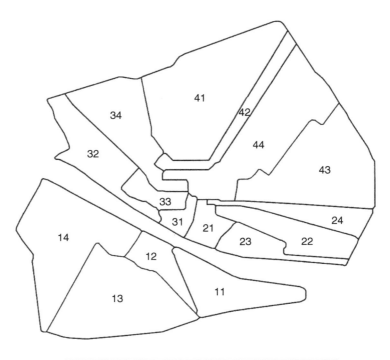

Number	Quarter	Gonfalone
11	Santo Spirito	Scala
12	Santo Spirito	Nicchio
13	Santo Spirito	Ferza
14	Santo Spirito	Drago Verde
21	Santa Croce	Carro
22	Santa Croce	Bue Nero
23	Santa Croce	Leon Nero
24	Santa Croce	Ruote
31	S. Maria Novella	Vipera
32	S. Maria Novella	Unicorno
33	S. Maria Novella	Leon Rosso
34	S. Maria Novella	Leon Bianco
41	San Giovanni	Leon d'Oro
42	San Giovanni	Drago
43	San Giovanni	Chiavi
44	San Giovanni	Vaio

Figure 4.3 Map of locations of Florentine gonfalone

Sources: Guido Carocci, ed., *L'Illustratore Fiorentino. Calendario Storico per L'Anno 1909* (Florence: Tipografica Pozienicana, 1908), 81–89; R. Burr Litchfield, *Florence Ducal Capital, 1530–1630* (New York: ACLS Humanities E-Book, 2008), map 1.02b, para. 162. Permanent Link: http://quod.lib.umich.edu/cgi/t/text/text-idx?c=acls;idno=heb90034; Ronald F. E. Weissman, *Ritual Brotherhood in Renaissance Florence* (New York: Academic Press, 1982), 8; Attilio Mori and Giuseppe Boffito, *Firenze nelle vedute e piante: Studio storico topografico cartografico* (Rome: Bonsignori, 1926); Consiglio comunale di Firenze, *Stradario storico e amministrativo della città e del commune di Firenze*, 2nd ed. (Florence: Enrico Ariani, 1929).

Other researchers are divided on whether the gonfalone or the parish is a better representative of Florentine neighborhoods. Kent and Kent, Trexler and Eckstein support gonfalone,[98] while Cohn and Sharon Strocchia support parishes.[99] Parishes were more numerous and generally smaller than gonfaloni: Florence was divided into 16 gonfaloni and between 57 and 62 parishes.[100] The typical gonfalone therefore contained several parishes or parts of parishes. This uncertainty regarding the identification of parishes is one reason discouraging their use. Nevertheless, the difference in size does offer two advantages for using the parish as the unit of analysis. First, the statistical results are presumably more reliable, because they arise from a larger sample size. Second, finer distinctions among Florentine neighborhoods would be visible, because the average unit size in the sample is smaller. Most gonfaloni extended from the center of the city to the periphery.[101] However, this difference would also cause a bias; the smaller the division, the more likely one is to find homogeneity and segregation, because there is less opportunity for variation. The key to choosing the correct unit of analysis, therefore, is to identify which definition of neighborhood better links location to community. There is some evidence that the gonfaloni and parishes were not so distinct in their community and governmental roles.[102]

There are three reasons to use gonfalone-level rather than parish-level data to analyze neighborhood composition. First, a person's gonfalone is a better indicator of his or her community membership. The gonfaloni were identifiable communities,[103] much more so than modern American census enumeration areas, which are often used to study neighborhood characteristics. For the purposes of taxation, households had to be physically resident in their gonfalone.[104] The studies of the Leon Rosso and Drago Verde neighborhoods described above reinforce the importance of the gonfalone in a Florentine's everyday life. In addition, Trexler is forceful on the relationship between gonfalone and community.[105] Second, parish membership only loosely indicates where householders actually lived. Members of a parish could, in theory, live anywhere within the city or even in outlying rural areas.[106] The parish organization itself could contribute to this bias by attracting parishioners from particular social groups. Using parish-level data could therefore highlight nonexistent social divisions in neighborhoods simply because particular

98 Kent and Kent, *Neighbours and Neighbourhood*, 13–19; Trexler, *Public Life*, 13; Nicholas A. Eckstein, "The Neighborhood as Microcosm of the Social Order," in *Renaissance Florence: A Social History*, ed. Roger J. Crum and John T. Paoletti (New York: Cambridge University Press, 2006), 219–39; Eckstein, *District of the Green Dragon*; Eckstein, "Addressing Wealth."

99 Cohn, *Laboring Classes*, 30; Strocchia, *Death and Ritual*, 88 and 92–94.

100 Carocci, *L'illustratore fiorentino*, 81–89; Firenze, *Stradario storico*, xxvi–vii. Cohn, *Laboring Classes*, 30–31. The assignments of parishes to gonfaloni also differs.

101 Litchfield, *Ducal Capital*, para. 28.

102 Kent and Kent, *Neighbours and Neighbourhood*, 128–36.

103 Kent and Kent, *Neighbours and Neighbourhood*; Eckstein, *District of the Green Dragon*; Eckstein, "Neighborhood as Microcosm."

104 Kent and Kent, *Neighbours and Neighbourhood*, 58 and 128–36.

105 Trexler, *Public Life*, 13.

106 Carmichael, *Plague and the Poor*, 70. Henderson reports the street-by-street boundaries of San Frediano. John Henderson, "The Parish and the Poor in Florence at the time of the Black Death: The Case of S. Frediano," *Continuity and Change* 3, no. 2 (1988): 250.

parishes at particular locations within the neighborhood may have catered to different social groups. This would therefore bias segregation and homogeneity upward. Third, the wide variation of parish sizes could cause problems of interpretation. The ratio of the sizes of the largest to the smallest was more than a dozen times greater among parishes than among gonfaloni.[107] Apparent differences could appear among parishes drawn from identical sets of parishioners simply because larger parishes would be more statistically representative samples of the city at large. This kind of bias is unlikely to occur with gonfaloni, which had less variation in size.[108]

The data come from two distinct types of sources. The 1352 and 1404 estimi data are from Stella.[109] Estimi were a direct tax assessed on fiscal households and were replaced by the catasto in 1427. The estimi data provide a count of households, some data about the household head and data about the tax burden. The 1427 catasto data come from the Herlihy and Klapisch-Zuber database.[110] The 1352 data's endpoint bias would tend to bias findings in favor of increasing inequality.

The primary indicator of a given neighborhood's standing is the relative number of *arte maggiore* members in that neighborhood. Arte maggiore members are clearly indicated in the estimi and catasti documents. The arte maggiore included the following: *Arte de Giudici e Notai* (Guild of Judges and Notaries), *Arte e Università de' Mercanti di Calimala* (Guild of Cloth Exporters), *Arte del Cambio* (Guild of Bankers and Money Changers), *Arte de Seta* or *Por Santa Maria* (Guild of Silk Merchants), *Arte e Università della Lana* (Guild of wool merchants), *Arte de' Medici e degli Speziali* (Guild of Doctors and Spice Merchants), and *Arte de' vaiai e pellicciai* (the guild of furriers and skinners).[111] The concentration indices measure the relative percentage of a group in a gonfalone compared to the overall citywide percentage.[112] A relative measure works well with historical data of this kind, as the counts might vary from year to year depending on the care of the authorities, but the variation should be consistent citywide. The arte maggiore do not precisely correspond to the wealthiest households. Among the top twenty wealthiest household heads in 1427, six were arte maggiore, thirteen had no occupation indicated and one, the richest, Palla di Nofri Strozzi, was a *messere* (knight).[113]

The fiscal household wealth data would not provide much insight to the questions in this chapter, because these data have little to say about whether or not there was greater

---

107 Cohn, *Laboring Classes*, 26; Strocchia, *Death and Ritual*, 88–89.

108 Heteroskedasticity is another potential statistical problem. It would be relevant for less robust statistical measures than those employed in this study.

109 Stella, *La Révolte des Ciompi*, 212.

110 Herlihy and Klapisch-Zuber, *Census and Property Survey*.

111 Edgcumbe Staley, *The Guilds of Florence: Illustrated after Miniatures in Illuminated Manuscripts and Florentine Woodcuts* (1906; New York: Benjamin Blom, 1967), 75, 105, 139, 170, 204, 236 and 274.

112 Concentration Index = $100 * \dfrac{\text{Percentage of all households in gonfalone}}{\text{Percentage of all households in citywide}}$.

113 Herlihy and Klapisch-Zuber, *Census and Property Survey*.

social separation in society. In addition, the limited data severely reduces its value as a trend. Only the 1427 tax returns could be considered complete. The earlier estimi returns were only estimates. The later catasti returns omit many assets (see Appendix 3A).

There are several potential sources of error in categorizing the households as arte maggiore. First, all occupational categories that were not explicitly arte maggiore, including missing observations, were included in the non–arte maggiore category. This should be a minor problem, because it is unlikely that arte maggiore membership would be systematically omitted. Second, the coding was lax with respect to notarial occupations.[114] This also should be a minor problem, because it is unlikely that many unidentified notaries were not also members of other arte maggiore. Finally, the relatively small number of arte maggiore might lead to problems of data sparseness. These guilds accounted for less than one-eighth of Florentine households. This also should be only a minor problem, because the sample sizes were still quite large.

Figures 4.4 and 4.5 map the relative concentration of arte maggiore at 1352 and 1404, respectively. There is no clear core and periphery distinction visible in 1352. The people living along the river to the north had the highest status, and those living in the western part of the city had the lowest status. Drago Verde and Leon Rosso were both among the lowest-status gonfaloni. However, a core and periphery distinction is visible in 1404. The area along the river to the north was still considered to have the highest status. Santo Spirito was generally lower status; Drago Verde was still among the lowest-status gonfaloni; and Leon Rosso had moved down to the middle half of gonfaloni.

Figures 4.6 through 4.8 map data based on a complete set of fiscal households for Florence from the 1427 catasto and, because of the greater amount of available data, provide a range of alternative representations of social standing. Figure 4.6 maps the relative concentration of arte maggiore in 1427 Florence and shows no clear distinction between core and periphery. By this time the outskirts were generally higher status. The area along the river near the center of the city was now lower status. Drago Verde was now among the highest-status gonfaloni in terms of its concentration of arte maggiori households. Leon Rosso was in the middle half of gonfaloni.

A comparison of figures 4.4 and 4.6 shows something interesting. The evolution of Florentine neighborhoods between 1352 and 1427 clearly contradicts what one would expect if there had been a continuous separation between the arte maggiore and the popolo minuto from the Trecento to the Quattrocento. It also suggests that the Ciompi revolt of 1378, where the popolo minuto rebelled against the arte maggiore, had little effect on the ecology of Florentine neighborhoods.

The 1427 neighborhood patterns can be analyzed in greater detail. Data on the relative numbers of migrants and *miserabili* (paupers) by neighborhood are available. The relative number of migrant households would be an indicator of low neighborhood social standing.[115] Cohn views immigration as another factor that helped form

---

114 Ibid.
115 Herlihy and Klapisch-Zuber, *Tuscans*, 113; Cohn, *Laboring Classes*, 91–113.

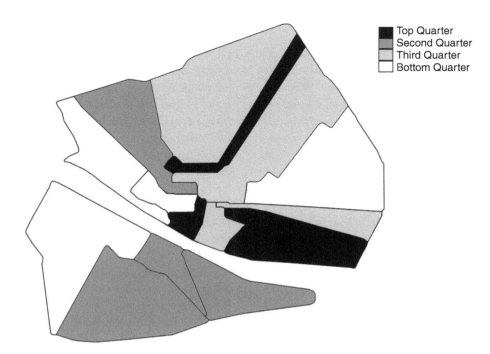

Figure 4.4 Map of index of arte maggiore to popolo minuto households by gonfalone, 1352
Source: Alessandro Stella, *La Révolte des Ciompi: Les hommes, les lieux, le travail* (Paris: Editions de l'Ecole des Hautes Etudes en Sciences Sociales, 1993), 212. See the text for the calculation of the concentration index.

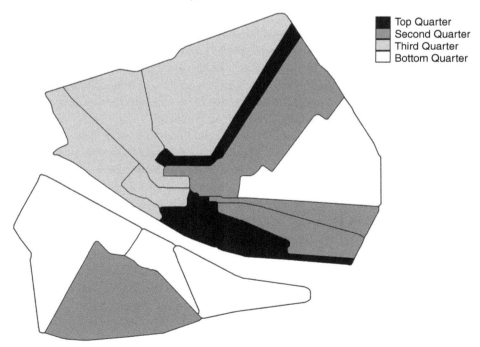

Figure 4.5 Map of index of arte maggiore to popolo minuto households by gonfalone, 1404
Source: Stella, *La Révolte des Ciompi*, 212. See the text for the calculation of the concentration index.

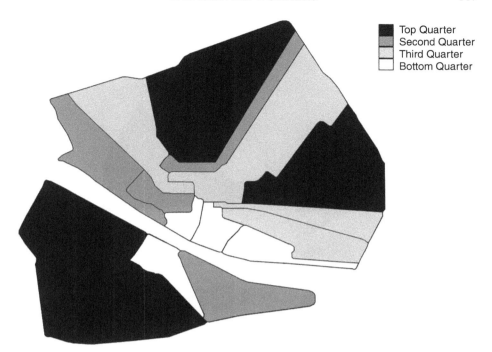

Figure 4.6 Map of index of arte maggiore to popolo minuto households by gonfalone, 1427
Source: Herlihy and Klapisch-Zuber, *Census and Property Survey*. See the text for the calculation of the concentration index.

Quattrocento ghettos. He claims that immigrants filled lower-end occupations and lived in the city's periphery.[116]

There are two possible sources of error in counting the number of migrant households. First, it is likely that not every migrant household was identified. However, the location of identified migrants should illustrate the general neighborhood pattern of all migrants. Second, data sparseness could be a problem. Immigrant households accounted for less than one-tenth of Florentine households.

Figure 4.7 maps the relative concentration of migrant households in 1427 and shows no clear core and periphery distinction. The area along the river to the northeast was generally considered to have the highest status. The outskirts were generally lower status. Drago Verde was now in the middle half of gonfaloni, while Leon Rosso was among the lowest-status gonfaloni.

The relative number of households with no taxable wealth, miserabili, is another indicator of low neighborhood social standing. Figure 4.8 maps the relative concentration of miserabili households in 1427 Florence and shows no clear core and periphery distinction. The outskirts were generally considered to have the highest status, while the core was generally

---

116   Cohn, *Laboring Classes*, 127 and 115–28.

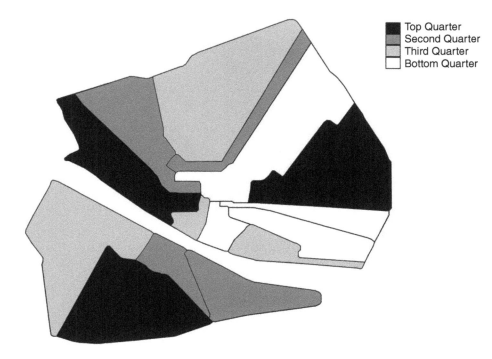

Figure 4.7 Map of index of migrant households by gonfalone, 1427
Source: Herlihy and Klapisch-Zuber, *Census and Property Survey*. The color scheme was adjusted from the other maps so that darker represents higher status rather than higher index of concentration. See the text for the calculation of the concentration index.

lower status. Drago Verde was in the highest quartile of poor household concentration among the gonfaloni. Leon Rosso was in the middle half of gonfaloni.

Summary statistics allow a more precise analysis of the neighborhood by neighborhood evolution of Florence. The change in the concentration index shows the ratio of the index from the later date compared to the earlier date.[117] Figure 4.9 maps the evolution of the relative concentration of arte maggiore households from 1352 to 1427. There was no clear trend toward status gains for the core of the city that is visible in the map. The outskirts generally had the highest gain in status. The core generally had the least gain in status.

Table 4.2 compares the relative concentration between core and periphery neighborhoods for 1352, 1404 and 1427. Three gonfaloni are located in the core. These are Carro, Leon Rosso and Vipera. The arte maggiore were not concentrated in the core in 1352 or 1427, but they were concentrated in 1404.

---

117   Change in Concentration Index $= 100*\dfrac{Concentration\ Index\ Later\ date}{Concentration\ Index\ Earlier\ Date}$.

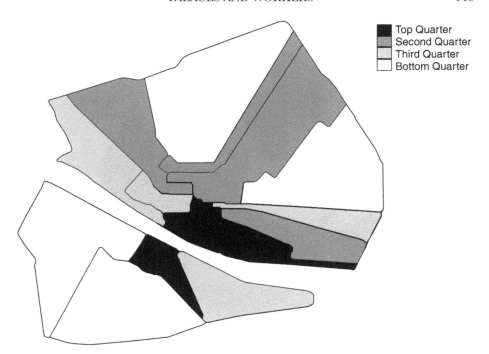

- ■ Top Quarter
- ▨ Second Quarter
- ▤ Third Quarter
- ☐ Bottom Quarter

Figure 4.8 Map of index of *miserabili* households by gonfalone, 1427
Source: Herlihy and Klapisch-Zuber, *Census and Property Survey.* The color scheme was adjusted from the other maps so that darker represents higher status rather than higher index of concentration. See the text for the calculation of the concentration index.

The concentration ratio shown in Table 4.3 is based on the Herfindahl-Hirschman Index, a standard concentration measure in economics.[118] The measure is the square of the percentage of arte maggiore in each of the gonfalone, and in this case ranges from 625 to 10,000.[119] A lower value implies a lower concentration of arte maggiore. As shown in the table, the neighborhoods were integrated in 1352, 1404 and 1427. The concentration ratios were all barely above the mathematical minimum.

The analysis of the data from the Trecento through the early Quattrocento shows that none of the three segregated neighborhood hypotheses fare well. Neighborhoods were clearly integrated, and there was no trend toward segregation. There was no statistically

---

118 George J. Stigler, "Measurement of Concentration," in *The Organization of Industry* (Chicago: University of Chicago Press, 1983), 31. For another, more standard example of the use of this measure, see chapter 7. This measure is the inverse of the Blau's measure of heterogeneity in sociology. Peter M. Blau, *Inequality and Heterogeneity: A Primitive Theory of Social Structure* (New York: Free Press, 1977), 9.

119 The maximum equals $10,000 = 100^2$. The minimum equals $625 = 100 * \left(\dfrac{100}{16}\right)^2$ [100 percent and 16 gonfaloni].

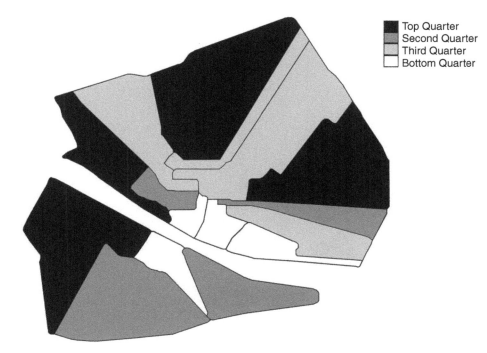

Figure 4.9 Map of change of index of arte maggiore to popolo minuto households, 1352–1427
Sources: Stella, *La Révolte des Ciompi*, 212; Herlihy and Klapisch-Zuber, *Census and Property Survey*. Calculation by author.

Table 4.2 Arte maggiore to popolo minuto core to periphery chi-squared, 1352–1427

Year	Chi-Squared	Significance
1352	0.152	0.697
1404	16.804	0.000
1427	0.532	0.466

Sources: Stella, *La Révolte des Ciompi*, 212; Herlihy and Klapisch-Zuber, *Census and Property Survey*. Calculation by author.

significant difference between core and periphery gonfaloni in 1352 and 1427. It is unclear why there was a difference in 1404.

From Early to Late Quattrocento Florentine Neighborhoods

The next step is to determine whether urban renewal led to any changes between 1427 and the late Quattrocento. Data from the 1427, 1458 and 1480 catasti are analyzed in

Table 4.3 Arte maggiore to popolo minuto ratio concentration, 1352–1427

Year	Concentration Ratio
1352	677
1404	733
1427	924

Sources: Stella, *La Révolte des Ciompi*, 212; Herlihy and Klapisch-Zuber, *Census and Property Survey*. Calculation by author. Calculated standardized percentage by gonfalone adjusting for different population levels and then used to estimate size of arte maggiore population by gonfalone.

this section. All data come from the Herlihy and Klapisch-Zuber database.[120] The 1458 and 1480 data are 10 percent samples of fiscal households from the 1458 catasto and the 1480 Decima Scalata. Only complete taxable fiscal households with living members were included. Households living outside Florence were included because household members may have remained even if the household head did not and because the domicile is a place of residence for purposes of city affairs. The 10 percent samples are large enough so that even without random sampling they should be generally representative. However, these samples tend to bias upward the variation across neighborhoods; this expectation has been corroborated. (See Appendix 3A for a more complete discussion of the 1458 and 1480 samples.)

Figures 4.10 through 4.12 present parallel information. All map the relative concentration of arte maggiore households. Figure 4.10 covers 1458, Figure 4.11 covers 1480 and Figure 4.12 presents the average of 1458 and 1480. These three figures show no clear core and periphery distinction. In 1458, both the highest- and lowest-status gonfaloni were spread across the city. Drago Verde and Leon Rosso were both in the middle half of gonfaloni. In 1480, the highest-status gonfaloni were spread across the city, and the lowest-status gonfaloni were to the west of the city. Drago Verde and Leon Rosso were both among the highest-status gonfaloni.

Figures 4.13 and 4.14 present the evolution of the relative concentration of arte maggiore households. Figure 4.13 covers the Quattrocento change starting from 1427, and Figure 4.14 covers the longer period starting from 1352 to the average of 1458 and 1480. Neither shows any clear trend toward status gains for the core.

Table 4.4 compares the relative concentrations of arte maggiore in the core and periphery for 1427, 1458 and 1480. It shows that they were not concentrated in the core in any year.

---

120   Herlihy and Klapisch-Zuber, *Census and Property Survey*.

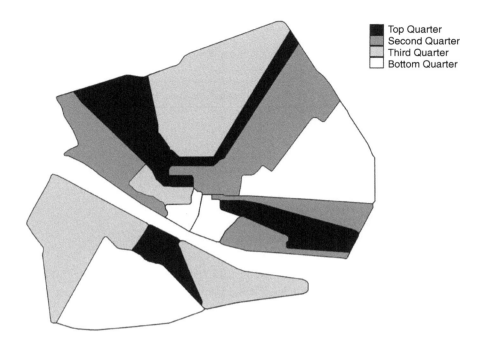

Figure 4.10 Map of index of arte maggiore to popolo minuto households, 1458
Source: Herlihy and Klapisch-Zuber, *Census and Property Survey*. See the text for the calculation of the concentration index.

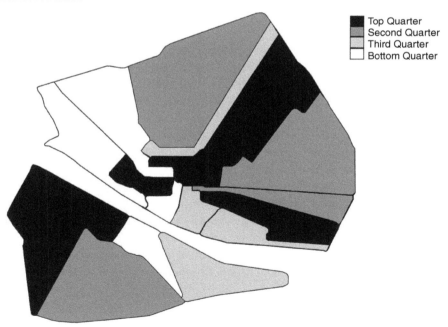

Figure 4.11 Map of index of arte maggiore to popolo minuto households, 1480
Source: Herlihy and Klapisch-Zuber, *Census and Property Survey*. See the text for the calculation of the concentration index.

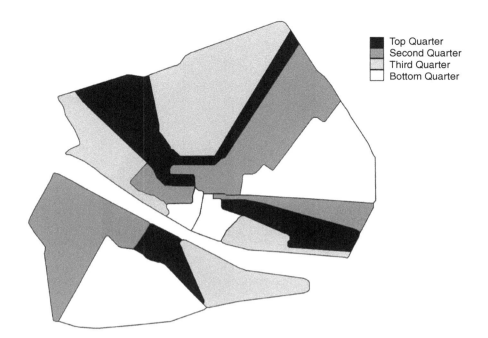

Figure 4.12 Map of index of arte maggiore to popolo minuto households, 1458 and 1480 average
Source: Herlihy and Klapisch-Zuber, *Census and Property Survey*. See the text for the calculation of the concentration index.

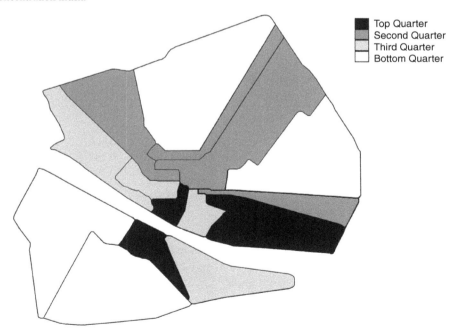

Figure 4.13 Map of change of index of arte maggiore to popolo minuto households, 1427–1458 and 1480 average
Source: Herlihy and Klapisch-Zuber, *Census and Property Survey*. Calculation by author.

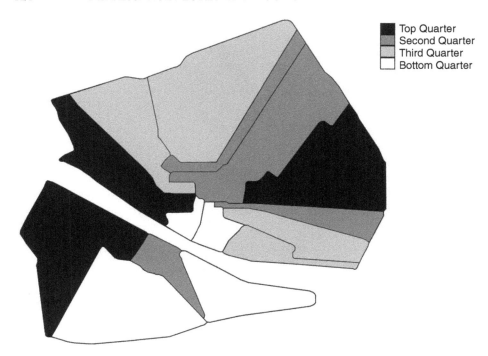

Figure 4.14 Map of change of index of arte maggiore to popolo minuto households, 1352–1458 and 1480 average
Sources: Stella, *La Révolte des Ciompi*, 212; Herlihy and Klapisch-Zuber, *Census and Property Survey*.

Table 4.4 Arte maggiore to popolo minuto core to periphery chi-squared, 1427–80

Year	Chi-Squared	Significance
1427	0.532	0.466
1458	2.071	0.150
1480	0.002	0.966

Source: Herlihy and Klapisch-Zuber, *Census and Property Survey*. Calculation by author.

Table 4.5, paralleling Table 4.3, presents Herfindahl-Hirschman Index numbers that show neighborhoods were integrated in 1458 and 1480. The concentration ratios were all barely above the mathematical minimum.

The three segregation hypotheses do not fare well in any of the maps or statistical tests. The neighborhoods were clearly integrated, and there was no difference between core and periphery neighborhoods and no trend toward segregation. These results imply, if anything, that the core was relatively less important during the Quattrocento than during the Trecento. This is exactly the opposite of what one would expect as a result of

Table 4.5 Arte maggiore to popolo minuto ratio concentration, 1427–80

Year	Concentration Ratio
1427	924
1458	838
1480	716
1458 and 1480 Average	685

Source: Herlihy and Klapisch-Zuber, *Census and Property Survey*. Calculation by author. This table uses the standardized percentage by gonfalone, which adjusts for different population levels. This was then used to estimate size of arte maggiore population by gonfalone.

Table 4.6 Summary of test of core versus periphery and segregation versus integration hypotheses

Year	Core or Periphery Advantage?	Integrated or Segregated?
1352	None	Integrated
1404	Core	Integrated
1427	None	Integrated
1458	None	Integrated
1480	None	Integrated
1458 and 1480	None	Integrated

Based on Tables 4.2 through 4.5.

urban renewal. The decrease in importance of the core could be associated with increasing homeownership rates (see Chapter 5 for more on this).

Conclusions

Florentine neighborhoods appear to have met Bruni's ideal and to have been well integrated across social levels during the second half of the Trecento and throughout the Quattrocento; therefore, there is no significant support for the segregation theory. Table 4.6 summarizes the results of the investigations in this study. In five out of six years (all except 1404), there were no discernibly higher-status neighborhoods in the core. The statistical tests in all six years demonstrate that the neighborhoods were integrated. Combining these results clearly shows that there was little discernible trend toward more homogeneous or segregated neighborhoods. This comparison implies that there is a long-term pattern to the social and economic relationships.

The integration of Florentine neighborhoods has several important implications. First, there is no apparent causal link between any Florentine urban planning and increasing neighborhood segregation. The new architecture and public art of the Renaissance did not segregate Florentine society, at least not noticeably. Burckhardt appears to be right when he envisions a thorough reconceptualization of the state during the Renaissance leading to greater equality.[121] Any darker side to the art of the Renaissance must be found elsewhere. Second, the city generally absorbed the influx of migrants. There were no migrant ghettos or slums. This implies, more broadly, that Florentine society during this period was extremely dynamic and that even major shocks could not disturb its equilibrium for long.

Finally, this integration shows that simple dichotomies, between rich and poor and between upper and lower class, are not applicable to Florentine urban ecology. The arte maggiore lived among the migrants and the miserabili. Neighborhood patterns neither held for long periods of time nor changed in predictable ways. The emergence of the Renaissance did not correspond with an increased division among the people. It seems much more likely that a wide range of the city's population continued to have regular contact with the greatness that became Burckhardt's vision of Florence.

---

121   Burckhardt, *Civilization of the Renaissance*; Julius Kirshner, "Introduction: The State is 'Back in'," *Journal of Modern History, Supplement: The Origins of the State in Italy, 1300–1600*, 67 (1995): S1–10.

Chapter Five

THE "STATE" MAKES A WORK OF ART: THE IMPACT OF THE *CATASTO* HOMEOWNER TAX LOOPHOLE ON THE QUATTROCENTO FLORENTINE PALAZZO BUILDING BOOM

Introduction

Florence is world famous in large part for its private palaces constructed during a *Quattrocento* building boom that ranks as one of the great events in art and architectural history. The results of this boom probably were part of what inspired Burckhardt to coin his famous phrase "the state as a work of art."[1] He writes that there was a thorough reconceptualization of the state during the Renaissance, which led to greater equality.[2] More recent economic and social historians debate whether this building boom was associated with an economic depression,[3] exacerbated class divisions[4] or was a significant and productive stimulant to the economy.[5]

The question remains, though, why were the private palaces constructed, and why were they constructed at that time? The study in this chapter provides evidence that a tax exemption in the Quattrocento *catasti* that subsidized homeownership explains the timing of the palace building as well as a simultaneous increase in the Florentine homeownership rate. Government interventions can have a major impact on homeownership rates. For example, in recent research, economic historians credit effective

---

1 Jacob Burckhardt, *The Civilization of the Renaissance in Italy*, 2 vols. (New York: Harper, 1973).

2 Ibid.; Julius Kirshner, "Introduction: The State Is 'Back in'," *Journal of Modern History, Supplement: The Origins of the State in Italy, 1300–1600*, 67 (1995): S1–10.

3 Robert S. Lopez, "Hard Times and Investment in Culture," in *The Renaissance, Medieval or Modern*, ed. Karl H. Dannenfeldt (Boston: D. C. Heath, 1959).

4 Samuel Kline Cohn Jr., *The Laboring Classes in Renaissance Florence* (New York: Academic Press, 1980), 50–63.

5 Richard A. Goldthwaite, *The Building of Renaissance Florence* (Baltimore: Johns Hopkins University Press, 1980); Goldthwaite, "The Florentine Palace as Domestic Architecture," *American Historical Review* 77, no. 4 (1972): 978; Goldthwaite, "The Economy of Renaissance Italy: The Preconditions for Luxury Consumption," *I Tatti Studies* 2 (1987): 15–39. For a non-economist comment on the distinctly different economic approaches of Lopez and Goldthwaite see: Anonymous, "An Editorial Comment to Richard Goldthwaite's 'The Economy of Renaissance Italy'," *I Tatti Studies* 2 (1987): 11–13.

government intervention with safeguarding American homeownership after the Great Depression began.[6] This study places Florentine palace construction in the long history of impacts from government interventions in the housing market.[7] The approach analyzes Florentine tax policy from a comparatively unusual perspective for Renaissance historiography. Most similar studies measure the aggregate burden to either the entire population or to some subset. This one, however, focuses on the changing relative tax burden.[8] Examining the relative rather than the absolute burden shifts the analysis to the impact of changing incentives on Florentine behavior.

The rest of this chapter develops this argument supporting the subsidy explanation. The timing fits the explanation: the palace-building boom happened at the same time as a striking increase in homeownership. An expanded access to homeownership also fits the explanation, as a wide range of measures shows that Florentines with less wealth and social status joined the ranks of the homeowners. Appendix 4A presents and discusses an opportunity cost model of homeownership that places the various possible explanations into a consistent and mathematical context.

Explaining the Palace-Building Boom

The study presented in this chapter focuses on the homeownership subsidy explanation of the palace-building boom. Other potential explanations include conspicuous consumption, decreased interest rates, increased population and increased wealth.[9] The homeownership subsidy began with the 1427 *catasto*, which represented a sweeping change in Florentine tax policy. Arbitrary assessments had been common under the *Trecento estimi*.[10]

---

6 Price Fishback, Jonathan Rose and Kenneth Snowden, *How the New Deal Safeguarded Home Ownership* (Chicago: University of Chicago Press, 2013).

7 Recent work includes Fishback et al., *How the New Deal Safeguarded Home Ownership*, and Eugene N. White, Kenneth Snowden and Price Fishback, eds., *Housing and Mortgage Markets in Historical Perspective* (Chicago: University of Chicago Press, 2014).

8 Bernardino Barbadoro, *Le finanze della Repubblica fiorentina: Imposta diretta e debito pubblico fino all'istituzione del Monte* (Florence: Olschki, 1929); Enrico Fiumi, "L'imposta diretta nei comuni medioevali della Toscana," *Studi in onore di A. Sapori* (Milan: Cisalpino, 1957), 327–53; Charles M. de La Roncière, "Indirect Taxes or 'Gabelles' at Florence in the Fourteenth Century," in *Florentine Studies: Politics and Society in Renaissance Florence*, ed. Nicolai Rubinstein (Evanston, IL: Northwestern University Press, 1968), 140–92; Anthony Molho, *Florentine Public Finances in the Early Renaissance, 1400–1433* (Cambridge, MA: Harvard University Press, 1971); Elio Conti, *L'imposta diretta a Firenze nel Quattrocento (1427–1494)* (Rome: Palazzo Borromini, 1984).

9 On conspicuous consumption, see Goldthwaite, *Building of Renaissance Florence*, 425; on population increase, see James R. Lindow, *The Renaissance Palace in Florence: Magnificence and Splendour in Fifteenth-Century Italy* (Aldershot, UK: Ashgate, 2007), 54. Other theories are based on general economic theory as described in Ann Dougherty and Robert Van Order, "Inflation, Housing Costs, and the Consumer Price Index," *American Economic Review* 72, no. 1 (1982): 154–64; Harvey S. Rosen, Kenneth T. Rosen and Douglas Holtz-Eakin, "Housing Tenure, Uncertainty, and Taxation," *Review of Economics and Statistics* 66 (1984): 407; Robert Topel and Sherwin Rosen. "Housing Investment in the United States," *Journal of Political Economy* (1988): 718–40.

10 Gene Brucker, *Renaissance Florence* (1959; Huntington, NY: Krieger, 1975), 143.

The catasto was the first impersonal tax in the city's history. It increased fairness, and its progressivity helped the poor by shifting the relative tax burden to the wealthy.[11] The catasto also introduced an exemption for the fiscal household's home and its furnishings. This exemption subsidized private palaces and works of art. In this context, Burckhardt's idea of the state as a work of art takes on an entirely new meaning. This exemption was not a minor change. The decision to delete the domicile led to 41 new volumes of corrections.[12] The exemption was effectively a subsidy, because assets were fungible.[13] For example, Francesco Sacchetti in his Trecento *Sposizione* 35 equates Monte credits with immovable assets.[14] Further, Monte credits could be encumbered and the cash applied elsewhere.[15] This fungibility allowed major shifts within Florentine portfolios.[16]

This direct subsidy effect was magnified by a pass-through tax on renters. The tax on property holdings created an indirect tax on renters above and beyond the direct subsidy on homeownership. This indirect tax effect would have further motivated increased homeownership and reduced renting. The subsidy's full impact might have taken a period of time to fully develop. There are several reasons for this. First, Florentines could not adjust their portfolios quickly enough, because the tax was new. In addition, the impact was based on prospective rather than retrospective tax savings. Therefore, before building, Florentines would have needed confidence that the exemption would remain in place for a significant period of time. The stability of the Medici regime, where the catasto was imposed more than two dozen times between 1427 and 1480, created this kind of confidence.[17] Finally, the increased progressivity starting in 1442 increased the subsidy for palaces.

The subsidy explanation correctly implies a set of observable facts about Florentine building and homeownership: that the greatest period of palace building began after 1427 and ended before 1500, that changes in the subsidy affected who was building as

---

11 Richard A. Goldthwaite, *The Economy of Renaissance Florence* (Baltimore: Johns Hopkins University Press, 2009), 378; James MacDonald, *A Free Nation Deep in Debt: The Financial Roots of Democracy* (Princeton, NJ: Princeton University Press, 2003), 104.

12 David Herlihy and Christiane Klapisch-Zuber, *Les Toscans et leurs familles: Une étude du Catasto Florentine de 1427* (Paris: Fondation nationale des sciences politiques, 1978), 94.

13 Julius Kirshner and Jacob Klerman, "The Seven Percent Fund of Renaissance Florence," in *Banchi pubblici, banchi private e monti di pietà nell'Europa preindustriale: amministrazione, tecniche operative e ruoli economici: Atti del convegno–Genova (1–6 ottobre 1990)* (Genova, Società Ligure di Storia Patria, 1991), 1: 367–98.

14 Julius Kirshner, " 'Ubi est ille?' Franco Sacchetti and the Monte Comune of Florence," *Speculum* 59, no. 3 (1984): 566.

15 Kirshner and Klerman, "Seven Percent Fund of Renaissance Florence."

16 Howell in a study of the Low Countries challenges the fungibility of assets in the late medieval world (Martha C. Howell, *Commerce before Capitalism in Europe, 1300–1600* [Cambridge, UK: Cambridge University Press, 2010]). Basic financial theory argues that real property is a preferred asset due to imperfect information (Frederic S. Mishkin, *The Economics of Money, Banking, and Financial Markets*, 4th ed. [New York: Harper Collins, 1995], 205–30). However, the active Monte secondary market in Florence casts doubt on the universality of her fungibility assertion (see chapter 2).

17 Conti, *L'imposta diretta*; Elio Conti, ed., *Matteo Palmieri ricordi fiscali (1427–1474)* (Rome: Palazzo Borromini, 1983).

well as how much they were building and that the building boom was broader than just the private palaces. The subsidy explanation also correctly implies that Florentine fiscal household sizes should have increased during the Quattrocento in order for people to pool resources to buy homes. This point stresses the fiscal and economic nature as opposed to the demographic aspects of the households in the catasti.

The other potential explanations—conspicuous consumption, decreased interest rates, increased population or increased wealth—have trouble explaining all the characteristics of the palace-building boom. Thorstein Veblen's conspicuous consumption theory seems an appealing choice to explain it. Conspicuous consumption and its associated bandwagon effect are simply the idea that the most affluent Florentines wanted to build bigger homes and that other leading families then followed them. Goldthwaite makes this point.[18] He implicitly assumes that tastes changed and that Florentines now simply preferred more art. The building boom "was a response to the rise of a new demand to a significant shift in the way wealthy men spent their money."[19] He further notes that "by introducing new criteria of luxury, they generated additional demand."[20]

The conspicuous consumption theory has wide support.[21] John Najemy argues that palace building was due to a bandwagon effect, which in turn led to a change in tastes. He writes that the "palace-building Medici grandeur generated emulation" and that "palace building was the ultimate in conspicuous consumption and advertisement of a patron's status and means."[22] Brucker argues that both values and economic pressures led to the palace building.[23] However, the conspicuous consumption theory faces a set of problems. Veblen originally coined the phrase "conspicuous consumption" to apply to 1890s American Gilded Age society.[24] It incorporates a range of behaviors, including a vicarious consumption of goods,[25] an emulation factor and a bandwagon effect. It is essentially unproductive.[26] The theory faces another set of problems when applied to Renaissance Florence. First, when applied within Goldthwaite's larger theory, it associates an unproductive conspicuous consumption with a productive palace building. This would appear to imply a kind of cancellation effect that would dilute both. Second, Veblen's connection of conspicuous consumption with conspicuous leisure leads to another problem: Quattrocento Florentine businessmen definitely did not consume conspicuous leisure.[27] There was no lavish spending on events.[28] Next, the theory can

---

18 Goldthwaite, *Building of Renaissance Florence*, 425.

19 Ibid., 422.

20 Ibid.

21 John M. Najemy, *A History of Florence: 1200–1575* (Malden, MA: Blackwell, 2006), 335–37; Paul N. Balchin, *Urban Development in Renaissance Italy* (Chichester, UK: Wiley, 2008), 364–66.

22 Najemy, *History of Florence*, 337 and 335.

23 Brucker, *Renaissance Florence*, 8.

24 Thorstein Veblen, *The Theory of the Leisure Class*, unabridged, Dover Thrift Edition (1899; New York: Dover Publications, 1994).

25 Ibid., 43.

26 Ibid., 44.

27 Ibid., 43.

28 Goldthwaite, *Economy of Renaissance Florence*, 380.

only be used to explain why a palace-building boom happened. It has nothing to say about the boom's timing or why there was a parallel boom among the general population. Finally, compounding the above issues, there is a theoretical issue. Simply assuming a change in tastes adds little to the understanding of an issue, since almost any change in preferences could have resulted from a change in tastes. It is, at best, difficult to test.[29] All of these issues are solely theoretical. They can be circumvented by assuming special circumstances. Nevertheless, it is dangerous to enlist a theory and then to reject inconvenient aspects of that theory.

The Timing of the Florentine Private Palace-Building Boom

The private palace-building boom was an increase in homeownership at the intensive margin. It is important to keep in mind that, although there were some public projects, this type of building was a private-sector phenomenon.[30] It is often called the Medicean period of palace building.[31] These private palaces were significantly larger than the previous homes. A set of homes that had housed many families would be bought and the land used to create one larger private palace.[32] The Medici palace replaced more than twenty homes;[33] the Strozzi palace was an entire block in size and replaced a large tower home, five other homes, and twelve shops, some of which also served as residences;[34] and the Bartolini palace replaced half a dozen homes and an inn.[35]

Each palace was associated with a particular family. There is debate about how closely private palaces can be associated with the creation of the modern nuclear family. Richard Goldthwaite and Isabelle Hyman argue that greater individualism led to palace construction.[36] According to Goldthwaite, "The palace represented a new world of privacy, and it was the privacy of a relatively small group."[37] He concludes that "the Florentine palace, then, was more often than not a residence of a single conjugal family,"[38] and indeed

29 George J. Stigler and Gary S. Becker, "De Gustibus Non Est Disputandum," *American Economic Review* 67, no. 2 (1977): 76–90.

30 Michael Baxandall, *Painting and Experience in Fifteenth-Century Italy: A Primer in the Social History of Pictorial Style* (Oxford: Oxford University Press, 1972); Richard A. Goldthwaite, *Wealth and the Demand for Art in Italy, 1300–1600* (Baltimore: Johns Hopkins University Press, 1993).

31 Francesco Gurrieri and Patrizia Fabbri, *Palaces of Florence* (New York: Rizzoli, 1996), 106–79.

32 Goldthwaite, *Building of Renaissance Florence*, 16; Cohn, *Laboring Classes*, 121.

33 Goldthwaite, *Building of Renaissance Florence*, 16.

34 Ibid.

35 Ibid.

36 Francis William Kent, *Household and Lineage in Renaissance Florence* (Princeton, NJ: Princeton University Press, 1977); Francis W. Kent, "Palaces, Politics and Society in Fifteenth-Century Florence," *I Tatti Studies* 2 (1987): 44; Francis W. Kent, "La famiglia patrizia fiorentina nel Quattrocento: Nuovi orientamenti nella storiografia recente," in *Palazzo Strozzi metà millennio, 1489–1989: Atti del convegno di studi*, Firenze, 3–6 luglio 1989 (Rome: Istituto della Enciclopedia Italiana, 1991), 159–66 and 70–91.

37 Goldthwaite, "Florentine Palace," 1004.

38 Ibid., 1003.

the internal layouts of the palaces clearly indicate they were built for single families.[39] Goldthwaite also links increased consumption with the development of the Renaissance individualism.[40] Francis Kent disagrees with Goldthwaite that palace building was associated with a modern-style nuclear family, pointing out that "no Renaissance palace was built by a *consorteria*, whereas a few older houses and some towers and loggias, remained the property of an entire clan."[41] Prior to the Quattrocento, wealthy Florentine families erected towers designed not so much to be impressive and a store of wealth, but rather as fortification for the family.[42] There were more than one hundred towers in the city,[43] but few rose to any significant level of architectural merit.[44] Some historians have seen palace building as a phenomenon that lasted the entire Quattrocento. Goldthwaite writes that "sometime after 1400, domestic architecture began to come into its own with the development of the private patrician palace."[45] However, Goldthwaite's dating is imprecise, and thus leads to interpretation problems.

It is possible to be much more precise. Little significant private palace construction began before 1427.[46] Niccolo da Uzzano had built the first private palace in 1411; however, no other significant palace appeared until 1446.[47] The conspicuous consumption explanation would imply that the Uzzano building should have set off a bandwagon effect and an early Quattrocento building boom. Instead, the private palace and artwork boom began decades later, well after Filippo Brunelleschi and Masaccio (Tommaso di Ser Giovanni di Simone) at the beginning of the century and well before Leonardo da Vinci and Michelangelo di Lodovico Buonarroti Simoni at the end of the century.[48] Palace building accelerated dramatically during the middle third of the Quattrocento. Leonardo Lisci estimates that of the 40 most significant palaces built during the 600-year period from 1300 to 1900, 15 of them (nearly 40 percent) were built during the 50-year period from 1450 to 1500.[49] Benedetto Dei wrote about these beautiful buildings in 1472, during the Florentine building boom. There were 33 palaces built in Dei's own time,[50] most by private citizens.[51] Palace building continued during the *Cinquecento*, but at a reduced rate. Benedetto Varchi, writing in 1545, cited

---

39 Ibid., 1004–6.
40 Richard A. Goldthwaite, "L'interno del Palazzo e il consume dei beni," in *Palazzo Strozzi metà millennio, 1489–1989: Atti del convegno di studi*, Firenze, July 3–6, 1989 (Rome: Istituto della Enciclopedia Italiana, 1991), 159–66.
41 Kent, "Palaces, Politics and Society," 48 and 45.
42 Gene Brucker, *Florence: The Golden Age, 1138–1737* (Berkeley: University of California Press, 1998), 38–39; Najemy, *History of Florence*, 33.
43 Brucker, *Golden Age*, 38–39; Najemy, *History of Florence*, 33.
44 Lisci, *Palazzi di Firenze*, 2: 800.
45 Goldthwaite, *Building of Renaissance Florence*, 14.
46 Lisci, *Palazzi di Firenze*, 2: 800.
47 Kent, "Palaces, Politics and Society," 66.
48 Lisci, *Palazzi di Firenze*, 2: 799–800.
49 Ibid., 800.
50 Benedetto Dei, *La cronica*, ed. Roberto Barducci (Florence: Papafava, 1984), 86–87.
51 Lindow, *Renaissance Palace*, 44.

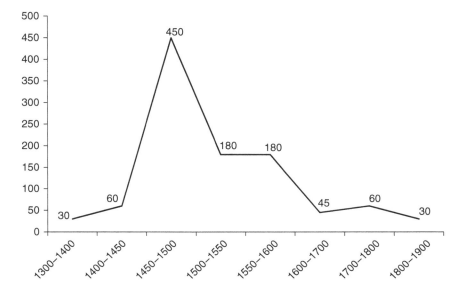

Figure 5.1 Index of date of construction of "most significant Florentine private palaces"
Source: Leonardo Ginori Lisci, *I Palazzi di Firenze nella storia e nell'arte* (Florence: Giunti, 1972), 2: 800.
Calculation by author.

30 palaces worthy of mention that had been built from 1450 to 1478, another 35 that had been built during the entire time before 1450, and 18 that had been built after 1478.[52] One prominent history of Florentine private palaces provides 3 examples from the age of tower houses, 9 examples from the "Great Period of the Medici," and 12 examples of "Aristocratic Homes in Grand Ducal Florence."[53] These differences are statistically significant.

Figure 5.1 shows this dramatically increased rate of palace construction.[54] The rate of "significant palace" building during the second half of the Quattrocento was nearly five times the average from 1300 to 1900.[55]

The accelerated palace building boom coincided with a tax rate change. The original catasto assessments from 1427, 1430 and 1433 imposed a flat rate. However, the next update of catasto rates in 1442 imposed a graduated rate (see Table 5.1).[56] This increased progressivity would have increased the subsidy for palace construction.

---

52 Ibid., 45.
53 Gurrieri and Fabbri, *Palaces of Florence*, 80–105, 106–79, 180–305.
54 A chi-squared test based on the difference between the 50 years of the late Quattrocento and the other 550 years is statistically significant at the 99 percent level.
55 All the numbers are in multiples of 15 due to an artifact of the data. There were 40 palaces constructed during a 600-year period. This is an average of one every 15 years.
56 Conti, *L'mposta diretta*, 199.

Table 5.1 Tax rate table of 1442 *diecina graziosa*

Assessment (*Fiorino di suggello*)	Relative Rate
1 to 50	4
To 100	7
To 150	8
To 200	10
To 250	12
To 300	14
To 400	16
To 500	18
To 600	20
To 700	22
To 1,000	25
To 1,200	28
To 1,500	31
Over 1,500	33 1/3

Based on assessment rates of August 16, 1442. The relative rate is in percentage terms.
Source: Elio Conti, *L'imposta diretta a Firenze nel Quattrocento (1427–1494)* (Rome: Palazzo Borromini, 1984), 199.

The Palazzo Medici is particularly important, because the Medici were the first family to build a significant palace.[57] Cosimo de' Medici began building it in 1446,[58] but this was part of a longer process that had started just after the catasto taxation system was initiated. The Medici already owned much of the land that was used for the Palazzo Medici.[59] By 1433, tenants in other buildings owned by the Medici had been moved out. No tenants are listed in the Medici account books after that time, and there is no rent from any of those buildings.[60] The Medici did not start to seriously acquire additional real estate until 1443.[61] The Medici family's great wealth and their government

---

57 Lisci, *Palazzi di firenze*, 1: 29. For more, see Dale V. Kent, *Cosimo de' Medici and the Florentine Renaissance: The Patron's Oeuvre* (New Haven, CT: Yale University Press, 2000), 217–38; Marvin Trachtenberg, *Dominion of the Eye: Urbanism, Art, and Power in Early Modern Florence* (Cambridge, UK: Cambridge University Press, 1997), 27–41; Vittorio Franchetti-Pardo, *Storia dell'urbanistica: Dal Trecento al Quattrocento* (Bari, Italy: Laterza, 1994), 541–54; Vittorio Franchetti-Pardo, "Cultura brunelleschiana e trasformazioni urbanistiche nella Firenze del Quattrocento," in *Storia dell'urbanistica: Dal Trecento al Quattrocento*, ed. P. Ruschi, G. C. Romby, and M. Tarassi (Florence: Vallecchi, 1979), 87–98; Carolyn Elam, "Lorenzo de' Medici and the Urban Development of Renaissance Florence," *Art History* 1 (1978): 43–66.

58 Hyman identified the 1446 date. Isabelle Hyman, *Fifteenth-Century Florentine Studies: The Palazzo Medici and a Ledger for the Church of San Lorenzo* (New York: Garland, 1977), 1. For the older 1444 date, see Lisci, *Palazzi di Firenze*, 29. Either date fits the subsidy hypothesis.

59 Hyman, *Fifteenth-Century Florentine Studies*, 85.

60 Ibid., 63.

61 Ibid., 54–84.

position allowed them to take greater risks with their money. Other families started building palaces later: the Pazzi family began construction in 1460, and the Gondi and Strozzi
families began in 1489.[62] These were among the wealthiest and most powerful families
in Florence. In general, the earliest adopters of something new, including products and
technologies, tend to be wealthier than average. This would imply that it was not unexpected that the Medici should build the first palace. It was not purely a sign of status but
also a point of leadership, as it demonstrated increased risk tolerance.

Palace construction also had a political aspect. Families with the Medici's favor could
follow them and build their own palaces,[63] and the Medici would also engineer the take-
over of palaces on behalf of their allies.[64] The patron-client relationship continued to
function as it had previously, so although the palaces were busy, they were not a way for
the owner to escape from client relationships.[65]

Shifting the building boom to the middle of the century is not to argue against the
existence of either the desire to live in private palaces or the magnificence of Florentine
architecture at earlier dates. Rather it is an argument solely about the timing and the rate
of construction. Florentine tastes did not change. The artistic vision and drive certainly
existed before large-scale private palace building began. The palaces did not represent
a significant break in the long-term cultural patterns of Florentine society. There was a
clear architectural relationship with the Trecento.[66] Preachers had extolled the benefits
of magnificent buildings from at least the 1420s.[67] However, that vision was not converted
into anything tangible until the middle of the Quattrocento.

Art patronage appeared before palace building, but later the two went hand in hand.
The Medici first became art patrons in 1418; however, their patronage of the arts developed slowly.[68] Private spending on the interiors of the homes would increase the home's
value as a potential tax shelter. Goldthwaite notes that "the palace was primarily an
expansion of interior private space" and that "all of these palaces considerably enlarged
the domestic space for the family."[69] Though art historians tend to focus on the public
displays of art, a statistically larger share of the murals were created in private homes.
More than 60 percent of the 23 famous Medicean-era mural artworks mentioned by
Benedetto Dei were painted in private homes.[70]

62 Lisci, *Palazzi di Firenze*, 29, 34; Brenda Preyer, "I documenti sulle fondamenta di Palazzo
    Strozzi," in *Palazzo Strozzi metà millennio, 1489–1989: Atti del convegno di studi*, Firenze, July 3–6,
    1989 (Rome: Istituto della Enciclopedia Italiana, 1991), 159–66, 195–213.
63 Najemy, *History of Florence*, 334.
64 Kent, "Palaces, Politics and Society," 68–69.
65 Ibid., 69.
66 Hyman, *Fifteenth-Century Florentine Studies*, 1–296.
67 Peter Howard, "Preaching Magnificence in Renaissance Florence," *Renaissance Quarterly* 61, no.
    2 (2008): 325–69.
68 H. M. Gombrich, "The Early Medici as Patrons of Art," in *Italian Renaissance Studies*, ed. Ernest
    Fraser Jacob (London: Faber and Faber, 1960), 281 and 279–311.
69 Goldthwaite, *Building of Renaissance Florence*, 15–16.
70 Dei, *La cronica*, 86.

Table 5.2 Estimates of fifteenth-century Florentine
population

Year	Population
1427	37,144
1458	37,369
1480	41,590

Sources: David Herlihy and Christiane Klapisch-Zuber,
The Tuscans and Their Families (New Haven, CT: Yale
University Press, 1985), 74; David Herlihy and Christiane
Klapisch-Zuber, *Les Toscans et leurs familles: Une étude du
Catasto Florentine de 1427* (Paris: Fondation nationale des
sciences politiques, 1978), 183.

There are other possible explanations for the palace-building boom besides a subsidy
or conspicuous consumption. The three key alternatives are an interest rate decrease, a
population increase or a wealth increase. Appendix 4A presents an equation that for-
malizes the choice between owning and renting and shows how all three are related to
the subsidy explanation. Decreasing interest rates could have made large capital expenditures more affordable. However, interest rates were high rather than low during the
period of the palace building boom (see Chapter 2). Increasing population could have
driven the need for palace building.[71] The problem is that the population, by all accounts,
did not increase substantially (see Table 5.2). Goldthwaite points out that the population was about constant during the Quattrocento, although the margins of error are
quite high.[72] Finally, increasing wealth could have led to the building boom, but this also
appears unlikely. First, per capita wealth actually appears higher when only towers and
not private palaces were built. Second, there is no clear evidence that wealth increased
during the Quattrocento.[73] The model of changing homeownership rates below adds
more support for this last point.

The Timing of the Florentine Homeownership Increase

Besides the increase in housing expenditures at the intensive margin, with an increase in
the size of homes through the private palace building, there was an increase in homeownership at the extensive margin, with an increase in the total number of homes. Overall
homeownership increased because homes became relatively less expensive. This exemption continued throughout the century, and the increasing progressivity of subsequent
catasti only accelerated it.[74]

---

71 Lindow, *Renaissance Palace*, 2007, 54.
72 Goldthwaite, *Economy of Renaissance Florence*, 337 and 563–64.
73 Gene A. Brucker, "The Economic Foundations of Renaissance Florence," in *Lorenzo il Magnifico
    e il suo mondo*, ed. Gian Carlo Garfagnini (Florence: Olschki, 1994), 3–15.
74 Conti, *L'imposta diretta*, 119–49, 247–61 and 281–93.

Table 5.3 Counts and percentages of owners and renters in Florence, 1427–80

Year	Est. No. of HHs	Owning	Renting	Neither	Unknown	Own/All HHs	Own/Own+Rent
1427	9,720	4,104	4,189	374	1053	42%	49%
1458	7,440	4,370	1,610	140	1320	59%	73%
1480	7,430	4,410	1,500	200	1320	59%	75%

HH: Fiscal household
Source: Herlihy and Klapisch-Zuber, *Census and Property Survey*. The counts for 1458 and 1480 are multiplied by ten because the data come from a 10 percent sample.

The homeownership level and rate can be analyzed using the Quattrocento Florentine catasti. The data come from a complete set of fiscal households in Florence from the 1427 catasto and 10 percent samples from the 1458 catasto and 1480 Decima Scalata.[75] The samples are large enough that even without precise random sampling, they should be generally representative. Only complete taxable fiscal households with living members are included. Some people with no wealth might have owned homes and not needed the deduction. In the statistics that follow, this group is included as renters, which serves to bias downward the ownership percentage. This bias does not appear to be significant, however, given the small number of people who belong to this category.

There are some complications when measuring the increasing breadth of homeownership. Any calculations have to take into account the missing data, the rate of which increased after 1427 due to the recognized decrease in data quality in the later catasti.[76] Data are missing more frequently from poorer and younger household heads, including migrant households, household heads with no occupation, female household heads, households of one person and households with heads age 25 and younger. The percentage of households neither owning nor renting was relatively constant. This is inconsistent with data errors, a consistent pattern of nonresponse or a shift in the supply curve, because in any of these cases most households would have been absorbed into one or the other category. These could represent subleasing.

There are two natural methods to estimate the homeownership rate using the catasto data. The first calculates the change in the number of owners from 1427 levels to the 1458/1480 levels. It is the most conservative calculation and is probably an underestimate of the change in the number of owner-occupied homes. The change is significant, growing from 4,104 owner-occupied homes in 1427 to an estimated 4,370 in 1458 and

75   David Herlihy and Christiane Klapisch-Zuber, *Census and Property Survey of Florentine Domains and the City of Verona in Fifteenth-Century Italy* [machine-readable data file]. Cambridge, MA: David Herlihy, Harvard University, Department of History and Paris, France: Christiane Klapisch-Zuber, Ecole Pratique des Hautes Etudes [producers], 1977. Madison: University of Wisconsin, Data and Program Library Service [distributor], 1981.
76   Raymond de Roover, *The Rise and Decline of the Medici Bank, 1397–1494* (Cambridge, MA: Harvard University Press, 1963), 24.

4,410 in 1480. The estimated increase between 1427 and 1480 is about 9.5 percent. The second method calculates the change in the share of households that are either owner occupied or renter occupied. This is a more liberal calculation and is probably an over-estimate. Using two variations of this calculation (see Table 5.3), it is possible to see that homeownership either increased from 42 percent in 1427 to around 59 percent later in the Quattrocento, an increase of about 40 percent, or from 49 percent to around 74 percent, an increase of nearly 50 percent. These calculations provide strong evidence for the subsidy explanation, since there was no change in the tax rates on housing between 1442 and 1480.

The significant homeownership increase suggests two points about Florentine society. First, there was significant capital market liquidity. Households were able either to accumulate capital or sell homes or to do both on a widespread basis. Second, there was no impermeable stratification; homeownership was within reach for a large portion of the population. For example, in order to be considered as a potential citizen, an immigrant had to own a home worth at least 150 florins.[77] This was much easier to achieve by the end of the century.

The palazzo construction and the increasing breadth of homeownership intersect in the apparent declining supply of housing stock during the Quattrocento. Though the population stayed about constant, the total housing stock appears to have decreased significantly sometime after 1427. The estimated number of occupied homes decreased from 9,261 in 1427 to 7,300 in 1458 and 7,230 in 1480, a citywide drop of more than 20 percent. The decline occurred in 15 of Florence's 16 civil divisions known as *gonfaloni*, increasing only in the central Vipera *gonfalone*. This could have been caused by both a consolidation of homes through the construction of palazzi, each replacing many homes, and by a consolidation of poorer households as they pooled assets to buy homes as a way to reduce taxes.[78]

The Quattrocento Florentine Homeownership Rates in Comparison

This section compares the Quattrocento homeownership rate with rates from other times and places, including Cinquecento Florence, the nineteenth- and twentieth-century United States and recent Organization of Economic Cooperation and Development (OECD) countries.

The first comparison is with 1561 Florentine data from the Decima, which assessed homes and businesses.[79] The rate of homeownership is based on reported households, so it is reasonably equivalent to the Quattrocento estimates from the previous section. The homeownership exemption was eliminated by that time, which probably reduced

77 Anthony Molho, ed., *Social and Economic Foundations of the Italian Renaissance* (New York: Wiley, 2005), 7.

78 Goldthwaite, *Economy of Renaissance Florence*, 379.

79 R. Burr Litchfield, *Florence Ducal Capital, 1530–1630* (New York: ACLS Humanities E-Book, 2008), para. 29. Permanent Link: http://quod.lib.umich.edu/cgi/t/text/text-idx?c=acls;idno=heb90034.

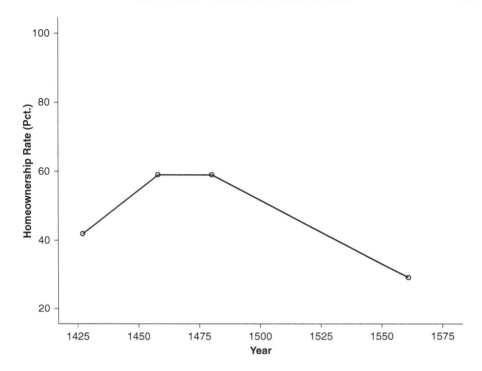

Figure 5.2 Florentine homeownership rates, 1427–1561
Sources: Herlihy and Klapisch-Zuber, *Census and Property Survey*; R. Burr Litchfield, *Florence ducal capital, 1530–1630* (New York: ACLS Humanities E-Book, 2008). Permanent Link: http://quod.lib.umich.edu/cgi/t/text/text-idx?c=acls;idno=heb90034, Table 7.4. Calculation by author.

homeownership rates.[80] Only 29 percent of all household heads owned their own home (see Fig. 5.2).[81]

Table 5.4 shows the homeownership rate in the United States during the nineteenth and twentieth centuries. Quattrocento Florentine homeownership rates were generally above nineteenth-century and about level with twentieth-century American nonfarm rates.[82]

Figure 5.3 provides a comparison between the twentieth-century United States and fifteenth-century Florence. The twentieth-century United States is an example of a long-term rapidly growing modern economy. The Florentine growth in homeownership during the Quattrocento is comparable to the growth in the United States between 1940 and 1970. This confirms that the Florentine housing market was highly liquid.

---

80 Lorenzo Cantini, *Legislazione toscana raccolta e illustrata (1532–1775)*, 32 vols. (Florence: Fantosini, 1800–1805) 4: 171 ("Decreto per la descrizione delle case di Firenze del di 17 Giugno 1561).
81 Litchfield, *Florence Ducal Capital*, table 7.4.
82 Lee Soltow, *Men and Wealth in the United States, 1850–1970* (New Haven, CT: Yale University Press, 1975), 50.

Table 5.4 Owner-occupied dwelling units as a percentage of all occupied dwelling units, United States, 1850–1970

	All	Farm	Nonfarm
Estimated			
1850	50%	–	–
1860	52%	–	–
1870	51%	65%	38%
Census Data			
1890	48%	66%	37%
1900	47%	64%	37%
1910	46%	63%	38%
1920	46%	58%	41%
1930	48%	54%	46%
1940	44%	53%	41%
1950	55%	66%	53%
1960	62%	74%	61%
1970	63%	–	–

Source: Lee Soltow, *Men and Wealth in the United States, 1850–1870* (New Haven, CT: Yale University Press, 1973), 50.

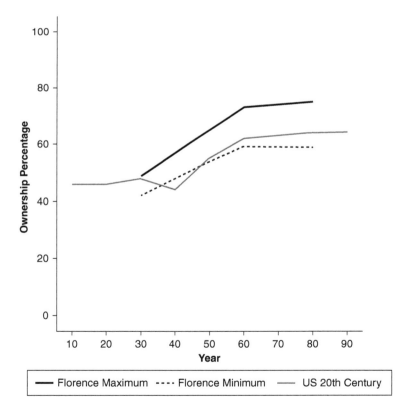

Figure 5.3 Homeownership rates: fifteenth-century Florence and twentieth-century United States. Florentine values calculated by author.
Sources: Herlihy and Klapisch-Zuber, *Census and Property Survey*; United States data: Soltow, *Men and Wealth*, 50.

Table 5.5 Homeownership rates in Organization of Economic Cooperation and Development (OECD) countries, circa 1992 and circa 2004

Country	ca. 1992	ca. 2004
Australia	71.4%	69.5%
Austria	46.3%	51.6%
Belgium	67.7%	71.7%
Canada	61.3%	68.9%
Denmark	51.0%	51.6%
Finland	65.4%	66.0%
France	55.3%	54.8%
Germany	36.3%	41.0%
Greece	83.1%	73.2%
Ireland	79.6%	81.4%
Italy	64.2%	67.9%
Luxembourg	71.6%	69.3%
Mexico	77.2%	70.7%
Netherlands	47.5%	55.4%
Spain	77.8%	83.2%
Switzerland	33.1%	38.4%
United Kingdom	67.9%	70.7%
United States	66.2%	68.7%

Source: D. Andrews and A. Caldera Sánchez, "Drivers of Homeownership Rates in Selected OECD Countries," *OECD Economics Department* (2011), 9. http://dx.doi.org/10.1787/5kgg9mcwc7jf-en. Not all the data are from 1992 or from 2004. Instead of 1992, the data are from: 1987 for Austria; 1990 for Spain; 1991 for Italy; 1994 for Canada, France, Germany, Mexico and the Netherlands; 1995 for Australia, Belgium, Finland, Greece and Ireland; 1997 for Luxembourg and the United States. Instead of 2004, the data are from: 2003 for Australia and 2007 for Germany and United States.

The final comparison is with contemporary homeownership rates from OECD countries. Table 5.5 shows Quattrocento Florentine homeownership rates on par with late twentieth- and early twenty-first century OECD homeownership rates.

If homeownership is taken as a key standard of well-being, then the Quattrocento Florentines were well-off. However, this idea should not be taken too far. Florentine houses were not that valuable compared to modern American and European markets due to low technology, high interest rates, lack of a mortgage market, the low quality of homes and other reasons.

The comparatively high homeownership rate and subsequent increase in that rate has significant implications for Florentine society. The access to real property is an important characteristic of an egalitarian society. Homeownership rates are a commonly used statistic to measure economic progress in the modern world. An increase in homeownership implies greater equality. Further, the ease of movement between owning and renting implies that there were significant opportunities to improve one's social position.

Table 5.6 Florentine share of households by demographic category, 1427–80

Share of Households	1427	1458	1480
Arte Maggiore	8%	7%	10%
Core Gonfalone	16%	18%	17%
Has Surname	37%	45%	52%
Female Headed	14%	16%	11%
Married Male	60%	63%	60%
Migrant	12%	6%	4%
No Occupation	46%	63%	62%
Sottoposti	12%	7%	5%

Source: Herlihy and Klapisch-Zuber, *Census and Property Survey*. Calculation by author.

Who Were the New Homeowners?

The demographic characteristics underlying homeownership changed during the Quattrocento as homeownership expanded into a broader segment of Florentine society. This section and the next examine those demographic changes using the same set of variables. The positive correlation among several of the variables permits greater confidence in this result. Increasing property assets are positively correlated with social status measures, such as having a surname and being a member of the *arte maggiore*. These alternative specifications mean that even if the interpretation of property holdings changes due to the changing tax base, the interpretation of these other variables does not. These other variables confirm the broadening homeownership in Florentine society.

Table 5.6 presents the households of Florence divided into key social categories. The arte maggiore households in this data set amounted to 9.05 percent in 1427, 8.33 percent in 1458 and 11.31 percent in 1480. The percentage of sottoposti and migrants dropped during this time. The percentages of women, sottoposti and migrants who were household heads also dropped, while the percentages of arte maggiore rose.

The percentage of those without occupations and who owned homes also rose. However, none of these changes was large enough, alone or in combination, to account for more than a small percentage of the change in homeownership rates.

The subsidy explanation would imply that homeownership broadened into new social groups, and this is exactly what happened (see Table 5.7). The 1427 homeownership rate was below the 1458 and 1480 average for every demographic category. The less wealthy tended to increase their homeownership rates the most. The sottoposti rate increased more than 30 percent, and the migrant rate also increased about 30 percent. Wealthier categories, such as arte maggiore and surnamed households, had smaller gains.

Tables 5.8A through 5.10B present the relationship of homeownership with a set of quantitative variables: household size, age of household head and property assets. Tables 5.8A and 5.8B present the relationship with household size. The 1427 homeownership rate was below the average in 1458 and 1480 for every size of household.

Table 5.7 Florentine homeownership by demographic category, 1427–80

Ownership Rates	1427	1458	1480
Arte Maggiore	58%	57%	74%
Core Gonfalone	47%	59%	56%
Has Surname	56%	58%	61%
Female Headed	41%	47%	52%
Married Male	45%	65%	65%
Migrant	30%	53%	20%
No Occupation	52%	57%	60%
Sottoposti	32%	74%	63%

Source: Herlihy and Klapisch-Zuber, *Census and Property Survey*. Calculation by author.]

Table 5.8A Florentine ownership rate by household size, 1427–80

Ownership Rate by Household Size	1427	1458	1480
1	37%	43%	43%
2	40%	61%	51%
3	38%	61%	65%
4	43%	54%	58%
5	46%	57%	66%
6–10	53%	66%	66%
11–15	74%	74%	77%
16–20	52%	100%	75%
20+	80%	100%	100%

Source: Herlihy and Klapisch-Zuber, *Census and Property Survey*. Calculation by author.

Table 5.8B Florentine owner and renter household size descriptive statistics, 1427–80

Household Size	1427		1458		1480	
	Owners	Renters	Owners	Renters	Owners	Renters
Mean	4.50	3.65	5.30	4.25	5.85	4.47
Std. Error	0.05	0.03	0.18	0.17	0.20	0.20
Std. Dev.	3.07	2.46	3.68	2.88	4.19	3.38
N	4104	5242	437	293	441	282

Std. Dev.: Standard deviation
N: Sample size
Source: Herlihy and Klapisch-Zuber, *Census and Property Survey*. Calculation by author.

Table 5.9A Florentine ownership rate by age, 1427–80

Ownership Rate by Age	1427	1458	1480
0–15	53%	59%	53%
16–24	43%	52%	52%
25–34	38%	57%	50%
35–44	41%	63%	63%
45–54	45%	63%	56%
55–64	47%	54%	68%
65+	51%	65%	71%

Source: Herlihy and Klapisch-Zuber, *Census and Property Survey*. Calculation by author.

Table 5.9B Florentine owner and renter age descriptive statistics, 1427–80

	1427		1458		1480	
Age	Owners	Renters	Owners	Renters	Owners	Renters
Mean	47.80	45.49	48.04	47.77	49.71	45.31
Std. Error	0.27	0.23	0.78	1.01	0.79	0.93
Std. Dev.	17.24	16.22	16.02	17.02	16.38	15.51
N	4104	5242	437	293	441	282

Std. Dev.: Standard deviation
N: Sample size
Source: Herlihy and Klapisch-Zuber, *Census and Property Survey*. Calculation by author.

Table 5.10A Florentine ownership rate by property assets level, 1427–80

Ownership Rate by Property Assets	1427	1458	1480
0	24%	58%	53%
1–249	45%	63%	58%
250–999	56%	68%	61%
1000–1999	69%	77%	76%
2000+	81%	81%	87%

Source: Herlihy and Klapisch-Zuber, *Census and Property Survey*. Calculation by author

The subsidy would induce fiscal households to pool assets to buy a home. This household consolidation could have led to an increase in the mean size of fiscal households. Both owner and renter household sizes increased over time. The mean size of owner households grew by 30 percent and renter households by 22 percent. There was no apparent increase in the number of servants or slaves. The renter households appear to have stopped growing after 1458. However, the owner households continued to grow in size between 1458 and 1480. This difference rules out some unknown factor increasing household size. The household size increase during the Quattrocento therefore supports the subsidy theory.

Table 5.10B Florentine owner and renter property assets level descriptive statistics, 1427–80

Property Assets	1427		1458		1480	
	Owners	Renters	Owners	Renters	Owners	Renters
Mean	683.26	228.65	231.63	105.92	582.41	352.25
Std. Error	22.51	7.56	34.13	21.86	41.10	28.16
Std. Dev.	1442.33	547.10	713.51	374.16	863.08	472.91
N	4104	5242	437	293	441	282

Std. Dev.: Standard deviation
N: Sample size
Source: Herlihy and Klapisch-Zuber, *Census and Property Survey*. Calculation by author.

The relationship with household head age is presented in Tables 5.9A and 5.9B. The 1427 homeownership rate was below the average in 1458 and 1480 for every age category. Homeownership increased for all age groups. Some children owned homes through the inheritance received by their fiscal household.

The relationship with household assets is presented in Tables 5.10A and 5.10B. In order to ensure comparability, this measure includes only the immovable assets from all three years. There should be a downward bias in immovable assets, because there was a drop in household immovable assets in 1480 due to a war in the years previous, and the changing list of tax exemptions between 1427 and later in the Quattrocento would have induced households to transfer wealth from property assets to other investments.[83] Owners were wealthier than renters. There was an active property market. Although they did not own homes, 52 percent of the renters in 1427 owned some property.[84] None of the statistics shown in this section contradict the subsidy explanation; rather, all of them generally support it.

A Model of Changing Homeownership Rates

This section presents a regression analysis of the changing Florentine homeownership patterns during the Quattrocento. A regression estimates an equation that explains a dependent variable, in this case homeownership, in terms of a set of independent variables. Here the independent variables include catasto date, wealth, age, household size and a set of demographic dummy variables as well as interaction terms by date.

Owners include only those households specifically coded as homeowners. The renters include households coded as renters and those without any coding. The missing households are those coded as people living with another fiscal household. Sensitivity

---

83 Anthony Molho, *Marriage Alliance in Late Medieval Florence* (Cambridge, MA: Harvard University Press, 1994), 363.
84 Herlihy and Klapisch-Zuber, *Census and Property Survey*. Calculation by author.

analyses were run using a variety of other specifications, and the results did not change appreciably.

A set of independent variables that help characterize the homeownership decision is included. A constant term is included in the regression. This measures the likelihood of homeownership during the Quattrocento in the absence of all other variables. A dummy variable (DUM) indicating whether the observation was from 1458 or 1480 (DUM5880) was included in the regression. The coefficients on the pure dummy variables should be positive. The 1458 and 1480 observations are not split, because the sample was bigger and the percentage differences between 1458 and 1480 were not great. Using just one time-period dummy is more parsimonious. This specification assumes the impact of the catasto itself as opposed to any differences between 1458 and 1480. Regressions were run with dummies for 1458 (DUM58) and 1480 (DUM80), and similar results were obtained.

The measure of wealth is the property (immovable) assets (VPROP). The underlying demographic variables are age (AGEHD) and household size (NPEO). The squared terms (XXX2) of all three were included. One would expect homeownership to increase as the age of the household head and as the household size increased.

Dummy variables for demographic characteristics of the household head were included in the regression. These were in the format XXXDUM and include holding a sottoposti occupation (SOTTODUM), holding no identified occupation (NOCCDUM), being a migrant (MIGDUM), having a family surname (FAMDUM) and being a female (FEMDUM). Being a member of an arte maggiore (AMDUM) was tested but left out of the presentation equation, because there is a large overlap between the AM and FAM variables. One would expect this because the arte maggiore were the leading business families of Florence, and the families with surnames had achieved some form of distinction either in the past or in the present (or both).

Each corresponding late Quattrocento interaction term is in the form of XXX5880 and equal to the DUM5880 multiplied by the associated variable. The XXX58 and XXX80, calculated similarly, were also tested but are not reported.

The subsidy explanation implies that the price of owning a home went down for everyone. This would imply that DUM5880 would be positive and significant. It would also imply that homeownership rates among poorer and lower social status households should increase with respect to wealthier and higher social status households. This implies that the regression should exhibit a form of mean reversion in the coefficients. In other words, an overall positive coefficient, such as in FAMDUM, should be matched by a negative coefficient on the corresponding late Quattrocento interaction term (FAM5880) and vice versa. Further, the coefficient on VPROP should be positive, and the interaction terms for 1458 and 1480 immovable assets (VPROP5880) should be negative and significant.

Table 5.11 presents the regression results for 'three regression specifications. The first includes only the wealth variables, and the results support the subsidy explanation. The coefficients on DUM5880 and on VPROP are positive, and the coefficient on the wealth interaction term, VPROP5880, is negative.

The second regression specification includes the wealth variables along with the variables of age and household size. These results also support the subsidy explanation. The dummy DUM5880 is positive and significant as expected. Homeownership with respect

Table 5.11 Quattrocento homeownership changes: logistic regression results

Dependent Variable: Homeownership			
N	10799	10,311	10,311
Log Likelihood	−6988.9039	−6,566.93	−6,462.51
Significance Level of LR	0.00	0.00	0.00
Variable	Coeff	Coeff	Coeff
Constant	−0.616***	−0.81***	−1.17***
DUM5880	0.88***	0.55	1.10***
VPROP	1.01E-03***	1.25E-03***	0***
VPROP5880	−5.08E-04***	−9.57E-04***	0***
VPROP2	−1.84E-08***	−1.02E-07***	0***
VPROP25880	2.29E-08	1.34E-07*	0
AGEHHHD		−0.019***	−0.01
AGE5880		0.014	0.01
AGEHHHD2		3.21E-04***	0***
AGE25880		−2.03E-04	0
NPEO		0.082***	0.11***
NPEO5880		0.034	-0.03
NPEO2		−3.40E-03*	0**
NPEO25880		8.36E-04	0
FAMDUM			0.12**
FAM5880			−0.37***
FEMDUM			−0.13
FEM5880			−0.11
MIGDUM			−0.71***
MIG5880			−0.12
NOCCDUM			0.44***
NOCC5880			−0.43***
SOTTODUM			−0.12
SOTTO5880			0.48*

N: Sample size
LR: Likelihood ratio
***Statistical significance at the 99 percent level.
**Statistical significance at the 95 percent level.
*Statistical significance at the 90 percent level.
Source: Herlihy and Klapisch-Zuber, *Census and Property Survey*. Calculation by author. Homeownership is defined in the text. The logistic regression was adjusted for heteroskedasticity.

to AGE and AGE2 had a slight U shape, declining at younger ages and increasing at older ages. This relationship did not change during the century. The household size, NPEO, is positive and significant as expected. Its curve did not change during the century. The property wealth, VPROP, is positive and significant, and the coefficient on VPROP5880 is negative.

The third regression specification had similar results and also confirms the subsidy explanation. The DUM5880, VPROPXXX, AGEXXX and NPEOXXX results were just as above. Homeownership with respect to AGE and AGE2 had a slight U shape, declining at younger ages and increasing at older ages. This relationship did not change during the century. The AGE and NPEO curves did not change during the century. The property wealth VPROP has a statistically significant inverted-U shape that exhibited mean reversion. The social status dummy coefficients are generally as expected. Having a surname (FAMDUM) and having no occupation (NOCCDUM) are positive and significant. Being a woman (FEMDUM) has no effect on homeownership, which could be a dowry effect. Being a migrant (MIGDUM) is negative and significant as expected. Working as a sottoposto (SOTTO5880) increased one's likelihood of owning a home as the century progressed compared with earlier years. A mean reversion effect is visible for the FAM, FEM, MIG, NOCC and SOTTO variables.

All three results fit the expectations of the subsidy explanation. Sensitivity analyses, including XXX58 and XXX80 dummies substituting for the XXX5880 dummy and all combinations of the social characteristics dummies, were run to increase the confidence in the results. None of the results from the other regressions contradict the results presented above.

Conclusions

This analysis leads to several conclusions. First, the Renaissance Florentine building boom was a price response to a subsidy and not a result of conspicuous consumption. Other potential explanations—an interest rate decrease, a population increase or a wealth increase—also do not fit the observations well. The palace construction was paralleled by a general homeownership increase.

The subsidy explanation fits better than the conspicuous consumption explanation for several reasons. To begin with, the construction primarily used private rather than public funds. In addition, the impact was broad and caused a citywide homeownership rate increase. Further, both the private palace construction and the homeownership increase occurred while the subsidy was in effect. Finally, the level of palace construction appears to have responded to the subsidy.

These results lead to a broader picture of the Florentine economy. The decrease in the wealth required to own a home implies that the price of homeownership decreased over the course of the Quattrocento. The impact of the subsidy also clearly implies that Florentine capital markets worked well. The ability to shift assets across categories implies market efficiency, competitiveness, freedom and liquidity.

Incentivizing artistic creation is somewhat ironic given the usual economists' picture of tax avoidance. William Fischel memorably points out that the avoidance of one especially high property tax led to hairy and ugly cattle in one New Hampshire locality.[85] The Florentine private palaces are a much more attractive example.

---

85   William A. Fischel, "Property Taxation and the Tiebout Model: Evidence for the Benefit View from Zoning and Voting," *Journal of Economic Literature* 30, no. 1 (1992): 171–77.

Viewing the building of the great Florentine private palaces as the result of a tax loophole rather than one of sudden, inexplicable, conspicuous consumption does not reduce their artistic value in any way. It simply provides an explanation that fits better in the larger context of Florentine history.

Next, two major strands of Florentine historiography are linked in an unexpected way. The catasto is widely seen either as a fair and progressive tax assessment or a result of the Quattrocento Florentine chronic shortage of government funds. The palace building and associated urban renewal are seen either as a great burst of creativity, an oppression of the poor or both simultaneously. This chapter's study implies that these strands were inextricably linked.

The result suggests that the relationship between creating a loophole for a wealth-inelastic asset and the perception of tax fairness and social distance in Florence is extremely complicated. Today, a homeownership tax exemption would be considered progressive. In some parts of the United States such a tax exemption is called a homestead exemption and is a populist idea. Some historians see palace building as a form of urban renewal.[86] The consolidation of many homes into one would have dislocated families and created a growing gap between rich and poor in Renaissance Florence, and it also would have changed how that gap was manifested. The increasing progressivity of the catasti during the Quattrocento would have increased the value of the owner-occupied-home tax loophole for wealthier households as opposed to poorer households. This would have been an additional incentive for the construction of private palaces.

In addition, the results shown in this study have implications for the history of art and Florentine society. Although the point has been amply demonstrated, the results here provide further proof that there was no semblance of a court culture that led to the start of the High Renaissance. The palace-building boom was a private-sector phenomenon influenced by decreasing relative prices, not increasing conspicuous consumption.

These results can be taken further to imply a broader context existed for Michael Baxandall's link between business and art. He observes that the cost of artists' paint in commissioned paintings is correlated with the status of the family and the importance of the figure in the painting.[87] These paintings were generally produced by families for their homes. Linking the price of the paint to a painting takes on new meaning if the painting was a way to take advantage of a kind of tax loophole. The results in this study combined with Baxandall's link also imply that the subsidy on homes and furnishings increased the number of artists and architects. This leads to several broader questions. Did the catasto accelerate the artistic Renaissance? Did the subsidy shift the creativity in business that had made Florentines so wealthy into artistic expression? These are questions for another study.

Finally, this study shows that tax laws could have a dramatic impact on the economy. If this loophole led to palace building, then the impact of this and other loopholes bears further examination.

---

86 Goldthwaite, *Building of Renaissance Florence*, 15; Cohn, *Laboring Classes*, 121–27.
87 Baxandall, *Painting and Experience*, 3–23.

Appendix 5A: Opportunity Cost Model of Homeownership

This appendix explains the opportunity cost model of homeownership and provides a rationale for its use. The idea is based on the observation that homeownership, as opposed to renting, is a choice. The assumption is that householders can either own or rent. The third option, moving in with another household, is discounted in modern economic theory; it seems unlikely that fiscal households would merge in this way. The 1427 catasto finds that few households took this third option.

The increasing ownership rate had to be due to either changing relative prices or to a shift outward of the entire curve.

The price of homeownership as opposed to renting, based on the Jorgensen model, is

$$P_t = \{[r_t V_t + T_t] + D_t + M_t - (dV/dt)_t\}/PL_t,$$

where
P: User costs of housing,
V: Market value of the house,
r: Individual's opportunity cost of capital,
T: Net taxes on housing (in Quattrocento Florence this is = 0 or < 0),
D: Depreciation,
M: Maintenance,
$(dV/dt)_t$: Expected capital gain in period t and
PL: General price level.[88]

One can assume that the change in PL, V, D and M is zero during the Quattrocento. Only the r_t and the T_t are subject to change.

This model provides a way to contextualize the five potential explanations brought up in this study. The shift in relative prices would imply either the subsidy explanation with a decrease in T_t or the interest rate explanation with a decrease in r_t. An outward shift of the curve could imply either the conspicuous consumption, population or wealth explanations.

---

88 This equation is based on Dougherty and Van Order, "Housing Costs"; Rosen, Rosen and Holtz-Eakin, "Housing Tenure"; Topel and Rosen, "Housing Investment."

Chapter Six

NOT GETTING AHEAD IN LIFE: THE LACK OF LIFE-CYCLE WEALTH ACCUMULATION IN QUATTROCENTO TUSCANY

Introduction

One of the bedrock empirical relationships in modern economics is that, except under rare circumstances, earnings, income and wealth increase as one ages. Beyond the obvious economic implications, this relationship has important social implications. Alberti's treatise on the family recognizes the importance of age when he assigns the father the leadership of the family.[1] The economic advantage of elders over juniors provides both the older a higher status and the younger an aspiration. This relationship appears entirely natural; older people can simply become richer if they are able to store their wealth over time. Natural economic production above subsistence level would seem to take care of the rest. Similarly, earnings and income increase by age if people build up their workplace skills over time. Research based on data from the nineteenth century and later confirms this relationship, but a lack of data has impeded work on earlier periods.

This chapter presents evidence of negligible life-cycle wealth accumulation in *Quattrocento* Tuscany in a series of steps. It begins by discussing the relevant economics literature. Next, it presents the results of the basic statistical analysis using data from the 1427 Florentine *catasto*.[2] Expanding on this, it attempts to determine whether problems with the data reduced the association between age and wealth. This analysis finds that none of these potential problems were significant. The final step extends the basic analyses above. First, it looks at the implied relationship between household size, wealth and age. Most historians accept that Quattrocento Tuscany was a Malthusian society; both wealth and age are strongly and positively associated with household size. This would normally imply, in turn, that wealth, age and household size are closely related due to transitivity. This section looks at the underlying mathematics that might create a lack of transitivity and examines possible explanations. Second, it starts from the joint assumptions that, despite the analyses and tests in part two, some portion of the household's

---

1 Leon Battista Alberti, *I Libri della Famiglia*, ed. Girolamo Mancini (Florence: G. Carnesecchi e Figli, 1908), 14–25; Alberti, *The Family in Renaissance Florence*, trans. Renée Neu Watkins (Columbia: University of South Carolina Press, 1969), 36–46.
2 The catasto was a net wealth tax applied to the city of Florence and to surrounding areas of Tuscany under Florentine control. (See appendix 3A for more information.)

wealth was unreported and that the standard modern model of life-cycle wealth accumulation holds. It then uses these assumptions to develop a simulation to measure how
much wealth would have been unreported had the life-cycle wealth accumulation profile
matched that of modern America. The unreported wealth seems too large to rehabilitate
the standard modern model. The chapter concludes by examining three possible explanations for the lack of a positive correlation beween age and wealth: vast missing assets,
extreme poverty and behavioral differences. The missing asset and poverty explanations
could form part of the story, but do not seem able to explain everything. Society-wide
behavioral explanations, such as gifting and dowries, charitable giving and a lack of
demand for life-cycle fhuman capital accumulation could make up the difference.

Life-Cycle Wealth Accumulation Theory

Numerous modern studies support an upward sloping relationship between life-cycle
and wealth accumulation.[3] This relationship holds for diverse modern populations and is
known to hold at least as far back as the mid-nineteenth century.[4] Occupation and status

3   J. Fisher, "Income, Spending, and Saving Patterns of Consumer Units in Different Age Groups,"
     in *Studies in Income and Wealth*, vol. 15 (New York: National Bureau of Economic Research,
     1952); M. A. King and L-D. L. Dicks-Mireaux, "Asset Holding and the Life-Cycle," *Economic
     Journal* 92 (1982): 247–67; M. Landsberger, "The Life-Cycle Hypothesis: A Reinterpretation
     and Empirical Test," *American Economic Review* 60 (1970): 175–84; John B. Lansing and John
     Sonquist, "A Cohort Analysis of Changes in the Distribution of Wealth," in *Six Papers on the
     Size Distribution of Income and Wealth*, ed. Lee Soltow (New York: National Bureau of Economic
     Research, 1969), 31–74; Harold Lydall, "The Life Cycle in Income, Saving, and Asset
     Ownership," *Econometrica* 23, no. 2 (1955): 131–50; Franco Modigliani and A. K. Ando, "The
     'Life-Cycle' Hypothesis of Saving: Aggregate Implications and Tests," *American Economic Review*
     53, no. 1 (1963): 55–84; K. Nagatani, "Life-Cycle Saving: Theory and Fact," *American Economic
     Review* 62 (1972): 344–53; A. F. Shorrocks, "The Age-Wealth Relationship: A Cross-Section
     and Cohort Analysis," *Review of Economics and Statistics* 57, no. 2 (1975): 155–63; Edward N.
     Wolff, "The Accumulation of Household Wealth over the Life-Cycle: A Microdata Analysis,"
     Review of Income and Wealth 27, no. 1 (1981): 75–79; Lingxin Hao, "Wealth of Immigrant and
     Native-Born Americans," *International Migration Review* 38, no. 2 (2004): 518–46.
4   David W. Galenson and Clayne L. Pope, "Precedence and Wealth: Evidence from Nineteenth-
     Century Utah," in *Strategic Factors in Nineteenth-Century American Economic History: A Volume to
     Honor Robert W. Fogel*, ed. Claudia Goldin and Hugh Rockoff (Chicago: University of Chicago
     Press, 1993), 225–42; J. R. Kearl and Clayne L. Pope, "Choices, Rents, and Luck: Economic
     Mobility of Nineteenth-Century Utah Households," in *Long-Term Factors in American Economic
     Growth*, ed. Stanley L. Engerman and Robert E. Gallman (Chicago: University of Chicago
     Press, 1986), 215–60, on life-cycle effects; David W. Galenson and Clayne L. Pope, "Economic
     and Geographic Mobility on the Farming Frontier: Evidence from Appanoose County, Iowa,
     1850–1870," *Journal of Economic History* 49, no. 4 (1989): 635–55, on life-cycle and migrancy-
     status effects; Jeremy Atack and Fred Bateman, "Egalitarianism, Inequality, and Age: The
     Rural North in 1860," *Journal of Economic History* 41, no. 1 (1981): 85–93, on life-cycle, gen-
     der and occupational effects; Joseph P. Ferrie, "The Wealth Accumulation of Antebellum
     European Immigrants to the U.S., 1840–60," *Journal of Economic History* 54, no. 1 (1994): 1–
     33, David W. Galenson, "Economic Opportunity on the Urban Frontier: Nativity, Work and

can affect wealth-accumulation patterns.[5] Much of the current debate is not about the upward slope of the curve, but rather about the existence and size of the downward-sloping portion of the curve during old age.[6] The only consistent modern exceptions occur among poor populations.[7] This observation has been put into practice. For example, Muhammad Yunus bases his microlending theory on the proposition that financial relationships are fundamentally different among the very poor.[8]

The life-cycle wealth accumulation relationship, however, does not appear to hold in Quattrocento Tuscany. Herlihy and Klapisch-Zuber, as part of their magisterial *Les Toscans et leurs familles*, published in 1978, note that household wealth did not increase with respect to the age of the household head.[9] Figure 6.1 presents a scatterplot of taxable wealth by age of household head for Florence in 1427. The lack of relationship, noted almost casually because it was so well supported by the data, directly contradicts virtually all studies of modern life-cycle earnings, income and wealth. The two authors attribute the lack of a relationship to inheritance; however, there is no strong evidence one way or the other on this point.[10] The relatively high percentage of youths owning homes (see Chapter 4) does highlight the importance of intergenerational wealth transfer. The role of inheritance in the relationship between age and wealth in the modern world is

---

Wealth in Early Chicago," *Journal of Economic History* 51, no. 3 (1991): 581–603; and Donald F. Schaefer, "A Model of Migration and Wealth Accumulation: Farmers at the Antebellum Southern Frontier," *Explorations in Economic History* 24 (1987): 130–57, on life-cycle, occupational and migrancy-status effects; J. R. Kearl, Clayne L. Pope and Larry T. Wimmer, "Household Wealth in a Settlement Community," *Journal of Economic History* 40, no. 3 (1980): 477–96, on life-cycle, gender, occupational and migrancy-status effects; Richard H. Steckel, "Poverty and Prosperity: A Longitudinal Study of Wealth Accumulation, 1850–1860," *Review of Economics and Statistics* 72, no. 2 (1990): 275–85, on occupational, migrancy-status and household-size effects.

5　For an analysis of and citations about the contemporary economy, see Lisa A. Keister, *Wealth in America: Trends in Wealth Inequality* (Cambridge, UK: Cambridge University Press, 2000), 204. For an analysis of the historical United States economy, see Atack and Bateman, "Egalitarianism, Inequality, and Age"; Ferrie, "Wealth Accumulation"; Galenson, "Economic Opportunity"; Schaefer, "Model of Migration and Wealth Accumulation"; Kearl, Pope and Wimmer, "Household Wealth in a Settlement Community"; Steckel, "Poverty and Prosperity."

6　Thad W. Mirer, "The Wealth-Age Relation among the Aged," *American Economic Review* 69, no. 3 (1979): 435–43; Keister, *Wealth in America*, 202–11.

7　On the differences between rich and poor, see Atack and Bateman, "Egalitarianism, Inequality, and Age"; Schaefer, "Model of Migration and Wealth Accumulation." On the differences between African Americans and the general population, see Mirer, "The Wealth-Age Relation"; James J. Heckman, "A Life Cycle Model of Earnings, Learning, and Consumption," *Journal of Political Economy* 84, no. 4, pt. 2 (1976): S11–44.

8　Muhammad Yunus, *Banker to the Poor: Micro-lending and the Battle against World Poverty* (1999; New York: Perseus Books Group, 2007), ix.

9　David Herlihy and Christiane Klapisch-Zuber, *Les Toscans et leurs familles: Une étude du Catasto Florentine de 1427* (Paris: Fondation nationale des sciences politiques, 1978), 492–93; David Herlihy and Christiane Klapisch-Zuber, *The Tuscans and Their Families* (New Haven, CT: Yale University Press, 1985), 306–7.

10　Herlihy and Klapisch-Zuber, *Les Toscans*, 491; Herlihy and Klapisch-Zuber, *Tuscans*, 303.

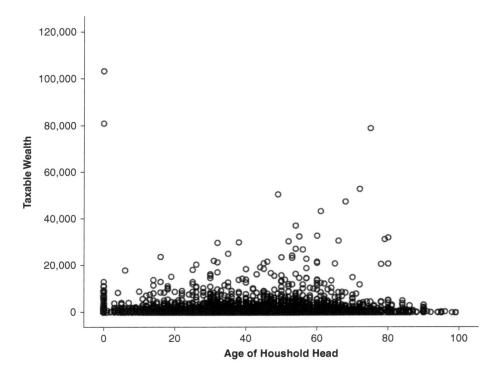

Figure 6.1 Scatterplot of taxable wealth by age of household head, City of Florence, 1427
Source: David Herlihy and Christiane Klapisch-Zuber. *Census and Property Survey of Florentine Domains and the City of Verona in Fifteenth-Century Italy* [machine-readable data file]. Cambridge, MA: David Herlihy, Harvard University, Department of History and Paris, France: Christiane Klapisch-Zuber, Ecole Pratique des Hautes Etudes [producers], 1977. Madison: University of Wisconsin, Data and Program Library Service [distributor], 1981. Calculation by author.

debated, with early research being conducted by scholars including John Brittain. More recently, Thomas Piketty has revived the debate, though Edward N. Wolff has shown the effect in modern America is limited.[11]

In comparison with a modern life-cycle income and wealth curve, the Florentine curve is strikingly flat (see Fig. 6.2). Since the age that people first enter the workforce differs between the two periods, age 21 was chosen as the initial age for study. Florentines generally entered the workforce at 16.[12] Figure 6.3 shows the relationship between the

---

11 John Brittain, *Inheritance and the Inequality of Material Wealth* (Washington, DC: Brookings Institution, 1978); Thomas Piketty, *Capital in the Twenty-First Century*, trans. Arthur Goldhammer (Cambridge, MA: Harvard University Press, 2014), 377–429; Edward N. Wolff, *Inheriting Wealth in America: Future Boom or Bust?* (Oxford, UK: Oxford University Press, 2015).

12 Paul F. Grendler, *Schooling in Renaissance Italy: Literacy and Learning, 1300–1600* (Baltimore: Johns Hopkins University Press, 1989), 75.

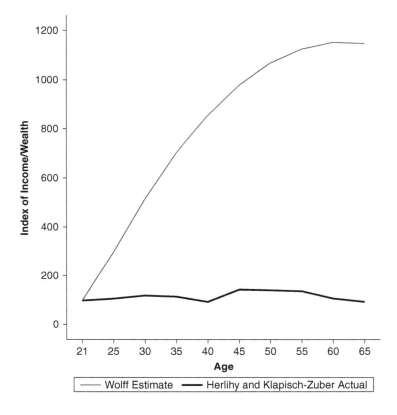

Figure 6.2 Comparison of Florence, 1427, taxable wealth with fitted household wealth by age, United States, 1979

Sources: Herlihy and Klapisch-Zuber, *Census and Property Survey*; Wolff, "Accumulation of Household Wealth over the Life-Cycle." Fitted wealth calculated based on best-fit equation of household wealth as a function of age from Wolff. Calculation by author.

mean taxable wealth and the mean age by occupation. There is no clear relationship between wealth and age. Wealthier occupations are not older, and poorer occupations are not younger. The occupations are largely clustered in one general location between ages 40 and 55 and between 0 and 1,000 florins. Many of the outliers represent occupations with a few or only one practitioner.

Any observed relationship between age and wealth would probably be long term. A flat age-wealth relationship at any point in time implies that the relationship had been flat, or approximately flat, for decades. In order to reach a flat distribution, people in their 50s would have had to experience no significant wealth accumulation over a span of nearly four decades. Similarly, a sudden shift among those just entering the workforce would take at least four decades to work through the system. This suggests that a total span of nearly a century is represented by these data.

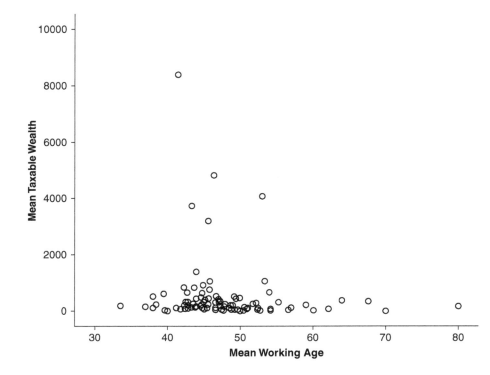

Figure 6.3 Scatterplot of mean taxable wealth by mean working age of occupation, City of Florence, 1427
Source: Herlihy and Klapisch-Zuber, *Census and Property Survey*. Calculation by author.

The Catasto Data

The analysis in this study is based on the standard regression model used to examine data from the nineteenth century onward in the life-cycle wealth accumulation literature.[13] The data here come from records of the Quattrocento Florentine catasto. (For more on the quality of these data, see Appendix 3A.) This model uses data on household head's gender and age and household wealth. The basic statistical model is a regression with a quadratic function of age as the independent variable and some measure of earnings, income or wealth as the dependent variable. In this context, age can be seen as the driving force of wealth accumulation. A constant is included to account for endowments or inheritance. The definition of a household head was well developed in contemporary law.[14]

---

13 Wolff, "Accumulation of Household Wealth over the Life-Cycle"; Atack and Bateman, "Egalitarianism, Inequality, and Age"; Schaefer, "Migration and Wealth Accumulation"; Mirer, "Wealth-Age Relation."

14 Rebecca Jean Emigh, "What Influences Official Information? Exploring Aggregate Microhistories of the Catasto of 1427," in *Small Worlds: Method, Meaning, and Narrative in Microhistory*, ed. James F. Brooks, Christopher R. N. DeCorse and John Walton (Santa Fe: School for Advanced Research Press, 2008), 208.

Close examination of the age data finds them generally reliable. Herlihy and Klapisch-Zuber find age heaping in the data but no particular bias.[15] In the context of the particular analysis in this study, age heaping would not be a problem if the errors are randomly distributed in a normal distribution with mean zero. Even with a nonnormal distribution of errors, there would be only a minor shift in the estimations based on ages. Using data from the 1480 catasto, the Decima Scalata, Molho conducts a comprehensive analysis and finds that young women's ages were generally biased downward; these women rarely headed households. Molho concludes, however, that the problem was not severe.[16] De Roover points out that the 1480 catasto was much less accurate than earlier catasti, suggesting that the Molho estimate of bias is probably an upper bound for bias in the 1427 data.[17] Together these observations imply errors in the age data that pose no significant problem. The regressions are restricted to working-age males in order to minimize outliers from younger households with large reported wealth. The reported regressions include only male household heads of age 16 and older.[18]

The dependent variable, wealth, is used in log form rather than level form.[19] There is good reason to believe the catasto wealth data are even more accurate than the age data. (See Appendix 3A.) The overall sample is skewed toward wealthier households, because the data come from tax returns. Poorer households are likely to be underrepresented, because the goal of the catasto was to raise revenue. The medieval fiscal household, in comparison with the modern census household, tended to bias upward the relationship between earnings and age. Younger children, even into adulthood, stayed in the household and continued to produce wealth that was aggregated as part of the fiscal household.

Household net wealth equals taxable assets net of liabilities where the assets equal the sum of three portfolio components: immovable assets, movable assets and Monte assets.[20] The home and its furnishings were exempt. The definitions of the asset categories differ from modern standards. Immovable assets or goods were mostly real estate. The category often included both urban and rural rental properties and sharecroppers. For example, the 1427 catasto declaration of Lorenzo Ghiberti, sculptor, who lived in Florence, includes "a piece of land in the parish of S. Donato in Fronzano [worth]

---

15 Herlihy and Klapisch-Zuber, *Les Toscans*, 352–70.
16 Anthony Molho, "Deception and Marriage Strategy in Renaissance Florence: The Case of Women's Ages," *Renaissance Quarterly* 41 (1988): 193–217. Molho's estimates are based on the 1480 catasto (Decima Scalata). De Roover points out that the 1480 catasto was much less accurate than earlier catasti. Raymond de Roover, *The Rise and Decline of the Medici Bank 1397–1494* (Cambridge, MA: Harvard University Press, 1963), 24. Hence, the Molho estimate of bias should be biased upward for the 1427 data.
17 De Roover, *Rise and Decline of the Medici Bank*, 24.
18 Regressions using the other age cutoffs were run with virtually identical results.
19 The variable in log form is multiplied by 10,000 in order to assist the rounding performance of the algorithm.
20 Sergio Tognetti, *Il Banco Cambini: Affari e mercati di una compagnia mercantile-bancaria nella Firenze del XV secolo* (Florence: Olschki, 1999), 13; Herlihy and Klapisch-Zuber, *Census and Property Survey*.

100 florins."[21] Movable assets or goods were mostly business materials. These included physical capital such as looms as well as inventories such as raw wool. The capital accumulation was short term. For example, most wool industry companies operated on renewable partnerships of three years. Of these, less than a quarter of companies operating in 1427 were running on a renewed partnership.[22] Movable assets could include anything from inventoried sculptures to weaving looms. A weaver might have had a loom worth 40 florins.[23] The same 1427 catasto declaration of Lorenzo Ghiberti notes he had "two pieces of bronze sculpture [...] made for a baptismal font in Siena." These were worth 400 florins. Ghiberti had been paid 290 florins, and he was owed 110 florins; therefore, the assessed valuation was 110 florins.[24] The implicit assumption here is that the payment for the sculpture had been converted into other assets or held in cash. The Monte assets category covers both Monte Comune and Monte delle doti holdings. The Monte Comune was the Florentine government bond market established in 1345. The Monte delle doti was a kind of dowry savings bond market established in 1425. (Chapter 2 covers these in greater detail.) Monte assets were widely held. Ghiberti had total Monte investments of 714 florins in 1427.[25] These three asset categories were not independent; there is substantial evidence that they were fungible. For example, Francesco Sacchetti in his *Sposizione* 35 equates Monte credits with immovable assets.[26] Further, there is extensive evidence that Monte credits could be encumbered by loans in order to purchase immovable and movable assets.[27]

Wealth was not consistently measured across the three categories of assets taxed by the catasto. Immovable assets, real property, were defined based on the income flow from real property assuming a 7 percent return. The value of the home was not included among the household's taxable assets. Movable assets, which included commercial assets and loans but excluded the value of animals and slaves, were assigned their fair market value. Monte assets, the Florentine version of public debt bonds, were valued at 50 percent of the face value.[28] The debts were also counted. The net wealth was the total assets minus

---

21 "The Declaration of Lorenzo Ghiberti, Sculptor," in *The Society of Renaissance Florence: A Documentary Study*, ed. Gene Brucker (New York: Harper & Row, 1971), 10; Giuseppe Gaye, *Carteggio inedito d'artisti dei secoli XIV, XV, XVI. Vol. 1: 1326–1500* (Florence: Giuseppe Molini, 1839), 104.

22 Hidetoshi Hoshino, *L'arte della lana nel basso medioevo in commercio della lana e il mercato dei panni fiorentini nei secoli XIII–XV* (Florence: Olschki, 1980), 228.

23 "The Declaration of Agnolo di Jacopo, Weaver," *Society of Renaissance Florence*, 12.

24 "Lorenzo Ghiberti," *Society of Renaissance Florence*, 10; Gaye, *Carteggio*, 104.

25 "Lorenzo Ghiberti," *Society of Renaissance Florence*, 11; Gaye, *Carteggio*, 104.

26 Julius Kirshner, "'Ubi est ille? Franco Sacchetti and the Monte Comune of Florence," *Speculum* 59, no. 3 (1984): 566.

27 Julius Kirshner and Jacob Klerman, "The Seven Percent Fund of Renaissance Florence," in *Banchi pubblici, banchi private e monti di pieta nell'Europa preindustriale: Amministrazione, tecniche operative e ruoli economici: Atti del convegno–Genova (1–6 ottobre 1990)* (Genova: Società Ligure di Storia Patria, 1991), 1: 367–98.

28 Otto Karmin, *La legge del Catasto fiorentino del 1427 (Testo, introduzione, e note)* (Florence: Bernardo Seeber, 1906), 17–18; Herlihy and Klapisch-Zuber, *Les Toscans*, 67; Herlihy and Klapisch-Zuber, *Tuscans*, 15.

the total debts.[29] These wealth components were not measured with equivalent accuracy. Monte asset values could be measured very precisely, because all ownership records were kept by the Florentine authorities. Immovable asset values could also be measured with relatively high precision, because they were based on rents that created matching assets and debts in two separate accounts. Movable asset values, however, were the most difficult to measure. The authorities recognized this fact and gradually eliminated them from taxation in the catasto. By 1458, movable assets were no longer assessed.[30]

The best measure of wealth in 1427 appears to be what the Florentine authorities considered taxable wealth, the net wealth with a floor at zero. As there was no incentive for the Florentine households to report, or authorities to validate, debts greater than assets, only those liabilities that would help to "zero out" assets would need to be counted. This is not a significant limitation, because long-term negative net wealth would be hard to sustain. Omission of the household's home is somewhat more problematic. However, various proxy measures for home value were conducted and found little effect. Although the analysis presented in this chapter at times uses as many as five different definitions of wealth, this is primarily due to an abundance of caution. Other research has used at most two definitions: total assets and taxable wealth.[31]

Overall, these differences between taxable wealth and net wealth should not pose a significant problem. Modern studies find a close connection between the life-cycle patterns of household earnings, income and wealth.[32] Earnings are income from labor provided, while net wealth is the total value of assets minus the total value of liabilities. Earnings and income are flow variables, while wealth is a stock variable. One would expect the connection between income and wealth to be closer in the Florentine than in the modern case. As noted above, the wealth data were largely calculated directly from income data. This relationship would have been reinforced by the labor-intensive production methods (see Appendix 3B for the example of the wool industry). The analysis in the next section runs regressions based on a decomposition of the total asset variable into these three components as a check of robustness.

The Statistical Results

This section analyzes the relationship between age and wealth in Quattrocento Tuscany using a variety of statistical specifications based on the standard model of life-cycle wealth accumulation. The 1427 City of Florence wealth is analyzed in aggregate and by components, the wealth in rural areas of Florentine Tuscany is analyzed in aggregate and immovable assets are analyzed for Florence during the mid and late Quattrocento.

---

29 Herlihy and Klapisch-Zuber, *Census and Property Survey*.
30 Elio Conti, *L'imposta diretta a Firenze nel Quattrocento (1427–1494)* (Rome: Palazzo Borromini, 1984), 258.
31 Rebecca Jean Emigh, *The Undevelopment of Capitalism: Sectors and Markets in Fifteenth-Century Tuscany* (Philadelphia: Temple University Press, 2009), xiv.
32 Gary S. Becker, *Human Capital: A Theoretical and Empirical Analysis, with Special Reference to Education*, 3rd ed. (Chicago: University of Chicago Press, 1993).

If the wealth accumulation patterns in Florence and the modern world were similar, then running equivalent regressions would get equivalent results. Regressions using nineteenth- and twentieth-century data generally yield two highly significant regression coefficients: a positive coefficient on the age variable and a negative coefficient on the age-squared variable. Together these result in the typical concave curve of earnings by age. The relative magnitude of the coefficient on the age-squared variable does vary.

Table 6.1 shows the relationship of taxable wealth to age for each of the various localities in Florentine Tuscany in 1427. Taxable wealth at age 16 is taken at a base index of 100 after age 16. Altogether, only 9 out of 25 localities show taxable wealth increasing with age.

The next step is to regress the logarithm of the wealth variable on the age and age-squared variables. Because of the lack of independence of observations, cross-sectional data sets tend to increase the apparent statistical significance of results and increase the likelihood of false positives. Therefore, all reported standard errors in the following tables are heteroskedasticity consistent.

Seven specifications were tested using City of Florence data. Florentine data from 1427 are more complete and detailed than those of other areas in Tuscany that were covered by the catasto (see Table 6.2). Three out of seven had positive coefficients on the age variable, and one, the City of Florence movable assets in 1427, was statistically significant.

An additional 24 specifications were tested using taxable wealth for each of the Tuscan regions that were outside Florence but under Florentine control in 1427. These are presented in Tables 6.3 through 6.5. It is well established that rural Tuscany was poorer than the city of Florence.[33] The Florentine contado (Table 6.3) had 3 out of 4 regions with positive coefficients and one statistically significant. Eastern Tuscany (Table 6.4) had 4 out of 7 regions with positive coefficients and one statistically significant. Western Tuscany (Table 6.4) had 9 out of 13 regions with positive coefficients and one statistically significant. In the modern world there is a consistent, strong and positive relationship between age and wealth. Here there are 12 negative coefficients on age out of 31 specifications. Age is clearly not a consistent, statistically significant predictor of wealth.

However, statistical significance is only part of the story. The growth of wealth during the life cycle is also important. The constant term in all the regressions is large, statistically significant and exceeds the age and age-squared portion of the regression, for reasonable ages, in every case and often by several orders of magnitude. This implies that the growth of wealth was insignificant compared to a household head's initial endowment.

Introduction to the Data-Quality Tests

The following sections examine the data used for the regressions in the last section. The objective is to eliminate possible explanations for the contradiction between the standard

---

33   Herlihy and Klapisch-Zuber, *Les Toscans*, 243.

Table 6.1 Indices of taxable wealth holding by region of the Florentine territories by age for males age 16 and older, 1427

Tuscan Region	Ages 16–20	Ages 21–25	Ages 26–30	Ages 31–35	Ages 36–40	Ages 41–45	Ages 46–50	Ages 51–55	Ages 56–60	Ages 61–65	Ages 66–70	Ages 71–75	Age 76+
City of Florence	100	63	66	83	60	70	81	107	83	59	59	93	78
Rural Quarter of Sta. Spirito	100	85	83	51	64	74	77	112	88	103	108	91	123
Rural Quarter of Sta. Croce	100	53	85	79	74	75	86	90	95	110	109	115	95
Rural Qtr. Sta. Maria de Novla.	100	86	70	87	85	86	83	95	84	104	107	80	87
Rural Quarter of Sta. Giovanni	100	53	51	59	57	68	57	66	74	86	80	95	85
City of Cortona	100	46	56	51	35	58	44	52	67	58	75	292	43
Countryside of Cortona	100	117	99	164	127	136	166	182	154	173	153	137	152
Castiglione Fiorentino,	100	93	38	55	40	44	35	35	27	40	53	50	43
Montepulciano and Ville	100	63	41	65	63	61	50	80	48	109	73	57	68
Countryside of Arezzo	100	147	145	182	138	216	151	180	143	165	155	201	149
City of Arezzo	100	113	49	57	59	47	83	81	44	61	45	198	48
Cortine of Arezzo	100	135	153	194	176	177	176	254	205	282	235	271	268
City of Pisa	100	76	51	80	80	54	98	87	87	97	74	108	65
Countryside of Pisa	100	75	77	105	87	95	90	97	101	96	88	102	100
City of Pistoia	100	66	85	85	77	74	77	144	73	64	48	63	54
Countryside of Pistoia	100	83	112	116	127	120	123	121	151	144	162	157	184
Mountains of Pistoia	100	106	92	124	155	135	177	123	153	258	162	186	203
Garfagnana	100	148	100	153	125	182	113	212	184	174	144	216	77
Val di Nievole	100	133	160	145	148	161	148	160	168	208	194	173	193
Val d'Arno di Sotto	100	41	46	82	65	77	69	90	78	71	69	41	64
San Gimignano	100	63	72	31	47	35	49	63	46	64	44	150	82
Colle	100	72	84	96	82	66	99	135	67	100	52	65	103
City of Volterra	100	268	553	482	283	333	334	913	362	481	266	397	957
Countryside of Volterra	100	199	239	194	359	345	273	295	302	218	338	388	349
Sillano and Montecastelli	100	77	200	82	130	115	184	112	168	300	163	146	72

Source: Herlihy and Klapisch-Zuber, *Census and Property Survey.* Calculation by author.

Table 6.2 Regressions of 1427 City of Florence asset/wealth holding by age for males age 16 and older

City of Florence	1427 Taxable Wealth	1427 Immovable Assets	1427 Movable Assets	1427 Public Debt Assets	1427 Total Assets	1458 Immovable Assets	1480 Immovable Assets
Constant	44180.95**	39639.55***	20134.55***	13982.04***	46888.37***	61842.90***	51798.98***
Age	−179.15	−102.83	676.40***	17.21	166.99	−250.02	−155.57
Age Sqd.	1.40	1.25	−7.88**	−0.79	−2.29**	3.25	1.14
R²	0.00	0.00	0.01	0.00	0.00	0.00	0.00
N	7684	7684	7684	7684	7684	125	627

Sqd.: Squared
R²: Measure of statistical fit.
N: Sample size
*** Statistical significance at the 99 percent level.
** Statistical significance at the 95 percent level.
* Statistical significance at the 90 percent level.
Source: Herlihy and Klapisch-Zuber, *Census and Property Survey.* Estimation by author.

Table 6.3 Regressions of 1427 Florentine contado taxable wealth holding by age for males age 16 and older

Contado of Florence	Rural Qtr. Santo Spirito	Rural Qtr. Santa Croce	Rural Qtr. Sta. Maria de Novella	Rural Qtr. San Giovanni
Constant	26822.65***	20068.54***	22260.40***	25095.00***
Age	−281.55***	78.73	−15.06	6.55
Age Sqd.	3.93***	0.68	1.33	1.12
R^2	0.01	0.02	0.01	0.01
N	6358	4271	6280	5838

Sqd.: Squared
R^2: Measure of statistical fit.
N: Sample size
Source: Herlihy and Klapisch-Zuber, *Census and Property Survey.* Estimation by author.
*** Statistical significance at the 99 percent level.
** Statistical significance at the 95 percent level.
* Statistical significance at the 90 percent level.

life-cycle wealth accumulation and this particular set of data. This series of tests expands on the work done by previous historians that was presented in Appendix 3A and in the Catasto Data section of this study. In particular, four possible data issues are investigated in detail.

First, the potential impact of missing ages in the sample is examined. This could lead to two possible problems: either there were a large number of missing ages or the wealth distribution of male household heads whose ages were missing was significantly different from that of the population used in the regression. When examined, neither appears to cause a problem.

Second, the impact of the home and its furnishings exemption are addressed in three ways. Did the homeownership rate increase with age and, if so, did it do so steeply? Did renters, who did not benefit from the home and furnishings tax exemption, show the same pattern between age and wealth? Did the private palaces provide a large store of wealth? When examined, none of these factors indicate a problem that could lead to the lack in correlation between age and wealth.

Third, the wealth variables are tested against Florentine social characteristics that one would expect to indicate increased wealth. The anticipated relationship between wealth and a measure of social status, either positive or negative, holds in every case. It is unlikely that a mixed distribution caused the regression results observed in Tables 6.2 through 6.5. One element of the distribution would have to have a strongly negative coefficient with respect to age if another part had a positive coefficient.

Finally, the life-cycle wealth accumulation patterns of the rich are examined independently from the poor. Research on modern populations finds that the correlation between age and wealth often disappears among the abject poor. Here only the top 10 percent wealthiest household heads are included. This regression test finds no significant life-cycle wealth accumulation.

Table 6.4 Regressions of 1427 Eastern Tuscany taxable wealth holding by age for males age 16 and older

Eastern Tuscany	City of Cortona	Cortona Countryside	Castiglione Fiorentino	Montepulciano and Ville	Arezzo Countryside	City of Arezzo	Cortine of Arezzo
Constant	41463.16***	23163.07***	43637.46***	32182.05***	28002.66***	40110.31***	32102.98***
Age	−224.48	356.13**	−200.02	204.35	107.87	58.91	−2.44
Age Sqd.	2.69	−2.98*	2.04	−1.38	−0.53	−0.66	1.11
R²	0.00	0.01	0.00	0.00	0.00	0.00	0.02
N	659	918	466	596	3003	837	1036

Sqd.: Squared
R²: Measure of statistical fit.
N: Sample size
*** Statistical significance at the 99 percent level.
** Statistical significance at the 95 percent level.
* Statistical significance at the 90 percent level.
Source: Herlihy and Klapisch-Zuber, *Census and Property Survey*. Estimation by author.

Table 6.5 Regressions of 1427 Western Tuscany taxable wealth holding by age for males age 16 and older

Western Tuscany	City of Pisa	Pisa Countryside	City of Pistoia	Pistoia Countryside	Pistoia Mountains	Garfagnana	Val di Nievole	Val d'Arno di Sotto	San Gimignano	Colle	City of Volterra	Volterra Countryside	Sillano and Montecastelli
Constant	26722.29***	23183.80***	36852.05***	33046.89***	27513.17***	40610.00***	39483.79***	29594.91***	42602.88***	41348.06***	28388.68***	28841.79***	21561.48***
Age	384.67*	124.70	65.35	-63.03	336.22	286.33	112.05	419.88	587.70	-137.40	3.96	-97.64	643.34***
Age Sqd.	-3.57*	-0.87	-1.23	1.51	-2.39	-2.35	-0.62	-3.28	6.96	0.93	0.86	2.09	-6.32***
R^2	0.00	0.00	0.00	0.01	0.02	0.01	0.00	0.01	0.02	0.00	0.00	0.01	0.05
N	1319	3287	930	1808	445	153	1034	534	504	454	652	670	105

Sqd.: Squared

R^2: Measure of statistical fit.

N: Sample size

*** Statistical significance at the 99 percent level.

** Statistical significance at the 95 percent level.

* Statistical significance at the 90 percent level.

Source: Herlihy and Klapisch-Zuber, *Census and Property Survey.* Estimation by author.

Table 6.6 Distribution statistics of male household heads by age category, Florence, 1427

Taxable Wealth	Age 0–15	Age 16+	Age Missing
Mean	1124.44	828.05	1512.36
Standard Error of Mean	131.52	30.23	478.23
Standard Deviation	2046.03	2650.25	8030.91
Total N	242	7687	282
Valid N	242	7687	282
Percentile 05	0	0	0
Percentile 25	183	0	0
Percentile 75	1109	650	525
Percentile 95	4086	3463	6824
Percentile 99	11534	11152	13062

N: Sample size
Source: Herlihy and Klapisch-Zuber, *Census and Property Survey*. Calculation by author.

The Impact of Missing Ages

Historians have found no significant problems with missing ages in the catasto data, but this section assesses problems that could have arisen. Since the entire focus of the research here is on life-cycle wealth accumulation, it is imperative that the age data are correct. There are two different kinds of possible problems. First, there could be a large number of household heads with missing ages.[34] The number of "Age Missing" cases is roughly 3 percent of the total number in the "Age 16+" category. In aggregate, the number of cases with missing ages does not cause a significant problem. Second, the missing ages, even though they might be few, might flag households with significantly more wealth than those included in the regressions.

Table 6.6 presents the distribution of wealth by age category. The wealth distribution of missing ages is represented by a set of statistical measurements, including the mean, standard error of mean and standard deviation. The distribution is then examined using the 5 percentile, 25 percentile, 75 percentile, 95 percentile and 99 percentile points. The distribution of wealth among household heads with missing ages looks generally like those with known ages 16 plus. The deviation is not statistically significant. The "Age Missing" category means that taxable wealth is less than a standard deviation greater for that category than it is for the "Age 16+" category. The percentile distribution points also indicate that the shape of the distribution of household heads with missing ages is not significantly different from those with reported ages.

The Effect of Exempting Home and Furnishings

This section assesses the magnitude of the problem in assessing the relationship between wealth and age caused by the homeownership exemption. There is no direct way to

---

34 There are no cases with missing wealth data.

assess this problem, as the value of the home is not reported anywhere. Assets that were considered part of the home were the building itself and the furnishings, including the art, in the home. This might explain the proliferation of Renaissance murals.

The regressions are based on the distribution of known assets. However, the functional form of the regression has an interesting property that tends to minimize the potential impact of missing assets. It is a logarithm of total wealth specification. The model first estimated in Tables 6.2 through 6.5 would be unaffected if the missing assets were a fixed ratio of taxable wealth. The missing assets would merely be accounted for in the constant term and would appear indistinguishable from the rest of the household's initial endowment. However, housing should be wealth inelastic, so one would expect the ratio of housing value to total wealth to decline as wealth increased. Therefore the regression would tend to bias upward the amount of housing.

Three indirect test methods are used here to assess the magnitude of the problem caused by the homeownership exemption. The first is the homeownership percentage by age. The regression assumptions suggest that there was only a small positive relationship between a household head's age and the likelihood of owning a home. Second, the regression is rerun excluding homeowners. Households where homeownership was noted in the tax return are simply excluded. This regression arrives at the same result that has been reported throughout this study—that is, it has no effect on the wealth-age correlation. Third, the timing of the private palace building boom is examined. Palaces could have sheltered a lot of wealth. The question is whether the construction boom of the great Renaissance Florentine private palaces occurred before or after the assessment of the 1427 catasto. It turns out that the construction boom came after 1427; therefore, there was no opportunity to shelter wealth.

The first test method uses the relationship between age and homeownership. The slope of the relationship is the important issue here. A positive correlation would imply that the wealth data are of high quality. The steepness of the correlation measures the strength of the homeownership exemption. Figure 6.4 shows that the curve of homeownership by age has a positive slope that does not increase steeply. The figure implies that, although including the value of the home as an asset could have flattened the curve, such flattening was probably not that significant. The positive but small correlation of homeownership with age validates this interpretation of the data.

The second test method runs the regression on only renters as opposed to all households. Multiple specifications were run. These regressions parallel the regressions run in Tables 6.2 through 6.5. Only male household heads age 16 and over were included. The regressions by household in 1458 and 1480 were removed due to small sample sizes. Table 6.7 shows that the relationship between age and wealth for Florentine renters was reasonably similar to the curve for all households. The results strongly suggest that the omission of the home value had little or no effect on the results.

The third test method looks at when famous private palaces were constructed. The question here is how much of the household wealth was taken "off the catasto books" by applying the home exemption to private palaces. At first glance, the private palaces seem

Table 6.7 Regressions of 1427 City of Florence asset/wealth holding by age for males age 16 and older who are not homeowners

City of Florence Nonowners	1427 Taxable Wealth
Constant	37254.67***
Age	−315.3
Age Sqd.	2.36
R²	0
N	4333

Sqd.: Squared
R²: Measure of statistical fit.
N: Sample size
*** Statistical significance at the 99 percent level.
** Statistical significance at the 95 percent level.
* Statistical significance at the 90 percent level.
Source: Herlihy and Klapisch-Zuber, *Census and Property Survey*. Estimation by author.

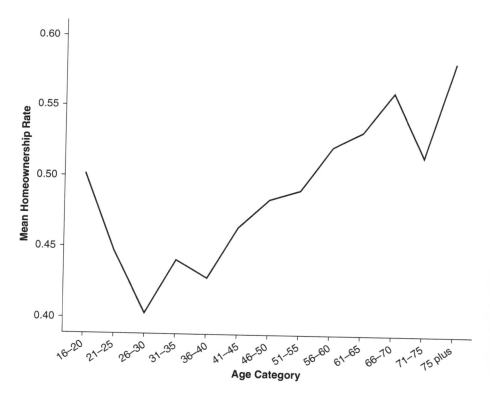

Figure 6.4 Homeownership rate by age, City of Florence, 1427
Source: Herlihy and Klapisch-Zuber, *Census and Property Survey*. Calculation by author.

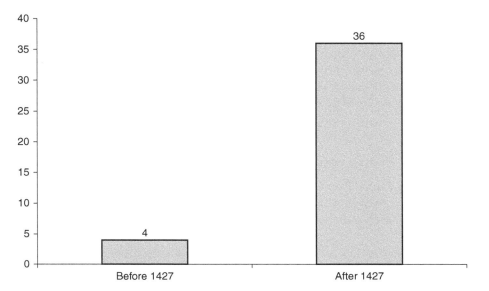

Figure 6.5 Number of "significant palaces" by date of building
Source: Leonardo Ginori Lisci, *I Palazzi di Firenze nella storia e nell'arte* (Florence: Giunti, 1972), 2: 800.

to have been a tremendous store of wealth in 1427 Florence. However, the key question is how much of the private palace construction occurred before 1427 and how much after. (Chapter 4 examines the reasons behind the building boom in greater detail.)

One would expect that the value of furnishings in private palaces was significantly more extravagant than in the household's previous home. Prior to the Quattrocento, wealthy Florentine families had erected more than 100 towers.[35] These were designed as fortifications rather than to be architecturally impressive and a store of wealth,[36] and their height was limited by statute.[37] They clearly had a lower value per square foot than the private palaces.

Leonardo Lisci's categorization of private palaces permits an estimate of the quantity of palace construction both before and after 1427. Lisci calls such private palaces "significant palaces,"[38] and they are the ones architectural historians study. Figure 6.5 shows that few significant palaces were completed before the 1427 catasto assessment, while 90 percent were completed after.[39] The private palaces do not appear to have sheltered wealth from taxation in 1427.

35 Gene Brucker, *Florence: The Golden Age, 1138–1737* (Berkeley: University of California Press, 1998), 38–39; John M. Najemy, *A History of Florence, 1200–1575* (Malden, MA: Blackwell, 2006), 33.

36 Brucker, *Golden Age*, 35–39; Najemy, *History of Florence*, 8; Leonardo Ginori Lisci, *I Palazzi di Firenze nella storia e nell'arte* (Florence: Giunti, 1972) 2: 800.

37 Brucker, *Golden Age*, 35.

38 This method is used in chapter 4.

39 Lisci, *Palazzi di Firenze*, 2: 800.

It appears that little wealth could have been moved into furnishings either. The 1427 catasto was the first Florentine tax that had a home and furnishings exemption.[40] It would have been nearly impossible to transfer much wealth to take advantage of the new tax rules. Furthermore, the assessment was conducted over a period of time, and with the back and forth between the assessors and household head and the reviews by neighbors, it seems unlikely that this kind of evasion would have been permitted. Finally, because the goal of the catasto was to create a fair assessment, obvious evasions of the tax would have been prevented.

Wealth and Its Expected Correlates

A household's wealth does not exist in a vacuum, and one would expect a household's wealth to be correlated with greater social status. This section assesses how well the wealth data matches up to measures of social status. Each measure should correlate with higher wealth.

The relationship is looked at from two directions. First, the mean and standard error of wealth are measured for household heads who are and who are not identifiable as having higher presumed social status based on a number of measures. Second, the wealthiest Florentine household heads are matched up with the most powerful Florentine household heads to see how well these correlate. Other research finds a high correlation between holding the office of prior in Florence from 1400 through 1494 and being one of the wealthiest households in Florence.[41]

The first test of whether wealth is correlated with other variables that one might expect it to be correlated with is to see whether social status is correlated with wealth. The measures of status used to evaluate wealth-holding patterns in this section are family status, occupational category, homeownership, migrancy status, gender and household size. Indicators of greater wealth and social status include surnames,[42] which became prominent in Florence only during the previous century,[43] arte maggiore membership,[44] homeownership, male household heads and larger households.[45] Migrant households should indicate less wealth and social status.

As noted earlier in Chapter 4, the catasto is less clear about who rented homes than who owned them. Three definitions of renters are used here. The narrow definition

40 Elio Conti, ed., *Matteo Palmieri Ricordi Fiscali (1427–1474) con due Appendici relative al 1474–1495* (Rome: Palazzo Borromini, 1983), 7.

41 R. Burr Litchfield, *Emergence of a Bureaucracy: The Florentine Patricians, 1530–1790* (Princeton, NJ: Princeton University Press, 1986), 19.

42 Anthony Molho, "Un aperçu statistique du quartier de Santo Spirito: Créditeurs de Florence en 1347," in *Firenze nel Quattrocento*, vol. 1: *Politica e Fiscalità* (Rome: Edizioni di Storia Letteratura, 2006), 97–112. This characteristic forms the basis for Najemy's study of the Florentine political system. Najemy, *Corporatism and Consensus*.

43 Anthony Molho, "Names, Memory, Public Identity in Late Medieval Florence," in *Firenze nel Quattrocento*, vol. 2: *Famiglia e Società* (Rome: Edizioni di Storia Letteratura, 2006), 89.

44 See chapter 3 for an extended discussion of this.

45 Herlihy and Klapisch-Zuber, *Les Toscans*, 309–15; Christiane Klapisch-Zuber, "Household and Family in Tuscany in 1427," in *Household and Family in Past Time*, ed. Peter Laslett and Richard Wall (Cambridge: Cambridge University Press, 1972), 277.

Table 6.8 Taxable wealth by household category, City of Florence, 1427

Category	Taxable Wealth		
	Mean	N	S. E.
All Households	772.07	9720	28.02
Arte Maggiore	2066.49	767	152.22
Non–Arte Maggiore	661.18	8953	27.17
Family Has Surname	1514.35	3578	69.51
No Surname	339.66	6142	15.63
Native	819.72	8519	31.27
Migrant	434.06	1201	46.17
Male	860.28	8211	32.97
Female	292.08	1509	14.82
Homeowner	1324.75	4104	61.02
Renter (Narrow Defn.)	346.47	4189	21.47
Renter (Middle Defn.)	360.15	5242	17.95
Renter (Broad Defn.)	368.19	5616	17.18

The mean, sample size (N), and standard error (S. E.) are included.
Defn.: Definition
Source: Herlihy and Klapisch-Zuber, *Census and Property Survey.* Calculation by author.

includes only those households specifically identified as renters. The middle definition expands the definition of renter to include those without any indication as to whether they rented or not. The broad definition includes all households not specifically iden-tified as homeowners and includes households living with family members and not renting.

The results of the tests correlating wealth and other indicators of social status are pre-sented in Table 6.8. All of the variables tested have the expected relationship with wealth. The families with surnames were wealthier than those without. The arte maggiore occu-pations were wealthier than non–arte maggiore occupations.[46] Native Florentines were wealthier than migrants. Male-headed households were wealthier than female-headed households. Homeowners were wealthier than renters. In this Malthusian economy there is also a clear relationship between greater household size and greater net wealth.

The second test is to see whether the richest Florentines in the catasto were also more likely to be government officeholders. Two sources for a list of government officeholders are the *Tratte*, a list of Florentine officeholders from 1282 through 1532,[47] and a listing

---

46 See chapter 3 for more details of the wealth differences between *arte maggiore* and *popolo minuto* households.

47 Online *Tratte* of Office Holders, 1282–1532, Florence, Italy. Florentine Renaissance Resources, Online *Tratte* of Office Holders, 1282–1532 [machine-readable data file]. David Herlihy, R. Burr Litchfield, Anthony Molho and Roberto Barducci, eds. Florentine Renaissance Resources/STG: Brown University, Providence, Rhode Island, 2002.

of families of officeholders compiled by Dale Kent.[48] The analysis matches observed wealthy households with members of the government or governing oligarchy.

The relationship between government service and wealth was complicated. First, service for the Comune typically fell on the youngest of good families, those with the least chance to become merchants or notaries.[49] Beyond this, becoming a member of the government was a two-step procedure. An individual must first be eligible. Eligibility was based on a variety of circumstances and was deliberately balanced to some extent by social rank. This guaranteed both a relatively wide representation and oligarchic control. It was also influenced by political allegiance. Opponents of leading families in power could be removed from the list. The second step for becoming a government member was a random draw among those who were eligible to determine who would serve. This procedure implies that the sample is representative of the most powerful families but that the exact membership should be random within those criteria. Cross-referencing the Kent list with the catasto data shows that 60 of the top 100 richest households and 115 of the 200 richest households were among the 355 most powerful families in Florence.[50] There is a clear correlation. Some prominent and wealthy families, such as the Del Bene and Pazzi families, are not on the list, because they were political enemies of the Medici. Kent's list includes only families with surnames.

The Tratte lists from 1282 through 1532 are readily accessible online.[51] The database includes the officeholder's name, position and often age. Matching the names on the Tratte with the wealthiest fiscal households has a significant complication. Service for the Comune often fell on the youngest member of important families, who had the least chance of becoming a merchant or notary.[52] This means that fiscal household heads were less likely to be on the Tratte lists. Therefore, one would expect a much higher than normal percentage of people with surnames on the Tratte lists and a much lower match rate with specific people. Both of these expectations appear to hold true. The 84 percent of the persons with surnames in the Tratte lists for 1427 is much higher than the 37 percent of the general population who had surnames and confirms the general correlation of surnames with power and with wealth. There were only seven exact matches between the 182 people in the 1427 Tratte list and the top 200 in the catasto, which supports the idea that the Tratte list mimics the catasto sample with respect to the roles of families, but that the roles of individuals are much less correlated.

Wealth Accumulation Patterns for Rich and Poor

The idea of different life-cycle wealth accumulation patterns between rich and poor is an appealing explanation of the lack of an overall correlation between age and wealth.

48 Dale Kent, "The Florentine *Reggimento* in the Fifteenth Century," *Renaissance Quarterly* 28 (1975): 624–32.
49 Herlihy and Klapisch-Zuber, *Les Toscans*, 84.
50 Kent list source: Kent, "*Reggimento*," 624–32. Catasto data: Herlihy and Klapisch-Zuber, *Census and Property Survey*.
51 Online Tratte of Office Holders.
52 Herlihy and Klapisch-Zuber, *Les Toscans*, 84.

This section examines whether the overall lack of a correlation was driven by widespread abject poverty. The idea is that mixing the poor and the rich in a single sample would drown out statistical indicators of life-cycle wealth accumulation among the wealthy. It is possible that the broad and deep poverty of medieval society drives the lack of any relationship between age and wealth. This pattern would have a modern parallel in that researchers have found that the standard life-cycle wealth accumulation relationship fails to hold with very poor populations.

There was a significant wealth gap between Florence and the surrounding regions. A poverty effect could explain the failure of the standard regression model to hold in the rural areas of Tuscany. However, it could not explain the general failure for the city of Florence.

These observations, the modern and the medieval, when combined suggest that it is natural to separate the rich from the poor. This analysis examines four different statistical specifications of the question: the wealthiest 10 percent of Florentines, arte maggiore members, families with surnames and homeowners. The wealthiest 10 percent of Florentines are defined as those fiscal households with a net taxable wealth of 1,737 florins and above.

Figure 6.6 presents a scatterplot of taxable wealth by age for City of Florence household heads among the top 10 percent in taxable wealth in 1427. There is no general upward trend.

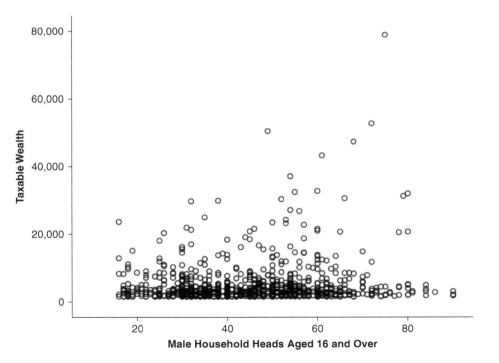

Figure 6.6 Scatterplot of taxable wealth by age of male household head age 16 and over for households among top 10 percent of taxable wealth, City of Florence, 1427
Source: Herlihy and Klapisch-Zuber, *Census and Property Survey*. Calculation by author.

Table 6.9 Regression of 1427 City of Florence taxable wealth by age for indicators of status and wealth (top 10 percent of households in taxable wealth, arte maggiore members, having a family surname and homeownership) headed by males age 16 and older

	Top 10%	Arte Mag.	Surnamed	Homeowner
Constant	83566.68***	35844.92***	3564.12***	60131.71***
Age	−73.81	925.49***	159.52	−135.35
Age Sqd.	1.01	−7.70***	1.66	−0.21
R²	0.00	0.02	0	0.01
N	869	738	2769	3354

Sqd.: Squared
R²: Measure of statistical fit.
N: Sample size
*** Statistical significance at the 99 percent level.
** Statistical significance at the 95 percent level.
* Statistical significance at the 90 percent level.
Source: Herlihy and Klapisch-Zuber, *Census and Property Survey*. Estimation by author.

Table 6.9 presents a regression of the top 10 percent of households, arte maggiore households, surnamed households and home-owning households in 1427 using taxable wealth on household head's age and age squared. There is no consistently statistically positive age relationship, but the regression for the arte maggiore is positive and significant. Although this holds in aggregate for arte maggiore households, the result does not hold consistently across all individual arte maggiore occupations. The regressions for the top 10 percent and homeowners are actually negative.

Household Size, Age and Wealth

The fourth part of this study's analysis, this section and the next, extends the earlier analyses by adopting a more sophisticated approach to the data. This section approaches the data from the perspective of Malthusian theory. Herlihy and Klapisch-Zuber argue strongly that Quattrocento Florence was Malthusian, and there is no significant debate on this matter.[53]

Malthusian theory predicts a strongly positive correlation between taxable wealth and household size. Klapisch-Zuber finds that this relationship holds true.[54] Figure 6.7 shows that the taxable wealth by household size follows a shallow U curve (quadratic with a positive curvature). The household size is relatively high at low levels of taxable wealth, then drops, and then rises dramatically at the highest levels. The drop in household size occurs at low levels. The nonlinearity is particularly strong between wealth and household size. The strongest positive correlation is among the wealthiest

---

53 Herlihy and Klapisch-Zuber, *Les Toscans*; Herlihy and Klapisch-Zuber, *Tuscans*.
54 Christiane Klapisch-Zuber, "Household and Family in Tuscany in 1427," in *Household and Family in Past Time*, ed. Peter Laslett and Richard Wall (Cambridge: Cambridge University Press, 1972), 277.

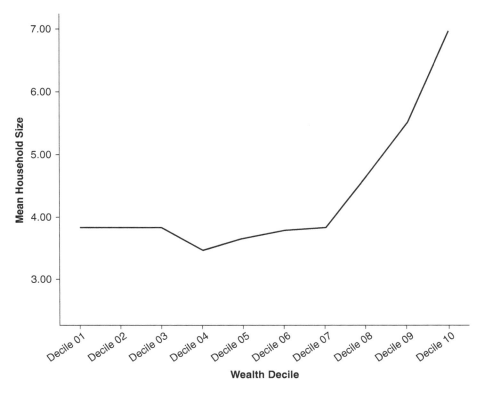

Figure 6.7 Mean household size by decile of taxable wealth, City of Florence, 1427
Source: Herlihy and Klapisch-Zuber, *Census and Property Survey*. Calculation by author.

households. The relatively large households at the bottom of the taxable wealth profile interrupt the typical Malthusian pattern. They probably represent a kind of floor for fiscal household size.

Figure 6.8 shows that the household size by age curve follows a shallow inverted-U curve (quadratic with a negative curvature). The peak is between ages 41 and 55. Based on transitivity, one would expect that positive correlations between age and household size and between wealth and household size, respectively, would imply a positive correlation between age and wealth. However, the lack of a positive correlation between age and wealth implies a lack of transitivity. The shapes of the two curves could cause this. Both are nonlinear. They are, in broad terms, mirror-image reflections centered on a single line. This implies that their product—the age by taxable wealth curve—should be a straight line. This could explain the flat age by taxable wealth curve and how all three curves are related.

A Simulation Estimating the Value of Missing Assets

At this point there are two reasonable answers to the question of why there is no correlation between age and wealth among Florentine households in the sample. First, the

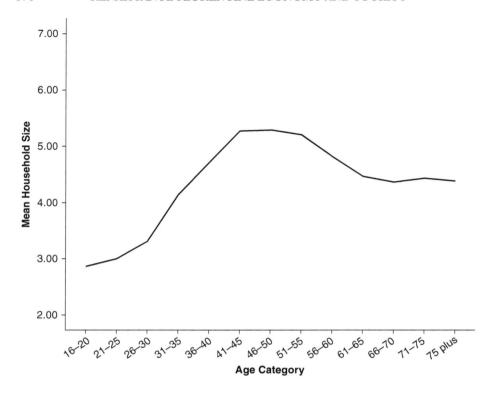

Figure 6.8 Mean household size by age category, City of Florence, 1427
Source: Herlihy and Klapisch-Zuber, *Census and Property Survey.* Calculation by author.

life-cycle wealth accumulation could have been flat and therefore widely at variance with modern experience. Second, a share of fiscal household assets could be missing from the data. This missing wealth would add enough at each age to guarantee that the relationship between age and taxable wealth was positive.

This section estimates the level of missing assets using simulations. Before going any further, it is important to point out that any estimated missing wealth would not significantly affect the results from Chapters 3 and 5, because the missing assets are probably correlated with recorded assets and because other proxies for wealth are included.

Two simulations, based on two natural sets of households, have been run here: all fiscal households and those who lived in their own home. The focus, as in previous sections, is on 1427 Florence, and the indices from Table 6.2 have been used. The standard of comparison as in Figure 6.2 is with Wolff's widely used estimate of the twentieth-century life-cycle wealth accumulation curve.[55] This opens the possibility that some intermediate curve might fit. Again, here, as earlier in this study, the effort has been to avoid any kind

---

55 Wolff, "Accumulation of Household Wealth."

Table 6.10 Simulation of missing household wealth: all fiscal households and only home-owning fiscal households with male household heads age 16 and older

Age Categories	Missing Assets in Florins	
	All Households	Homeowners Only
21–25	0	0
26–30	641	1149
31–35	1123	2284
36–40	1890	3881
41–45	2227	4521
46–50	2383	4955
51–55	2340	5146
56–60	2626	5548
61–65	3055	6285

Sources: Florentine data: Herlihy and Klapisch-Zuber, *Census and Property Survey;* Twentieth-century life-cycle wealth accumulation simulation based on data from Wolff, "Accumulation of Household Wealth over the Life-Cycle." Estimates based on Figure 6.2 and Table 6.1. Calculation by author.

of data mining just to get a result. It should also be noted that, because most of the estimated curves are flat, any small increment could create a positively sloping curve. The possibility of this kind of mathematical manipulation makes it even more important to use a well-established pattern.

The larger the estimated amount of missing assets, the less likely the modern relationship between age and wealth holds in the data. It is unlikely both that a household's combined assets in land, business and government debt would be less than that of some other asset and that this other asset would have remained untaxed in response to the Florentine financial crises of the late 1420s.

Table 6.10 shows that the estimated missing assets would need to form an extremely large share of taxable wealth. This should be intuitively plausible based on earlier results. The gap in Figure 6.2 would imply that any estimated missing assets should grow disproportionately by age. The simulations indicate that at nearly every age the mean value of the missing assets alone could move a fiscal household from miserabili well past the minimum level to be part of the top 10 percent of households in taxable wealth at 1,737 florins. The consistently increasing estimated missing assets immediately rule out some form of random error by officials.

The missing assets could fall into one or more of three categories: housing, cash or assets hidden from the officials. None of these would seem to be the source of the missing assets. Assets hidden from the officials would probably vary randomly rather than systematically by age.

Housing was the most prominent untaxed asset and could vary systematically by age and wealth. However, housing seems an unlikely source of missing assets. The demand for housing is typically wealth inelastic. As the household head aged and became wealthier, the share of assets in housing should have decreased. Housing should be a safer investment than others, and the demand for housing per household member is limited. If housing were the source of missing assets, then households would have shifted assets into housing and away from wealth-elastic investments as their wealth increased by age.[56] There is some evidence on this point from the previous section. Figure 6.7, where the household size increased disproportionately among the top wealth deciles, implies that at extreme wealth the effect of household size could outweigh the wealth-inelasticity effect. However, Figure 6.8, where the size of the household first increased and then decreased with the age of the household head, makes this explanation less likely.

Cash is another, though unlikely, possibility to explain missing assets, as it could be hidden relatively easily.[57] However, the Florentines thought any untaxed cash holdings were likely to be small, because cash made no return and because any hidden cash subsequently used for a large transaction would be noticed.[58] In addition, the demand for cash due to liquidity should be wealth inelastic, since increased wealth is associated with decreased risk aversion. This would imply that liquidity demand should decrease as wealth increases.

It appears unlikely that sufficient missing assets existed to shift the life-cycle wealth accumulation curves to modern levels. The estimated missing assets are extremely large and cannot be easily explained. They could not have been the result of data error. Neither housing nor cash would seem to be likely sources of the estimated missing data.

Conclusion and Discussion

This study has found that, in Renaissance Florence and its territories, contrary to research of modern populations, there is no positive relationship between age and wealth. It is not clear exactly what explains this observation. At this point in time, there are three broad approaches to an explanation. First, there could be a problem with the data. In particular, the missing data could be systematically correlated with age. The missing homes and cash could be the reason for the lack of life-cycle wealth accumulation among Tuscans. The last section examined this possibility using simulations, which circumscribe the possible characteristics of the missing assets. They show that the Florentine relationship between age and wealth would have to be much less steep than that in modern America.

Second, there could be a systematic explanation. Florence could just have been a very poor society. In the modern world, only very poor societies demonstrate this kind of age-wealth profile.[59] Although this is the simplest explanation that fits with economic theory,

---

56   There is an extensive theory about this pattern. Seminal work includes John R. Hicks, "Liquidity," *Economic Journal* 72, no. 288 (1962): 787–802; John W. Pratt, "Risk Aversion in the Small and in the Large," *Econometrica* 32, no. 1/2 (1964): 122–36; Kenneth Joseph Arrow, "The Theory of Risk Aversion," in *Essays in the Theory of Risk-Bearing* (Chicago: Markham, 1971), 90–120.

57   Julius Kirshner, "Custom, Customary Law, and Ius Commune in Francesco Guicciardini," *Bologna nell'età di Carlo V e Guicciardini* (2002): 163–76.

58   Niccolò Machiavelli, *Florentine History*, trans. W. K. Marriott (1909; London: Dent, 1976), 156.

59   Atack and Bateman, "Egalitarianism, Inequality, and Age"; Schaefer, "Migration and Wealth Accumulation"; Mirer, "Wealth-Age Relation"; Heckman, "Life Cycle Model."

it is not plausible. Few would believe that Quattrocento Florence, with its private palaces and artistic splendor, was everywhere a deeply poverty-stricken society. Alternatively, the 10 percent cutoff that was used to flag who was truly wealthy could have been too low, but any other cutoff would not make sense in the context of the other data (see Chapters 3, 4 and 5). For example, the wealth distribution does not indicate that a corresponding level of inequality existed.

Third, there could be a behavioral explanation. This would most plausibly take one of three forms. The large intergenerational wealth transmission through gifting or dowries could flatten the curve. Though the dowry impact would have been largest for men starting in their 50s, gifting could have begun earlier.[60] The high rate of charity, possibly increasing as one aged, could also flatten the curve.[61] Finally, the lack of significant life-cycle human capital accumulation in Quattrocento Florence could flatten the curve. Modern researchers find a strong correlation among life-cycle earnings, income and wealth.[62] If the wealth curve was flat, then the earnings and life-cycle human capital accumulation curve would also be flat. Some guilds, those which established fixed prices, which limited the possible returns, would have limited the value of acquiring human capital over one's lifetime. The high late medieval interest rates (relative to modern rates)[63] would have reduced the value of holding any form of capital, human or physical.[64] Economic theory suggests that human capital formation can be the basis for economic growth.[65] However, empirical research is divided over whether human capital formation drove early modern economic growth.[66] A low rate of human capital accumulation could

---

60 Herlihy and Klapisch-Zuber, Les Toscans, 393–419; Herlihy and Klapisch-Zuber, The Tuscans, 202–31; Julius Kirshner and Anthony Molho, "The Dowry Fund and the Marriage Market in Early *Quattrocento* Florence, *Journal of Modern History* 50 (1978): 403–38; Anthony Molho, *Marriage Alliance in Late Medieval Florence* (Cambridge, MA: Harvard University Press, 1994).

61 For discussions of how charity was routine, see: Ronald F. E. Weissman, *Ritual Brotherhood in Renaissance Florence* (New York: Academic Press, 1982); John Henderson, *Piety and Charity in Late Medieval Florence* (Chicago: University of Chicago Press, 1994).

62 Jacob Mincer, *Schooling, Experience, and Earnings* (Chicago: National Bureau of Economic Research, 1974); Becker, *Human Capital*; Heckman, "Life Cycle Model."

63 Sidney Homer, *A History of Interest Rates* (New Brunswick, NJ: Rutgers University Press, 1963); Sidney Homer and Richard Sylla, *A History of Interest Rates*, 4th ed. (Hoboken, NJ: Wiley, 2005).

64 Heckman, "Life Cycle Model."

65 Gary S. Becker, Kevin M. Murphy and Robert Tamura, "Human Capital, Fertility, and Economic Growth," *Journal of Political Economy* 98, no. 5, pt. 2 (1990): S12–37; Robert E. Lucas Jr., *Lectures on Economic Growth* (Cambridge, MA: Harvard University Press, 2006).

66 For studies that support the human capital and growth thesis, see Stephan R. Epstein, "The Late Medieval Crisis as an 'Integration Crisis,'" in *Early Modern Capitalism: Economic and Social Change in Europe, 1400–1800*, ed. Maarten Prak (London: Routledge, 2001), 25–50; Stephan R. Epstein, "Property Rights to Technical Knowledge in Pre-Modern Europe," 1300–1800, *American Economic Review* 94, no. 2 (2004): 382–87. For studies that see this thesis as problematic, see Robert C. Allen, "Progress and Poverty in Early Modern Europe," *Economic History Review*, new ser., 56, no. 3 (2003): 403–43; Gregory Clark, "Human Capital, Fertility, and the Industrial Revolution," *Journal of the European Economic Association* 3, nos. 2/3 (2005): 505–15; Gregory Clark, "The Condition of the Working-Class in England, 1209–2004," *Journal of*

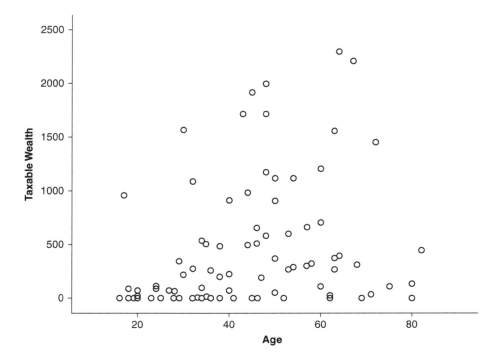

Figure 6.9 Scatterplot of taxable wealth by age for workers in gold and jewels, City of Florence, 1427
Source: Herlihy and Klapisch-Zuber, *Census and Property Survey*. Calculation by author.

explain the exceptionally low premodern economic growth rates. There is some evidence for the lack of life-cycle human capital accumulation hypothesis. Whereas the life-cycle accumulation is insignificant, or negative, for nearly all the occupations, it is positive and possesses the right shape for two: gold and jewelry workers and tailors. See Figures 6.9 and 6.10 and Table 6.11. Workers in both occupations would tend to benefit from experience because there would be no necessary upper bound in quality. Workers in other occupations, whose returns are circumscribed by guild regulations, would have seen less benefit from increasing their human capital.

These approaches are not exclusive. For example, systematic tax avoidance by the very wealthy combined with a fundamentally poor society for others could explain the pattern. The behavioral explanations could function together or independently or in combination with the data and poverty approaches. However, taking the behavioral

Political Economy 113, no. 6 (2005): 1307–40; Gregory Clark, *A Farewell to Alms: A Brief Economic History of the World* (Princeton, NJ: Princeton University Press, 2007); Margaret C. Jacob, *The First Knowledge Economy: Human Capital and the European Economy, 1750–1850* (Cambridge, UK: Cambridge University Press, 2014).

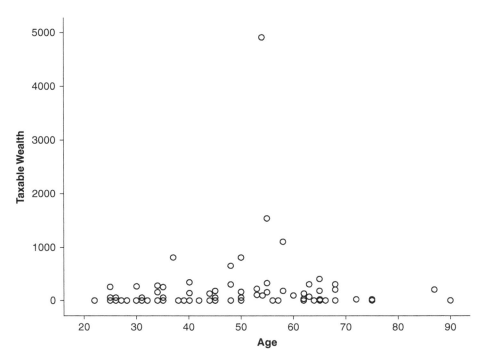

Figure 6.10 Scatterplot of taxable weath by age for tailors, City of Florence, 1427
Source: Herlihy and Klapisch-Zuber, *Census and Property Survey*. Calculation by author.

Table 6.11 Regressions of 1427 City of Florence taxable wealth holding by age for males age 16 and older by occupation

	Workers in Gold & Jewels	Tailors
Constant	−22624.39	−36271.51
Age	2529.86***	2262.30**
Age Sqd.	−21.08**	−18.52**
R².	0.17	0.09
N	87	95

Sqd.: Squared
R²: Measure of statistical fit.
N: Sample size
*** Statistical significance at the 99 percent level.
** Statistical significance at the 95 percent level.
* Statistical significance at the 90 percent level.
Source: Herlihy and Klapisch-Zuber, *Census and Property Survey*. Estimation by author.

explanations as either the exclusive or predominant explanations present issues. They require accepting the data substantially as they are and proposing that the late medieval and early modern world had a very different economy than the modern world. At this point none of these three approaches to explaining the results is completely satisfactory. More research is necessary.

Part III

WORK

Chapter Seven

JUST DOING BUSINESS: TESTING COMPETITION IN THE RENAISSANCE FLORENTINE WOOL INDUSTRY

Introduction

The organization and efficiency of Florentine business is a key question in the study of the Renaissance. The city's businesses made the money that paid for the art and architecture of the Florentine Renaissance. Views of Florentine economic efficiency are widely split. Whether or not the industry was competitive has important implications about how one views the Florentine economy. Markets can range fromcompetitive through gradations of monopsony power to simple monopolies. Florentine wool industry firms operated in two markets: an input market and an output market. These were distinct. A competitive industry has a number of implications besides not being a monopoly. There is a type of equality among the firms. No firm or subset of firms dominates or leads the industry or has a significant influence on prices. Economists would call these firms price takers. They accept the prices as they are on the market and are unable to change them. This implies that production is efficient and that the owners do not receive any economic rent, excessive profits. A competitive industry also has implications for society. It both allocates resources efficiently and prevents extraction by the rich from the poor. Since Florentine businesses were essentially family proprietorships, a competitive industry would imply that the marketplace was fair.

A competitive market does not imply that the guild was meaningless. However, it is important to be careful in defining the market. Organizations that possess monopoly power that have individual members without monopoly power are common in today's world. For example, a seat on a stock exchange is expensive and membership is limited. Exchange membership is valuable because only members can buy and sell stocks directly. Nevertheless, the stock markets are competitive.

An analysis of competition in the Renaissance Florence wool industry is presented in the rest of this chapter. Both the source and the method largely drive the results from previous studies of Florentine competitiveness. Further, methods that ignore the dynamic nature of economies seem more likely to find a less competitive business environment. From this foundation, two methods are used to examine competitiveness in the Florentine wool industry. It describes the theory, specifies the tests and presents the findings of these two approaches together. As a baseline, wool industry monopoly power is calculated using a wide range of specifications based on the standard concentration measure approach. These results also strongly support the idea that the industry was competitive. Next, the core of this study tests neoclassical production theory using a regression model of the substitution matrix for a Cinquecento Florentine firm. Empirical tests of perfect competition are generally limited by the available data. In some cases they look only at outputs and ignore inputs. In other cases the firm is treated as a black box, where the internal structure is invisible. The organization of the Florentine wool industry allows one to avoid both limitations. In many ways the Cinquecento Florentine wool industry company is a better subject to test the modern theory of perfect competition than are modern firms. The typical wool industry firm's operations, inputs, outputs and internal structure are all visible. This test further differs from the first set of tests because it incorporates the joint assumption of rationality. In general, neoclassical production theory performs well throughout. Four appendices that discuss the mechanics of the regression model in greater detail are at the end of this chapter.

Florentine Business Efficiency

The modernity and efficiency of Florentine business has been debated for more than a century. Much of this has been viewed retrospectively through the lens of the success of the Industrial Revolution in northern Europe. Those who question the capabilities of the Florentine people target their culture, their competence, their economic rationality and the city's market structure.

The Florentines' Catholic culture was the first target. Max Weber and Werner Sombart see inherent but different conflicts between capitalism and Italy's Catholicism. Weber's *Protestant Ethic and the Spirit of Capitalism* promotes the importance of Protestantism to the development of capitalism.[1] Catholicism was seen as antithetical to capitalist development. It held the Florentines back and prevented economic growth. Sombart's *Der moderne Kapitalismus* is similar but focuses on the role of Jews instead of Protestants.[2] Neither of these works holds up today. One hundred years later it is clear there are many industrialized Catholic economies.

The Florentines' competence is the second target of critique. Sombart develops four broad theses about Italian merchants in general: (1) merchants did not like or have much talent for writing, (2) even the best business records were only untidy jottings, (3) account books were deliberately kept in an obscure manner and (4) there were never any exact accounts in the books.[3] However, Sombart's pessimistic theses about Italian merchants do not stand up to scrutiny. Not only did Italian merchants enjoy writing and have a talent for it, but also their business records were more than untidy jottings. They were clear, easy to read and were kept exactly. In addition, Florentine businessmen had high rates of literacy and numeracy. Raymond de Roover, Armando Sapori and Gunnar Dahl all find

---

1   Max Weber, *The Protestant Ethic and the Spirit of Capitalism and Other Writings*, ed. and trans. Peter Baehr and Gordon C. Wells (New York: Penguin, 2002).

2   Werner Sombart, *Der moderne Kapitalismus: Historisch-systematische Darstellung des gesamteuropäischen Wirtschaftslebens von seinen Anfängen bis zur Gegenwart*, 3 vols. (Munich: Duncker & Humblot, 1924–27).

3   Armando Sapori, *The Italian Merchant in the Middle Ages*, trans. Patricia Ann Kennen (New York: Norton, 1970), 28–29.

a high level of numeracy in Florentine account books.[4] Robert Black has found that at least 69 percent of all Florentine fiscal household heads in 1427 were functionally literate,[5] and Alison Brown demonstrates that many Florentine businessmen were erudite.[6] The Italian Sapori even takes on the biases of the German Sombart directly and points out that German merchants of the time were not as literate as Italian merchants.[7]

The Florentines' rationality and market structure is the third target. Though these two points are theoretically distinct to economists, they are often linked in the work of economic historians. Some historians see a lack of rationality among businessmen that impeded smooth market functioning and assert that they were stuck in a medieval or noncapitalist mind-set. In addition, the economic structure was rigid and uncompetitive due to guild regulations. Finally, a skewed wealth distribution inhibited the economy.[8] Other historians see a competitive Florentine economy with broadly integrated markets; an efficient use of resources; and competitive, profit-maximizing firms.[9] Its institutional structure favored competitive markets. Contemporary jurists and moralists supported competitive markets, opposed collusion and cartelized behavior and preferred freedom of bargaining.[10] The city put these principles into practice,[11] and its financial market behavior was similar to that of comparable markets today.[12]

Research on this question has taken a variety of forms. Available documents include statutes, notarial documents, chronicles and commercial records, including account books, letters, commercial handbooks, memoirs and journals.[13] However, the documents

4   Ibid.; Raymond de Roover, "The Story of the Alberti Company of Florence, 1302–1348," in *Business, Banking, and Economic Thought*, 58; Gunnar Dahl, *Trade, Trust, and Networks: Commercial Culture in Late Medieval Italy* (Lund, Sweden: Nordic Academic Press, 1998), 280.

5   Robert Black, *Education and Society in Florentine Tuscany: Teachers, Pupils, and Schools, c. 1250–1500* (Leiden, the Netherlands: Brill, 2007), 1: 35.

6   Alison Brown, *Bartolomeo Scala, 1430–1497, Chancellor of Florence: The Humanist as Bureaucrat* (Princeton, NJ: Princeton University Press, 1979).

7   Sapori, *Italian Merchant*, 30.

8   Cf. Carlo M. Cipolla, "The Economic Depression of the Renaissance?," *Economic History Review* ser. 2, 16, no. 3 (1964): 518–24; Samuel K. Cohn Jr., *The Laboring Classes in Renaissance Florence* (New York: Academic Press, 1978); Alfred Dören, *Studien aus der Florentiner Wirtschaftgeschichte*, vol. 1: *Die Florentiner Wollentuchsindustrie vom Vierzehnten bis zum Sechzehnten Jahrhundert* (Stuttgart: J. G. Cotta'sche Buchhandlung Nachfolger, 1901); Sombart, *Der moderne Kapitalismus*.

9   Cf. Gene Brucker, *Renaissance Florence* (1959; Huntington, NY: Krieger, 1975); Richard A. Goldthwaite, "The Economy of Renaissance Italy: The Preconditions for Luxury Consumption," *I Tatti Studies* 2 (1987): 15–39; Raymond de Roover, "A Florentine Firm of Cloth Manufacturers," in *Business, Banking, and Economic Thought in Late Medieval and Early Modern Europe*, ed. Julius Kirshner (1938; Chicago: University of Chicago Press, 1974), 85–118; De Roover, "Story of the Alberti Company," 39–84; Sapori, *Italian Merchant*.

10 Raymond de Roover, "Labour Conditions in Florence around 1400: Theory, Policy, and Reality," in *Florentine Studies: Politics and Society in Renaissance Florence*, ed. Nicolai Rubinstein (Evanston, IL: Northwestern University Press, 1968), 313.

11 Ibid.

12 G. Geoffrey Booth and Umit G. Gurun, "Volatility Clustering and the Bid-Ask Spread: Exchange Rate Behavior in Early Renaissance Florence," *Journal of Empirical Finance* 15 (2008): 131–44.

13 Sapori, *Italian Merchant*, 92–105.

can dictate the scope of the analysis. The documents and methods being used must match as closely as possible the underlying theory being tested, and the theoretical assumptions being tested must be reasonable. Three key studies of Florentine wool industry market structure and competitiveness define the debate. Alfred Dören examines the laws that regulated the wool industry, rather than its actual behavior, and finds a monopolistic industry.[14] De Roover examines account books that reveal dynamic behavior and finds a competitive industry.[15] Paul McLean and John Padgett examine net wealth tax returns and find some monopolistic power.[16]

Dören's 1901 work examines city laws and guild regulations.[17] He does not conduct a quantitative test, thus his view of the economy is an idealized one. He claims that the wool industry was a monopoly with large firms running large workshops.[18] In his research he uses Arte della Lana guild records and adopts their perspective. This explains why he observed a large centralized manufacturing operation. Using only guild documents gave him the impression that there was too much power in the hands of the Arte. It is now known that the guild statutes must be used carefully.[19] They can only characterize a static situation, and any analysis using them is therefore biased against finding a competitive market. The optimal test of competition uses dynamic data.

De Roover's 1938 paper corrects Dören's overreliance on statutes and concludes that the industry was competitive.[20] His work is a significant methodological improvement over previous studies, as he conducts a detailed analysis based on mid-Cinquecento account books.[21] Account books provide a better source of data than laws and guild records, because they allow a researcher to observe individual behavior. They also provide a dynamic view of the firm. De Roover neither conducts statistical tests nor quantifies the level of monopoly power in the industry. Such tools were not then in wide use. Florence Edler's observations match De Roover's.[22] Later work follows De Roover's method and extends his results.[23]

---

14 Dören, *Wirtschaftgeschichte*, vol. 1.
15 De Roover, "Florentine Firm of Cloth Manufacturers."
16 Paul D. McLean and John F. Padgett, "Was Florence a Perfectly Competitive Market? Transactional Evidence from the Renaissance," *Theory and Society* 26, nos. 2/3 (1997): 209–44.
17 Dören, *Wirtschaftgeschichte*, vol. 1.
18 Ibid.
19 Florence Edler de Roover, "Andrea Banchi, Florentine Silk Manufacturer and Merchant of the Fifteenth Century," *Studies in Medieval and Renaissance History* 3 (1966): 223; Sapori, *Italian Merchant*, 93.
20 De Roover, "Florentine Firm of Cloth Manufacturers," 85–118.
21 Ibid.
22 Florence Edler, *Glossary of Medieval Terms of Business: Italian Series, 1200–1600.* Medieval Academy of America (1934; New York: Kraus Reprint Co., 1970), 335–426.
23 Federigo Melis, *Aspetti della vita economica medievale: Studi nell'Archivio Datini di Prato* (Siena, Italy: Monte dei Paschi di Siena, 1962), 455–634; Richard A. Goldthwaite, "The Florentine Wool Industry in the Late Sixteenth Century: A Case Study," *Journal of European Economic History* 32, no. 3 (2003): 527–54; Francesco Ammannati, "L'Arte della Lana a Firenze nel Cinquecento: crisi del settore e risposte degli operatori," *Storia economica: Rivista quadrimestrale*, 11, no. 1 (2008): 5–39, esp. 34; Ammannati, "Francesco di Marco Datini's Wool Workshops,"

It is hard to argue with De Roover's specific results. He concludes that the individual woolen-cloth production companies were small; only a handful of people were employed in any one firm. In addition, the individual subcontractor operations were mostly small and involved just one or a few people. The only exceptions were the guild-subsidized workshops that provided various services to all wool industry companies. Subsequent work by Hidetoshi Hoshino and Franco Franceschi bear this out. Their data clearly show that the market was comprised of many small companies.[24] (These points and related research are discussed in Appendix 3B.)

McLean and Padgett's 1997 paper tests the hypothesis of perfect competition. It looks at the wool industry from the perspective of the tax collector. Although their paper appeared decades after De Roover's, they apply a static approach. The analysis is based on a set of transactions: credit and debt contracts above a minimum size from the 1427 catasto.[25] The two researchers base their test on three conditions that George Stigler argues "are enough to insure that a single price will rule in a market": that the market is unconcentrated, that trading is impersonal and that traders have complete knowledge.[26] They test the market concentration and impersonal trading conditions on four Florentine industries: banking, cloth retailing, silk manufacturing and wool manufacturing.[27]

It is important to note that these conditions are theoretically sufficient but not necessary. If all initial conditions are met, the market will be perfectly competitive. However, if one or more conditions are not met, nothing is implied. This, in and of itself, implies that the McLean and Padgett test is theoretically incomplete. They test industry concentration first. They follow Stigler, who points out that perfect competition requires that firms in the industry be relatively small.[28] They find that banking and cloth retailing were concentrated, while wool and silk manufacturing were not.[29] Their concentration standard is only relative, however. Two of the studied industries are more concentrated and two of them are less concentrated. McLean and Padgett do not compare their results with accepted absolute concentration level standards.

They next test for impersonal trading, which they identify with anonymity.[30] They assert that transactions are anonymous when they are randomly distributed across firms.

in *Francesco di Marco Datini. The Man the Merchant*, ed. Giampero Nigro (Florence: Firenze University Press, 2010), 489–514; Ammannati, "Production et productivité du travail dans les ateliers laniers florentins du XVIe siècle," in *Les temps du travail. Normes, pratiques, évolutions (XIVe–XIXe siècle)*, ed. Corine Maitte and Didier Terrier (Rennes: Presses Universitaires de Rennes 2014), 225–49.

24 Hidetoshi Hoshino, *L'arte della lana nel basso medioevo in commercio della lana e il mercato dei panni fiorentini nei secoli XIII–XV* (Florence: Olschki, 1980), 228; Franco Franceschi, *Oltre il "Tumulto": I lavoratori fiorentini dell'Arte della Lana fra Tre e Quattrocento* (Florence: Olschki, 1993), 6–28.

25 McLean and Padgett, "Perfectly Competitive Market."

26 George J. Stigler, "Competition," in *The Organization of Industry* (Chicago: University of Chicago Press, 1968), 6.

27 McLean and Padgett, "Perfectly Competitive Market," 232.

28 Stigler, "Competition," 5.

29 McLean and Padgett, "Perfectly Competitive Market," 232.

30 McLean and Padgett, "Perfectly Competitive Market"; Stigler, "Competition," 5–6.

Table 7.1 Summary of tests of Florentine wool industry market competitiveness

Information	Dören	De Roover et al.	McLean/Padgett
Source of Data	Laws	Account Books	Census/Tax Records
Type of Test(s)	Firm Organization	Firm Organization	Concentration & Anonymity
Qualitative or Statistical?	Qualitative	Qualitative	Statistical
Direct or Indirect?	Indirect	Direct	Indirect
Behavioral Test?	No	Yes	Yes
Dynamic or Static?	Static	Dynamic	Static
Finding	Monopoly	Competitive	Mixed

Source: Table based on discussion in the text of: Dören, *Wirtschaftgeschichte*, vol. 1; De Roover, "Florentine Firm of Cloth Manufacturers;" Melis, *Aspetti*; Hoshino, *L'artedellalana*, 228; Franceschi, *Oltreil "Tumulto"*; Goldthwaite, "Florentine Wool Industry;" Ammannati, "L'Artedella Lana;" Ammannati, "Datini's Wool Workshops;" Ammannati, "Production et productivité" McLean and Padgett, "Perfectly Competitive Market."

This hypothesis leads to what they call the ball-throwing model of perfect competition.[31] Using a test based on this model, they claim that the wool industry had significant monopoly power. However, there is a problem with this analysis. McLean and Padgett take Stigler's concept of "impersonal" in his expression "perfect competition is *impersonal*" to be a synonym for anonymous. However, Stigler defines it differently; to him impersonal means "the fortunes of any one firm are independent of what happens to any other firm."[32] Seen in this context, the definition of anonymity used by McLean and Padgett adds a second, much stronger requirement to the one in Stigler's definition. Not only are the long-term results independent, but also the set of transactions are statistically independent. This biases the test against finding perfect competition. Instead of the ball-throwing model, Stigler's theory of impersonal behavior seems to require a test of dynamic time series behavior or some similar approach.

The concept of anonymity in the McLean and Padgett model is also anachronistic. It is based on a very specific and modern assumption about firm structure and extent. Modern American manufacturing firms generally operate using primarily employees and not subcontractors. They transact with sellers of inputs and buyers of outputs. Florentine silk and wool companies, however, employed mostly subcontractors rather than employees, because they produced using the putting-out system. (Appendix 3B and Chapter 9 look at this arrangement in greater detail.) Their transactions would include individuals that modern firms would categorize as employees. Assuming that the relationship of these subcontractors to the company was random is an additional assumption that biases the test.

Table 7.1 summarizes the research discussed in this section. De Roover's work is based on dynamic data and finds that the wool industry was highly competitive. Account books provide the best kind of data to test the competitiveness of the wool industry, because they allow a direct examination of the behavior of the firm. Although De Roover uses account

---

31 McLean and Padgett, "Perfectly Competitive Market," 234–35.
32 Stigler, "Competition," 6; emphasis in original.

books, his work was solely descriptive. Dören and McLean and Padgett base their work on static data and suggest that the wool industry had some level of monopoly power. The improvement of social scientific methodology over a century is one difference between the studies. Dören does not analyze actual behavior, but McLean and Padgett do. However, both approaches are fundamentally limited, because neither uses dynamic data.

Analysis of Wool Industry Market Structure

This section calculates three separate concentration measures to assess the Florentine wool industry market structure. Concentration measures essentially tests whether the industry is composed of a large number of small firms. The measure is a valuable tool that is widely used to assess monopoly power because for a large number of small firms it is both harder to collude and easier to violate regulations and evade detection. That Florentine firms kept secret account books is testament to the efficacy of the latter characteristic. The first measure is based on a complete set of data available for the sizes of all companies in the market in 1427. The second is a reanalysis of the McLean and Padgett data in the context of economic theory. The third is a time series composed of tests to see whether concentration was reasonably possible at any point during a three-century period in which the wool industry operated.

The concentration measures are all based on the Hirschman-Herfindahl Index, which is a reasonable approximation of a given industry's monopoly power and is widely used by governments and law courts around the world. It equals the sum of the squares of the market share percentages for all companies in a market. Stigler recommends its use.[33] The common standards to categorize an industry's competitiveness are where a value under 1,500 is considered competitive and a value above 2,500 is considered concentrated. The maximum possible value is 10,000.[34] The index accurately measures monopoly power if enforced collusion to form a cartel was difficult or impossible. The primary method of enforcing collusion would have been through the Arte della Lana, which effectively enforced production regulations,[35] but was unable to enforce a cartel.[36]

---

33 Stigler, "Measurement of Concentration," 29–38.
34 Ibid., 31. The current scale used in legal cases is as follows: 0 to 1,500 being unconcentrated, 1,500 to 2,500 being moderately concentrated and 2,500 and above being concentrated. This scale is discussed in US Department of Justice and the Federal Trade Commission, "Market Concentration in Horizontal Merger Guidelines, Issued August 19, 2010," sec. 5.3. http:// www.justice.gov/atr/public/guidelines/hmg-2010.html#5c. The older US Department of Justice and Federal Trade Commission standard is used in the chart: 0 to 1,000 being unconcentrated, 1,000 to 1,800 being moderately concentrated and 1,800 and above being concentrated. This scale is discussed in Federal Reserve Bank of Minneapolis, "A Widget Example of the Herfindahl-Hirschman Index," FedGazette (January 2000). http://research.mpls.frb.fed. us/publications_papers/pub_display.cfm?id=2389; Elizabeth S. Laderman, "Changes in the Structure of Urban Banking Markets in the West," Economic Review Federal Reserve Bank of San Francisco no. 1 (1995): 21–34.
35 De Roover, "Florentine Firm of Cloth Manufacturers," 94.
36 Brucker, Renaissance Florence, 64–65.

Simply as a practical matter, collusion would have been difficult to coordinate among a large number of independently owned companies.[37]

The first analysis is based on data gathered by Hoshino from the balance sheets of the lanaiuoli, included in the 1427 catasto.[38] These include the period of operation, the total production and the annual average production of the 26 companies operating. The data appear to be of high quality. Companies submitted balance sheets.[39] They had a strong incentive to submit balance sheets that were believable but not necessarily precisely accurate. (See the evaluation of the catasto data in Appendix 3A.) The list of firms appears to be comprehensive.[40] The index is computed directly using the annual average production figures of all companies that were operating (Table 7.2). The index of 442 implies a competitive market.

The second analysis applies the standard measure of monopoly power to the McLean and Padgett estimates discussed above.[41] (See Fig. 7.1.) All were well below the moderately concentrated standard, with indices of 374 for banking, 376 for silk manufacturing, between 207 and 436 for wool manufacturing and 659 for cloth retailing.[42]

The third analysis is more complicated. It gauges whether the wool industry could be even moderately concentrated. It creates an upper bound on concentration—the maximum reasonable Hirschman-Herfindahl Index—based on the numbers of companies organized by year and the known size distribution of wool industry companies.

The industry's general organization remained essentially constant through these three centuries. The companies were small and not vertically integrated.[43] A sample from a wide range of dates shows a remarkable consistency over time.[44] The largest company produced about ten times as much per year as the smallest. Removing the extreme quarters of the data reduces the variation to about two and a half times as much per year. Since the companies are small and all about the same size, the number of companies in a particular industry can approximately measure industry concentration. A company had to register with the guild before it could do business. Several sources provide industrywide lists of companies from 1308 through 1627, but not the production figures of individual companies. These company counts include those that were currently producing or were potential entrants.[45] The entry rates appear to have been relatively low. Hoshino

---

37 Mancur Olson, *The Logic of Collective Action: Public Goods and the Theory of Groups* (Cambridge, MA: Harvard University Press, 1971).

38 Hoshino, *L'Arte della Lana*, 228.

39 De Roover, "The Development of Accounting Prior to Luca Pacioli According to the Account Books of Medieval Merchants," in *Business, Banking, and Economic Thought in Late Medieval and Early Modern Europe*, ed. Julius Kirshner (Chicago: University of Chicago Press, 1974), 158.

40 McLean and Padgett, "Perfectly Competitive Market," 216.

41 Ibid., 232.

42 Ibid., 224.

43 De Roover, "Florentine Firm of Cloth Manufacturers," 85–118.

44 Edler, *Glossary of Medieval Terms*, 335–426; De Roover, "Florentine Firm of Cloth Manufacturers"; Raymond de Roover, *The Rise and Decline of the Medici Bank, 1397–1494* (Cambridge, MA: Harvard University Press, 1963), 173, 175 and 183; Melis, *Aspetti*; Goldthwaite, "Florentine Wool Industry," 527–54; Hoshino, *L'arte della lana*, 228.

45 See chapter 9 for more on this point.

Table 7.2 Florentine wool industry production shares by company, 1427

Company	(Number of Cloths Produced by Company)		(Company's Production as a % of Industry Total)		
	Total Production	Annual Average	Total Production	Annual Average	No. of Years in Ave. (to 1427)
Albizzi	111	47	1.43%	2.15%	2.36
Altoviti	290	75	3.73%	3.43%	3.87
Barbadori	517	161	6.64%	7.37%	3.21
Benivieni	366	91	4.70%	4.16%	4.02
Biliotti	250	96	3.21%	4.39%	2.60
Bischieri	223	46	2.86%	2.10%	4.85
Capponi, A.	340	123	4.37%	5.63%	2.76
Capponi, N.	315	116	4.05%	5.31%	2.72
Cardini	60	61	0.77%	2.79%	0.98
Cocco	76	16	0.98%	0.73%	4.75
Corbinelli, G.	147	67	1.89%	3.06%	2.19
Corbinelli, Pa.	202	105	2.60%	4.80%	1.92
Corbinelli, Pi.	71	50	0.91%	2.29%	1.42
Da Ghiacceto	126	90	1.62%	4.12%	1.40
Dietisalvi	76	57	0.98%	2.61%	1.33
Doffi	93	83	1.19%	3.80%	1.12
Fortini	1692	83	21.74%	3.80%	20.39
Giugni, D.	90	124	1.16%	5.67%	0.73
Giugni, N.	370	134	4.75%	6.13%	2.76
Popoleschi	150	85	1.93%	3.89%	1.76
Ridolfi	182	79	2.34%	3.61%	2.30
Rucellai, A.	243	48	3.12%	2.20%	5.06
Rucellai, A.	1100	83	14.13%	3.80%	13.25
Salvi	157	82	2.02%	3.75%	1.91
Velluti	400	126	5.14%	5.76%	3.17
Vettori	137	58	1.76%	2.65%	2.36

Herfindahl-Hirschman Index based on average annual production: 442.
Herfindahl-Hirschman Index based on total production: 903.
Source: Hoshino, *L'arte della lana*, 228. Production prior to 1427 is used. The total production and annual average production were calculated by Hoshino. The number of years was calculated by the author.

found that only 26 of 132 companies (about 20 percent) in the 1427 catasto had detailed balance sheets.[46] The large number of potential entrants significantly reduced the possibility of monopoly power.

Calculating the minimum number of companies needed for the industry to be guaranteed to be competitive is straightforward. First, assume the distribution of company sizes that is most likely to cause monopoly power. Since an index less than 1,500 indicates that an industry is competitive, a minimum of 10 companies would be required for a competitive industry. This is a realistic estimate. Doubling this to 20 companies gives a

---

46 Hoshino, *L'arte della lana*, 229.

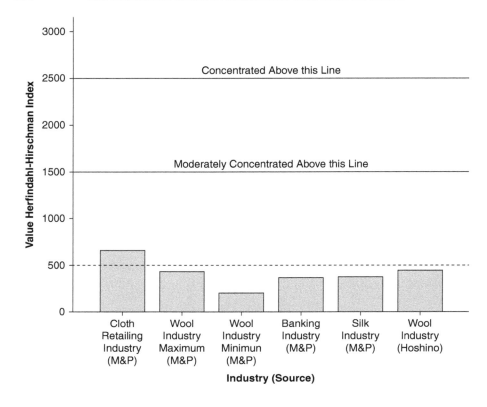

Figure 7.1 MacLean and Padgett concentration measures when compared to common standards of industry concentration and competition
Sources: Paul D. McLean and John F. Padgett (M&P), "Was Florence a Perfectly Competitive Market? Transactional Evidence from the Renaissance," *Theory and Society* 26, nos. 2/3 (1997), 224; Hoshino, *L'arte della lana*, 228. See the text for discussion of the methodology. Calculation by author.

conservative minimum. It is safe to conclude that the wool industry was not concentrated any time the number of companies surpassed either level.

Figure 7.2 presents the results of the analysis of companies. The line at the bottom represents the conservative estimate of 20 companies. There were between 200 and 300 companies ready to enter the industry during the *Trecento*, between 132 and 270 during the *Quattrocento*, between 63 and 153 during the Cinquecento and between 52 and 120 during the *Seicento*.

The lack of monopoly power persisted even as the industry declined. Far more companies operated than could possibly exist in a concentrated industry. The number of registered wool industry companies nevertheless remained greater than 50. Even assuming a 20 percent entry rate, the numbers almost always exceeded the conservative threshold of 20 and always exceeded the realistic threshold of 10 in order to prevent significant monopoly power. Of course, the large pool of potential entrants would reduce any monopoly power.

Figure 7.2 Florentine wool industry companies by year, 1308–1627
Sources: For years 1308, 1338, 1495, 1537, 1586, 1596, 1604 and 1627: Gene Brucker, *Florence: The Golden Age, 1138–1737* (Berkeley: University of California Press, 1998), 105.
For years 1382, 1427, 1458, and 1469: Hoshino, *L'arte della lana*, 227, 229 and 283.
For 1561: R. Burr Litchfield, *Florence Ducal Capital, 1530–1630* (New York: ACLS Humanities E-Book, 2008), Table 5.2. Calculation by author.

George Stigler's survivorship principle asserts that if a market structure persists for a long period of time, then that structure is in some sense optimal for that industry.[47] This principle is widely used in studies of industrial organization.[48] Smaller companies could not possibly have survived over the long term if the industry tended toward concentration and companies exhibited monopoly power. The persistently large number of companies combined with the survivorship principle suggests that the industry was competitive and that a low level of concentration was the optimal wool industry structure.[49]

---

47 George J. Stigler, "The Economies of Scale," *Journal of Law and Economics* 1 (1958): 54–71.
48 Dennis W. Carlton and Jeffrey M. Perloff, *Modern Industrial Organization*, 4th ed. (Boston: Addison Wesley, 2005), 42–43.
49 Stigler, "Economies of Scale."

A Test of Production Theory

The remainder of this study presents another test of whether the wool industry was perfectly competitive. This tests the combination of neoclassical production theory and perfect competition. This approach intertwines the economic rationality and perfect competition hypotheses regarding Florentine businessmen. The result is a more stringent set of requirements than either one hypothesis would impose alone. It is important to keep in mind that a model is a deliberate, and usually very significant, simplification of reality. Appendix 7A presents a supplemental discussion of the relationship between neoclassical production theory and Seemingly Unrelated Regressions (SUR).

This examines the factor markets for a particular wool industry company. Since this is a test of the input market, it is, technically, a test of monopsony, not monopoly power. The data are from 1550s Medici-Tornaquinci wool industry account books. The key advantage of using account books is that the individual production steps, which were completed serially, can be easily distinguished. Production theory usually models the firm as a black-box process, because the firm uses inputs and produces outputs. Here both are visible, and the researcher can see inside the black box. The model, however, implies that the producer would have been able to foresee any changes in the prices of the inputs and of the final cloth. Failure of this assumption would mean the test in this study is biased against acceptance of the model. Appendix 7B discusses this in greater detail.

Most of the data concern the partnership of Francesco di Giuliano de'Medici and Company, wool merchants, 1556–59, because it has the most complete set of books in the collection. These account books were kept by the family and so can be presumed to be their secret account books. These would be more likely to reveal the actual behavior, since they would have no need to conceal violations or revenue. Of seven of the eight account books used by a typical mid-Cinquecento wool merchant's firm, only one book has been lost. This is the Book of Weavers (*Libro di tessitori*).[50] Additional data on weavers is therefore included, as necessary, from the Book of Weavers of another firm, that of Giuliano di Raffaello de'Medici and Company, wool merchants, 1547–52.[51] Francesco di Giuliano de'Medici and Company produced ten lots of woolen material, each a batch of 3 to 12 similar cloths, for a total of 71 cloths for the whole period. It produced four types of cloth, ranging in quality from the *rascia*, a very fine cloth, to shorts, the cheap odds and ends that were a by-product of the production process. The period during which this company operated is reasonably representative of long-term industry characteristics. The industry was producing at the long-term wool industry average level, and the concentration level was low. Litchfield finds 153 extant companies in 1561.[52] This particular company,

---

50 Edler, *Glossary*, 386. The surviving account books from this company are as follows: Book of Spinners (*Libro di filatori*), Book of Weavers (*Libro di tessitori*), Book of Dyers and Workmen (*Libro di tintori e laboranti*), Wastebook (*Quadernaccio*), Journal (*Giornale*), Book of Income and Outgo and Cash Book (*Libro di entrata e uscita e Quaderno di cassa*), Wage Ledger (*Quaderno di manifattori*) and General Ledger (*Libro debitori e creditori*).

51 De Roover, "Florentine Firm of Cloth Manufacturers," 97–98; Edler, *Glossary*, 419. The manuscript used will be Medici-Tornaquinci, Ms. 560 (5).

52 R. Burr Litchfield, *Florence Ducal Capital, 1530–1630* (New York: ACLS Humanities E-Book, 2008), table 5.2. Permanent Link: http://quod.lib.umich.edu/cgi/t/text/text-idx?c=acls;idno=heb90034.

however, was relatively unsuccessful. The company bought an abnormally small amount of wool compared with similar companies in the Medici-Tornaquinci collection, and the partnership contract was not renewed when the initial contract expired after three years. This lack of success implies that the company was probably not efficiently managed and was therefore less likely to appear competitive. Appendix 7B presents a supplemental discussion of how the data were processed prior to inclusion in the statistical test.

Before covering the statistical results, it is useful to note that the account books provide important insights about the Arte della Lana and the firms that operated within its marketplace. Though a guild is often seen as a monopoly in the modern sense, that is not an accurate picture. Gary Richardson provides a cautionary note regarding English guilds in his handling of the changing usage of the term "monopoly" and how those changes are associated with modern theoreticians' handling of guilds. He argues against use of the modern term monopoly to describe guilds.[53] Arte della Lana regulations did not regulate wages or piece rates until the Cinquecento.[54] For example, regulations setting prices for spinners were established in 1547 and reissued in 1557.[55] The need to reissue this implies it was not followed. Nevertheless, as a practical matter, some of the payments to workers could vary.[56] For example, the piece rates paid by *lanini* to the spinners varied.[57] Weaving piece rates[58] and dyeing prices[59] also varied.

The results of the joint test of perfect competition and neoclassical production theory do not reject the hypothesis. The joint test is not rejected in seven out of ten specifications. The results are summarized in Table 7.3. Overall, the model held up well considering all the biases built into the test against it. In particular, the behavioral assumptions fit well.

Conclusions

The evidence clearly demonstrates that the Renaissance Florentine wool industry was competitive. The descriptive evidence is overwhelming. The companies were small, and there were always a large number of them. Moreover, the neoclassical production theory model of perfect competition is generally supported despite strong statistical biases imposed against its acceptance. These findings lead to more general implications for

---

53 Gary Richardson, "A Tale of Two Theories: Monopolies and Craft Guilds in Medieval England and Modern Imagination," *Journal of the History of Economic Thought* 23, no. 2 (2001): 217–42.

54 Francesco Ammannati, "Craft Guild Legislation and Woollen Production: The Florentine Arte della Lana in the Fifteenth and Sixteenth Centuries," in *Innovation and Creativity in Late Medieval and Early Modern European Cities*, ed. Karol Davids and Bert De Munck (Farnham: Ashgate, 2014), 55–79.

55 Lorenzo Cantini, *Legislazione toscana*, 32 vols. (Florence: Albizzini, 1800–1804), 1: 366–9 and 3: 217; Edler, *Glossary*, 149–50 and 279–80.

56 Goldthwaite, "Florentine Wool Industry in the Late Sixteenth Century," 553.

57 Medici-Tornaquinci, Ms. 567 (4).

58 Medici-Tornaquinci, Ms. 560 (5).

59 Medici-Tornaquinci, Ms. 567 (7).

Table 7.3 Summary of test results by choice of proxy for spinning production step and overall

Restriction	Lanini	Stamaiuoli	Overall
Negative slope	pass	pass	pass
Negative semidefinite	pass	pass	pass
Symmetry	fail	pass	unclear
Negative slope given symmetry	pass	pass	pass
Negative semidefinite given symmetry	pass	pass	pass
Symmetry given negative slope	fail	pass	unclear
Combined	fail	pass	unclear

This table summarizes the results in Tables 7.5 through 7.8 in Appendix 7C.

early modern industry. The simpler, behavioral implications of neoclassical production theory are consistent with observed behavior. However, the more mathematical implications, in particular symmetry, seem only partly applicable.

The behavioral predictions of neoclassical production theory are broadly consistent with production by the Renaissance Florentine wool industry. The model used in this study includes the joint assumptions of functioning markets for all major inputs in the production process and a lack of monopoly, or monopsony, power in the marketplace.

These results suggest that if perfect competition and capitalism can be equated, then Renaissance urban capitalism was well developed even if there are questions about rural capitalism.[60] This particular point opens several areas of research that are beyond the scope of this study.

Together, these findings should encourage further application of quantitative techniques to the preindustrial world, as well as motivate the gathering of more detailed data on early modern enterprises. As always, it is important to model the data carefully.

Appendix 7A: Supplemental Discussion of the Theory and Model Used in Test of Production Theory

This appendix expands on the brief discussion in Section 4 of this chapter in order to provide more insight into the theory, the model, the statistical test and how each is incorporated into the analysis.

The statistical test uses SUR, sometimes referred to as "Zellner's method."[61] This is a joint test of perfect competition and neoclassical production theory. The study here also uses a standard version of the neoclassical production theory model. A successful model must both accurately represent human behavior and have a mathematical solution.[62]

---

60 Rebecca Jean Emigh, *The Undevelopment of Capitalism: Sectors and Markets in Fifteenth-Century Tuscany* (Philadelphia: Temple University Press, 2009).

61 Arnold Zellner, "An Efficient Method of Estimating Seemingly Unrelated Regressions and Tests for Aggregation Bias," *Journal of the American Statistical Association* 57, no. 298 (1962): 348–68.

62 For a formal statement of the model, see Hal R. Varian, *Microeconomic Analysis*, 3rd ed. (New York: Norton, 1992), chaps. 2–6.

A key set of assumptions underlies the model, its mathematical space and the functions on that space. All of these mathematical constructs either have real-world analogues or are included to improve statistical tractability. The assumptions here are that (1) a given firm is perfectly competitive and cannot influence the prices it pays or receives, (2) the firm has perfect foresight about future events and (3) every input can be replicated without cost. Obviously, these assumptions are not absolutely true. The theory asserts that together they describe production reasonably well.

Neoclassical production theory, though usually presented in a mathematical language, can be explained with relatively little use of mathematics. A mathematical space is assumed to be regular, monotonic and convex; a regular space has no corners. In economics terms this means that every incremental change has some effect. A monotonic space has curves that slope in only one direction. This means that as the inputs increase, the outputs should not decrease. A convex space is such that if two points are in the space, then every point on a line connecting those two points is in the space. This means that, if two sets of inputs can be used to produce a particular output, then the weighted combination of those inputs will produce at least that amount of output. Since firms can vary their inputs, they can produce all affordable outputs. The regularity of the space makes the mathematics more intuitive. Its monotonicity and convexity make the model more realistic.

The production, cost and profit functions, basic to neoclassical production theory, are defined in the context of the mathematical space. The production function expresses the relationship between the various sets of possible inputs and the corresponding maximum outputs. The cost function minimizes the total cost of the inputs, given the input prices and the total output. The profit function maximizes profit, given input and output prices. The profit function is defined contingent on the cost function, which, in turn, is defined contingent on the production function. Minimizing the cost function is equivalent to maximizing the profit function.[63] The substitution matrix associates the changes in price of inputs and outputs with the changes in quantity for all inputs and outputs. It requires no further assumptions about the functional form of the production, cost or profit functions. Every functional form that satisfies the above assumptions is equivalent.

The assumptions about the space and the functions lead to five testable hypotheses about firm behavior. First, the output function of the firm is positive semidefinite, which means if the price of the output increases, the producer firm will not reduce supply of that output. Second, the input-demand function of the firm is negative semidefinite, which means if the price of an input increases, the producer will not increase demand for that input. The firm's demand curves do not slope up. The negative slopes of these curves are a necessary but not sufficient condition for negative semidefiniteness. Third, the cross-effects between inputs do not dominate the own effects of the inputs. This means the relative effect of a change in price of an input on the quantity of that input will always be greater than the effect of the price change of another input. Fourth, the cost and profit functions are homogeneous of degree one, which means the firm's production can be scaled up or down. This is equivalent to assuming that the firm's production process brings

63 Varian, *Microeconomic Analysis*, 43–45 and 74.

constant returns, neither economies nor diseconomies, to scale in the region where the firm is producing. Section 3 showed that in the long term the wool industry was composed of small companies with few scale economies. Fifth, and last, the substitution matrix is symmetric, which means the function that the substitution matrix represents is smooth and without corners. For all input sets, the derivatives exist in every direction, and these derivatives are continuous. This last hypothesis simply makes the model more easily usable mathematically and does not contain any significant behavioral implications.

The model is tested here using the SUR method, which in this case is natural, intuitively reasonable and which precisely fits the mathematical structure of the underlying theory. The SUR is a system of simultaneous interrelated equations. No independent variable occurs as a dependent variable in any other regression in the system. The coefficients calculated in this regression are precisely the partial derivatives of the hypothesized substitution matrix.

Three hypotheses are tested: the behavioral hypothesis of downward sloping input-demand curves and the two mathematical hypotheses of negative semidefiniteness and symmetry. These are tested independently and then jointly. Negative semidefiniteness and symmetry is tested by constraining the matrix element estimates, using the Lagrange multiplier method.[64] This method provides global constraint results and is a commonly used model in economics. The SUR is then estimated subject to linear constraints implied by neoclassical production theory. The mean squared error (MSE) criterion was chosen as the most appropriate standard to evaluate the results. It is similar to the commonly used gravity-style model and approximates the L_2 metric (a functional distance measure) criterion.[65] The MSE uses a noncentral F-statistic, which is calculated by using the R^2 (a measure of statistical fit) result, as recommended by Marjorie McElroy.[66] A noncentral F-statistic is appropriate because the constraints in the Lagrangian method create a bias in the estimation. The MSE criterion weights the bias and error effects equally. The test is run to determine whether or not the restrictions affect the estimated coefficients at the 5 percent level of significance. It uses the noncentral F-statistic table published by James Goodnight and T. D. Wallace and also recommended by McElroy.[67]

The applications of the two constraints are carried out in different ways. The application of the symmetry constraint using this specification of the model is straightforward, since the symmetric coefficients are simply constrained to equality. The application of the negative semidefiniteness constraint is somewhat less straightforward. If any of the diagonal elements in the estimated matrix were greater than zero, the SUR was reestimated with the aberrant parameter or parameters constrained to zero.

---

64 S. D. Silvey, "The Lagrangian Multiplier Test," *Annals of Mathematical Statistics* 30, no. 2 (1959): 389–407a; David G. Luenberger, *Optimization by Vector Space Methods* (New York: Wiley, 1969), chap. 8.

65 Luenberger, *Optimization*, 29–32.

66 Marjorie McElroy, "Weaker MSE Criteria and Tests for Linear Restriction in Regression Models with Non-Spherical Disturbances," *Journal of Econometrics* 6, no. 3 (1977): 389–94.

67 James H. Goodnight and T. D. Wallace, "Weaker Criteria and Tests of Linear Restrictions in Regressions," *Econometrica* (1972): 699–709.

Appendix 7B: Supplemental Discussion of the Data Used in Test of Production Theory

This appendix expands on the brief discussion of the data used in the test of production theory and how the relationship between them and the model and test.

Not all of the implications of the theory and parts of the industry can be examined. Lack of data on product quantities prevents testing the hypothesis of positive semidefiniteness of the product-supply function. Lack of data covering every step in the production process prevents testing if the entire production process exhibits homogeneity of degree one. The inability to run certain tests poses a significant problem. Statistically reliable methods are used to mitigate this problem and construct the tests. In these cases the statistical tests are uniformly, and sometimes strongly, biased against the hypothesis of perfect competition. Several other limitations arise from using data from only one firm: (1) there is no method for checking the robustness of the findings; (2) there is no reliable method for examining the market demand for woolen cloth based on data from only one firm; and (3) time series analyses are impossible, because the company was in business for such a short time. However, it is possible to test for monopsony power because the company interacted with all aspects of the wool industry's labor (factor) market.

However, there are two key advantages to focusing research on account book data, The first advantage is that the various specialized artisans worked independently, so the data should allow the statistical identification of the firm's input-demand curves. The second advantage of using account book data is that it eliminates aggregation bias. The test uses individual cloths as the basic unit of data. This decision motivates all criteria used in the data preparation and selection. Each cloth in each lot received an identification number at the moment the company assigned the material to the warper. Individual cloths can thus be tracked from warping to final sale in the firm's account book. Materials were distinguished by lot in the spinning process as well.

Only the spinning, weaving and dyeing of the cloth are included in the test. It is not feasible to include the purchases of wool, the warping or the sales of cloth. There are too few purchases of wool (only six purchases consisting of four types of wool) to permit a statistical estimation. All warping work was priced identically, so no statistical distinction among cloths is possible. The sales of cloth were made individually. No measurement of quantity sold—for example, length—is available. Only the cloth quality is available. The preparing and finishing steps are also not included in the analysis, because there are too few or no usable data. Most of these data would have been listed in the Book of Dyers and Workmen, which had a large portion ripped out.[68]

The data on spinning were gathered from the Book of Spinners, which contains data for both lanini and *stamaiuoli*.[69] Each cloth in a particular lot was assigned the mean price and quantity of spun threads for that lot. One must then assume that each lot's cloth was spun in a similar manner so that the added value from the spinning on each piece of cloth was identical. Given that the Book of Spinners does not provide a more detailed

---

68 The only steps for which data remain are dyeing, those involving *capodieci* and washing.
69 Medici-Tornaquinci, Ms. 567 (4).

Table 7.4 Construction of weaving proxy variable: regression results

no. of days	=	8.828	+3.111P	−0.083P²	+0.001P³
		(9.950)	(1.102)	(0.036)	(0.000)
R² = 0.0646					
no. of pounds	=	−14.395	+13.572P	−0.345P²	+0.002P³
		(8.882)	(0.984)	(0.032)	(0.000)
R² = 0.7367					
N = 309					

P: Price of cloth
P²: Price of cloth squared
P³: Price of cloth cubed (std. dev.)
R²: Measure of statistical fit
Sources: Medici-Tornaquinci, Mss. 560 (4) and 560 (5). Estimation by author.

description of the process, this assumption is plausible. Corrections, done by reducing the quantity of cloth, were made only for obviously short cloths.

As one would expect, the prices and quantities reported by the lanini and stamaiuoli are highly correlated; therefore, they are included in separate specifications. Separating them should somewhat lessen the magnitude of the negative semidefiniteness in the substitution matrix, because there is less possibility for substitution between the spinning steps. These specifications appropriately bias the findings against the hypothesis of the symmetry of the substitution matrix. The variation is reduced through this averaging process, which further biases the findings against accepting the model.

The weaving data are primarily from the Book of Weavers of Giuliano di Raffaello de'Medici and Company, 1547–52. However, most of the data are gathered from the wage ledger, an account book that summarizes all payments to subcontractors.[70] The prices for weaving the cloth are gathered from lists in the Book of Weavers, which contains the tally of cloths woven for each weaver. These cloths are listed only by type, with no identification numbers. If the original Book of Weavers still existed, then each cloth in the analysis could be identified. Lacking such identification, and in order to derive a proxy formula for the prices of individual cloths, the prices for weaving are assumed to be the mean for each type of cloth. This assumption requires that the weaving process be almost identical for each type of cloth. As the wage ledger makes no distinction among cloths other than by type, this is a reasonable assumption. The data on spinning and the data on weaving are statistically independent, because the sets of data for each step were compiled on a different basis: spinning data were compiled by lot and weaving data were compiled by type of cloth.

All of the weaving quantities are single cloths that cannot be used unadjusted as the quantity of weaving. A proxy for the quantity of weaving must therefore be created. The results of this are shown in Table 7.4. In order to create a proxy for the quantity of cloth woven for the price listed in the Book of Weavers, a sample of weaving quantities,

---

70 Wage Ledger: Medici-Tornaquinci, Ms. 567 (11); Book of Weavers: Medici-Tornaquinci, Ms. 560 (5).

with their corresponding prices from the 1547–52 company was gathered. The objective was to calculate the best fit using regression and substituting the price of the cloth for the quantity of weaving to be used in the test. Note that this method intentionally includes the quality of the work as part of the quantity variable. This is effectively, then, an efficiency-adjusted quantity. The results are listed in Table 7.4. The R^2 criterion was used in order to minimize variation that was unaccounted for. A cubic equation of the weaving price per cloth was regressed on the weight of the cloth and the number of days. The cubic form was used to avoid orthogonality (collinearity) problems between the dependent and independent variables in the final form of the statistical test. The cloths were not separated by type. The pounds of cloth provide a better statistical fit and so are used. As in the case of the spinning data, the statistical processing of the weaving data introduces biases against both negative semidefiniteness and symmetry.

The data on dyeing are from the Book of Dyers and Workmen.[71] The quantity of dyeing work is difficult to determine, because it was measured on the basis of one cloth per job. This implies a quality measure that better represents what the lanaiuoli received back from the dyer. Therefore, the final sales price of the cloth is used as a proxy for the quantity of dyeing. The final sales price varied significantly within lots and across types of cloth but allows sufficient degrees of freedom in the test. The specification is computationally equivalent to the assumption that the dyeing process produced florins—in other words, profits—which is reasonable because the quantity and quality of the cloth and the quality of the dye were important determinants of the final sales price of the cloth.

The dyeing prices are listed individually for most cloths. The remaining cloths were dyed in large batches. Apparently the same price was charged for each cloth, because the total price was an exact multiple of the number of cloths dyed. The average for each batch is incorporated in the price of dyeing. That price is calculated by dividing the dyeing price by the final sales price of the cloth, which should factor out any correlation. As before, the biases here are also against negative semidefiniteness and symmetry. There should be a bias against the negative semidefiniteness hypothesis, because an inexact proxy for the quantity is used in the test.

As noted above, the exact data cannot be gathered in all cases; thus, the use of imputed values is sometimes required. In practice, these values are the means over some subset of production. This process creates a step function (see Fig. 7.3). Since the theory and estimation procedure assume a smooth function, the added roughness caused by the imputed data reduces the fit and increases the bias against the theory.

These missing data do not cause problems in estimating the matrix if the prices used for each of these three steps—spinning, weaving and dyeing—and unknown prices of the omitted steps are linearly independent. This is a reasonable assumption because the prices of the steps not included in the analysis were generally fixed, while the prices used for the three steps in the regression were variable. The prices were fixed by statute or had limited flexibility. Frequent credit and discount provisions in transactions would have increased the competitive nature of the market.[72]

---

71 Medici-Tornaquinci, Ms. 567 (7).
72 Edler, *Glossary*, 396–406.

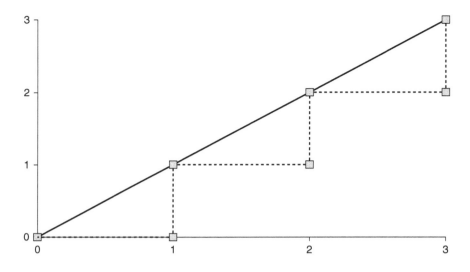

Figure 7.3 Contrasting a step function with a smooth function

Appendix 7C: Supplemental Discussion of the Statistical Results from Test of Production Theory

This appendix presents the detailed results of the joint test of perfect competition and neoclassical production theory. The setup of the SUR is straightforward. The idea, following neoclassical theory, is that the quantities are based on the observed output and factor prices. The price vectors are regressed on the quantities of all three steps in the production process, in combination, to estimate the best least-squares fit over all equations simultaneously. A 3 x 3 matrix is tested, with the spinning, weaving and dyeing quantities being the dependent variables and their prices being the corresponding independent variables in each equation in the matrix. A 3 x 3 matrix is the minimum size for a nontrivial test of the substitution matrix. Each step originates in a different stage in the production process, which reduces the possibility of collinearity. The tests use the two spinning proxies in separate specifications of each statistical test in order to increase the estimation's robustness. Overall, six tests have been run. Each theoretical assumption is tested as a restriction on the acceptable values. If the restriction is rejected then the theoretical assumption is rejected.

The joint test is not rejected in seven out of ten specifications. The results are summarized in Table 7.3 in the body of Chapter 7 and provided in detail in Tables 7.5 through 7.8. The fully restricted stamaiuoli specification is not rejected. The fully restricted lanini specification fits the data well, based on the R^2s, even though the imposition of the restriction caused a statistically significant reduction in the quality of the statistical fit.

Table 7.5 Results of the Lanini tests

Test	Negative semidefinite	Symmetry	Negative semidefinite given symmetry	Symmetry given negative semidefinite	Combined
R^2	0.9647	0.8052	0.8052	0.8052	0.8052
R^{*2}	0.0026	0.1621	0	0.1595	0.1621
MT-K	168	168	168	168	168
J	1	3	1	3	4
(MT-K)/J	168	56	168	56	42
$(R^2 - R^{*2})/(1 - R^2)$	0.0795	4.957	0	4.878	4.957
F-stat	13.35	277.6	0	273.16	208.2
Result	pass	fail	pass	fail	fail

MT-K: Degrees of freedom
J: Constraints
R^2: Measure of statistical fit
R^{*2}: Constrained R^2
Sources: Medici-Tornaquinci, Mss. 560 (5), 567 (4), 567 (7), and 567 (11). Estimation by author.

The behavioral implications of neoclassical production theory are borne out quite well. All input-conditional demand curves slope downward. Higher prices were not associated with increases in demand. The constraint of negative or zero terms along the diagonal has no significant effect on the regression. These results are presented in Tables 7.6 and 7.8, respectively.

In addition, the model fits quite well. The wool industry appears competitive. Both of the fully restricted estimates of the substitution matrices have high R^2s. These estimates provide a rough measure of how well the theory predicts the data. The results of the estimates are presented in Tables 7.6 and 7.7 and in greater detail in Tables 7.6 and 7.8, respectively. The individual regression diagnostics confirm the good statistical fit. The R^2 in all the tables indicates that the model explains more than 70 percent of the variation. This high percentage implies that the data fit the theory well. The significance levels of the t-statistics confirm this.

The two mathematical implications of neoclassical economic theory do less well but still acceptably given all the biases against them that are built into the test. The results are summarized in Table 7.3 in the body of Chapter 7. Negative semidefiniteness was not rejected in any specification of the test. This result is presented in Tables 7.5 and 7.7 and in greater detail in Tables 7.6 and 7.8, respectively. Symmetry did not hold for the specifications of the test involving the lanini proxy for spinning. This result is presented in Table 7.5, and the statistical failure is presented in greater detail in Table 7.6.

Table 7.6 Estimation of unrestricted and restricted seemingly unrelated regressions equations for Lanini

Estimated Coefficients in the Lanini Unrestricted Model
Dependent Variables

	Constant	P spinning	P weaving	P dyeing
Q spinning	1.13**	1.01**	9.87**	−15.79**
Q weaving	323.61**	−25.14**	−151.68**	11.40
Q dyeing	1.72**	−0.11**	−0.15*	−1.38**
R² = 0.9673				

Estimated Coefficients in the Lanini Negative Semi-Definite-Restricted Model
Dependent Variables

	Constant	P spinning	P weaving	P dyeing
Q spinning	8.71**	0.00***	6.58**	−17.29**
Q weaving	329.60**	−25.94**	−154.28**	10.21
Q dyeing	1.90**	−0.13**	−0.23**	−1.42**
R² = 0.9647				

Estimated Coefficients in the Lanini Symmetry-Restricted Model
Dependent Variables

	Constant	P spinning	P weaving	P dyeing
Q spinning	38.79**	−3.69**	−13.20**	0.01
Q weaving	236.92**	−13.20**	−113.96**	0.10
Q dyeing	0.95**	0.01	0.10*	−1.35**
R² = 0.8052				

Estimated Coefficients in the Lanini Fully Restricted Model
Dependent Variables

	Constant	P spinning	P weaving	P dyeing
Q spinning	38.79**	−3.69**	−13.20**	0.01
Q weaving	236.92**	−13.20**	−113.96**	0.10
Q dyeing	0.95**	0.01	0.10*	−1.35**
R² = 0.8052				

Q spinning: Quantity of spinning
Q weaving: Quantity of weaving
Q dyeing: Quantity of dyeing
P spinning: Price of spinning
P weaving: Price of weaving
P dyeing: Price of dyeing
R²: Measure of statistical fit
*** Constrained.

** Significant at the 95% level.

* Significant at the 90% level.

Sources: Medici-Tornaquinci, Mss. 560 (5), 567 (4), 567 (7), and 567 (11).

Table 7.7 Results of the Stamaiuoli tests

Test	Negative semidefinite	Symmetry	Negative semidefinite given symmetry	Symmetry given negative semidefinite	Combined
R^2	0.7861	0.7404	0.7404	0.7404	0.7404
R^{*2}	0	0.0457	0	0.0457	0.0457
MT-K	168	168	168	168	168
J	1	3	1	3	4
(MT-K)/J	168	56	168	56	42
$(R^2 - R^{*2})/(1 - R^2)$	0	0.2136	0	0.2136	0.2136
F-stat	0	11.96	0	11.96	8.97
Result	pass	pass	pass	pass	pass

MT-K: Degrees of freedom
J: Constraints
R^2: Measure of statistical fit
R^{*2}: Constrained R^2
Sources: Medici-Tornaquinci, Mss. 560 (5), 567 (4), 567 (7), and 567 (11). Estimation by author.

Table 7.8 Estimation of unrestricted and restricted seemingly unrelated regressions equations for Stamaiuoli

Estimated Coefficients in the Stamaiuoli Negative Unrestricted Model
Dependent Variables

	Constant	P spinning	P weaving	P dyeing
Q spinning	106.03**	−4.54	4.35	−107.20**
Q weaving	102.53**	143.98**	−177.11**	56.15
Q dyeing	0.76**	0.72**	−0.34**	−1.19**
$R^2 = 0.7861$				

Estimated Coefficients in the Stamaiuoli Negative Semi-Definite-Restricted Model
Dependent Variables

	Constant	P spinning	P weaving	P dyeing
Q spinning	106.03**	−4.54	4.35	−107.20**
Q weaving	102.53**	143.98**	−177.11**	56.15
Q dyeing	0.76**	0.72**	−0.34**	−1.19**
$R^2 = 0.7861$				

Estimated Coefficients in the Stamaiuoli Symmetry-Restricted Model
Dependent Variables

	Constant	P spinning	P weaving	P dyeing
Q spinning	116.54**	−76.78**	52.95**	−0.07**
Q weaving	125.39**	52.95**	−106.22**	0.25**
Q dyeing	0.94**	−0.07	0.25*	−1.22**
$R^2 = 0.7404$				

continued

Table 7.8 continued

Estimated Coefficients in the Stamaiuoli Fully Restricted Model
Dependent Variables

	Constant	P spinning	P weaving	P dyeing
Q spinning	116.54**	−76.78**	52.95**	−0.07
Q weaving	125.39**	52.95**	−106.22**	0.25
Q dyeing	0.94**	−0.07	0.25*	−1.22**
R² = 0.7404				

Q spinning: Quantity of spinning
Q weaving: Quantity of weaving
Q dyeing: Quantity of dyeing
P spinning: Price of spinning
P weaving: Price of weaving
P dyeing: Price of dyeing
R²: Measure of statistical fit
*** Constrained
** Significant at the 95% level
* Significant at the 90% level
Sources: Medici-Tornaquinci, Mss. 560 (5), 567 (4), 567 (7), and 567 (11). Estimation by author.

Appendix 7D: On the Correspondence between the Neoclassical Production Theory Substitution Matrix and Seemingly Unrelated Regressions

There is a mathematical correspondence between the SUR statistical model and neoclassical production theory substitution matrix.[73] The results from both are equivalent. In particular, the coefficients of the SUR equal the partial derivatives of the derived factor demands.

The SUR equation system is a set of simultaneous equations without any instrumental variables. The SUR equation system is then the following :[74]

$$Q_S = \frac{\partial QS}{\partial PS} P_S + \frac{\partial QS}{\partial PW} P_S + \frac{\partial QS}{\partial PD} P_D$$

$$Q_W = \frac{\partial QS}{\partial PS} P_S + \frac{\partial QS}{\partial PW} P_S + \frac{\partial QS}{\partial PD} P_D$$

$$Q_D = \frac{\partial QS}{\partial PS} P_S + \frac{\partial QS}{\partial PW} P_S + \frac{\partial QS}{\partial PD} P_D$$

---

73 This approach is largely motivated by Arnold Zellner's Economics 414, University of Chicago, Fall 1983.

74 George G. Judge et al., *The Theory and Practice of Econometrics*, 2nd ed. (New York: Wiley, 2005), 465–508.

Where:

Q_S: Quantity of spinning.

Q_W: Quantity of weaving.

Q_D: Quantity of dyeing,

P_S: Price of spinning,

P_W: Price of weaving and

P_D: Price of dyeing.

The coefficients of the SUR are the matrix of derived factor demands. The SUR equation system can be made to represent the substitution matrix. The regression coefficients match up to the elements of the matrix for the derived demand. The elements of the matrix for derived factor demands are the following:[75]

$$
\begin{matrix}
\dfrac{\partial QS}{\partial PS} & \dfrac{\partial QS}{\partial PW} & \dfrac{\partial QS}{\partial PD} \\[2mm]
\dfrac{\partial QW}{\partial PS} & \dfrac{\partial QW}{\partial PW} & \dfrac{\partial QW}{\partial PD} \\[2mm]
\dfrac{\partial QD}{\partial PS} & \dfrac{\partial QD}{\partial PW} & \dfrac{\partial QD}{\partial PD}
\end{matrix}.
$$

---

75 P. R. G. Layard and A. A. Walters, *Microeconomic Theory* (New York: McGraw Hill, 1978), chap. 9; Hal Varian, *Microeconomic Analysis*, 3rd ed. (New York: Norton, 1992), chap. 2.

Chapter Eight

TIME FOR IT ALL: WOMEN IN THE RENAISSANCE FLORENTINE WOOL INDUSTRY

Introduction

The role of women in society and how that role evolved over time is a fundamental question in Italian Renaissance historiography. Finding whether that role was expanding, contracting, unchanged or moving into new areas provides an important insight into discovering the heart of what the Renaissance means. The role of working women is a critical component of any such research agenda because it occupies the most common and frequently observed margin between the worlds of men and of women.

Burckhardt's nineteenth-century observation that women gained increasing equality during the Renaissance began the discussion.[1] However, his view has been challenged in recent years. Joan Kelly-Gadol questions whether women even had a Renaissance and whether the term can mean anything for women. She argues that the new Renaissance society, better suited to a world with an expanding urban economy and shrinking nobility, reduced options for women.[2] Cohn argues that Burckhardt overestimated the social changes in the case of Renaissance Florence.[3] However, Herlihy argues persuasively that women did have a Renaissance in at least one area—that of charisma. The roles in society assumed by Catherine of Siena and Joan of Arc were unique to that time.[4]

Much of the research to date has concentrated on big-picture examinations of the Renaissance. Those results have been applied then to individual cases. This approach can leave surprising lacunae. For example, Goldthwaite points out that working women in Renaissance Florence have not been well studied.[5] Given the great regional diversity in government structures and social conventions in Europe during the late medieval and

1   Jacob Burckhardt, *The Civilization of the Renaissance in Italy* (New York: Harper, 1973), 2: 389–95.
2   Joan Kelly-Gadol, "Did Women Have a Renaissance?," in *Becoming Visible: Women in European History*, ed. Renate Bridenthal and Claudia Koonz (Boston: Houghton Mifflin, 1977), 137–64.
3   Samuel K. Cohn Jr., *Women in the Streets: Essays on Sex and Power in Renaissance Italy* (Baltimore: Johns Hopkins University Press, 1996).
4   David Herlihy, "Did Women Have a Renaissance?" in *Women, Family, and Society in Medieval Europe: Historical Essays, 1978–1991*, ed. Anthony Molho (Providence, RI: Berghahn, 1995), 33–56.
5   Richard A. Goldthwaite, *The Economy of Renaissance Florence* (Baltimore: Johns Hopkins University Press, 2009), 370.

early modern periods, some specificity regarding the place and time of the research focus is clearly important.

This chapter's study exploits a source of dynamic data to reveal that women used their time differently than men. As in Chapter 7, the Medici-Tornaquinci wool industry account books are used, this time to study working women from the mid-Cinquecento Florentine wool industry. The more commonly used static data sources could not permit this kind of analysis.

Though it examines other occupations held by women, this study focuses on weavers.

Research on late medieval and Renaissance working women often necessitates using small samples. Even work based on the voluminous late medieval Italian notarial records often results in a distillation down to a small set of applicable cases.[6] The study presented in this chapter, like much of the work on this subject, is based on a relatively small sample of working women and is necessarily limited in its scope. Therefore it should be viewed as a preliminary investigation that demonstrates the value of using a dynamic approach to study Renaissance working women.

The analysis is presented in the rest of the chapter. Different sources can change the results, and the effects of this are examined. The current state of what is known about working women is presented in this context. Women in Renaissance Florence worked in different occupations, tended to have smaller operations and engaged in different types of contracts. Household production theory helps explain some of these observations. Women usually worked at home, but this fact did not control their behavior. Where a woman was in her life cycle appears to have been a key determinant. Human capital theory also explains some of the behavior of working women.[7] Here, the focus turns to weaving. Weaving was the one occupation in which significant numbers of both men and women worked. Women received equal pay for equal work but wove less valuable cloths

---

6   This opinion has been expressed elsewhere, including Anna Bellavitis and Linda Guzzetti, "Introduzione," in *Donne, lavoro, economia a Venezia e in Terrafirma tra medioevo ed età moderna*, ed. Anna Bellavitis and Linda Guzzetti, *Archivio veneto* 143 (2012): 6–7. For examples, see Georges Jehel, "Le rôle des femmes et du milieu familial a Gênes dans les activités commercials," *Revue de l'histoire économique et sociale* 53 (1975): 193–215; Geo Pistarino, "La donna d' affari a Genova nel secolo XIII," in *Miscellanea di storia Italiana e mediterranea per Nino Lamboglia*, ed. G. Pistarino (Genoa: Università di Genova, 1978), 155–69; Carmela Maria Rugolo, "Donna e lavoro nella Sicilia del basso Medioevo," in *Donne e lavoro nell'Italia medievale*, ed. Bruno Andreolli, Paola Galetti and Maria Giuseppina Muzzarelli (Turin: Rosenberg & Sellier, 1991), 67–82; Eleanor S. Riemer, "Women, Dowries, and Capital Investment in Thirteenth-Century Siena," in *The Marriage Bargain: Women and Dowries in European History*, ed. Marion A. Kaplan (New York: Institute for Research in History, 1985), 59–79; Linda Guzzetti, "Gli investimenti delle donne veneziane nel medioevo," in *Donne, lavoro, economia a Venezia e in Terrafirma tra medioevo ed età moderna*, ed. Anna Bellavitis and Linda Guzzetti, *Archivio veneto* 143 (2012): 41–66; Marcello Della Valentina, "'Parone': Donne alla guida di una bottega artigiana a Venezia nel '700'," in *Donne, lavoro, economia a Venezia e in Terrafirma tra medioevo ed età moderna*, ed. Anna Bellavitis and Linda Guzzetti, *Archivio veneto* 143 (2012): 145–64.

7   For a comprehensive discussion of human capital theory see: Gary S. Becker, *Human Capital: A Theoretical and Empirical Analysis, with Special Reference to Education*, 3rd ed. (Chicago: University of Chicago Press, 1993).

and therefore were paid less for each cloth. This would seem to suggest that women were less skilled than men. However, women's skills equaled men's when they were doing exactly the same work. This creates a paradox. Why would women accept lower pay when their skills were equal to those of men? This paradox is resolved by the different use of time by gender. Women generally worked part-time, whereas men were usually employed full-time. Women also worked less frequently than men and took less time to complete cloths. This gender difference could have been revealed only by the use of dynamic data.

Sources on Medieval and Renaissance Working Women

In large part the sources that provide the information under study determine the results of research on late medieval and early modern working women. This can pose a significant limitation. Studies of working women based on static sources tend to possess a frozen-in-amber quality, where women appear stuck and immobile.

In general, four broad types of sources are used to write the history of working women. The primary type is surveys, which includes censuses, guild registers and tax records. These sources provide comprehensive coverage of a city or a region's industry at any particular time. However, they are limited and can provide only snapshots of conditions at the time. Another type is laws, including guild regulations and legal collections. These can provide some information about behavior. However, as shown in Chapter 7, researchers have to separate the ideals shown in the laws and regulations from the reality of the marketplace. It is best to read these laws and regulations in the context of other data sources.[8] A third type is legal records, including court cases and notarial records. These are something of an intermediate source. Court cases can provide extremely detailed behavioral data, and notarial records are often used much as if they were surveys. The final type is account books. Florentine *ricordanze*—essentially, family diaries—are part of this category, although they do not include quantitative information. This type of source is generally less comprehensive than censuses and guild registers but nevertheless provides dynamic data. The sample sizes can be limited; however, as shown in Chapter 7, the much broader range of questions that dynamic data can answer compensates for much of this deficiency. Most of the research to date on working women in Renaissance Florence has been based on one or more of the first three types of records.

It seems reasonable to start any analysis of working women by asking what they did. The range of women's occupations a historian finds in a particular city or region can be largely determined by the choice of sources. Censuses and guild registers provide comprehensive but selective data. The Parisian *tailles* (tax registers) of 1292 and 1313 show that women worked predominantly as servants, but several also ran businesses.[9]

---

8   For an excellent example of how to weave these two disparate strands together, see Florence Edler, *Glossary of Medieval Terms of Business: Italian Series, 1200–1600*, Medieval Academy of America (1934; New York: Kraus Reprint Co., 1970), 419–26.

9   David Herlihy, *Opera Muliebria: Women and Work in Medieval Europe* (Philadelphia: Temple University Press, 1990), 146; Hercule Gerard, ed., *Paris sous Philippe le Bel* (1837; Tübingen: Max Niemeyer

The fifteenth-century Parisian *roles d'impôt* (tax registers) show that most working women ran their own businesses.[10] This was probably not the result of an improvement in women's working conditions, but rather due to a difference in the sources used for analysis. Occupations held by very poor or very rich women, such as servants and nobility, respectively, seem to be missing from the labor force.[11] This limitation has affected research on Florence. The *Trecento estimi* report only household heads.[12] The *catasto*, from 1427, reports all household members, but rarely reports the occupations of nonhousehold heads.[13]

The implications of the data can be influenced by larger events.[14] As noted previously in this book, the Black Death's impact on society affected data collected during its immediate aftermath. These data can help document the event's impact, but provide much less information about larger trends. Using such data as a baseline for future changes would create an endpoint problem. This is not theoretical.[15] For example, Florentine sources show a large drop in the number of working women between 1352, just after the Black Death, and 1427, nearly a century later.[16] There was probably not a dramatic loss in work opportunities for women; instead, a more likely explanation comes from the nature and timing of the sources. Women's occupations were generally listed in either survey only if they were household heads. The loss of life from the Black Death disrupted many households and made many women household heads. Once everything got sorted out demographically—75 years later is plenty of time—working women disappeared from view, because far fewer of them would be household heads.

Although survey and notarial data are most frequently used to study women's occupations, account book data can provide a very different type of data that answers very different questions. For example, the number of female spinners and weavers shown in the 1427 catasto survey is much lower than the numbers implied by contemporary account books. Those earlier numbers were reduced because in order to be counted,

---

Verlag, 1991); Karl Michaelsson, ed., *Le Livre de la Taille de Paris: L'an 1297* (Göteborg: Elanders Bokriyckeri Aktiebolag, 1962); Karl Michaelsson, ed., *Le Livre de la Taille de Paris: L'an 1313* (Göteborg: Werner and Kerbers, 1951).

10 Herlihy, *Opera Muliebria*, 176; Jean Favrier, ed., *Les contribuables Parisiens a la fin de la guerre de cent ans: Les roles d'impôt de 1421, 1423, et 1438* (Geneva: Librairie Droz, 1970).

11 Herlihy, *Opera Muliebria*, 136.

12 For example, Ildefonso il San Luigi, *Delizie degli Eruditi Toscani*, 16 and 125–60.

13 David Herlihy and Christiane Klapisch-Zuber, *Census and Property Survey of Florentine Domains and the City of Verona in Fifteenth-Century Italy* [machine-readable data file]. Cambridge, MA: David Herlihy, Harvard University, Department of History and Paris, France: Christiane Klapisch-Zuber, Ecole Pratique des Hautes Etudes [producers], 1977. Madison: University of Wisconsin, Data and Program Library Service [distributor], 1981.

14 Chapters 1 and 5 contain examples of this type of phenomenon.

15 Anna Bellavitis, "Apprendiste e maestre a Venezia tra Cinque e Seicento," in *Donne, lavoro, economia a Venezia e in Terrafirma tra medioevo ed età moderna*, ed. Anna Bellavitis and Linda Guzzetti, *Archivio veneto* 143 (2012): 144.

16 Isabelle Chabot, "La réconnaissance du travail des femmes dans la Florence du bas Moyen Âge: Context idéologique et réalité," in *La donna nell'economia, secc. XIII–XVIII*, ed. S. Cavaciocchi (Florence: Le Monnier, 1990), 565.

women had to be household heads.[17] The 1427 catasto shows that 4 percent of weavers were women,[18] but a 1431 account book implies that two-thirds were women.[19] The gap is a ratio of nearly twenty to one, and is too large to be explained by sampling error. One can reduce the gap somewhat by counting a few additional women who were not heads of households yet had an occupation listed, but that ad hoc adjustment does not begin to make up the difference. However, it is clear that many working women are missed in the 1427 catasto when only household heads are included. An entire employment category could be missed if married women, who were not household heads and therefore unobservable, held different occupations than unmarried or widowed women.

Account books also contain dynamic information that surveys lack. If censuses and guild registers are akin to snapshots, then account books are like movies. Although De Roover does not use the term "dynamic," he points out that business records, particularly account books, "tell us how the system actually worked."[20] Using account books as if they were censuses and guild regulations and as only static sources wastes valuable information.[21] Dynamic elements of work are important, because much of the difference between women's work and men's work stemmed from the dynamic nature of work. Actual work activities as well as its character are interesting to historians; however, the dynamic characteristics of women's work have not been sufficiently studied. As an example, Herlihy looks at how different sources can be used to study the social and economic history of women, but he does not examine the difference between dynamic and static sources.[22]

Late Medieval and Renaissance European Working Women

Earlier studies identify several characteristics of working women that appear to hold throughout late medieval and early modern Europe. Women usually performed work that had relatively low social standing.[23] The occupations open to women included servant, prostitute, wet nurse, midwife, a variety of textile industry occupations, alewife, baker, innkeeper, service in religious orders, commodities middleperson and

---

17 Isabelle Chabot, "La réconnaissance."
18 Among weaver household heads, 12 out of 269 were women. See Herlihy and Klapisch-Zuber, *Census and Property Survey*.
19 Medici-Tornaquinci, Ms. 496.
20 Raymond de Roover, "A Florentine Firm of Cloth Manufacturers," in *Business, Banking, and Economic Thought in Late Medieval and Early Modern Europe*, ed. Julius Kirshner (Chicago: University of Chicago Press, 1974), 85–86.
21 Cf., Judith Brown and Jonathan Goodman, "Women and Industry in Florence," *Journal of Economic History* 40, no. 1 (1980): 79.
22 David Herlihy, "Women and Sources of Medieval History: The Towns of Northern Italy," in *Women, Family, and Society in Medieval Europe: Historical Essays, 1978–1991*, ed. Anthony Molho (Providence, RI: Berghahn, 1995), 13–32.
23 Barbara A. Hanawalt, Introduction to *Women and Work in Preindustrial Europe*, ed. Barbara A. Hanawalt (Bloomington: Indiana University Press, 1986), viii.

unskilled work at construction sites.[24] Sheilagh Ogilvie argues that women did a wide range of work in seventeenth-century Württemberg, Germany, but that women were prevented from engaging in certain forms of production. She further argues that wage ordinances capped the pay on certain women's occupations.[25] Women's work opportunities were also limited because they were poorer. Some occupations required large capital outlays that restricted female entry.[26]

---

24 On servants, see Christiane Klapisch-Zuber, "Women Servants in Florence during the Fourteenth and Fifteenth Centuries," in *Women and Work in Preindustrial Europe*, ed. Barbara A. Hanawalt (Bloomington: Indiana University Press, 1986), 56–80; Herlihy, *Opera Muliebria*, 159; Steven Epstein, "Labour in Thirteenth-Century Genoa," *Mediterranean Historical Review* 3 (1988): 131. On wet nurses, see Klapisch-Zuber, "Women Servants"; Leah L. Otis, "Municipal Wet Nurses in Fifteenth-Century Montpellier," *Women and Work*, 83–93; Epstein, "Labour in Thirteenth-Century Genoa," 131. On midwives, see Merry E. Wiesner, "Early Modern Midwifery: A Case Study," *Women and Work*, 94–114. On prostitutes, see Richard Trexler, "La prostitution Florentine au 15e siècle," *Annales E. S. C.*, 1981, 983–1015. On textile industry occupations: in Italian cities the specific occupations included silk spinning in thirteenth-century Lucca as reported in Edler, *Silk Trade of Lucca*; silk spinning and weaving in fifteenth- and sixteenth-century Venice as reported in Luca Molà, "Le donne nell'industria serica veneziana del Rinascimento," in *La seta in Italia dal Medioevo al Seicento: Dal baco al drappo*, ed. Luca Molà, Reinhold C. Mueller and Claudio Zanier (Venice: Marsilio, 2000), 423–60; gold thread spinning in thirteenth-century Genoa as reported in Epstein, "Labour in Thirteenth-Century Genoa," 132; and woolen cloth carding, combing, dyeing, weaving and company ownership in thirteenth-century Genoa as reported in Epstein, "Labour in Thirteenth-Century Genoa," 132; combing and spinning in 1395 Bologna as reported in Herlihy, *Opera Muliebria*, 96; warping and weaving in fourteenth- through sixteenth-century Florence as reported in Edler, *Glossary* and in Herlihy, *Opera Muliebria*, 159. On alewives, see Barbara A. Hanawalt, "Peasant Women's Contribution to the Home Economy in Late Medieval England," *Women and Work*, 8; Judith M. Bennett, "The Village Ale-Wife: Women and Brewing in Fourteenth-Century England," *Women and Work*, 20–37. On bakers, see Carmela Maria Rugolo, "Donna e lavoro nella Sicilia del basso Medioevo," in *Donne e lavoro nell'Italia medievale*, ed. Bruno Andreolli, Paola Galetti and Maria Giuseppina Muzzarelli (Turin: Rosenberg & Sellier, 1991), 74. On inn keepers, see Anna Esposito, "Perle e coralli: credito e investimenti delle donne a Roma (XV-inizio XVI secolo)," in *Dare credito alle donne: Presenze femminili nell'economia tra medioevo ed età moderna*, ed. Giovanna Petti Balbi and Paola Guglielmotti (Asti: Centro studi Renato Bordone sui Lombardi, sul credito e sulla banca, 2012), 248. On religious orders, see Herlihy, *Opera Muliebria*, 159. On commodities middlemen, see Maryanne Kowaleski, "Women's Work in a Market Town: Exeter in the Late Fourteenth Century," *Women and Work*, 145–64; Hanawalt, "Peasant Women's Contribution," 8; Bennett, "Village Ale-Wife," 25; Rugolo, "Donna e lavoro nella Sicilia," 75. On construction sites, see Shelley R. Roff, "'Appropriate to Her Sex'? Women's Participation on the Construction Site in Medieval and Early Modern Europe," in *Women and Wealth in Late Medieval Europe*, ed. Theresa Earenfight (New York: Palgrave Macmillan, 2010), 109–34.

25 Sheilagh C. Ogilvie, *A Bitter Living: Women, Markets, and Social Capital in Early Modern Germany* (Oxford: Oxford University Press, 2003), 321 and 346–51.

26 Judith C. Brown, "A Woman's Place Was in the Home: Women's Work in Renaissance Tuscany," in *Rewriting the Renaissance: The Discourses of Sexual Difference in Early Modern Europe*, ed. Margaret W. Ferguson, Maureen Quilligan and Nancy J. Vickers (Chicago: University of Chicago Press, 1986), 217.

Guilds usually served as industrial regulators where they often limited work opportunities for women. Herlihy concludes that the formation of guilds hampered women's work prospects,[27] and Hanawalt states as a general rule, "the greater the regulations on production, the more likely the women were to lose employment."[28] Marian Dale's study of fourteenth-century English silk workers finds that women, unlike men, did not form guilds. She notes further that men refused to do the work that women did.[29] These regulations would have provided an economic benefit, economic rent, to men. However, the resulting economic inefficiency was a net drag on the overall society. Ogilvie argues that the limitations on women's work harmed everyone in the society, as such restrictions reduced not only the welfare of the women involved but also the flexibility of the overall economy.[30]

Guilds were part of the larger social apparatus of late medieval and early modern Europe. Martha Howell argues that the social patriarchy was an important determinant of employment relations.[31] Ogilvie argues that gender-based "social capital" differences helped to exclude women.[32] Merry Wiesner looks at the impact of social, economic and ideological factors on women's work during the sixteenth and seventeenth centuries and concludes that guilds restricted work for women.[33] These guilds were an important source of values in society that led to these restrictions.[34]

Guilds apparently did not always restrict women's work opportunities, however. P. J. P. Goldberg's study of English working women finds that women could have significant status in the workplace.[35] The legal subordination of women did not mean a significant exclusion from the economy in early modern Norway.[36] E. Dixon's examination of the list of thirteenth-century Parisian guild regulations, called the *Livre des Métiers*, finds no laws that discriminated against women. She does find, however, that women were prohibited from occupations requiring hard physical labor.[37] Although market forces generally led

---

27 Herlihy, *Opera Muliebria*, 162 and 190–91.
28 Hanawalt, Introduction, xv.
29 Marian K. Dale, "The London Silkwomen of the Fifteenth Century," *Economic History Review* 24, no. 3 (1933): 335.
30 Ogilvie, *Bitter Living*, 346–51.
31 Martha C. Howell, *Women, Production, and Patriarchy in Late Medieval Cities* (Chicago: University of Chicago Press, 1986).
32 Ogilvie, *Bitter Living*.
33 Merry E. Wiesner, *Working Women in Renaissance Germany* (New Brunswick, NJ: Rutgers University Press, 1986).
34 Merry E. Wiesner, "Guilds, Male Bonding, and Women's Work in Early Modern Germany," in *La Donna nell'Economia Secc. XIII–XVIII*, ed. Simonetta Cavaciocchi (Prato: Le Monnier, 1990), 655–69.
35 P. J. P. Goldberg, *Women, Work, and Life Cycle in a Medieval Economy: Women in York and Yorkshire, ca. 1300–1520* (Oxford: Clarendon Press, 1992), 325.
36 Solvi Sogner and Hilde Sandvik, "Minors in Law, Partners in Work, Equals in Worth? Women in the Norwegian Economy in the 16th to the 18th Centuries," in *La Donna nell'Economia Secc. XIII–XVIII*, ed. Simonetta Cavaciocchi (Prato: Le Monnier, 1990), 633–53.
37 E. Dixon, "Craftswomen in the *Livre des Métiers*," *Economic History Review* 5, no. 18 (1895): 209.

to equal pay for men and women, statutes could enact unequal pay, and Hanawalt shows that English women were paid less than men by law.[38]

The kinds of work women did in northern Europe varied by location. On the one hand, Howell's studies of Cologne, Douai, Frankfurt, Leiden and Lier show that late medieval European women's work "was determined by ways in which the sex-gender system intersected with the economic system."[39] However, Ogilvie argues that restrictions and limitations on women were less strict in England and the Netherlands. In those countries women were able to increase the time they allocated to economic production. This is connected to Jan de Vries's "industrious revolution" that preceded the modern industrial society.[40]

There has been some limited examination of women's substitution of time between the marketplace and the household or their tendency to work at home. Wiesner claims that women adapted their work to family responsibilities.[41] Alice Clark argues that the restriction of women's work to the home was a key factor that limited opportunities in seventeenth-century England.[42] Hanawalt implies that the substitution of time is an important factor in women's work behavior, but she does not expand on this theme.[43] The changing seasons had some impact on women's work. Servants were single women, and their work was not seasonal;[44] however, wage-earning jobs for married women were often seasonal. Such seasonality implies that household production was relevant. Natalie Davis finds that in Lyons seasonal work variations meant that women held multiple occupations.[45]

Italian guilds had an important role in dictating the terms of women's employment. Guild regulations created a market for employment and ensured production quality. The impact of guilds on employment varied. Maureen Mazzaoui finds that in the Italian cotton industry, skilled men held the guild occupations, and women joined less skilled men in less attractive nonguild seasonal labor. Indeed, women are not listed in the membership of the cotton guilds despite the guilds' prevailing open-membership policy, which often brought employers and employees into the same guilds.[46] Brown and Goodman argue that guilds did not greatly restrict women's work decisions in the Renaissance Florentine silk and wool industries.[47]

---

38 Hanawalt, "Peasant Women's Contribution," 12.

39 Howell, *Women, Production, and Patriarchy*, 173.

40 Jan de Vries, *The Industrious Revolution: Consumer Behavior and the Household Economy, 1650 to the Present* (Cambridge: Cambridge University Press, 2008), x; Ogilvie, *Bitter Living*, 346–51.

41 Wiesner, *Working Women in Renaissance Germany*, 196.

42 Alice Clark, *Working Life of Women in the Seventeenth Century* (1919; Abingdon, UK: Frank Cass, 1968), 290.

43 Hanawalt, Introduction.

44 Clark, *Working Life of Women*, 66.

45 Natalie Zemon Davis, "Women in the Crafts in Sixteenth-Century Lyons," in *Women and Work*, 187.

46 Maureen Fennell Mazzaoui, *The Italian Cotton Industry in the Later Middle Ages, 1100–1600* (Oxford: Oxford University Press, 1983), 110.

47 Brown and Goodman, "Women and Industry," 79–80.

Since northern Italy was more industrially advanced than northern Europe throughout this period, it is better to study northern Italian working women separately from those of northern Europe. Surveys show that northern Italian women worked in a range of industrial, religious and low-status occupations, but this range is narrower than what is seen in northern Europe. Northern Italian women, specifically those from Florence, were much more likely to be employed in industrial, particularly textile, occupations than women from northern Europe. A 1395 Bolognese survey listing all household members shows that the few identifiable working women included spinners, beggars and prostitutes.[48] Fifteenth- and sixteenth-century Veronese surveys show women as spinners and weavers in the textile industry, but list no women as business heads.[49]

The 1427 Florentine catasto shows that few women were employed. It lists women working as servants, serving in religious orders (both uncloistered and as dependents of a religious house) and working in the textile industry as spinners and weavers.[50] Nevertheless, textile industry employment was important to Florentine women.[51] Simona Laudani finds that women were incorporated into the guild apprenticeship system, such as the Florentine silk guild of Arte di Por Santa Maria.[52] According to the catasto, many working women in Florentine Tuscany wove some kind of cloth, which Herlihy suspects was silk.[53] Women usually worked on the margins of the markets and not at the center, and only a few women were listed as owning business capital.[54]

The concentration of women's employment in the industrial sector could have limited the range of work opportunities that historians observe. Some suggest that this industrial development limited women's opportunities. Goldberg suggests that women had more employment flexibility in sixteenth-century York, England, than in 1427 Florence.[55] Herlihy argues that Renaissance Italian urban conditions in general reduced women's work opportunities.[56] Roberto Greci argues, more specifically, that the development of the Italian textile industry restricted women's work options.[57]

Comparisons with the modern world can shed light on these issues. Claudia Goldin's research of economies during the modern era finds that the evolution of female labor force participation follows a U-shaped curve over time as a country or region develops

---

48 Herlihy, *Opera Muliebria*, 155–58; Paolo Montanari, ed., *Documenti su la popolazione di Bologna alla fine dell' Trecento* (Bologna: Istituto per la Storia di Bologna, 1966).

49 Herlihy, *Opera Muliebria*, 160–61.

50 Herlihy and Klapisch-Zuber, *Census and Property Survey*; Herlihy, *Opera Muliebria*, 158–60.

51 Goldthwaite, *Economy of Renaissance Florence*, 372.

52 Simona Laudani, "Mestieri di donne, mestieri di uomini: le corporazioni in età moderna," in *Il lavoro delle donne*, ed. Angela Groppi (Rome: Laterza, 1996), 183–205.

53 Herlihy, *Opera Muliebria*, 159–61.

54 Goldthwaite, *Economy of Renaissance Florence*, 370–72.

55 Goldberg, *Women, Work, and Life Cycle*, 325.

56 David Herlihy, "Deaths, Marriages, Births, and the Tuscan Economy," in *Population Patterns in the Past*, ed. R. D. Lee (Cambridge: Cambridge University Press, 1977), 163.

57 Roberto Greci, "Donne e corporazioni: la fluidità di un rapporto," in *Il lavoro delle donne*, ed. Angela Groppi (Rome: Laterza, 1996), 71–91.

economically.[58] Labor force participation is high in undeveloped countries, and low in developing countries, because women are excluded from the labor market, and then it is high again in developed countries as women reenter the labor force.[59] Goldin's women's labor market growth curve resembles the Kuznets curve of income inequality.[60]

The first two stages in Goldin's model of women's work and economic evolution resemble, respectively, northern Europe and northern Italy during the Renaissance. Labor markets appear less open to women in industrial Italy than in northern Europe. However, the observation of a limited number of choices for women does not imply that choices were limited. There was not necessarily either a lack of opportunities or a lack of economic value. The concentration of working women in a few industrial occupations could be seen as good news for women. Women were limited to a few occupations that often employed men as well. This implies that their pay could not have been too bad in comparison to men's pay for doing the same work. The higher-paying industrial occupations lured women away from the lower-paying menial occupations. It is very possible that this shift in northern Italy increased salaries and drew women into fewer, but higher paying, occupations.

Although these results seem appealing, historians should be careful drawing conclusions. The problem with the sources in such analyses is that usually only the final choices are observed and not the wage rates. Any limitation in the number of working women's occupations, or, more generally, in what women did for work, could simply be a corner solution. This could have implications regarding the extensive literature claiming that women were worse off than men during the Renaissance.[61]

Women's Work in the Renaissance Florentine Wool Industry

This section describes how Florentine working women fit into the wool industry's occupational structure. Table 8.1 shows the division of labor between men and women among wool industry occupations. As shown in the table, women participated in a smaller set of occupations than men; they are represented only in spinning, warping and weaving. All of these jobs were performed using the putting-out system, an independent handicraft that was a one-person job. The small scale implies that working women had relatively less capital to invest in business than men. There was no statistically observable seasonality.

Women's specialization in piece-rate work has broader implications. Piece-rate work is sometimes seen, like sharecropping, as a form of risk sharing. As such, one expects workers to progress up a ladder of occupations as they became wealthier and less risk averse—from wage laborer, to piece-rate worker, to shop renter, to shop owner. Such a

58 Claudia Goldin, "The U-Shaped Female Labor Force Function in Economic Development and Economic History," in *Investment in Women's Human Capital*, ed. T. Paul Schultz (Chicago: University of Chicago Press, 1995), 61–90.
59 Ibid.
60 Simon Kuznets, "Economic Growth and Income Inequality," *American Economic Review* 45, no. 1 (1955): 1–28. The Kuznets curve is discussed in Chapter 3.
61 Compare: Kelly-Gadol, "Did Women Have a Renaissance?"

Table 8.1 Wool industry occupation by gender

Step	Occupation	Gender
Preparing	Sorting	Male
	Washing	Male
	Beating	Male
	Combing	Male
	Carding	Male
Spinning	Spinning	Female
Weaving	Warping	Female/Some Male
	Weaving	Male/Female
Finishing	Burling	Male
	Fulling	Male
	Stretching	Male
	Teaseling	Male
	Shearing	Male
	Mending	Male
Dyeing	Dyeing	Male

Sources: De Roover, "Florentine Firm of Cloth Manufacturers," 103; Edler, *Glossary*, 329–30. Occupations listed in order of steps to completion.

ladder is reminiscent of the agricultural ladder hypothesis observed at times and in places as different as the American South and Thailand.[62] The wealth data for wool industry workers presented in Chapter 3 supports the ladder hypothesis. It implies that working women were not always at the bottom of the employment ladder. As noted in the previous section, women sometimes worked as servants, but their primary market occupations involved piece-rate work. Many men worked for daily wages, but women almost never did. This might have been because working women came from two-income households, and it was therefore thought to be unnecessary for them to be daily wage workers. This also suggests that the minimum cost to enter the labor market as daily wage workers could have been higher for women than men. These results, combined with research by Julius Kirshner and Thomas Kuehn on the impact of the life cycle on women's role in society, suggest that further research on this point is needed.[63]

---

62 W. J. Spillman, "The Agricultural Ladder," *American Economic Review: Papers and Proceedings* 9 (1919): 170–79; Lawanda S. Cox, "Tenancy in the United States, 1865–1900: A Consideration of the Validity of the Agricultural Ladder Hypothesis," *Agricultural History* 18 (1944): 97–105; Laurence Stifel, "Patterns of Land Ownership in Central Thailand during the Twentieth Century," *Journal of Siam Society* (1976): 237–74; Lee Alston and Robert Higgs, "Contractual Mix in Southern Agriculture since the Civil War: Facts, Hypotheses, and Tests," *Journal of Economic History* 42, no. 2 (1982): 327–53.

63 See, for instance, Julius Kirshner, "The Morning After: Collecting Monte Dowries in Renaissance Florence," in *From Florence to the Mediterranean and Beyond: Essays in Honor of Anthony Molho*, ed. Diogo Ramada Curto, Eric R. Dusteler, Julius Kirshner and Francesca Trivellato (Florence: Olschki, 2009), 1: 29–61; Thomas Kuehn, *Law, Family, and Women: Toward a Legal*

All spinners in the sample from the Medici-Tornaquinci account books were rural women. The work did not require highly skilled labor.[64] Self-employed male intermediaries dealt directly with the spinners. Piece rates were paid to the intermediaries and to the spinners. The *lanaiuoli* distributed the wool, divided into pieces, to the *lanini* and *stamaiuoli*. The weight of the wool differed minimally from piece to piece.[65] The Medici account books record the number of pieces given out to each woman. No apparent distinction is made for pieces that were used to make finer cloths. The average payment for spinning a piece of cloth did not vary significantly by cloth quality. Piece rates based on weight were set by guild regulation; however, in practice the amount per piece paid out decreased as the number of pieces distributed to a spinner at a particular time increased.[66]

The warpers reported directly to the company, and their work was closely linked to that of the weavers. Warping was performed almost exclusively by women, and the piece rate for the warps to be woven into a single cloth varied little. Weaving was the only occupation that employed both men and women in this sample.[67] The weaving process was straightforward. The wool to make the cloth was dispensed to the weaver, usually in several batches. Each batch was supposed to be weighed as it was dispensed. Occasionally the weaver returned for more warps of wool. The completed work was returned as a single cloth and weighed again. The weight of the cloth entered in the account books when it was returned was always a more rounded number than when it was dispensed.[68] The mean of the distribution of differences between the out and in weights, at less than 1 percent of the mean of the out weights, is insignificantly different from 0.

The cloths ranged in price and quality and adjusted to changing markets over time. During the mid-Cinquecento the industry appears to have mostly produced six kinds of cloth, which can be grouped into three categories based on quality. The highest-quality category is called *rascia*. It includes both rascia (rash) and *saia* cloths, the finest cloths made by the Medici. The next level is called *accordelato* and includes both accordelato (corduroy) and *perpignano* (as in the city of Perpignan in Catalonia) cloth. At the lowest level are shorts, a category that includes the shorts of the accordelato and perpignano lots. These three categories—rascia, accordelato and shorts—are used throughout this study to distinguish cloth quality.

Anthropology of Renaissance Italy (Chicago: University of Chicago Press, 1991); Thomas Kuehn, "Daughters, Mothers, Wives, and Widows: Women as Legal Persons," in *Time, Space, and Women's Lives in Early Modern Europe*, ed. Anne Jacobson Schutte, Thomas Kuehn and Silvana Seidel Menchi (Kirksville, MO: Truman State University Press, 2001), 97–115.

64 De Roover, "Florentine Firm of Cloth Manufacturers," 96.

65 The weights of the stamaiuoli pieces are provided in the accounts. For the lanini pieces, no weight is given in the accounts. De Roover writes that these pieces appear to have been identical. De Roover, "Florentine Firm of Cloth Manufacturers," 96. Edler does not dispute this, but points out that the piece rates in the account books would have been by weight. Edler, *Glossary*, 149 and 414. The varying prices per piece that were paid to the lanini imply that the weights varied.

66 Edler, *Glossary*, 149, 279 and 414.

67 Ibid., 419.

68 Ibid., 421–22.

The company had a distinct weaving demand curve for each type of cloth. The prices for weaving rascia cloth were flexible and generally ranged from around 55 to 65 lire per cloth woven. Prices were generally determined by the length and the fineness of the cloth.[69] There was no correlation, either positive or negative, between the price and the time required to weave the cloths. Other cloths were woven at fixed prices: the saia cloths were 44 lire per cloth, the accordelato were 26 lire, the perpignano were 24 lire, the accordelato shorts were 12 lire and the perpignano shorts were 10 lire. These payments were all in silver currency.

The restriction of women working in the wool industry to a set of three occupations allows one to use broader patterns to infer narrower results. This method leads to an interesting result. The total value of payments for spinning and for warping and weaving by a firm more than doubled between the late Trecento and late Cinquecento.[70] Given the industry's organization of production and its competitive nature (see Chapter 7), it is hard to imagine that a share of this increase did not go to women.

Household Production and Working Women

This section applies household production theory from economics to analyze the work behavior of Florentine women. The theory is based on the idea that persons make decisions and actions in the context of their household and not solely as individuals. It does more than acknowledge the existence of nonmarket or household production. The theory implies a trade-off between production for the home and production for the market. Women's household work and market work were both valuable. The trade-off between these determined the minimum payment, or reservation wage, required before women would enter the labor force given the household decision process. Household production theory describes both the preference for goods by the household[71] and the allocation of time within the household.[72]

The Renaissance Florentine legal system complicates any effort to distinguish legal barriers from household limitations. This body of family law made the woman's labor force participation decision subject to the family. As such, the theory is well suited to examine the Florentine *pater familias*. The Florentine institution of the *mundualdus* dictated that men would sign off on women's transactions.[73] For example, women could invest on

---

69 Ibid., 422.

70 Richard A. Goldthwaite, "The Florentine Wool Industry in the Late Sixteenth Century: A Case Study," *Journal of European Economic History* 32, no. 3 (2003): 540–41.

71 Seminal works on household production theory are: Kelvin J. Lancaster, "A New Approach to Consumer Theory," *Journal of Political Economy* 74 (1966): 132–157; Richard F. Muth, "Household Production and Consumer Demand Functions," *Econometrica* (1966): 699–708. For a more textbook-style approach, see: Gary S. Becker, *A Treatise on the Family* (Cambridge, MA: Harvard University Press, 1981), esp. 14–37.

72 Seminal works that connect time and household production are: Gary S. Becker, "A Theory of the Allocation of Time," *Economic Journal* 75 no. 299 (1965): 493–517; Robert A. Pollak and Michael L. Wachter, "The Relevance of the Household Production Function and Its Implications for the Allocation of Time," *Journal of Political Economy* 83, no. 2 (1975): 255–78.

73 Kuehn, *Law, Family, and Women*, 212–37.

their own through their reputation, but could sell shares of the Monte only with a procurator.[74] Similarly, a woman's entry into the workforce was subject to the men in her family.

The father was the typical head of the Florentine family. Alberti begins his work *Libri della famiglia* with the proper role of the father in the family.[75] Gene Brucker's fiercely independent Lusanna fighting through the Florentine legal system for justice was probably a rare figure.[76] Several studies highlight the important influence of the family on Florentine economic life. For example, Francis Kent studies the Florentine extended family.[77] Goldthwaite implicitly assumes that families were important decision-making units in his research on the Florentine economy.[78] Najemy focuses on the family as the basic unit of the Florentine political system.[79]

The institution of pater familias in Florence has led many to consider Florentine women to have lived under the rigid control of Florentine men. Throughout her life, a Florentine woman was surrounded by male relatives who constantly influenced her decisions. These familial relationships were reinforced by legal ones. Roman law created legal restrictions, through the pater familias principle in particular. Under this principle, an unmarried woman was under the authority of her father, and a married woman was under the authority of her husband. This meant few women were independent of their family obligations. However, it is important to distinguish between the prescriptions made by laws and how people and families adjusted their behavior in response to those laws.

Klapisch-Zuber argues that the family and household was the key determinant of women's behavior. Men and women had clearly defined roles. Women were subordinated, which limited their opportunities. They "remained under command of level-headed males." Another force that brought women under the influence of male householders arose from the common practice of Florentine men to marry much younger women. In this case the man generally died before the woman, which often left the woman obligated to two families: she was born into her father's family and therefore had some obligations to them, but she also had to raise her husband's children.[80]

---

74 Thomas Kuehn, *Heirs, Kin, and Creditors in Renaissance Florence* (Cambridge, UK: Cambridge University Press, 2008), 43–44.

75 Leon Battista Alberti, *I libri della famiglia*, ed. Girolamo Mancini (Florence: G. Carnesecchi e Figli, 1908), 14–25; Alberti, *The Family in Renaissance Florence*, trans. Renée Neu Watkins (Columbia: University of South Carolina Press, 1969), 36–46.

76 Gene Brucker, *Giovanni and Lusanna: Love and Marriage in Renaissance Florence* (Berkeley: University of California Press, 1986).

77 Francis William Kent, *Household and Lineage in Renaissance Florence* (Princeton, NJ: Princeton University Press, 1977); Anthony Molho, "Visions of the Florentine Family in the Renaissance," *Journal of Modern History* 50, no. 2 (1978): 304–11.

78 Richard A. Goldthwaite, *The Building of Renaissance Florence* (Baltimore: Johns Hopkins University Press, 1980).

79 John M. Najemy, *Corporatism and Consensus in Florentine Electoral Politics, 1280–1400* (Chapel Hill: University of North Carolina Press, 1982).

80 Christiane Klapisch-Zuber, "The 'Cruel Mother': Maternity, Widowhood, and Dowry in Florence in the Fourteenth and Fifteenth Centuries," in *Women, Family, and Ritual in Renaissance Italy*, trans. Lydia G. Cochrane (Chicago: University of Chicago Press, 1985), 117–31; quote on 118.

Careful examination of the laws and how they were interpreted provides a more nuanced view. Kuehn applies a sophisticated legal analysis to the condition of women in Renaissance Florence and finds that laws could be interpreted creatively.[81] He argues that women were neither as subordinate as Klapisch-Zuber or Kent suppose nor as free as Brucker claims in his *Giovanni and Lusanna* book.[82]

This approach is borne out in the way the laws actually functioned. The laws that restricted what women could do economically were flexible.[83] Historians have used bequests to wives and daughters, as represented by wills and dowries, to examine this question. Together, they provide strong evidence that Florentine males were altruistic. Wills tend to show that household heads were altruistic. Isabelle Chabot's quantitative analysis of wills shows that, despite the patrimony, widows shared in the inheritance.[84] Future widows were taken care of in 80 percent of wills.[85] Further, wills were structured to take into account the needs of the widow and children.[86] Those who required more received more. Women had additional legal avenues. Some research sees wills as immutable and effectively the final word on the distribution of property from one generation to the next.[87] However, widows could go to court and change wills if necessary. Kuehn points out that wills could be successfully challenged and a wide range of legal strategies were available.[88] Dowries provided another way to transmit wealth to women outside this legal structure. Examination of the institution of the dowry is central in the recent reassessment of Klapisch-Zuber's work.[89] Maristella Botticini's quantitative analysis of dowries reinforces Kuehn's legal observations.[90] In fact, altruism toward daughters appears to have driven large dowries in Tuscany.[91] The dowries were a significant share of the ultimate bequests.[92]

---

81 Kuehn, *Law, Family, and Women*, 9.
82 Kuehn, *Law, Family, and Women*, 5, 7 and 14.
83 Kuehn, *Heirs, Kin, and Creditors*, xiv–xv.
84 Isabelle Chabot, *Le dette des familles: Femmes, lignage et patrimonie à Florence au XIVe et XV siècles* (Rome: École Française de Rome, 2011), 273–309.
85 Chabot, *Le dette des familles*, 273.
86 Chabot, *Le dette des familles*, 273, 275, 277 and 280.
87 Samuel Kline Cohn, Jr., *Death and Property in Siena: 1205–1800* (Baltimore, MD: Johns Hopkins University Press, 1988; Steven Epstein, *Wills and Wealth in Medieval Genoa: 1150–1250* (Cambridge, MA: Harvard University Press, 1984).
88 Kuehn, *Law, Family, and Women*, 15. For a detailed study of one aspect of inheritance, repudiation, see: Kuehn, *Heirs, Kin, and Creditors*.
89 See, for instance, Kirshner, "Morning After," 29–61; Stanley Chojnacki, "Getting Back the Dowry, Venice c. 1360–1530," in *Time, Space, and Women's Lives in Early Modern Europe*, ed. Anne Jacobson Schutte, Thomas Kuehn and Silvana Seidel Menchi (Kirksville, MO: Truman State University Press, 2001), 77–115; Julius Kirshner, "Women Married Elsewhere: Gender and Citizenship in Italy," in *Time, Space, and Women's Lives in Early Modern Europe*, ed. Anne Jacobson Schutte, Thomas Kuehn and Silvana Seidel Menchi (Kirksville, MO: Truman State University Press, 2001), 117–149; Kuehn, "Daughters, Mothers, Wives, and Widows," 97–115.
90 Maristella Botticini, "A Loveless Economy? Intergenerational Altruism and the Marriage Market in a Tuscan Town, 1415–1436," *Journal of Economic History* 59, no. 1 (1999): 104–21.
91 Maristella Botticini and Aloysius Siow, "Why Dowries?" *American Economic Review* 93, no. 4 (2003): 1385–98. There is additional analysis of dowries in Appendix 3C.
92 Botticini, "Loveless Economy."

Analyses of labor markets can be used to elaborate this approach. Following the standard approach of labor economists, the combined effect of income and prices on women's labor supply can be more usefully divided into an income effect and a substitution effect. A substitution effect implies that an increase in the wage rate, holding income constant, would increase the amount of work demanded. An *income effect* implies that an increased income would decrease the amount of work supplied and increase the woman's reservation wage. A classic income effect is observed by Herlihy, who points out that Florentine women who were independent were usually well-off and rarely considered working.[93] The structure of the Florentine household means that the income and substitution effects one would see in a modern labor market have to be balanced with returns from household production. This raised the importance of substitution of the woman's time between market and home work.[94] Related to this, the dowry system created an income effect that distinguished widows from nonwidows. The reclaimed dowry increased the income of widows. Dowries affected a widow's behavior in a general sense.[95]

Chabot argues that labor scarcity led to an increase in women's participation in the workforce between 1352 and 1427.[96] This suggests that the higher wage rates lured women into the labor market through a substitution effect.[97] However, Chabot's own data undercut this specific argument. They actually suggest that widows had a higher reservation wage than nonwidows.[98] This implies that it was an income effect that drove the different participation rates. In both 1352 and 1427, about 40 percent of nonwidow and about 10 percent of widow household heads were in the workforce.[99] These rates were the same despite the large-scale structural changes forced on society by the Black Death. Kuehn has also found this kind of variation of activities across the life cycle.[100] Widows had more money and wanted less work. This result is consistent with the dowry and inheritance research presented above.

It appears that an income effect also influenced women's work decisions during the Cinquecento. None of the women working for the Medici-Tornaquinci during the 1550s appear to come from surnamed families, a marker that would indicate wealth (see

---

93   David Herlihy, "Marriage at Pistoia in the Fifteenth Century," in *Cities and Society in Medieval Italy* (London: Variorum, 1980).

94   Brown, "Woman's Place Was in the Home," 206–24.

95   Kuehn, "Women as Legal Persons," 97–115; Esposito, "Perle e coralli," 247–48.

96   Chabot, "La réconnaissance."

97   Charles M. de La Roncière, *Florence Centre Économique Regional au XIVe siècle: Le marché des denrées de première nécessité à Florence et dans sa champagne et les conditions de vie des salariés (1320–1380), I, Le Marché des Deurées de Première Nécessite à Florence et dans sa Compagne et les Conditions de View des Salaires (1320–1380)* (Aix-en-Provence: S.O.D.E.B., 1976), 417–54; Charles M. de La Roncière, *Florence Centre Économique Regional au XIVe siècle: le marché des denrées de première nécessité à Florence et dans sa champagne et les conditions de vie des salariés (1320–1380), IV, Notes et Documents* (Aix-en-Provence: S.O.D.E.B., 1976), 451–500. A later edition is Charles M. de La Roncière, *Prix et salaires à Florence au 14e siècles: 1280–1380* (Rome: Ecole Française de Rome, 1982).

98   Chabot, "La réconnaissance," 566–67.

99   Ibid.

100   Kuehn, "Women as Legal Persons."

Table 8.2 Location of work in the wool industry by occupation and by gender, fourteenth through sixteenth centuries

Step	Occupation	Men	Women
Preparing	Sorting	Central Workshop	N/A
	Washing	Rented Space	N/A
	Beating	Central Workshop	N/A
	Combing	Central Workshop	N/A
	Carding	Central Workshop	N/A
Spinning	Spinning	N/A	Home
Weaving	Warping	Central Workshop	Home
	Weaving	Home	Home
Finishing	Burling	Central Workshop	N/A
	Fulling	Rented Space	N/A
	Stretching	Rented Space	N/A
	Teaseling	Private Workshop	N/A
	Shearing	Private Workshop	N/A
	Mending	Central Workshop or Private Workshop	N/A
Dyeing	Dyeing	Private Workshop	N/A

Sources: De Roover, "Florentine Firm of Cloth Manufacturers," 103; Edler, *Glossary*, 329–30. Occupations listed in order of steps to completion.

Chapters 5 and 6).[101] Evidence from later centuries indicates that the dowry's income effect did not always keep women out of the labor force.[102]

It is well established that most women worked at home. On a microscale the data in Table 8.2 confirm that women who worked in the wool industry usually worked at home. On a macroscale the percentage of women in a given occupation was correlated with the likelihood of workers to do that work at home.

Human Capital and Working Women

Some researchers argue that gender-based human capital differences limited women's work.[103] Katrina Honeyman and Jordan Goodman and Ogilvie argue that medieval European working women had lower skills than men.[104] Brown and Goodman argue that

---

101 Medici-Tornaquinci Mss. 558 (5), 560 (4), 560 (5).
102 Beatrice Zucca Micheletto, "Reconsidering the Southern Europe Model: Dowry, Women's Work, and Marriage Patterns in Pre-industrial Urban Italy (Turin, Second Half of the 18th Century)," *History of the Family* 16 (2011): 354–70; Della Valentina, "'Parone'," 161–64.
103 Brown, "Woman's Place Was in the Home," 215.
104 Katrina Honeyman and Jordan Goodman, "Women's Work, Gender Conflict, and Labour Markets in Europe, 1500–1900," *Economic History Review* 44, no. 4 (1991): 613; Ogilvie, *Bitter Living*, 45–47.

because women in Florence tended to weave lower-quality cloths, they were therefore less skilled.[105]

Brown elsewhere argues that factors besides human capital and skills determined which occupations women worked in.[106] She is certainly right about this. For example, the social requirement that women work at home restricted their employment opportunities. Brown ventures into less solid ground when she argues that the human capital argument cannot explain why skilled *taferta* weavers, who were mostly women, made 70 *soldi* a week, while unskilled male construction workers made a daily wage of 20 soldi (meaning a weekly wage of 100 soldi).[107] Though human capital cannot explain this difference, market forces can. Rates of pay are based on marginal returns rather than average returns. Job uncertainty sometimes explains different levels of pay in modern labor markets. Semiskilled and unskilled construction workers in twenty-first-century America are sometimes paid far more than professors; however, construction workers receive that pay only when they can find work.

A gender-based skill difference would lead to a number of implications. Lower skills could help explain why women worked in different occupations than men.[108] Lower skills could be due to a lack of training and guild regulations.[109] The argument that women had lower skills faces a number of hurdles. First, if women's skills were uniformly less than those of men, women would have been paid less for the same work; however, studies find that women received equal pay for equal work. Bronislaw Geremek and Dixon independently observe equal pay for equal work in fourteenth-century Paris.[110] Clark also finds no pay difference between genders in seventeenth-century England.[111]

Second, a wide range of market factors pushed for skills equality between genders. Women weavers faced the same pressures as men to guarantee product quality. The Arte della Lana established, monitored and enforced fixed prices and minimum quality standards.[112] Women doing the same jobs as men should have been able to meet the minimum standards of the Arte. This implies that their general skill level should not be

---

105 Brown and Goodman, "Women and Industry," 80; Brown, "Woman's Place Was in the Home," 218.

106 Brown, "Woman's Place Was in the Home," 215.

107 Ibid., 218.

108 Brown and Goodman, "Women and Industry," 80.

109 On lack of training, see Clark, *Working Life of Women*, 290; Ogilvie, *Bitter Living*, 158–59 and 235–36. On guild regulations, see Hanawalt, Introduction, xv; Ogilvie, *Bitter Living*, 153 and 230.

110 Bronislaw Geremek, *Le Salariat dans L'artisanat Parisien aux XIIIe–XVe Siècles* (Paris: Mouton, 1968); Dixon, "Craftswomen in the *Livre des Métiers*," 216.

111 Clark, *Working Life of Women*, 290.

112 The figure of 275 days comes from the early Trecento. Anna Maria E. Agnoletti, ed., *Statuto dell'Arte della Lana in Firenze (1317–1319)*, Fonti e Studi sulle Corporazioni Artigiane del Medio Evo, vol. 1 (Florence: Felice Le Monnier, 1940); De Roover, "Florentine Firm of Cloth Manufacturers," 422. The figure of 250 days comes from a calculation by the author based on Mario Bernocchi, *Le Monete della Repubblica Fiorentina, IV: Valute del Fiorino d'Oro 1389–1432* (Florence: Olschki, 1978).

Table 8.3 Gross pay by lot by gender of weaver for Giuliano di Rafaello de'Medici and Company, wool manufacturers, 1547–53

| Lot | Women | | | Men | | | Comparison |
	Cls.	Wvn.	μ Pay	Wvn.	Ident.	μ Pay	Pay Adv.
2	29	1	59.10	28	28	57.15	Female
5	24	3	24.00	21	21	24.00	Equal
6	10	2	26.00	8	8	25.90	Female
9	21	1	59.10	20	20	58.30	Female
17	7	1	26.00	6	6	26.00	Equal
21	23	2	10.00	21	11	10.00	Equal
25	7	1	12.00	6	6	12.00	Equal
26	6	1	10.00	5	3	10.00	Equal
27	6	1	12.00	5	5	12.00	Equal
29	6	3	10.00	3	2	10.00	Equal
30	5	1	44.00	4	3	44.00	Equal
32	8	2	26.00	6	6	26.00	Equal
34	10	1	56.15	9	9	58.55	Male

Lot: Lot number
Cls.: Total number of cloths in lot
Wvn.: Number of cloths woven by that gender
μ Pay: Mean pay for that gender per cloth
Ident.: Number of identical cloths woven by men
Pay Adv.: Pay advantage—that is, gender listed received a higher average piece-rate pay for work done on that lot
Sources: Medici-Tornaquinci, Mss. 560 (4) and 560 (5). Calculation by author.

significantly below that of men. It is unlikely that companies would knowingly hire weavers who were significantly less skilled and then pay them the same prices.

Third, women could have had equal or greater skill to men but instead chose to specialize in work requiring less skill due to nonmarket considerations. Edler observes that Lucchese women silk weavers specialized in different kinds of cloth than men. It was not the case that few women achieved high skill. It was rather that less of the work done by women was on cloths that required a high level of skill.[113]

This pattern can be observed in Florence. Table 8.3 shows that women almost always received the same pay for the same kind of cloth woven as men. It applies not just to the same type of cloth but also extends to the individual lot of cloth woven. Most of the variation in pay, in fact, was in favor of women.

No woman was penalized by the Medici for poor workmanship, and only 1 of the 51 men was penalized. This suggests that, at least in this firm, women weavers were not less skilled than men and that quality was maintained throughout the production process.

Table 8.4 shows that men and women wove different kinds of cloths. Men tended to weave higher-quality cloths, while women tended to weave lower-quality cloths. The chi-squared test of the data in Table 8.4 is statistically significant.

---

113 Edler, *Silk Trade of Lucca*.

Table 8.4 Type of cloth produced by gender of weaver for Giuliano di Rafaello de'Medici and Company, wool manufacturers, 1547–53

Gender	Total Weavers	Total Cloths	Cloths/ Weaver	Share Shorts	Share Accordelato	Share Rascia
Men	51	288	5.65	17%	39%	44%
Women	6	21	3.50	43%	38%	19%
Total	57	309	5.42	19%	39%	42%

Sources: Medici-Tornaquinci, Mss. 560 (4) and 560 (5). Calculation by author

Table 8.5 Days between weaving and sale by type of cloth for Giuliano di Rafaello de'Medici and Company, wool manufacturers, 1547–53

Statistic	Population	Men	Women
Sample Size	297	276	21
Mean	294.36	293.84	301.1
Std. Error	17.02	17.44	75.45
Coeff. of Var.	99.65	98.59	114.83

Std. Error: Sample standard error
Coeff. of Var.: Coefficient of variation; the value equals the sample standard deviation divided by the mean, then the resulting quotient multiplied by 100
Sources: Medici-Tornaquinci, Mss. 560 (4) and 560 (5). Calculation by author.

Dynamic data can help resolve the issue of why men wove higher-quality cloths than women. The time required by the lanaiuolo to sell the cloth after it was woven should measure the skill of the weaver. Lower-quality weaving should have been more difficult to sell if all cloths were assigned a set price based on quantity. The results in Chapter 7 imply that the weaving and cloth markets were sufficiently efficient to identify and to evaluate differences based on workmanship.

The time between completing the weaving and the final sale of the cloth is an inexact measure of the time each cloth spent in inventory and the time to finish and dye the cloth. This is not as problematic as it might at first seem, since the finishing and dyeing steps were usually relatively quick and predictable. The data in Table 8.5 show no signifi-cant difference in sales time between the cloths woven by men and women. This implies that there was no significant difference in skill and thus justifies the equal pay for equal work noted above.

The results appear to present a kind of paradox. The industry clearly failed to notice any skill difference; however, women seem to have voluntarily accepted less pay despite equal skills. The next section resolves this paradox: women used their time differently.

Part-Time Work

There were important differences between how men and women weavers worked. Each woman weaver, on average, provided less work product, in terms of total value, for the firm than did each man. Women wove lower-quality cloths and fewer cloths, only about two-thirds the number that men wove. (See Table 8.4.) Nevertheless, the division of labor was incomplete, as both men and women wove all three general types of woolen cloth.

This leads to the next question: how did women use their time? Today most workers are paid either by the hour or they are on salary. Renaissance women were paid a piece rate; this is the cost to the employer. The cost to the worker of being employed is measured by the cost per unit of time.

Day rather than hour is the most relevant unit of time to use when examining wage rates of this period. The regular work year consisted of between 250 and 275 days.[114] The standard workday lasted from sunrise to sunset with one interruption for the noon meal in winter and two interruptions in summer.[115] It is not clear how precisely women kept to this daily schedule.

The length of time to weave a single cloth was the one key variable that was unregulated by the guild; thus, it was open to variation. Guild regulations set the weaving market prices, the length of the cloth and the fineness of the cloth.[116] The weight of the cloth was constrained, therefore, by the length and the fineness requirements. The weights tended to cluster around means determined by the type of cloth.

Women deliberately spent less time working for the firm. The women would use their time to spin, warp or weave. Spinning and warping could generally be completed in only a few days, while weaving took longer. Other researchers have also found that warping work took relatively little time to complete and significantly less than weaving.[117] This appears to have been a basic characteristic of the production process—holding from the 1390s until at least the 1560s. Table 8.4 shows that women wove fewer cloths, on average, and a higher percentage of shorts. Figure 8.1 shows that shorts took two-thirds the time to weave as other cloths.

Taking less time for each project led to a more irregular work schedule. It appears that the women and not the company initiated this schedule, since men worked more regularly. All the companies operated relatively efficiently, with many companies in the market and with low concentration levels.

---

114 Agnoletti, *Statuto dell'Arte della Lana*, 153–57; Raymond de Roover, *The Rise and Decline of the Medici Bank, 1397–1494* (Cambridge, MA: Harvard University Press, 1963), 185.

115 Agnoletti, *Statuto dell'Arte della Lana*, 175–77.

116 Edler, *Glossary*, 421–22.

117 Federigo Melis, *Aspetti della vita economica medievale: Studi nell'Archivio Datini di Prato* (Siena, Italy: Monte dei paschi di Siena, 1962), 633; Francesco Ammannati, "Francesco di Marco Datini's Wool Workshops," in *Francesco di Marco Datini. The Man the Merchant*, ed. Giampero Nigro (Florence: Firenze University Press, 2010), 507; Ammannati, "Production et productivité du travail dans les ateliers laniers florentins du XVIe siècle," in *Les temps du travail. Normes, pratiques, évolutions (XIVe-XIXe siècle)*, ed. Corine Maitte and Didier Terrier (Rennes: Presses Universitaires de Rennes 2014), 242–44.

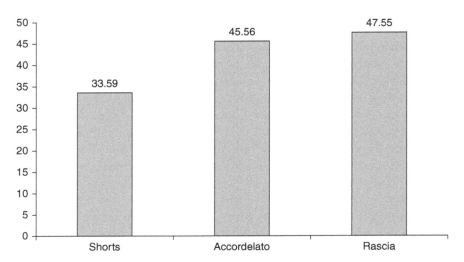

Figure 8.1 Weaving time by type of cloth for Giuliano di Rafaello de'Medici and Company, wool manufacturers, 1547–53
Sources: Medici-Tornaquinci, Mss. 560 (4) and 560 (5). Calculation by author.

These observations are part of a broader pattern. Women maintained a more flexible schedule and saved time to do something else. This pattern of less time spent working is more likely to be related to their marginal substitution of time than an income effect for nonwidows. The trade-off could come either from working multiple occupations or from household production; however, the multiple occupations explanation does not appear to fit the Florentine case. These observations are corroborated by the work of Francesco Ammannati, who presents data showing Florentine women's warping work was irregular and concentrated into periods of heavy work separated by periods of no work.[118] This is related to the observation by Davis that women worked at multiple occupations in sixteenth-century Lyons.[119] However, this was a seasonal effect, and the Florentine wool industry work was not seasonal.

Household production seems the most plausible explanation for the differences in time management. These observed irregularities could easily correspond to the pregnancy cycle, to children's life cycles or to other causes. Recent labor market studies of the United States, Japan and developing countries observe similar behavior by women and successfully use maternity and the number of children as explanatory factors.[120]

---

118 Francesco Ammannati, "Production et productivité du travail dans les ateliers laniers florentins du XVIe siècle," in *Les temps du travail. Normes, pratiques, évolutions (XIVe-XIXe siècle)*, ed. Corine Maitte and Didier Terrier (Rennes: Presses Universitaires de Rennes 2014), 43.

119 Davis, "Women in the Crafts in Sixteenth-Century Lyons," 187.

120 For example, see Suganya Hutaserani and James Roumasset, "Institutional Change and the Demographic Transition in Rural Thailand," *Economic Development and Cultural Change* 40, no. 1 (1991): 75–100.

Conclusion

The study described in this chapter uses dynamic data to examine women's work in Renaissance Florence. Previous research, based on survey sources, such as censuses and guild registers, claimed that the labor market differences between men and women resulted largely from guild laws and skill differences. This study comes to a more nuanced conclusion. In short, working women used their time differently than men did. This difference could only be discovered using dynamic data. Florentine women matched the men in skill; however, they did not always take the opportunity to demonstrate their skills. Women worked from home; received equal pay for equal work; worked in lower-paying but less time-consuming occupations; worked irregularly but quickly; and produced a product comparable to that of men. Together, and independently, these findings suggest that women attempted to schedule their time differently than did men. Therefore, Florentine working women must have engaged in some unobserved activity whose exact nature is not clear. The women were probably performing some kind of complementary production for their household—caring for children is one of many possibilities—and had to minimize their time spent traveling and working.

These results imply that Florentine men and women had different labor supply functions. The income effect was a critical determinant in a woman's decision to participate in the labor force. Both the very limited number of working widows and the existence of two-income families also support this conclusion.

Household production requirements determined the way women worked. Women without households to care for could certainly have worked more regularly and more frequently, just as men did. Women doing household work would have had less time and would have had to substitute time working for the market for time working for their households. This seems reasonable and explains most of the observed phenomena. Women's work in the Renaissance Florentine wool industry would have been what Goldin terms "nonlinear work."[121]

These different gender-based labor supply functions could correspond to different social roles. As Kuehn suggests, it is possible that women had different occupations at different stages in their life cycle. Alternatively, something now unobservable by historians was strongly influencing their work behavior. The absence of detailed demographic data, however, precludes examining precise reasons for women's behavior.

---

121 Claudia Goldin, "A Grand Gender Convergence: Its Last Chapter," *American Economic Review* 104, no. 4 (2014): 1091–119.

Chapter Nine

WHY WERE RENAISSANCE FLORENTINE WOOL INDUSTRY COMPANIES SO SMALL?

Introduction

The Renaissance Florentine wool industry employed an uncommon production system that presents a paradox of industrial organization. On the one hand, the firms in the industry were clearly profitable. It is no exaggeration to state that their profits funded much of the Florentine Renaissance, from the paintings and sculptures to the private palace architecture. This profitability made the industry large—indeed, it was by far the largest employer in Florence—with, at any given time, dozens of firms participating. (See Appendix 3B.) On the other hand, the industry's production used a putting-out production system organized by a guild. Though this system was widely used throughout late medieval and early modern Europe, a long tradition of economists and historians argue that both the guild and the putting-out system were hopelessly inefficient.[1] Their ends in many ways signaled the beginning of the Industrial Revolution. Nevertheless, the wool industry was resilient. Over the course of three centuries, it experienced dramatic swings, but adapted by substantially changing its mix of inputs and products and its cost structure in response to each new challenge.[2]

The small size of the companies would have amplified these effects. By any reasonable standard the companies within the wool industry were extremely small. They were small both in space—only a few people worked directly for the company—and in time, with the partnerships being time limited, generally only three years. This small size increased the already high transaction costs. This makes the investment, the long position in investment jargon, shorter both in size and in time. The paradox becomes even more apparent in the context of the survivor principle, which should apply here.[3] That principle is designed to analyze business behavior in a competitive industry. Chapter 7 showed that the Florentine wool industry was competitive during the Renaissance. The principle, as

1 Adam Smith, *The Wealth of Nations*, ed. Alan Krueger (1776; New York: Bantam Dell, 2003), bk. 1, chap. 10, pt. 2, 164–97; Charles Babbage, *On the Economy of Machinery and Manufactures*, 4th ed. (1835; New York: A. M. Kelly, 1971).
2 John H. Munro, "The Rise, Expansion, and Decline of the Italian Wool-Based Cloth Industries, 1100–1730: A Study in International Competition, Transaction Costs, and Comparative Advantage," *Studies in Medieval and Renaissance History* 9 (2012): 45–207; Patrick Chorley, "*Rascie* and the Florentine Cloth Industry during the Sixteenth Century: A Case Study," *Journal of European Economic History* 32, no. 3 (2003): 514.
3 George J. Stigler, "The Economies of Scale," *Journal of Law and Economics* 1 (1958): 54–71.

used here, has no normative implications. The current debate about merchant guilds is an entirely different issue.[4]

This study shows how this set of seemingly independent and clearly paradoxical aspects were actually all part of a single comprehensive response to a fundamental aspect of the medieval economy: risk. These institutional arrangements were complementary and, instead of decreasing overall efficiency, acted together. They allowed the company to hedge and reduce its aggregate commitment, thus providing a form of insurance. Small firms lead to a reduction in risk because of their smaller capital outlays. In essence, they place much less at risk. The form of the companies in the wool industry therefore has implications for why Renaissance Florence was so wealthy.

The dynamic nature of the wool industry is well recognized.[5] Risk is necessarily dynamic because it is intrinsically connected with the movement of time and the unknown future. The structure of the Arte and company permitted dynamic business trade-offs. This study uses dynamic data to make clear the relationship of risk with the wool industry. The static view implicitly assumes steady activity over time. Dynamic data reveal significant variations over time.

This study approaches the problem from a different direction: the contractual framework within which the firm operated. Previous work generally emphasizes the guild and its regulations[6] or the firm's manufacturing technology and organization of production.[7] This framework opens up a new perspective by allowing a formal analysis of firm, guild and subcontractors simultaneously as a set of relationships. Important to this analysis is a careful distinction among the firm, the shop (*bottega*) and the company (*compagnia*) that

---

4   See Avner Greif, *Institutions and the Path to the Modern Economy: Lessons from Medieval Trade* (Cambridge, UK: Cambridge University Press, 2005); Sheilagh Ogilvie, *Institutions and European Trade: Merchant Guilds, 1000–1800* (Cambridge, UK: Cambridge University Press, 2011).

5   Raymond de Roover, "A Florentine Firm of Cloth Manufacturers," *Business, Banking, and Economic Thought in Late Medieval and Early Modern Europe*, ed. Julius Kirshner (1938; Chicago: University of Chicago Press, 1974), 85–118; Richard T. Lindholm, "Studies of the Renaissance Florentine Woolen Industry," PhD diss., University of Chicago, 1993, chap. 5; Richard A. Goldthwaite, "The Florentine Wool Industry in the Late Sixteenth Century: A Case Study," *Journal of European Economic History* 32, no. 3 (2003): 527–54; Richard A. Goldthwaite, *Economy of Renaissance Florence* (Baltimore: Johns Hopkins University Press, 2009), esp. 329–30.

6   Alfred Dören, *Studien aus der Florentiner Wirtschaftsgeschichte*, vol. 1: *Die Florentiner Wollentuchsindustrie vom Vierzehnten bis zum Sechzehnten Jahrhundert* (Stuttgart: J. G. Cotta'sche Buchhandlung Nachfolger, 1901); Francesco Ammannati, "Craft Guild Legislation and Woollen Production: the Florentine Arte della Lana in the Fifteenth and Sixteenth Centuries," in *Innovation and Creativity in Late Medieval and Early Modern European Cities*, ed. Karol Davids and Bert De Munck (Farnham: Ashgate 2014), 55–79.

7   De Roover, "A Florentine Firm of Cloth Manufacturers;" Federigo Melis, *Aspetti della vita economica medievale: Studi nell'Archivio Datini di Prato* (Siena: Monte dei Paschi di Siena, 1962), 455–634; Goldthwaite, "Florentine Wool Industry"; Francesco Ammannati, "L'Arte della Lana a Firenze nel Cinquecento: Crisi del settore e risposte degli operatori," *Storia economica: Rivista quadrimestrale*, 11, no. 1 (2008): 5–39; Ammannati, "Datini's Wool Workshops;" Ammannati, "Production et productivité."

is not commonly made. This distinction motivates many of the results that follow. In this chapter "firm" is used in the economic theory sense and is the entity that produces the product. The Arte della Lana guild and putting-out system performed functions that are usually carried out inside the modern firm. The "shop" is the place where production is controlled and is a physical location. It has been the focus for much of the recent research by economic historians.[8] The "company" was the business itself. A specific contract among the partners defines the company. This distinction is essential for the subsequent analysis.

The solution advanced here is that the combination of the guild and the putting-out system was essential. Risk is not cheap to eliminate, and costly behavior, such as open fields in medieval English agriculture, have been adopted as a conscious technique to reduce risk.[9] The putting-out system decreased risk, but increased transaction costs. The guild, separately, reduced transaction costs. Together they created a system resilient enough to function essentially unchanged for centuries.[10]

The framework is developed in the rest of the chapter. First, the foundation for the analysis is built. It describes the current state of the theory of craft guilds. There is a debate over whether guilds were good or bad for the overall economy. This debate provides a framework for analysis. The basic economic theories of the firm starting with the transaction cost theory are explained. This is then tied to the costs associated with the division of labor and the putting-out system. Next, these two theoretical approaches are connected to the wool industry. The transaction cost approach shows that the Arte reduced transaction costs by establishing minimum training and production standards, fixing prices, monitoring quality and providing work locations for craft workers. This chapter next introduces and describes the need for risk reduction and the response of the wool industry. The wool industry faced high ex ante risk and low ex post risk. Both the company and crafts workers reduced risk in the wool industry. The company appears to deliberately minimize the extent of the risk as well as any consequent risk. Such risk was small and created using only a short-term contract. Although many companies were established, few were active at any one time. Craft workers shared risk with the companies through piece-rate production. They made only short-term contracts, had easy entry and exit in the labor market and were able to work discontinuously and for multiple companies. Finally, a brief example that shows the potential of this framework is provided at the end of the chapter. This work creates a framework that allows a deeper analysis of the wool industry and its history.

---

8 Cf. Melis, *Aspetti*; Goldthwaite, "Florentine Wool Industry," 527–54; Goldthwaite, *Economy of Renaissance Florence*, 265–340; Gene Brucker, *Florence: The Golden Age, 1138–1737* (Berkeley: University of California Press, 1998), 105.

9 Donald N. McCloskey, "The Open Fields of England: Rent, Risk, and the Rate of Interest, 1300–1815," in *Markets in History: Economic Studies of the Past*, ed. David W. Galenson (Cambridge, UK: Cambridge University Press, 1989), 5–51.

10 See appendix 3B for more details.

General Theories of Craft Guilds

The criticism of craft guilds in modern economic theory can be traced to Adam Smith's 1776 *Wealth of Nations*.[11] Their theoretical inefficiency leads naturally to the question of why they existed in the first place. Economic historians and economists have not yet agreed on the answer. One obstacle to a conclusive answer is the variation of guilds across localities and across industries within each locality. The internal structure of guilds varied widely. This was true in both early modern Italy and the Low Countries.[12] The wide variety of guilds implies local conditions, certainly including economic, influenced the structure.

Guilds provided economic and social benefits. The economic benefits included monopoly power and production services. Industrial organization theory leads to the most common economic explanation of why guilds existed. Guilds helped create monopoly power when they created cartels,[13] established quality standards[14] and limited entry in order to benefit members.[15] Guilds are sometimes seen as almost protolabor unions.[16] By limiting competition, they would have provided a kind of implicit insurance to their members.[17] However, Richardson argues that English guilds did not have legal monopolies[18] and that this belief was due to a misunderstanding among theoretical economists.[19]

Some argue that guilds also provided economic benefits. Along the lines of Coase and Williamson, Ulrich Pfister applies the transaction cost approach to the early modern firm. He uses predominantly German examples.[20] He views the firm and

11 Smith, *Wealth of Nations*, bk. 1, chap. 10, pt. 2, 164–97.

12 Paola Massa, "Presentazione," in *Dalla corporazione alla società di mutuo soccorso*, ed. Paola Massa and Angelo Moioli (Milan: Franco Angeli 2004), 9–11; Angelo Moioli, "I risultati di un'indagine sulle corporazione nell città italiane in età moderna," in *Dalla corporazione alla società di mutuo soccorso*, ed. Paola Massa and Angelo Moioli (Milan: Franco Angeli 2004), 15–31; Jan Lucassen, Piet Lourens and Bert de Munck, "The Distribution of Guilds in the Low Countries, 1000–1800," in *Dalla corporazione alla società di mutuo soccorso*, ed. Paola Massa and Angelo Moioli (Milan: Franco Angeli 2004), 33–56; Luca Mocarelli, "Guilds Reappraised: Italy in the Early Modern Period," *International Review of Social History* 53, no. S16 (2008): 159–78.

13 G. Mickwitz, *Die Kartellfunktionen der Zünfte und ihre Bedeutung bei der Enstehung des Zunftwesens* (Helsingfors: Societas scientiarum Fennica, 1936).

14 Bo Gustafsson, "The Rise and Economic Behaviour of Medieval Craft Guilds," in *Power and Economic Institutions*, ed. Bo Gustafsson (Aldershot, UK: Edward Elgar, 1991), 69–106; Gary Richardson, "Brand Names before the Industrial Revolution," *National Bureau of Economic Research*, no. 13930 (2008).

15 Karl Gunnar Persson, *Pre-Industrial Economic Growth: Social Organization and Technological Progress in Europe* (Oxford: Blackwell, 1988), 75–76; C. R. Hickson and E. A. Thompson, "A New Theory of Guilds and European Economic Development," *Explorations in Economic History* 28, no. 1 (1991): 127–68.

16 Unwin, *Industrial Organization*, chap. 8; Steven A. Epstein, *Wage Labor and Guilds in Medieval Europe* (Chapel Hill: University of North Carolina Press, 1991).

17 Persson, *Pre-Industrial Economic Growth*, 75–76.

18 Gary Richardson, "Guilds, Laws, and Markets for Manufactured Merchandise in Late-Medieval England," *Explorations in Economic History* 41, no. 1 (2004): 1–25.

19 Gary Richardson, "A Tale of Two Theories: Monopolies and Craft Guilds in Medieval England and Modern Imagination," *Journal of the History of Economic Thought* 23, no. 2 (2001): 217–42.

20 Ulrich Pfister, "Craft Guilds and Economic Development in Early Modern Europe," in *Dalla corporazione alla società di mutuo soccorso*, ed. Paola Massa and Angelo Moioli (Milan: Franco Angeli 2004), 293–98.

guild as alternative organizations.[21] Guilds reduced the firm's transaction costs, and their monitoring decreased the number of barriers to entry.[22] He argues that the benefits of guilds[23] include delegated monitoring[24] and multiple measurement and vertical integration.[25] Pfister notes that there is little research on the economic effects of guilds on the daily practice of various industries—in other words, the dynamic element of production with guilds is omitted.[26] Some go so far as to argue that guilds aided long-term growth. Guilds were an important aid in technology transfers.[27] Stephan Epstein argues that not only did they transfer technology[28] but they also promoted the production of human capital.[29] Luca Mocarelli argues that guilds protected customers, stabilized the local market and cut transaction and organization costs.[30]

Guilds provided social as well as economic benefits.[31] Early modern German guilds were an important source of values in society.[32] Guilds providing mutual aid as a primitive form of insurance was important in Italy.[33]

---

21 Pfister, "Theory of the Firm," 44.
22 Ibid., 42.
23 Pfister, "Economic Development," 293–98.
24 Ibid., 293–95.
25 Ibid., 295–98.
26 Pfister, "Theory of the Firm," 50.
27 Giorgio Gottardi, "Ruoli della corporazioni artigiane nella promozione dell'innovazione tecnologica," in *Dalla corporazione alla società di mutuo soccorso*, ed. Paola Massa and Angelo Moioli (Milan: Franco Angeli 2004), 275–85; Edoardo Demo, "L'industria tessile nel Veneto tra XV e XVI secolo: Tecnologie e innovazione dei prodotti," in *Dalla corporazione alla società di mutuo soccorso*, ed. Paola Massa and Angelo Moioli (Milan: Franco Angeli 2004), 329–41; Ulrich Pfister, "Craft Guilds and Economic Development in Early Modern Europe," in *Dalla corporazione alla società di mutuo soccorso*, ed. Paola Massa and Angelo Moioli (Milan: Franco Angeli 2004), 298–307.
28 Epstein, "Apprenticeship and Technological Change"; Stephan R. Epstein, "Property Rights to Technical Knowledge in Pre-Modern Europe, 1300–1800," *American Economic Review* 94, no. 2 (2004): 382–87; Stephan R. Epstein and Maarten Prak, Introduction to *Guilds, Innovation, and the European Economy, 1400–1800* (Cambridge, UK: Cambridge University Press, 2008), 4–24.
29 Stephan R. Epstein, "Craft Guilds in the Pre-Modern Economy: A Discussion," *Economic History Review* 61, no. 1 (2008): 155–74.
30 Luca Mocarelli, "Guilds Reappraised: Italy in the Early Modern Period," *International Review of Social History* 53, no. S16 (2008): 178.
31 There is large literature that discusses this characteristic from many perspectives. For more information, see the studies in: Alberto Guenzi and Paola Massa, "Introduction," in *Guilds, Markets and Work Regulations in Italy, 16th–19th Centuries*, ed. Alberto Guenzi, Paola Massa and Fausto Piola Caselli (Brookfield, VT: Ashgate Publishing Company, 1998), 2; Alberto Guenzi, Paola Massa and Fausto Piola Caselli, eds. *Guilds, Markets and Work Regulations in Italy, 16th–19th Centuries* (Brookfield, VT: Ashgate Publishing Company, 1998), 395–475; Paola Massa and Angelo Moioli, eds. *Dalla corporazione alla società di mutuo soccorso* (Milan: Franco Angeli 2004), 443–516, 523–745.
32 Merry E. Wiesner, "Guilds, Male Bonding, and Women's Work in Early Modern Germany," in *La Donna nell'Economia Secc. XIII–XVIII*, ed. Simonetta Cavaciocchi (Prato: Le Monnier, 1990), 655–69.
33 There is a large literature that discusses this characteristic from many perspectives. For more information, see the studies in: Alberto Guenzi, Paola Massa and Fausto Piola Caselli,

Social organizational theories lead to another set of explanations for the existence of guilds. Bo Gustafson argues that guilds equalized returns for members.[34] Karl Persson, C. R. Hickson and E. A. Thompson, and Sheilagh Ogilvie argue that guilds increased the welfare of members.[35] Persson and Hickson and Thompson assert that the existence of guilds was a net positive,[36] while Ogilvie asserts that the increased welfare for guild members harmed others more than it helped guild members.[37] Ogilvie believes that guilds helped create social capital that benefited only members with higher social status.[38]

Ogilvie brings social capital theory to the study of guilds. She views much of the discussion on the existence of guilds as simply a justification for their existence.[39] The guilds' rent-seeking behavior transferred value to its members at the expense of others and the overall economy. Ogilvie's work implies that guilds were a constant and significant drain on an already small economy. Such a long-term drain suggests that guilds and the putting-out system should not have lasted long.

These observations are consistent with recent developments in the theory of institutions. Ogilvie argues that guilds arise through political conflicts about distribution.[40] Ogilvie writes, "Guilds, I will argue, provide strong support for the view that institutions arise and survive as a result of political conflicts over distribution."[41]

The Putting-Out System and Firm Structure

The Renaissance Florentine wool industry produced cloth using an extensive division of labor operating in a putting-out system, a system that later disappeared when placed in competition with modern industrial methods. (See Appendix 3B.)

---

eds. *Guilds, Markets and Work Regulations in Italy, 16th–19th Centuries* (Brookfield, VT: Ashgate Publishing Company, 1998), 395–475; Paola Massa and Angelo Moioli, eds. *Dalla corporazione alla società di mutuo soccorso*, (Milan: Franco Angeli 2004), 443–516, 523–745.

34 Bo Gustafsson, "The Rise and Economic Behavior of Medieval Craft Guilds," in *Power and Economic Institutions: Reinterpretations in Economic History*, ed. Bo Gustafson (Aldershot, UK: Edward Elgar, 1991), 69–106.

35 Persson, *Pre-Industrial Economic Growth*, 75–76; Hickson and Thompson, "New Theory of Guilds"; Sheilagh C. Ogilvie, "'Whatever Is, Is Right'? Economic Institutions in Pre-Industrial Europe," *Economic History Review* 60, no. 4 (2007): 649–84.

36 Persson, *Pre-Industrial Economic Growth*, 75–76; Hickson and Thompson, "New Theory of Guilds."

37 Ogilvie, "'Whatever Is, Is Right'?"

38 Sheilagh C. Ogilvie, *A Bitter Living: Women, Markets, and Social Capital in Early Modern Germany* (Oxford, UK: Oxford University Press, 2003); Sheilagh C. Ogilvie, "Guilds, Efficiency, and Social Capital: Evidence from German Proto-Industry," *Economic History Review*, 2nd ser., 57, no. 2 (2004): 286–333; Ogilvie, "'Whatever Is, Is Right'?"

39 Epstein, "Craft Guilds in the Pre-Modern Economy"; Sheilagh C. Ogilvie, "Rehabilitating the Guilds: A Reply," *Economic History Review* 61, no. 1 (2008): 175–82.

40 Sheilagh Ogilvie, "The Economics of the Guild," *Journal of Economic Perspectives* 28, no. 4 (2014): 169–92.

41 Ibid., 170.

The division of labor is a core concept in economics. Stigler forcefully demonstrates that "the division of labor [is limited by the extent of the market and] is not a quaint practice of eighteenth-century pin factories; it is a fundamental principle of economic organization."[42] The extent of the market can vary dramatically from place to place. In Industrial Revolution Britain, the extent of the market could be quite large. For example, Birmingham gun workers divided production into highly specialized steps and worked in close proximity.[43] In contrast, colonial America's market was much smaller than Britain's. Benjamin Franklin told the story of colonial American failures to successfully lure British expertise to the American colonies because the colonial market was too small.[44] The extremely detailed division of labor in the Florentine wool industry implies that its market was very large (see Appendix 3B).[45]

Transaction costs can be applied in a variety of ways. Munro's history of the rise, expansion and decline of the Italian wool industries places emphasizes the importance of transaction costs in this process.[46] His definition of transaction costs, however, is limited to the external costs the firm faces as it delivers its product and well outside of its production process. The present study examines the impact of transaction costs inside the production process on the actual purpose of the work—to do work in order to make money.

The transaction costs theory of firm size is based largely on work of R. H. Coase and Oliver Williamson.[47] Coase argues that transaction costs limit the extent of the firm,[48] which will expand to the point where the marginal transaction costs balance the marginal benefits of getting bigger. The firm itself organizes production within the firm. The market's price mechanism operates outside the firm and is costly to use.[49] It requires the firm to search for the product, negotiate the price, agree to contract terms, monitor the quality and complete the transaction. Coase writes that the marketing and organizing costs determine the number of products and quantity of each produced.[50] He expands

---

42 George Stigler, "The Division of Labor Is Limited by the Extent of the Market," *Journal of Political Economy* 59, no. 3 (1951): 185–93; quote on 193.

43 Ibid., 192–93.

44 Ibid., 193.

45 The early modern gun industry is a fertile source of examples of the organization of production. For example, Belfani shows corporate organization in a rural area and the protection and conservation of technical knowledge of craftsmen in the gun industry. (Carlo Marco Belfani, "A Chain of Skills: The Production Cycle of Firearms Manufacture in the Brescia Area from the Sixteenth to the Eighteenth Centuries," in *Guilds, Markets and Work Regulations in Italy, 16th–19th Centuries*, ed. Alberto Guenzi, Paola Massa and Fausto Piola Caselli (Brookfield, VT: Ashgate Publishing Company, 1998), 266–83.).

46 Munro, "Italian Wool-Based Cloth Industries," 153–73 and 179.

47 See particularly R. H. Coase, "The Nature of the Firm," in *The Firm, the Market, and the Law* (Chicago: University of Chicago Press, 1988), 33–56; Oliver E. Williamson, *Markets and Hierarchies: Analysis and Antitrust Implications* (New York: Free Press, 1975); Oliver E. Williamson, *The Economic Institutions of Capitalism* (New York: Free Press, 1985).

48 Coase, "Nature of the Firm," 33–56.

49 Ibid., 36 and 39.

50 Ibid., 53.

on this and argues that if there were no transaction costs, then there would be no reason to have a firm.[51] Alfred Chandler has applied this to the development of the modern firm, writing, "The visible hand of management replaced what Adam Smith referred to as the invisible hand of market forces."[52]

The division of labor and transaction cost approaches can be linked in a natural way. The division of labor creates transaction costs, which prevent an arbitrary division of labor within the firm. It improves the production process but requires a corresponding market for the product. The Florentine division of labor was based on the putting-out system, but classical and modern economists attack the putting-out system as inefficient. Poor inventory management is a primary criticism of the putting-out system. The nineteenth-century industrialist and economic theorist Charles Babbage famously attacked the system on this point, arguing that it created lags throughout the production process.[53] Modern economists tend to agree with their classical counterparts and say the system needs buffer inventories to keep the product flowing.[54] Each portion of the product has to be sent from one step to the next in discrete shipments rather than continuously.[55] Economic historians, however, are not unanimous in their criticism of inventory management. Fernand Braudel, upon an examination of early modern documents, claims that generally there was quick inventory turnaround.[56]

Williamson places the putting-out system in a larger framework when he compares it to the modern industrial production, the "capitalist authority relation," using simple efficiency criteria.[57] The putting-out system led to higher transaction costs, because the firm did so little production internally. Table 9.1 summarizes Williamson's analysis by listing all eleven types of transaction costs that Williamson envisions.[58] He claims that the capitalist authority relation is more efficient for six types of costs: transportation expense, buffer inventories, interface leakage, contracting, local responsiveness and system responsiveness. The efficiency levels are tied for three types of costs: station, leadership and equipment utilization. And the putting-out system is more efficient for two types of costs: work intensity and local innovation. Overall, the differences create a large gap that worked against the putting-out system.[59]

High transaction costs combined with redistribution costs should have killed the system early on. However, both the guild system and the putting-out system lasted for centuries, in Florence for example, implying that there was some level of optimality somewhere.[60]

---

51 Ibid., 14.
52 Alfred D. Chandler Jr., *The Visible Hand: The Managerial Revolution in American Business* (Cambridge, MA: Harvard University Press, 1977), 1.
53 Babbage, *Machinery and Manufactures*.
54 Williamson, *Economic Institutions of Capitalism*, 223n15.
55 Ibid., 227.
56 Fernand Braudel, *The Wheels of Commerce (Civilization and Capitalism 15th–18th Century)* (New York: Harper and Row, 1982), 2: 140.
57 Williamson, *Economic Institutions of Capitalism*, 223–31.
58 Ibid., 226.
59 Ibid.
60 Stigler, "Economies of Scale," 54–71.

Table 9.1 Williamson efficiency criteria: comparison of modern industrial capitalist authority relation with medieval putting-out system

	Capitalist Authority Relation	Putting-Out System
Transportation Expense	Efficiency	Lack
Buffer Inventories	Efficiency	Lack
Interface Leakage	Efficiency	Lack
Contracting	Efficiency	Lack
Local Responsiveness	Efficiency	Lack
System Responsiveness	Efficiency	Lack
Station	Efficiency	Efficiency
Leadership	Efficiency	Efficiency
Work Intensity	Lack	Efficiency
Equipment Utilization	Efficiency	Efficiency
Local Innovation	Lack	Efficiency

Source: Oliver E. Williamson, *The Economic Institutions of Capitalism* (New York: Free Press, 1985), 223–26. The costs associated with each are:
Transportation expense: physical transport from one work station to another is costly
Buffer inventories: want to economize on buffer inventory
Interface leakage: losses of product during production
Station assignments: match people with job best suited
Leadership: costs of coordination
Contracting: minimizing the amount of contracting per work
Work intensity: worker malingering is a cost
Equipment utilization: equipment abuse and neglect are costly
Local shock responsiveness: cost and time to recover from illness or machinery
Local innovation: want to promote local cost economizing and process changes
System responsiveness: cost to adapt to changing market circumstances

The theoretical transaction cost and the empirical survivor principle approaches therefore appear to be at odds. The guild system had to increase product for someone and could not continually reduce aggregate economic product year after year. The criterion that the existence of the extra product matters, and not how it was subsequently distributed, is frequently used in the field of law and economics to justify legal standards.[61]

The Arte della Lana

The Arte della Lana guild produced wool cloth using a putting-out system. The Arte was a sophisticated umbrella guild organized by the lanaiuoli to coordinate production from a wide range of other occupations.[62] A high level of organization underlay umbrella guilds, which is why they were comparatively uncommon.[63] Somewhat similar but much

---

61 Richard A. Posner, *The Economics of Justice* (Cambridge, MA: Harvard University Press, 1983), 91–94.
62 The term "umbrella guild" is used by Stephan R. Epstein, "Craft Guilds, Apprenticeship and Technological Change in Pre-Modern Europe," *Journal of Economic History* 53, no. 3 (1998): 690.
63 Epstein, "Technological Change," 690; Ammannati, "Craft Guild Legislation," 59.

less sophisticated umbrella guilds included the burrellers' (cloth makers') in contemporary London[64] and the Florentine silk guild, the *Arte di Por Santa Maria*.[65] The Arte system was not the only way to organize wool cloth production, let alone the only one used in Tuscany. The Datini used a *Verlagssystem* type of production where they organized their own system of artisan subcontractors.[66] This system was common in Northern Europe.[67] The Datini created a monopsony in the labor market. Though they used the same manufacturing technology and organization of production as the Arte, the different contractual structure has implications. It probably affected the labor market and increased risk for contractors, making them more reluctant to travel all the way to Prato for work.

The research on individual woolen industry firms has traditionally focused on how they produced cloth: what one could call a production approach.[68] There is a difference between a production approach and a contract approach. The production approach emphasizes the manufacturing technology and the organization of production. At least equally important to this production process is to examine the firms from the perspective of the contract that established the company. An emphasis on the contract instead places the focus on the actual purpose of the work: making profit.[69] Some work sees the industries as investment opportunities, which is, at least implicitly, a contract approach.[70]

Although there is a tendency to look at Arte della Lana companies as if they were modern firms with long-term commitments that grew over time, these companies were, in reality, set up as short-term contracts.[71] The companies were partnerships of Arte

---

64 Epstein, "Technological Change," 690; George Unwin, *Industrial Organization in the Sixteenth and Seventeenth Centuries* (Oxford, UK: Clarendon Press, 1904), 28–30; E. M. Carus-Wilson, *Medieval Merchant Venturers*, 2nd ed. (London: Methuen, 1967), 234–35; and Edward Miller and John Hatcher, *Medieval English Towns: Commerce and Crafts, 1086–1548* (London: Longman, 1995), 112–13.

65 Florence Edler, *Glossary of Medieval Terms of Business, Italian Series, 1200–1600* (Cambridge, MA: Medieval Academy of America, 1934), 330–31; Girolamo Gargiolli, *L'arte della seta a Firenze Trattato del secolo XV* (Florence: G. Barbera, 1868); Florence Edler de Roover, *L'arte della seta a Firenze nei secoli XIV e XV* (Florence: Olschki, 1999).

66 This is clear from Melis, *Aspetti*, 496–634; Ammannati, "Datini's Wool Workshops." This has been widely recognized: Giorgio Borelli, "A Reading of the Relationship between Cities, Manufacturing Crafts and Guilds in Early Modern Italy," in *Guilds, Markets and Work Regulations in Italy, 16th–19th Centuries*, ed. Alberto Guenzi, Paola Massa and Fausto Piola Caselli (Brookfield, VT: Ashgate Publishing Company, 1998), 19–31.

67 Peter Kriedte, Hans Medick and Jürgen Schlumbohm. *Industrialization before Industrialization*, trans. Beate Schempp (Cambridge, UK: Cambridge University Press, 1981; orig. German, 1977.), xi.

68 De Roover, "A Florentine Firm of Cloth Manufacturers;" Melis, *Aspetti*, 495–634; Goldthwaite, "Florentine Wool Industry;" Ammannati, "L'Arte della Lana;" Ammannati, "Datini's Wool Workshops;" Ammannati, "Production et productivité."

69 This emphasis on profit here is not to minimize the importance of charity in the society.

70 Jordan Goodman, "Financing Pre-modern European Industry: An Example from Florence 1580–1660," *Journal of European Economic History* 10, no. 2 (1981): 415–36; Goldthwaite, "Florentine Wool Industry," 548.

71 Edler, *Glossary*, 335–47.

members generally set up for three years at a time. The contract limited the size and length of capital committed. These contracts are also, in many ways, the most fundamental part of the production process. They determined the work to be done and calculated the profit shares from the business. This stresses their short-term and limited nature. Other contracts, explicit and implicit, with the Arte and the subcontracting artisans, provide a convenient analytic framework.

Transaction Cost Reduction

Modern economic theory studies the management of the firm as a single entity. The Florentine wool industry, however, divided the management functions of the modern firm between two legally constituted entities: the company and the Arte. The company was based on the legally constituted partnership agreement between lanaiuoli and directed the production. The Arte provided the environment within which the company operated. The production system was therefore much larger than the company.

The transaction cost theory of the firm implies that transaction costs determine the production structure. The putting-out system increased the relative transaction costs. The off-site work that prevented the manufacturer's direct supervision increased the agency costs and created a moral hazard problem. There were issues with both petty theft and unnecessarily high wastage of material.[72] The manufacturer could observe what typical levels were but could never verify compliance.

The Florentine Arte putting-out system involved a large number of steps. Figure 9.1 shows how the standard woolen-cloth manufacturing production process repeatedly transported the product to the place of work and then brought it back into the company. There were 30 separate movements. (See Figure 9.1.) As a further complication, each occupation's specific relationship to the company varied widely.[73]

Companies produced cloth using a large number of small-scale contracts with individual craft workers. Jurists and moralists frowned on the minor guilds negotiating as a unit with the Arte or the company and preferred freedom of bargaining.[74]

The Arte and the company reduced transaction costs in a number of ways. First, the Arte established minimum entrance requirements for all occupations.[75] Entry (and reentry) was relatively easy for craft work once those minimum requirements had been met. The Arte prepared lists that typically included all available and qualified workers.[76]

---

72 De Roover, "Florentine Firm of Cloth Manufacturers," 93.

73 Franco Franceschi, *Oltre il "Tumulto": I lavoratori fiorentini dell'Arte della Lana fra Tre e Quattrocento* (Florence: Olschki, 1993), 88–92.

74 Raymond de Roover, "Labour Conditions in Florence around 1400: Theory, Policy, and Reality in Florentine Studies," in *Politics and Society in Renaissance Florence*, ed. Nicolai Rubinstein (Evanston, IL: Northwestern University Press, 1968), 313.

75 Anna Maria E. Agnoletti, ed., *Statuto dell'Arte della Lana in Firenze (1317–1319)*, Fonti e Studi sulle Corporazioni Artigiane del Medio Evo, vol. 1 (Florence: Felice Le Monnier, 1940).

76 R. Burr Litchfield, *Florence Ducal Capital, 1530–1630* (New York: ACLS Humanities E-Book, 2008), para. 275. Permanent Link: http://quod.lib.umich.edu/cgi/t/text/text-idx?c=acls; idno=heb90034.

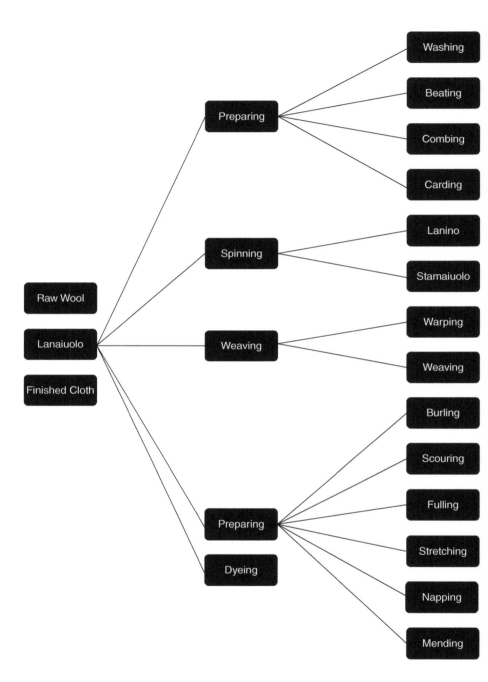

Figure 9.1 Movement of material between wool manufacturing steps for the typical sixteenth-century firm
Source: De Roover, "Florentine Firm of Cloth Manufacturers," 103.

Second, the Arte often established legally binding prices and contracts for many occupations.[77] Fixed prices reduced search costs and the need for negotiation. For example, each phase of production used one or more new craft workers who otherwise would have required a new contract. Not all rates were fixed.[78] Some rates paid to weavers were regulated by ordinance,[79] but the prices could sometimes be adjusted.[80] Arte della Lana regulations did not regulate wages or piece rates until the Cinquecento.[81] For example, regulations setting prices for spinners were established in 1547 and reissued in 1557.[82] Finally, the Arte established and regulated production-quality standards for all subcontractors.[83] The strict regulations attempted to reduce or essentially eliminate agency and transaction cost problems.[84] These regulations included penalties for poor workmanship by weavers.[85] The Arte had drastic punishments for moral hazard violations, such as banishment from work with the Arte.[86]

The company and Arte together generally reduced ex post transaction costs. Both the company and the Arte monitored quality. The Arte had an advantage over the companies, because monitoring exhibited economies of scale. The Arte could use its coercive legal power to guarantee payments and compliance with regulations.

The company directly monitored several steps, including dyeing, warping and weaving, and delegated some monitoring to factors, independent contractors who performed market-making services (see Table 9.2).[87] The typical lanaiuolo hired five kinds of factors: *capodieci, fattori di cardo, fattori di pettine*, lanini and stamaiuoli. Factors were more continuously employed by the companies when production was higher.[88]

The marketplace and strong competitive pressures did reduce the need for monitoring. Craftsmen had a relatively small marketplace for their product and needed repeat business. Efficiency differences would almost certainly have been noticed.

In addition, the company and the Arte provided workspace for some occupations. Table 9.3 shows where each of the different subcontractors involved in the production process worked during the Cinquecento. At that time, the wool washers, cloth scourers, fullers and stretchers used space in large establishments owned by the Arte.[89] The

---

77 Edler, *Glossary*, 422.
78 Goldthwaite, "Florentine Wool Industry," 553.
79 De Roover, "Florentine Firm of Cloth Manufacturers," 98; Edler, *Glossary*, 422.
80 Medici-Tornaquinci, Ms. 560 (5).
81 Ammannati, "Craft Guild Legislation," 55–79
82 Lorenzo Cantini, *Legislazione toscana*, 32 vols. (Florence: Albizzini, 1800–1804), 1: 366–9, 3: 217; Edler, *Glossary*, 149–50 and 279–80.
83 Agnoletti, *Statuto dell'Arte della Lana*.
84 De Roover, "Florentine Firm of Cloth Manufacturers," 94.
85 Medici Ms 560 (4).
86 See Agnoletti, *Statuto dell'Arte della Lana*, 145 and 152. Additional documentation can be found in Alfred Dören, *Studien aus der Florentiner Wirtschaftgeschichte*, vol. 2: *Das Florentiner Zunftwesen vom 14 bis zum 16 Jahrhundert* (1908; Aalen: Scientia Verlag, 1969), 249–54.
87 De Roover, "Florentine Firm of Cloth Manufacturers," 95.
88 Ibid., 95n4.
89 Edler, *Glossary*, 229 and 409.

Table 9.2 Wool manufacturing production steps with those that employed factors noted

Major Step	Minor Step	*Cinquecento* Monitoring
Preparing	Washing	*Arte*
	Beating/Cleaning	Company factor
	Combing	Company factor
	Carding	Company factor
Spinning	Lanini	Company factor
	Stamaiuoli	Company factor
Weaving	Warping	Company direct
	Weaving	Company direct
Finishing	Burling	Company direct
	Scouring	*Arte*
	Fulling	*Arte*
	Stretching	*Arte*
	Napping/ Shearing	Company direct
	Mending	Company direct
Dyeing	Dyeing	Company direct

Sources: De Roover, "Florentine Firm of Cloth Manufacturers," 103; Edler, *Glossary*, 329–30; Franceschi, *Oltre il "Tumulto,"* 33–37. Occupations listed in order of steps to completion.

lanaiuolo supplied workspace for other occupations.[90] During the Cinquecento, only beating, carding and combing were done on the premises of the lanaiuolo.[91] This system could vary slightly over time. During the *Quattrocento*, fullers rented space from large landowners outside the city, and the stretchers were small-scale masters working in family businesses.[92]

The teamwork between the Arte and the company reduced overall costs. The analysis presented here confirms that Pfister's broad European picture in which guilds reduced the firm's transaction costs also applies to Florence. Teamwork meant that the extent of the wool industry firm was not clearly defined. The effective extent of the firm, including the company and all the components of the Arte, was much larger than the company alone. Most workers were contractors, not employees. The lack of a clear definition of the firm can be clarified by reexamining some material from Chapter 7. The work by Dören and by De Roover shows how the firm could appear both large and small at the same time. The size of the firm depends on the researcher's perspective. Dören's use of laws and guild regulations emphasized the integration of production.[93] This led him to

---

90 Ibid., 330.
91 Raymond De Roover, *The Rise and Decline of the Medici Bank, 1397–1494* (Cambridge, MA: Harvard University Press, 1963), 171.
92 De Roover, "Florentine Firm of Cloth Manufacturers," 99.
93 Dören, *Wirtschaftgeschichte*, vol. 1.

Table 9.3 Location of work by step in wool manufacturing production process

Step	Centralized Manufacture	Home	Large Establishment	Private Shops
Preparing				
Washing	X			
Beating/Cleaning	X			
Combing	X			
Carding	X			
Spinning				
Lanini		X		
Stamaiuoli		X		
Weaving				
Warping	X	X		
Weaving		X		
Finishing				
Burling	X			
Scouring			X	
Fulling			X	
Stretching			X	
Napping/Shearing				X
Mending	X			X
Dyeing				
Dyeing				X

Sources: De Roover, "Florentine Firm of Cloth Manufacturers," 103; Edler, *Glossary*, 329–30. Occupations listed in order of steps to completion.

conclude that the companies were large. De Roover's use of account books, however, finds small companies.[94] Larger firms were feasible, because some horizontal consolidation did occur, but the survivor principle implies that such consolidation was not generally optimal.[95] As the above analysis makes clear, the Arte was large and expensive to establish and keep running. Florence, however, created the Arte instead of larger firms. This implies that larger firms would have been too costly and that there is an additional cost to consolidation beyond just transaction costs.

The Risk Facing the Company

Examining the level of risk facing the company introduces a new perspective on Renaissance industry. Risk is generally left out of the modern economic theory of the firm, and a recent literature review finds little role for risk in the theory of the firm.[96]

---

94 De Roover, "Florentine Firm of Cloth Manufacturers."
95 Stigler, "Economies of Scale."
96 Francine LaFontaine and Margaret Slade, "Vertical Integration and Firm Boundaries: The Evidence," *Journal of Economic Literature* 45, no. 3 (2007): 629–85.

Williamson explicitly assumes that the firm is risk neutral, but that assumption is unlikely to hold in the case of the wool industry.[97] Each company was a family business and much more likely to be risk averse than risk neutral.

In contrast to modern economists, late nineteenth- and early twentieth-century economists saw a role for risk in the firm's production process. The idea was that the risk experienced by large firms was reduced due to the law of large numbers.[98] A larger firm was less susceptible to random fluctuations. This approach has a number of limitations that explain why it is not used much by modern economists. For the purposes here, the key limitation is that it assumes the firm operates continuously. (Chapter 7 has more about how not all constituted companies were continuously active.)

The ex ante and ex post risk must be distinguished in the case of the wool industry. The ex ante risk is the projected risk that the company would have faced without risk mitigation. The ex post risk is the actual risk faced after mitigation. In general, ex post risk is more easily observed. The ex ante risk, however, often has to be inferred. Ex ante nondiversifiable risk would have affected household decisions and required some form of costly insurance or hedging. Any mitigated risk would become invisible to the historian. The apparent level of ex ante risk would be much less than the actual.

There are reasons to believe the ex ante risk was large. First, the level of risk had an important impact on economies during this period.[99] Risk had significantly affected the organization of institutions during the feudal period.[100] Later, a decline in risk was a key factor in the Dutch economic rise.[101] Second, the woolen-cloth industry's risky export market led to large industry fluctuations.[102] Finally, the manufacturers did not have all the modern legal tools that are now used to diversify risk. There were no limited liability partnerships until the Seicento.[103] Owners were liable for the full extent of any losses, and the partners' risk exposure grew as the firm grew. This unlimited liability increased the risk for owners of early modern companies in comparison with that for owners of

---

97 Williamson, *Economic Institutions of Capitalism*, 388.

98 Edward A. Ross, "Uncertainty as a Factor in Production," *Annals of the American Academy of Political and Social Sciences* 8 (1896): 115–19; Irving Fisher, *The Nature of Capital and Income* (New York: Macmillan, 1906), 265–98 and 408–9; Charles Oscar Hardy, *Risk and Risk Bearing*, 2nd ed. (Chicago: University of Chicago Press, 1931), 17 and 20–21; Frank H. Knight, *Risk, Uncertainty, and Profit*, 4th ed. (1957; 1921; Mineola, NY: Dover, 2006), 257.

99 De Roover, *Rise and Decline of the Medici Bank*; Armando Sapori, *The Italian Merchant in the Middle Ages*, trans. Patricia Ann Kennen (New York: Norton, 1970).

100 Marc Bloch, *French Rural History: An Essay on Its Basic Characteristics*, trans. Janet Sondheimer (Berkeley: University of California Press, 1966), 55; Donald N. McCloskey, "The Open Fields of England: Rent, Risk, and the Rate of Interest, 1300–1825," in *Markets in History: Economic Studies of the Past*, ed. David W. Galenson (Cambridge, UK: Cambridge University Press, 1989), 5–52.

101 Jan de Vries and A. van der Woude, *The First Modern Economy: Success, Failure, and Perseverance of the Dutch Economy, 1500–1815* (Cambridge, UK: Cambridge University Press, 1997), 670–71.

102 De Roover, *Rise and Decline of the Medici Bank*, 172 and 185; Goldthwaite, *Economy of Renaissance Florence*, 265.

103 Edler, *Glossary*, 347.

modern firms for which the standard economic theories were built. This means that, all other things being equal, a smaller venture with less capital and less contractual commitment was relatively less risky and, consequently, more preferable than it would be today.

Although the industry's ex ante risk was apparently very high, the corresponding ex post risk for the company appears low.[104] This is paradoxical, at least from the perspective of a modern economist. In modern economies it is more likely to be the other way around. This reversal implies that the systematic industry risk was largely eliminated.[105] Risk management seems the most plausible explanation of this paradox. The techniques were well developed in the international trade of the period.[106] International merchants had led the way in the new techniques, including *commenda* and *societies maris* partnership contracts (used for shipping and trading), marine insurance and long-term venture companies.[107] These extensive efforts at risk reduction imply that the risk was high in these markets, the very same markets in which the final product of Florentine wool manufacturers had to be sold.

The extent of the modern firm can change with the market conditions. For example, during business cycles when the economy is good, a firm will first add hours for existing employees, then add temporary employees and finally add full-time employees. When the economy is bad, this process is works in reverse. This relationship holds so broadly that these phases are part of the leading, coincident and lagging business-cycle indicator model widely used by government and private economists for decades. This relationship is also a form of hedging. A firm with a larger share of full-time employees over temporary workers will therefore face greater risk, ceteris paribus, during a bad economy.

Reducing the Company's Risk

The risk-reduction techniques in the production and labor markets are the subject of this section and the next. Renaissance Florentine wool industry companies appear to have deliberately minimized their extent of their internal operations and in so doing incurred substantial costs. Besides the riskier business environment, two factors increased risk for Florentine businessmen compared with their modern counterparts: (1) the company was much more like a risk-averse household than a risk-neutral corporation, and (2) there was no such thing as limited liability in Cinquecento Florence. Both of these factors would have made the small-size company operating with piece rates seem a better alternative to creating a much larger firm that incorporated all the craft workers working for day wages.

104   De Roover, *Rise and Decline of the Medici Bank*, 172; Goldthwaite, *Economy of Renaissance Florence*, 306–7 and 456–57.

105   Harry Markowitz, "Portfolio Selection," *Journal of Finance* 7 (1952): 77–91; James Tobin, "Liquidity Preference as Behavior Towards Risk," *Review of Economic Studies* 25 (1958): 65–86.

106   Edwin S. Hunt and James M. Murphy, *A History of Business in Medieval Europe, 1200–1500* (Cambridge, UK: Cambridge University Press, 1999); Greif, *Institutions and the Path to the Modern Economy*.

107   Hunt and Murphy, *Business in Medieval Europe*, 60–62.

The putting-out system allowed the company a series of advantages that reduced its exposure to risk. First, the company could divide and conquer its labor management commitments and gradually ramp up its production. The company was able to leverage a small office staff to create a much larger firm, because it did not have to manage everything all at once. Labor management could be divided into more controllable portions. Production was divided into 15 separate steps, 16 if the raw wool purchases are included. This allowed the limited central control resources of the company to be maximized throughout the entire production process.

In addition, the putting-out system combined with the Arte organization allowed the company to leverage its small number of employees into a much larger number of workers. This also reduced the company's exposure to risk. Companies typically hired a very large number of employees who did not work in the central office.[108] Typically, no more than three or four people worked directly for the company, including the partners. However, a single company could use more than 80 weavers alone. Table 9.4 shows how the number of weavers employed by the Medici-Tornaquinci series of companies varied over time. One could add to this number between one to several dozen spinners, a handful of warpers and several additional workers at each of the other steps of the production process. Each factor had to manage at least one, and probably several, other workers. Therefore, at an absolute minimum this adds up to 19 additional employees. If we take the minimum number of weavers (2) and add the minimum of 19 additional workers, we get a total of 4 workers in the office and 21 external employees. This quick calculation implies that at the absolute minimum the size of the company is no more than 16 percent of the effective extent of the firm. If, however, we look to a more reasonable production scale, then there are a total of 50 spinners, 5 warpers and 50 weavers, and if each centralized manufacturer and large establishment employed 10 and each private workshop employed 5, then the total number of workers would increase to 200 external workers. This would reduce the size of the company to no more than 2 percent of the effective extent of the firm.

Second, Arte membership allowed firms a certain flexibility to time their production. One factor that increased this competitiveness was that, though guild membership was fixed, members were allowed free entry and exit of firms into act of production. Guild membership permitted this flexibility. Companies could time entry with low factor prices, high cloth prices or both. Goldthwaite has noted that "this market structure functioned to assure the wool manufacturer of the security of his investment. He could sell bolts of cloth as they were finished to any merchant-exporter who would buy them; and any slack in demand could be met simply by ceasing production."[109] The entry rate at any one particular appears to have been relatively low. Only about 20 percent of the established companies in 1427 appear to have actually been in operation.[110]

---

108 Goldthwaite, "The Florentine Wool Industry," 543; Ammannati, "Production et productivité," 238.
109 Goldthwaite, "Florentine Wool Industry," 546–47.
110 Hidetoshi Hoshino, *L'arte della lana nel basso medioevo in commercio della lana e il mercato dei panni fiorentini nei secoli XIII–XV* (Florence: Olschki, 1980), 229.

Table 9.4 Number of weavers employed by Medici-Tornaquinci companies, 1431–1558

Years	Weavers
1431–34	9
1441–44	15
1444–49	8
1458–61	2
1461–64	10
1464–67	7
1467–69	9
1468–72	23
1473–83	29
1476–86	34
1482–86	16
1486–95	14
1490–94	11
1491–92	7
1534–43	86
1547–53	57
1552–56	15
1556–58	21

Sources: Medici-Tornaquinci, Mss. 496, 498, 499, 501, 504, 505, 506, 507, 508, 509, 510, 511, 513, 514, 558 (5), 560 (2), 560 (5) and 567 (8).

Finally, the putting-out system allowed the company to gradually increase its total capital. This further reduced the exposure to risk. To begin with, the putting-out system freed him from any investment in plant and equipment.[111] Goldthwaite writes, "Inasmuch as the capital needs of a wool firm were primarily for start-up funds to maintain cash flow until income from sales reached a certain pace, a firm at the end of the sixteenth century represented a much larger investment."[112] Figure 9.2 shows how the company gradually committed to additional costs. This kind of gradual commitment would only be possible in a putting-out system. The close connection between production steps in the modern industrial firm compresses the timing of work too much to allow this kind of gradual commitment. In addition, the expenses were back-loaded rather than being either front-loaded or evenly distributed through the production process. Approximately 40 percent of the labor production costs were finishing and dyeing costs that did not have to be committed to until the very end. In Figure 9.2, two late Cinquecento companies' share and timing of costs during the production process are presented.

Goldthwaite notes that there was a "fragmentation and fluidity of the larger structures in which the firm operated, and in this it falls in line with the traditions of the Florentine wool industry."[113]

---

111 Goldthwaite, "Florentine Wool Industry," 547.
112 Ibid., 539.
113 Ibid., 546.

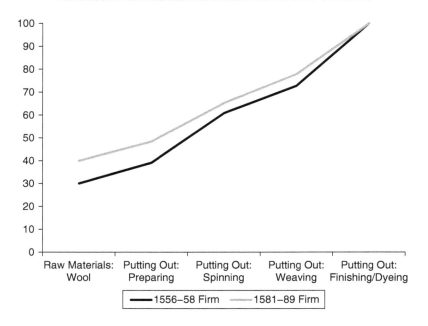

Figure 9.2 Share of accumulated costs by stage of production
Source: Richard A. Goldthwaite, "The Florentine Wool Industry in the Late Sixteenth Century: A Case Study," *Journal of European Economic History* 32, no. 3 (2003): 537. Calculation by author.

Reducing Craft Worker Risk

The craft workers, like the companies, minimized their risk of losing all work. This fluidity has been noticed before.[114] Goldthwaite argues that it was driven by the employer's needs;[115] however, the fluidity reduced ex post risk for employer and employee alike. Craft workers used several strategies to reduce risk. First, the company and workers shared risk through the piece-rate payments in the putting-out system. Risk sharing was a major risk-reduction tool implemented by Italian businessmen of the period in the putting-out system. Historians such as Goldthwaite have recognized this fact, although he does not take the next step, namely seeing it as a form of risk reduction through hedging. The putting-out and the sharecropping systems, the predominant urban and rural production methods, respectively, were both types of hedges.

Second, the company made short-term contracts with the craft workers. The terms of payment varied. Sometimes craft workers may have received retainers during slack periods at approximately one-quarter of their regular salary.[116]

Third, there was easy entry and exit for craft workers as the account books demonstrate. This meant the Arte lists typically included all potential workers, many more

---

114   Goldthwaite, *Economy of Renaissance Florence*, 329–30.
115   Ibid.
116   Medici-Tornaquinci, Ms. 558 (5).

names than a list of those working at any one time.[117] It appears that entry and exit into work for a particular wool industry firm by spinners, warpers and weavers (the subcontractors with the greatest total employment) were relatively easy. This kind of observation cannot be made using just the static (snapshot) data found in the catasto documents. The fluidity of weavers' work schedules was noticeable.[118]

Fourth, employment was discontinuous. Ammannati has also found that production was done in bursts.[119] The company's irregular work would have increased unemployment if craft workers worked for only one company. However, there was other work. Weavers rarely worked full-time for a single company and for long periods of time. The impact of this work pattern was significant. The weavers in the sample produced far fewer cloths for a particular company than the average rate of production would suggest. A weaver working full-time would weave at least ten cloths per year. Data from the Medici-Tornaquinci Book of Weavers implies that a typical cloth would take between 30 and 45 days to weave (see Fig. 8.1).[120] This means an average of eight to twelve cloths per year for a full-time weaver. In addition, using aggregate Seicento statistics, Brown and Goodman report that there were 544 weavers in 1663 and that approximately 6,000 cloths were produced in an average year during the 1630s.[121] Simple division yields about 11 cloths per weaver.

Finally, workers diversified by working for multiple companies. Each weaver produced fewer than 3 cloths per year for a particular company, far below the overall estimated average annual production of about 10 cloths per year. One Medici-Tornaquinci company hired 25 weavers to produce 71 cloths.[122] Based on the above analysis of annual averages, one would expect no more than ten weavers to have been employed to produce that number of cloths. In another Medici-Tornaquinci firm, the mean number of cloths woven per weaver was 2.84. This is about one cloth per year, or less than 10 percent of the mean annual production per weaver. In a third Medici-Tornaquinci firm, the mean number of cloths per weaver was 5.72. This, again, is about one cloth per year, or about 10 percent of the annual mean. It is probably not a coincidence that the two averages match up so closely. Finally, a company from the Brandolini family operating a generation later produced 450 cloths using 71 weavers.[123] This yields a mean of 6.34 cloths per weaver and is about 2 cloths per year. This gap would have been even greater for migrants working in Florence. These workers might have been less skilled or less connected to the market and, consequently, produced fewer cloths than the annual average. The wages could have been so much higher in Florence than in the countryside, or in many places in Europe, that even part-time work was better than the alternative of no work at all.[124]

117 Litchfield, *Florence Ducal Capital*, para. 275.
118 Goldthwaite, "Florentine Wool Industry," 544.
119 Ammannati, "Production et productivité," 240, 243 and 247.
120 Edler, *Glossary*, 421; Medici-Tornaquinci, Ms. 560 (4).
121 Judith Brown and Jonathan Goodman, "Women and Industry in Florence," *Journal of Economic History* 40, no. 1 (1980): 78 and 77.
122 Medici-Tornaquinci, Ms. 560 (5).
123 Goldthwaite, *Economy of Renaissance Florence*, 329.
124 Larry A. Sjaastad, "The Costs and Returns of Human Migration," *Journal of Political Economy* 70, no. 5, pt. 2 (1962): 80–93.

The system guaranteed that high-quality workers would be available for firms operating in Florence.[125] Consistent employment would help guarantee the kind of pay that would motivate these workers. The Datini firm of the 1390s, as noted above, was not part of the Arte and therefore did not benefit from its system. They consequently had trouble getting quality workers, which implies there is a significant value to being in Florence and connected with the Arte[126] There are a number of possible reasons. One could have been that the cost to travel from Florence to Prato was too high. However, based on the above analysis, it is very possible the Arte system would have led to an increasing value over a one-time wage rate and allowed Florence to keep the best workers there.

Applying the Framework

The theoretical framework constructed in this study has a number of applications. This section briefly discusses one of them: the Seicento decline of the wool industry and its failure to recover.[127] The industry lost both its Mediterranean and northern European markets[128] and was, eventually, reduced to serving only local markets.[129]

The final decline of the wool industry coincided with the rise of the silk industry in Tuscany and the development of joint-stock companies in England. This section will compare the structures of a wool industry company, a silk industry company and the new English joint-stock companies and propose a reason why the Arte della Lana never rose again.

A wide range of causes has been offered for the industry's decline. These include the increasing price of wool as one of these. This would have reduced the incentive to produce wool cloth.[130] Though the resulting problems with cash flow have been observed, it would also have decreased the incentive to invest in the first place because of the increased risk.[131]

Levant Joint-Stock Company

The joint-stock companies, such as the Levant Company, were set up as royal monopolies. The joint-stock companies were the result of a long evolution from the Italian

---

125   Ammannati, "Datini's Wool Workshops," 495.

126   Ibid.

127   Please see appendix 3B for more information and references about the decline of the wool industry and potential explanations.

128   Paolo Malanima, *La decadenza di un'economia cittadina: L'industria di Firenze nei secoli XVI–XVIII* (Bologna: Il Mulino, 1982), 289–305, esp. 304; Ruggiero Romano, "A Florence au XVIIe siècle: Industries textiles et conjuncture," *Annales: Histoire, Sciences Sociales* 7, no. 4 (1952): 508–12.

129   Chorley, "Florentine Cloth Industry during the Sixteenth Century," 514.

130   Patrick Chorley, "*Rascie* and the Florentine Cloth Industry during the Sixteenth Century: A Case Study," *Journal of European Economic History* 32, no. 3 (2003): 509; Ammannati, "L'Arte della Lana," 38; Ammannati, "Florentine Woolen Manufacture in the Sixteenth Century: Crisis and New Entrepreneurial Strategies," *Business and Economic History On-Line*, 7 (2009): 9.

131   Goldthwaite, "Florentine Wool Industry," 548.

medieval Societas and Commendas contracts,[132] the corporate ideal instilled in English businessmen[133] and the recent English Merchant Adventurers companies.[134] The earliest joint-stock companies included the East India Company, Levant Company and Muscovy Company. The African Company and the Hudson's Bay Company were created near the end of the seventeenth century. The Levant Company was created out of the previous Turkey and Venice companies. It received its charter in 1592 and its permanent charter in 1605.[135] The arrival of the Levant Company significantly affected the Mediterranean wool trade. The company set up its Mediterranean base of operations very near Florence at the Tuscan city of Livorno (Leghorn).[136]

The joint-stock companies are usually analyzed as rent-seeking entities,[137] similarly to guilds. The differences between guilds and joint-stock companies resemble those between medieval city states and early modern national states. Adam Smith opposed mercantilism.[138] Smith was also against joint-stock companies.[139] This opposition was motivated by the same reasons as his opposition to guilds.[140] This reasoning parallels Ogilvie's argument for guilds as political entities.[141] However, rent-seeking for the monarchy was not everything. The monarchy could not simply set up a monopoly and just order shareholders to buy into it. There must have been a profit somewhere.

The contractual forms of the companies of the Arte and the joint-stock companies were significantly different and embodied their own approaches to risk management and transaction costs. The Arte was a guild that functioned as an association where companies were small. Joint-stock companies had a corporate governance structure and system of equity ownership that acted to reduce the transaction costs and risk to the owners. The company was controlled by governors and assistants.[142] The Board of Governors was designed to provide strong internal control. It was originally an unwieldy system.[143]

132 William Robert Scott, *The Constitution and Finance of English, Scottish and Irish Joint-Stock Companies to 1720: Volume 1: The General Development of the Joint-Stock System to 1720* (Cambridge, UK: Cambridge University Press, 1912), 1–2.

133 Ibid., 2–5.

134 Ibid., 5–10.

135 Mordecai Epstein, *The Early History of the Levant Company: Its Foundation and Its History to 1640* (New York: Burt Franklin, 1968; London: Routledge and Sons, 1908), 16, 20, 25, 26, 36 and 57; Alfred Cecil Wood, *A History of the Levant Company* (London: Frank Cass and Co., 1964), 11, 18, 19, 20 and 39.

136 Gigliola Pagano De Divitiis, *English Merchants in Seventeenth-Century Italy. Cambridge,* trans. Stephen Parkin (Cambridge, UK: Cambridge University Press, 1997).

137 Robert B. Ekelund Jr., and Robert D. Tollison, "Mercantilist Origins of the Corporation," *Bell Journal of Economics* 11, no. 2 (1980): 715–20; Ekelund and Tollison, *Mercantilism as a Rent-Seeking Society: Economic Regulation in Historical Perspective* (College Station: Texas A&M University Press, 1981).

138 Smith, *The Wealth of Nations*, 539–703.

139 Scott, *Constitution and Finance*, 448–55.

140 Ibid., 448–53.

141 Ogilvie, "The Economics of the Guild."

142 Scott, *Constitution and Finance*, 150–52.

143 Ibid., 152–55.

The efficiency of chartered companies is debated.[144] This debate focuses on the inability to monitor employees. The problem is similar to that which the Arte tried to solve. The centralized control in the joint-stock company contrasted with the small central office of the Arte.

The joint-stock companies also, like the companies of the Arte, were set up to reduce risk for the owners. They did this through a number of methods, though not including limited liability. The Arte's methods were detailed above. The joint-stock companies went much further and essentially eliminated any level of long-term commitment for owner-ship. Although the joint-stock company shares were long-lived, they were highly liquid and could be readily disposed of in a relatively free market for shares.[145] Shares were also traded and not alienated. This acted to increase liquidity and decrease risk. The managers were sensitive to this. Early on, the value of the East India Company, another joint-stock company, increased so rapidly that the high value of individual shares signifi-cantly reduced their market. This defeated the purpose of the free market for shares. In response, the East India Company reduced the share denominations.[146] These fractional shares allowed more capital to be invested.[147] Scott notes that "it was only by the right of freedom of sale or purchase of shares that the joint-stock company was distinguishable from the regulated type."[148]

The fundamental difference between the Arte della Lana and the joint stock companies was one of resulting scale. This was entirely caused by their different contractual forms that permitted different techniques to reduce risk. The Arte reduced risk for its member com-panies by reducing each company's capital at risk. The production was discontinuous, the contract period was only three years and the putting-out system allowed incremental invest-ment. The joint-stock company used a very different method. It reduced risk for its share-holders by allowing each individual shareholder to reduce their position, both by increasing the liquidity of investments by making shares tradable and by decreasing the size of mini-mum positions (from shares to fractional shares). This last point created a fundamental dif-ference. Whereas, the Arte companies were small and unable to invest sizable amounts on their own, the joint-stock companies were large and very capable, and willing, of investing large amounts. There was effectively no limit to the amount of capitalization in a joint-stock company.

This implies that the ability of the English to create firms that operated at a scale much larger than those in Florence was a key to their success on the actual purpose of the

---

144 Arguing for their economic efficiency: Ann M. Carlos and Stephen Nicholas, "Theory and History: Seventeenth-Century Joint-Stock Chartered Trading Companies," *Journal of Economic History* 56, no. 4 (1996): 916–24. Arguing for their economic inefficiency: S. R. H. Jones and Simon P. Ville, "Efficient Transactors or Rent-Seeking Monopolists? The Rationale for Early Chartered Trading Companies," *Journal of Economic History* 56, no. 4 (1996): 898–916.

145 Scott, *Constitution and Finance*, 442–43.

146 Ibid., 155.

147 Ibid., 442–43.

148 Ibid., 443.

work— to do work in order to make money. Munro attributes the final decline of the Italian, particularly the Venetian, wool industry to the novel organization of the English Levant Company.[149] Braude argues that the Levant Company won markets through dumping.[150] If correct, this would probably be possible due to the significant capital advantage of the Levant Company.

Silk Industry Rise

The silk industry rose in place of the wool industry during the Seicento.[151] The Seicento silk industry was much larger than the Quattrocento silk industry.[152] However, unlike the differences between the Arte and the Levant Company, the silk industry was organized similarly to the wool industry. Both had a major guild, called the Arte di Por Santa Maria in the case of the silk industry, which coordinated a putting-out system. The partnerships generally were short term like the wool industry partnerships.[153] A Quattrocento company examined by Edler De Roover had three partners[154] and employed about 100 persons.[155] This amounted to a ratio of approximately 30 to 1—the same order of magnitude as wool industry companies. Goldthwaite finds a similar leverage of labor.[156] Smaller companies and higher transactions costs were accepted in return for risk reduction. However, the silk industry was much less complex with only four steps, winding and throwing, boiling and dyeing, warping and weaving, compared with fifteen for wool.[157] This highlights a difference between the two industries. On the one hand, fewer steps probably meant lower transaction costs. On the other hand, fewer steps would have permitted less flexibility once the production decision was made.

---

149 Munro, "Italian Wool-Based Cloth Industries," 153–65.

150 Benjamin Braude, "International Competition and Domestic Cloth in the Ottoman Empire, 1500–1650: A Study in Undevelopment," *Review (Fernand Braudel Center): Research Foundation of SUNY* 2, no. 3 (1979): 437–51.

151 Paolo Malanima, *La decadenza di un'economia cittadina: L'industria di Firenze nei secoli XVI–XVIII* (Bologna: Il Mulino, 1982), 305–21; Jordan Goodman, "Financing Pre-modern European Industry: An Example from Florence 1580–1660," *Journal of European Economic History* 10, no. 2 (1981): 415–36.

152 Gino Corti and J-Gentil Da Silva. "Note sur la production de la soie à Florence, au XVe siècle." *Annales. Histoire, Sciences Sociales*, 20, no. 2 (1965): 309–11; Paolo Malanima, *La decadenza di un'economia cittadina: L'industria di Firenze nei secoli XVI–XVIII* (Bologna: Il Mulino, 1982): 311, 314 and 316–20.

153 Florence Edler de Roover, "Andrea Banchi, Florentine Silk Manufacturer and Merchant of the Fifteenth Century," *Studies in Medieval and Renaissance History* 3 (1966): 228.

154 Ibid., 231.

155 Ibid., 259.

156 Richard A. Goldthwaite, "An Entrepreneurial Silk Weaver in Renaissance Florence," *I Tatti Studies* 10 (2005): 93.

157 Edler, *Glossary*, 330–31; Gargiolli, *L'arte della seta*; Edler de Roover, "Andrea Banchi," 241–56; William Caferro, "The Silk Business of Tommaso Spinelli, Fifteenth-Century Florentine Merchant and Papal Banker," *Renaissance Studies* 10, no. 4 (1996): 426–49; Goldthwaite, "Entrepreneurial Silk Weaver," 75–80.

Wool Industry Decline

The wool industry was resilient. It had survived multiple downturns prior to the arrival of the Levant Company. The industry had coped with changes in its wool supply, changes in its cloth customers and changes in the political world as well as plagues, wars and other disasters.

Munro sees changing patterns of transaction costs driving these cycles.[158] However, whereas this approach explains the cycles of decline and recovery, it has limited explanatory power in the case of the final Seicento decline of the industry. Based on the transactions cost framework, one would expect an eventual recovery of the industry. For example, the Peace of Westphalia in 1648 should have led to growth comparable to that of Cateau-Cambresis in 1559 by reopening northern markets. Instead, it did not, and the industry never recovered.

The real question is not only why the Florentine wool industry declined but also why it did not rise again. The Levant Company clearly led to the decline of the nascent Venetian wool industry, but one could argue its growth also blocked a later Florentine recovery as well. The contractual framework implies that the massive size, permitted by the joint-stock company system, closed the door on any attempt to regain any market share anywhere and blocked any future Florentine recovery.

The creation of the joint-stock companies did not directly lead to the end of the Arte della Lana-style organization of production, The silk industry maintained this system long after the wool industry had become only a local producer. The switch to silk industry dominance in the Seicento implies that economic, not political, reasons were the cause for the shift. The flow of investment capital went to the silk industry and away from the wool industry.

Conclusion

This study has looked at the determinants of the size of the Renaissance Florentine wool industry company. Rather than being an inefficient burden on the production process, the Arte and the putting-out system allowed a firm to reduce its risk exposure. This helped the Florentines respond to the risky late medieval and early modern world. The company employed a production system using the putting-out system organized by the Arte. This is a puzzle. Both the putting-out system and the Arte are considered inefficient on their own, and combining the two would seem doubly inefficient; however, together they helped reduce risk. The guild system provided the necessary flexibility and risk reduction for workers. Advantages of the guild system included risk sharing, short-term contracts, easy entry and exit and discontinuous employment with potentially multiple employers. The putting-out system allowed the firm great flexibility in its extent. For example, the ability to scale up the production incrementally and to share risk made this structure attractive.

---

158   Munro, "Italian Wool-Based Cloth Industries."

The one period, or static, view implicitly assumes that the firm was engaged in continuous operations. This study demonstrates that adopting a multiperiod dynamic view can resolve a wide range of issues. Manufacturing production since the Industrial Revolution has essentially been done continuously. It would seem reasonable to assume that preindustrial production was also done continuously, but it was not. That assumption falsely implies that the wool industry performed like a less efficient version of the modern factory. This leads directly to the modern opinion of guilds and the putting-out system.

In reality, wool industry production was discontinuous. This has two significant implications. First, the costs to workers to move among companies must have been relatively low. This means that, alongside the competitive industry shown in Chapter 7, the Arte functioned to reduce transaction costs in a labor market for its members. Second, the discontinuity allowed companies to vary quantity dramatically in response to demand shocks.

The wool industry developed in a way to handle the high ex ante risk. The ex post risk in wool manufacturing was significantly less than the ex ante risk from the international markets. The financial theory of projects can help explain the paradox of creating small companies that increased total transaction costs. A larger firm required a larger investment and therefore places more value at risk. This resembles taking a long position in an asset, where an investor is not hedged and suffers gains and losses in proportion to the total investment and not some smaller portion. In such a marketplace the extent of the firm is correlated with the risk underlying its operation. This risk is a new kind of transaction cost that limits the extent of the firm.

The research presented here is necessarily the first step in a larger research agenda. An example of the work in this agenda is presented in the last section. The decline of the wool industry is seen from the perspective of its industrial organization, which had been viable for centuries, being unable to rise up to compete with the joint-stock company organization. The continued viability of the Arte's sophisticated umbrella guild structure is demonstrated by the survival of the silk industry, which was not a target of the joint-stock companies. The Levant Company did not cause the final decline of the Arte della Lana. However, it probably helped make sure the Arte did not get back up.

Future research would develop a formal model of the risk-reduction strategies of the Arte. This risk-reduction model could be used to examine a variety of issues that are more central to Renaissance Italian historiography. The sophisticated umbrella guild structure of the Arte clearly allowed the companies to be so small. For example, did this risk-reduction strategy contribute to the ability of Arte members to expropriate from members of the *popolo* minuto or the *sottoposti*? Did different risk-reduction strategies affect the evolution of the relative sizes of the silk industry and wool industry? Did the cost of implementing this risk-reduction strategy lead to a failure of Italian industry in the face of the Industrial Revolution? These questions can only be answered once the necessary factual and theoretical frameworks have been developed.

CONCLUSION

This book touches on a wide range of subjects: economics, finance, geography, history, mathematics, sociology and statistics. The topics and methods in this book were chosen in order to demonstrate the diversity of topics and potential methods available for quantitative studies.

Each of the nine studies in this book tackles a question in Renaissance Florentine economic and social history using a suitable quantitative method. The results from these individual studies can be combined to reveal larger themes. Several Renaissance Florentine themes recur. Above all is that the city's economy and society were dynamic. On the one hand, unfolding events are discussed that see Florentines fleeing the plague, facing evolving interest rates and increasing their demand for owning homes. On the other hand, the wool industry shows that the underlying economic and social structure itself was dynamic.

Further, Florentine society was one of flexibility subject to constraints. For example, not everyone owned a home, but homeownership was within the reach of many households. Women worked in the market with equal pay for equal work, but they were limited, though not prevented, in how they could work by family and by law. Although a *popolo minuto* household could attain significant wealth, it was still rare for one to reach the levels of the *arti maggiori*. Related to this flexibility is the important impact of risk. The recurring plague, the wide interest rate swings and the exceptional risk-minimization efforts taken by the wool industry all highlight this important feature of life in the Renaissance.

Finally, the inequality of Florentine wealth was real, but it did not divide society. The wealth difference that distinguished the arti maggiori from the popolo minuto was neither manifested in segregated homogeneous neighborhoods nor did it stop Florentine from wanting a more equal society. Their support for both progressive tax rates and a homeownership exemption in the catasto resemble contemporary tax policies more than the export and poll taxes common in the period. The irony is that the increased homeownership that resulted was paralleled by an increased spending on art and architecture. The latter has attracted the notice of historians much more than the former, and this has obscured the underlying process. The palace-building boom has often been seen as the symptom of wealth and a desire for segregation rather than the result of a larger process that brought homeownership within reach of the masses.

Two larger themes in European economic and social history recur. The new institutional economics is studied from two widely separated perspectives. At the grand historical end, there are comments on the recent literature on state formation where interest rates are used to assess the confidence in a government. At the microeconomic end, there are comments on the recent literature on firm structure where transaction costs are used to analyze how firms are organized. In both cases the simple applications of the theory were insufficient, and the historical circumstances needed to be plumbed in greater depth.

Guilds are studied from several different directions. Recent debates have focused on their ills or blessings. A range of studies in this book illuminates this question. First, the studies of wealth accumulation and distribution also provide insights into the impact of guilds on society. Since household wealth was largely determined by initial conditions and the difference between major and minor guilds was a key determinant of wealth, then guild membership appears to have acted to reinforce lifetime wealth differences between households. Second, the internal functioning of the Arte della Lana guild in the marketplace also provides insight. Since wool industry production was done competitively and the guild reduced risk and transaction costs, then the companies operated in a highly flexible and resilient market. Taken together, all of these imply a further result. Workers in each of the occupations faced initial conditions that were hard to escape. However, given those initial conditions, the guild provided many kinds of benefits. The overall result is balanced and takes an intermediate position between those who argue for the ills of guilds and those who argue for their blessings.

Several larger themes in historical methodology recur. First, this book implicitly argues throughout that there is little fundamentally different between qualitative and quantitative methods. To underscore this, figures are frequently used to present the quantitative results. This is intended as a way to highlight the inherently qualitative aspects of the results of quantitative methods. It is often necessary to visualize the quantitative data on the surface in order to see the deeper qualitative relationships.

Second, an overly narrow concentration on laws and regulations is inadvisable. The picture of the world based solely on the laws on the books can create a view that exists very far from any recognizable reality. A large part of this is related to the differences between dynamic and static analysis. The use of quantitative methods makes this distinction clear. Laws can help define the tools of analysis, such as showing how to calculate the true interest rate. However, they have their limitations. The role of women in society can only be understood when people's actual behavior in the legal environment is studied. Early work on the Florentine wool industry based solely on the prevailing legal structure showed large-scale monopolists and was wrong. Further, even understanding that industry's guild regulations requires a dynamic analysis.

Third, explicit theoretical structures can help illuminate the data. Often historians are rightly skeptical of overly elaborate structures. However, structures that are explicitly presented and carefully linked to the context can be invaluable as a kind of torch to illuminate quantitative data. For example, the theory of financial market information illuminates behavior during a plague. A more precise definition of interest rates creates a picture of significant change rather than one of rarely changing values. The analysis of relative tax burdens, rather than just absolute tax burdens, reveals how a tax loophole drove an art and architecture boom. A careful analysis of the theory of perfect competition can lead to consistent and valuable results. And the theory of the firm can be applied to study the evolution of Florentine industry.

Finally, the studies in this book have implications for the application of big data techniques. As of this writing, many see big data as the ultimate expression of quantitative methods where vast quantities of data are processed. The techniques are more familiar as a tool used by business and government, rather than by historians, though the range of applications expands daily. The Google Books project is one prominent example. The practical application of big data often proceeds in the opposite direction to that of an explicit theoretical structure and creates a kind of theory-free data where both explicit theory and context are ignored. This book points out some of these dangers. The large-scale analysis of state formation is one. The research on late medieval and early modern Europe standardizes interest rate calculations across many cities and places in order to provide a consistent analysis. This standardization, in the case of Florence, grossly distorts the actual circumstances. The large-scale analysis of wealth inequality is another. Since the relative burden of a particular tax can significantly change behavior, such as homeownership and purchases of art and architecture, then extremely long-term analyses of the wealth distribution that are constructed by linking tax data over time can be hazardous. This has implications for a wide range of studies that cover the world from the late medieval world to contemporary policy.

In the end, this collection of studies is designed to open new questions. Several stand out. The interest rate time series calculated in Chapter 2 can be refined and linked to specific events. The framework developed to analyze the Arte della Lana guild in Chapter 9 can be used to study a range of topics, both related to the Florentine guilds and to guilds in other locations and at other times. The exploration of the creation of wealth in Chapters 3 and 6 can be expanded in a number of directions. Most readily, they can assess the impact of guilds on wealth creation and how human capital was accumulated during the life cycle in Florence. The urban ecological analysis in Chapter 4 can be expanded to gain a better understanding of location effects in the economy, the differences in neighborhood dynamics and relationships between art and architecture and social divisions. The analysis of the impact of taxes in Chapter 5 can be used to examine other economic impacts of taxes. The varieties of the Florentine tax system, from the late medieval through the early modern periods, provide a fruitful place to explore the impact of Florentine government policies. The approaches here lead to a wide range of topics, only a few of which are mentioned above. The hope is that this book will spur additional interest in these topics.

GLOSSARY

absolute value (math.): The distance of a number from the origin (zero). Never negative.

arbitrage (finl.): Taking advantage of a price difference between markets.

***Arte della Lana*:** The woolen cloth manufacturers' guild in Florence. It was one of the seven arte maggiore.

***Arte maggiore* (plural *arti maggiori*):** One of the seven major guilds of Florence. It included international traders, wool manufacturers, silk manufacturers and notaries.

asymmetric information (econ.): See "information."

asymptote (-ic) (math.): A line approached, but not intersected, by a particular curve.

average (stat.): The center of a distribution. The **mean** equals the sum of values over all observations divided by the number of observations. The **median** equals the value where half the values are greater and half are less.

base industry: Industries that do not export their products.

Base occupations: Occupations in base industries. The base versus export classification is a concept from regional science.

bet (econ.): A **fair bet** is one where the net expected return is zero. An **unfair bet** is one where the net expected return is negative.

***Bianchi* (lit. the white ones):** The Bianchi were participants in a religious pilgrimage in 1399 that began in northwest Italy and concluded in Rome. See "White Death."

black-box model (econ.): An economic model where only the inputs and outputs are observed, but the process of conversion is not.

Black Death: The first and deadliest plague, which arrived in Florence in 1348.

***Calimala*:** The international traders' guild in Florence. The guild was one of the arte maggiore. They primarily traded woolen cloths.

***cambiatore* (pl. *cambiatori*):** Money changer; member of the Arte del Cambio guild.

cartel (econ.): A group of buyers or sellers who collude to set a market price.

***catasto* (pl. *catasti*):** The Florentine net wealth tax that was collected from 1427 through 1494.

chi-squared statistic (stat.): A test statistic that estimates the probability that two categorical variables are not associated. It has an exact solution when both variables have exactly two categories. It is based on the chi-squared distribution.

Cinquecento: The sixteenth century.

Ciompi **revolt**: A popular revolt in Florence (1378–82), predominantly by wool workers against the arte maggiore.

coefficient of variation (stat.): Equals the standard deviation divided by the mean. It measures the volatility as a percentage of the size of the center of the distribution (relative volatility).

collinear (stat.): Two dependent variables X and Y are collinear if one variable is a linear function of another, such as $X = aY$. This can be generalized to more than two dimensions, such as where any single variable equals a linear combination of other variables, such as $X = aY + bZ$, where X, Y and Z are variables and a and b are coefficients. A basic assumption of multiple linear regression theory is that the independent variables are not collinear.

compagnia **(pl. *compagnie*)**: A company; a partnership established by a contract for a set period of time.

complement (econ.): Two goods are complementary if they are used together. An example would be left and right shoes. In general, complements are the opposite of substitutes.

composizione: The fund of retired Monte credits.

concave function (math.): A function that when pictured in a graph is shaped like an overturned bowl. It first increases and then decreases. An inverted-U curve has a positive first derivative and a negative second derivative. It is often associated with finding the maximum of a function.

concentration: (i) (econ.): A measure of monopoly/monopsony power based on the theory that greater market share is associated with greater control of the price.

(ii) (geog.): The inverse of dispersion.

conditional (stat.): An estimate calculated contingent on the value of another variable; **unconditional** is where the estimate is not contingent.

consistent (stat.): A statistical estimator that converges to a particular estimate as the number of observations increases.

contado **(lit. county)**: The countryside surrounding a city. In general, the contado was considered part of the city's core territory. The Florentine contado was divided into four quarters—San Giovanni, Santa Croce, Santa Maria Novella and Santo Spirito—that mirrored the four quarters within the city. Other major cities in the Florentine distretto, such as Arezzo and Pisa, each had an associated contado.

convex function (math.): A function that when pictured in a graph is shaped like a bowl. It first decreases and then increases. A U curve has a negative first derivative and a positive second derivative. This is often associated with finding the minimum of a function.

corner (math.): An extreme point that does not fit smoothly with the rest of a space. One can lead to a nonintuitive result, because the range of possibilities suddenly stops.

C. Solution: The case where one extreme point is optimal and is chosen. This reduces the variation across observations.

cost function (econ.): The cost to produce a particular output. This can be represented in an equation where $C(x) = \sum_i xi^*wi$, where C is the cost function, there is a set of inputs, the x_i are the quantities and w_i are the prices or wages of inputs.

coupon (finl.): The coupon is the regular payment offered by a bond. The **coupon rate** is the total coupon value per year divided by the face value. See *"Paga."*

cross effects (econ.): The effects of one good or input on other goods or inputs as might be captured in a substitution matrix.

cross-sectional data (stat.): Observations of members of a set collected at a particular point in time.

debasement (econ.): The reduction in value of a commodity currency or coin by reducing the share of the precious metal.

decile (stat.): See "quantile."

Decima Scalata: The 1480 catasto assessment.

***denaro* (pl. *denari*):** See "money."

dependent variable (stat.): The variable estimated by a function. The value of that variable is dependent on the values of the independent variables.

derivative (math.): The rate of change of a function. There are two types of derivatives: total and partial. A **total derivative** is calculated based on all dimensions of a function. A **partial derivative** is based on a single dimension of a function. A **first derivative** is the derivative of the function. A **second derivative** is the derivative of the first derivative. The second derivative is often associated with the curvature, the concavity or convexity, of a function.

difference (stat.): The **first difference** is the change between periods and equals the value in the subsequent period minus the value in the current period. The **second difference** is a difference between first differences and so on.

discount rate (econ./finl.): The rate per unit of face value paid for bonds. Generally, this was much less than 100 percent during the Quattrocento.

distretto: The portion of the Florentine domain beyond the contado. These areas were not considered part of the core Florentine territory.

distribution (stat.): The frequency of each value a particular variable takes on.

diversification (finl.): The action of distributing the total assets among a set of assets leading to a reduction in risk. The idea is that these different assets have some degree of independence from one another.

division of labor (econ.): The division of specialized tasks among workers in order to increase efficiency.

***Dugento*:** The thirteenth century.

dummy variable (stat.): A variable that takes on the values of one or zero where a particular state is, respectively, true or false. For example, a dummy variable for female takes on the value of one if the person is a female and zero if the person is not a male.

economic rent (econ.): The amount paid in excess of what is required to keep something at the current level of use.

efficiency (econ.): This adjusts for productivity or quality differences between two similar quantities. For example, although both a skilled worker and an unskilled worker provide labor, the skilled worker generally provides more per hour. An efficiency-adjusted skilled worker might be equal to two unskilled workers.

elasticity (econ.): The percentage response of one economic variable with respect to a percentage change in another economic variable. **Elastic** is where the elasticity is greater than one. **Inelastic** is where the elasticity is less than one. For example, necessities, such as food and housing, are typically income inelastic and luxury items, such as jewelry, are typically income elastic. The **elasticity of substitution** measures the ease of substitution between two goods or inputs.

endpoint problem: The problem that results from the choice of an unusual baseline for comparison, either at the beginning or the end of a time series, under the assumption that it is typical. Usually the problem can be identified, and often solved, by examining the data from intermediate dates.

***estimo* (pl. *estimi*):** The Florentine direct taxes prior to the catasti. The assessments were based on estimates of the fiscal household's net worth.

expected return (econ.): The mean of the distribution of possible future returns.

expiration date (finl.): The date when the option right to do something expires.

extent of the market (econ.): The breadth, scale or size of the market.

face value (finl.): The nominal or official value of an asset.

factor (econ.): (i) An individual or firm hired as an intermediary for a company. A factor is an agent working for a principal. **(ii)** An input to a production function.

firm (econ.): An economic entity formed to produce something. The extent of the firm and the scope of the firm are alternative terms for the firm's size.

fiscal household: A household defined using financial rather than demographic relationships.

florin: See "money."

forced loan (law): An involuntary loan made in lieu of taxes in Florence.

f-statistic (stat.): A test statistic that estimates the likelihood that all coefficients of a regression equation in a particular set, usually all the coefficients in an equation, are equal to zero. The F-statistic for a single coefficient equals the t-statistic. It is based on the F-distribution.

function (math./econ.): The relationship between variables where the value of one or more variables determines the value of one or more other variables. A supply function is the quantity supplied based on the price paid and other variables. A labor supply function is the hours of work supplied based on the wage rate and other variables.

Gabelles: The Florentine sales taxes assessed on a wide range of items, including contracts and salt. Most goods taxed had inelastic demands.

Gambler's Ruin (finl.): The notion that after a sufficiently large number of fair gambles any starting point with a fixed level of wealth will equal zero at least once.

Gini coefficient: A measure of the wealth distribution. A greater Gini coefficient is associated with greater wealth inequality. The Gini coefficient equals the difference between the cumulative share of wealth of a perfectly equal distribution of wealth and the cumulative share of wealth that actually exists. The latter curve is below the former, because the wealthier possess a greater share of wealth.

gonfalone **(pl.** *gonfaloni***):** One of the 16 civil divisions of Florence during the late medieval and Renaissance periods. They were formed in 1343. Previously the city had been divided into six *sesti*.

grosso: See "money."

hedge (finl.): A way to reduce a portfolio's risk exposure. Generally this is done by buying an asset whose value moves in the direction that is opposite to that of the rest of the portfolio.

Herfindahl-Hirschman Index (econ.): A measure of concentration. It equals the sum of squares of the shares of each component. Its minimum is determined by the number of components. Its maximum is 10,000.

heteroskedastic (-ity) (stat.): Heteroskedasticity is where the variance of a distribution varies across the distribution. It violates a basic assumption of multiple linear regression theory.

horizontal integration (econ.): Concentration among firms in a particular stage of production. See "vertical integration."

household production (econ.): Production within the household as opposed to market.

human capital (econ.): The skills a person possesses. It is distinct from physical capital (the assets) and social capital (the connections) a person possesses.

immovable assets: Property assets.

imperfect information (econ.): See "information."

independent variable (stat.): The variables that are the inputs in a regression estimate of a functional relationship.

information (econ./finl./stat.): The set of observations used to estimate a quantity. **Perfect information** is the case where all information is available. **Imperfect information** or **limited information** is the case where not all information is available. **Asymmetric information** is where two economic actors have different information sets.

income effect (econ.): The effect on demand or supply byan individual or household due to changing income holding price constant. Often people with greater incomes or wealth will supply less labor than they otherwise would have for the given wage rate. In this case the income effect would be negative and would reduce labor supplied. See "substitution effect."

interest rate (finl.): The annual amount of payment for a financial asset from the debtor to the creditor.

inverted-U curve (math.): See "concave."

Kaufsystem (hist.): A system of production where the merchant buys from the artisan. The artisan owns the means of production.

labor force participation rate: The share of a particular population working.

Lagrange Multiplier Method (math.): A method of finding a maximum or a minimum of a function subject to a constraint based on another function. For example, a firm minimizes the cost to produce a particular output.

***Lanaiuolo* (pl. *lanaiuoli*): *i*:** A woolen cloth manufacturer; a member of the Arte della lana.

***Libri dei morti*: (lit. Books of the Dead):** The lists of burials in Florence.

likelihood ratio: See "logit."

limited information (econ.): See "information."

liquidity (finl.): The ease of sale of an asset.

Liquid (econ./finl.): An asset that is easy to sell.

Illiquid (finl.): An asset that is difficult to sell.

***lira* (pl. *lire*):** See "money."

logit (logistic regression) (stat.): A limited dependent variable regression where the coefficient estimates allow the calculation of log likelihoods.

Log likelihood (stat.): The likelihood estimate from a logit regression that allows the calculation of the percentage increase in likelihood of the dependent variable based on a specified change in one of the independent variables.

Likelihood ratio (stat.): A measure of statistical significance. Can be seen as the logistic regression version of R^2.

longitudinal data (stat.): A set of observations of members of a set collected at a particular point in time.

Malthusian: A world described by the economic theory of Thomas Malthus.

margin (econ.): Extensive m.: An increase in supply or demand in terms of quantity of units. **Intensive m.:** An increase in supply or demand in terms of size of units.

market maker (finl.): An intermediary who facilitates trades of an asset or product.

Market yield: The return from a financial asset.

matrix (math.): A two-dimensional array showing a quantitative relationship. The diagonal elements are reflexive relationships (down the diagonal).

maturity date (finl.): The date a financial contract expires.

maximum (math.): The maximum value of a function. A **global maximum** is the maximum for an entire mathematical space. A **local maximum** is the maximum in some subspace of a mathematical space.

maximum likelihood estimation (stat.): A method of statistical estimation that determines the most likely estimate.

mean (stat.): See "average."

mean reversion (stat.): The characteristic where the values in a time series converge over time to the mean. It is said that the values "revert to the mean."

mean squared error (MSE): A measure of the total error of an estimate. It equals the sum of the variance and the square of the bias.

median (stat.): See "average."

messere: A title referring to knights; ecclesiastical officials, such as bishops; and those possessing a university degree.

metric (math.): A way to measure distance on a mathematical space. For example, the Euclidean metric is based on the Pythagorean theorem and in a two-dimensional space is $\sqrt{x^2 + y^2}$. The **L_2 metric (math.)** is based on the Lebesgue measure. It is a version of the Pythagorean theorem designed to measure the difference between either functions or sets of values. The associated criterion minimizes the difference between the set of values and the estimates.

minimum (math.): The minimum value of a function. A **global minimum** is the minimum for an entire mathematical space. A **local minimum** is the minimum for some subspace of a mathematical space.

***miserabili* (lit. the miserable ones):** Fiscal households having zero net assets.

money: Money was measured in moneys of account during the Florentine Renaissance period. These moneys of account were consistent, and well-defined official standards were used to simplify trade using the large number of coins in circulation in Florence that were minted in Florence, other Italian cities and beyond. The currency system was bimetallic with gold and silver currencies. The **florin** was the gold currency of Florence, which was first minted in 1252.

Fiorino d'oro: A Florentine gold coinage.

Fiorino suggello: A Florentine gold coinage; the coins were certified and then sealed in a box.

Grosso **(lit. Groat)**: The Florentine white, high, silver coinage.

Quattrino: A Florentine black silver, base metal, coinage. It had a lower silver content. Florence used the Carolingian system of denomination.

Lira **(pl. *lire*)**: The measure of value of the Florentine silver coinage, equivalent to a pound.

Soldo **(pl. *soldi*)**: There were 20 soldi per pound or lira, equivalent to a shilling.

Denaro **(pl. *denari*)**: There were 12 denari per soldi, equivalent to a penny.

monopoly (econ.): The case where the seller is able to set the market price. It is then said that the seller possesses market power and receives an economic rent (unearned profit).

monopsony (econ.): The case where the buyer is able to set the market price. It is then said that the buyer possesses market power and receives an economic rent (unearned profit).

monotonic (math.): A mathematical function whose value moves either up or down, but not both. It is either nondecreasing or nonincreasing.

Monte Comune: The government bond market of Renaissance Florence, which started in 1345. The principal deposited either came voluntarily or through forced loans.

Monte vecchio **(lit. old mountain)**: The original Florentine government bonds where the face value equaled the principal deposited.

Monte dell'uno due: A bond issued by Florence where the face value equaled double the principal deposited.

Monte dell'uno tre: A bond issued by Florence where the face value equaled triple the principal deposited.

Monte della doti **(lit. mountain of the dowries)**: The Florentine dowry insurance market. It was separate from the Monte Comune.

moral hazard (econ.): A situation where an economic actor can gain from dishonesty.

movable assets: Personal and business assets, not including government bonds

negative semi-definite (math.): A multidimensional function possessing this characteristic is concave. It is associated with the ability to find a minimum.

nominal interest rate (finl.): An interest rate not adjusted for inflation.

normalized (math.): A value that is measured in terms of a particular standard.

n. s.: New style. The dates were converted to new style from old style. Florence used the Julian (old style) calendar during the time period covered by this book. That mean New Year's Day was March 25. Dates from January 1 through March 24 are the previous year as March 25 in old style and the same year in new style.

option (finl.): The right, but not the obligation, to do something. A **European option** allows exercise of the option at only one particular time or date. An **American option** allows exercise of the option up to and including a particular time or date. **A call option** is the right to buy an asset. A **put option** is the right to sell an asset. A **real option** is a nonfinancial option.

Exercise (of an option): The buying or selling of an asset based on holding an option right.

own effects (econ.): The impact of a changing price of a good or input on its own quantity demanded or supplied. See "substitution matrix."

***Paga* (pl. *paghe*) (lit. payment):** Monte bond coupons.

***palazzo* (pl. *palazzi*) (lit. palace):** Renaissance private palace.

perfect competition (econ.): The case where no individual or group is able to set the market price. The price contains all necessary information, and neither the buyer nor the seller makes an unearned profit (economic rent).

perpetuity (finl.): A bond without a maturity date. The consol, which, unlike the Monte, had no coupons, was the original British version.

***popolo minuto* (lit. little or thin people):** They were those who were not members of an arte maggiore.

premium (finl.): (i) The portion of the price paid in excess of the competitive market price. **(ii)** The price paid to purchase an option.

***prestanze*:** A forced loan.

primary market (econ.): The initial market where an asset is sold.

principal (finl.): The capital of a loan or bond as opposed to the interest.

principal and agent (econ.): An agent works for a principal in order to perform a specific task. See "factor."

production function (econ.): The engineering relationship between the inputs and the output of that firm. This can be represented in an equation as $f(x)$, where f is the production function and x is the set of inputs.

profit function (econ.): The difference between the revenue function and the cost function. This can be represented in an equation where $i = \dfrac{c}{d}$, where $\prod$ is the profit, R(y) is the revenue function based on sales vector "y" and C(x) is the cost function based on input vector "x."

quadratic (math.): A function of the form $a + bX + cX^2$, where X is a variable and a, b and c are coefficients.

quantile (stat.): An **n-tile** is a method that divides a distribution into n parts with equal numbers of observations. A **quartile** contains four parts divided into fourths. Similarly, a **decile** contains ten equally sized parts.

quartile (stat.): See "quantile."

***Quattrino*:** See "money."

***Quattrocento*:** The fifteenth century.

R² statistic (stat.): A test statistic that measures the share of total variance explained by a regression. It is mathematically similar to correlation. It measures how well the estimate fits the actual values.

random walk (finl./stat.): A time series where the next observation is not predictable based on current and previous observations. Equivalent terminologies are "an integrated time series" or "a time series with a unit root."

real interest rate (finl.): An interest rate adjusted for inflation.

redemption (bond) (finl.): The purchase of an asset, often a bond, by a debtor from a creditor.

regression (stat.): An equation that summarizes a set of observations. The term refers to the equation's lower dimensionality (regression) compared to the number of observations.

regular space (math.): A mathematical space is regular if it is well behaved in a relatively minimal sense. A Hausdorf space is the minimum regular space and is the usual space used in the mathematical analysis of random walks in finance.

reservation level (econ.): The minimum level in order to induce an economic actor to do something.

Reservation wage: The minimum wage necessary to induce a worker to enter the workforce or to perform a particular occupation.

Reservation mortality: As used in the text, it is the minimum expected mortality rate necessary to induce someone to flee.

return: The return is what one makes from a completed project. The **expected return** is what one expects to make from a project not yet finished.

revenue function (econ.): The function that calculates the total revenue of a firm. This can be represented in an equation where, where R is the revenue function, there is a set of outputs j, the y_j are the quantities and p_j is the prices of outputs.

risk management (finl.): The effort to reduce or manage risk.

robust (stat.): Something that is statistically significant under a wide range of specifications and underlying assumptions.

scale economy (econ.): A case where the production increases more than. proportionately to the increase of inputs.

Economy of scale: a case where there is a scale economy.

secondary market (econ.): Any market after the initial market where an asset is sold.

seemingly unrelated regressions (SUR) (stat.): A multivariate system of linear regression equations that are not necessarily related. This method is related to simultaneous equations. However, there is no specified relationship between the regression equations.

Seicento: The seventeenth century.

sensitivity (stat.): The amount of change in a result if the underlying assumptions are changed.

ser: A title identifying a notary, judge or priest.

smooth (math.): A mathematical space is smooth if the derivatives are continuous. This assumption makes many mathematical analyses easier.

soldo (pl. *soldi*): See "money."

sottoposto (pl. *sottoposti*): Wool industry workers.

space (math.): A mathematical space is a set of quantitative values. An example is the Cartesian plane. A **subspace** of a particular space is not greater than the entire space.

specification (stat.): A variation in the function that allows a researcher to test how the statistical significant varies dependent on changes in the underlying assumptions.

spread (finl.): The difference between the bid and ask prices. The **bid-ask spread** is another term for the spread. The **bid** is the price offered to buy something. The **ask** is the price demanded to sell something.

standard deviation (stat.): Essentially, this is the square root of the variance, so it has the same dimensions as the observations in the distribution.

standard error (stat.): Essentially, this is the square root of the mean squared error, so it has the same dimensions as the observations in the distribution.

stationary (stat.): A time series processed so that it is stable (no trend or unit root). This characteristic simplifies time series analyses. For example, the Box-Jenkins approach uses first (or more) differences to make the time series stationary and refers to the resulting time series as integrated.

statistical significance (stat.): An estimate that a relationship exists based on some form of statistical test. The standard of 95 percent confidence is used throughout this book. The results of tests based on other levels of confidence, 90 percent and 99 percent, are also reported in order to provide supplemental information.

subsidy (econ.): The opposite of a tax. The government provides a relative benefit to make a transaction.

substitute (econ.): Two goods are substitutes if they are used instead of one another. Examples of substitutes are butter and margarine. In general, substitutes are the opposites of complements.

substitution effect (econ.): The effect on demand due to changing prices while holding income and wealth constant. See "income effect."

substitution matrix (econ.): The functional relationship between a set of individual inputs.

survivor principle (econ.): The idea that if a particular economic practice survives a long time, then it is in some sense optimal.

systematic risk (finl.): The nondiversifiable risk in an economy.

t-statistic (stat.): The difference from the hypothesized value, usually taken as zero, in multiples of the standard error. This usually provides the probability that a particular regression equation coefficient is equal to zero.

time series (stat.): A series of observations ordered by dates or times.

transaction cost (econ.): The cost of conducting a transaction.

transitivity (math.): The property of a mathematical relationship that if it holds for A and B and it holds for B and C, then it holds for A and C. For example, if $A = B$ and $B = C$, then $A = C$.

***Trecento*:** The fourteenth century.

U curve (math.): See "convex."

variance (stat.): A measure of the spread of a distribution. The variance is the second moment of a distribution. See "standard deviation."

Verlagssystem (hist.): A system of production where the artisan works only upon being commissioned by a merchant. This is a putting-out system where the artisan and merchant have a direct relationship.

vertical integration (econ.): Concentration among firms that buy and sell inputs for a product. See "horizontal integration."

White Death: The plague that hit Florence in 1400. It was the second-deadliest plague to hit Florence, behind only the Black Death. The Florentines named it after the 1399 Bianchi. See *"Bianchi."*

yield to maturity (finl.): A measure of the interest rate.

BIBLIOGRAPHY

Archival Sources

Catasto. Archivio di Stato, Florence. Vols. 64–69, 72–81.
Medici-Tornaquinci Collection. Harvard Baker Library, Boston, MA.
Monte Comune Archivio di Stato, Florence. Vol. 1939.

Other Sources

Abbott, Walter F. "Moscow in 1897 as a Preindustrial City: A Test of the Inverse Burgess Zonal Hypothesis." In *Urban Patterns: Studies in Human Ecology*, rev. ed., edited by George A. Theodorson, 398–405. University Park: Pennsylvania State University Press, 1982.

Achtman, M., G. Morelli, P. Zhu, T. Wirth, I. Diehl, B. Kusecek, A. J. Vogler et al., "Microevolution and History of the Plague Bacillus, *Yersinia pestis.*" *Proceedings of the National Academy of Sciences* 101, no. 51 (2004): 17837–42.

Ackerman, James S., and Myra Nan Rosenfeld. "Social Stratification in Renaissance Urban Planning." In *Urban Life in the Renaissance*, edited by Susan Zimmerman and Ronald F. E. Weissman, 21–49. Cranbury, NJ: Associated University Presses, 1989.

Agnoletti, Anna Maria E., ed. *Statuto dell'Arte della Lana in Firenze (1317–1319)*. Vol. 1, Fonti e Studi sulle Corporazioni Artigiane del Medio Evo. Florence: Felice Le Monnier, 1940.

Aiden, Erez, and Jean-Baptiste Michel. *Uncharted: Big Data as a Lens on Human Culture.* New York: Riverhead Books, 2013.

Alberti, Leon Battista, *The Family in Renaissance Florence.* Translated by Renée Neu Watkins. Columbia: University of South Carolina Press, 1969.

———. *I libri della famiglia.* Edited by Girolamo Mancini. Florence: G. Carnesecchi e Figli, 1908.

Alfani, Guido. "Economic Inequality in Northwestern Italy: A Long-Term View (Fourteenth to Eighteenth centuries)." *Journal of Economic History* 75, no. 4 (2015): 1058–96.

———. "Prima della curva di Kuznets: Stabilità e mutamento nella concentrazione di ricchezza e proprietà in età moderna." In *Ricchezza, valore, proprietà in età preindustriale 1400–1850*, edited by Guido Alfani and Michela Barbot, 143–67. Venice: Marsilio, 2009.

———. "Proprietà, ricchezza e disugualianza economica." In *Ricchezza, valore, proprietà in età preindustriale 1400–1850*, edited by Guido Alfani and Michela Barbot, 11–22. Venice: Marsilio, 2009.

———. "Wealth Inequalities and Population Dynamics in Early Modern Northern Italy." *Journal of Interdisciplinary History* 40, no. 4 (2010): 513–49.

Alfani, Guido, and Francesco Ammannati. "Economic Inequality and Poverty in the Very Long Run: The Case of the Florentine State (Late Thirteenth–Early Nineteenth Centuries)." No. 70. Dondena Working Paper (2014). ftp://ftp.dondena.unibocconi.it/WorkingPapers/Dondena_WP070.pdf.

Alfani, Guido, and Michela Barbot, *Ricchezza, valore, proprietà in età preindustriale 1400–1850* (Venice: Marsilio, 2009).

Alfani, Guido, and Wouter Ryckbosch. "Was There a 'Little Convergence' in Inequality? Italy and the Low Countries Compared, ca. 1500–1800." No. 557. CEPR Working Paper (2015). http://www.igier.unibocconi.it/files/557.pdf.

Allen, Robert C. "Progress and Poverty in Early Modern Europe." *Economic History Review*, n.s. 56, no. 3 (2003): 403–43.

Alston, Lee J., Thráinn Eggertsson and Douglass C. North, eds. *Empirical Studies in Institutional Change*. Cambridge, UK: Cambridge University Press, 1996.

Alston, Lee J., and Robert Higgs. "Contractual Mix in Southern Agriculture since the Civil War: Facts, Hypotheses, and Tests." *Journal of Economic History* 42, no. 2 (1982): 327–53.

Ammannati, Francesco. "L'Arte della Lana a Firenze nel Cinquecento: Crisi del settore e risposte degli operatori." *Storia economica: Rivista quadrimestrale*, 11, no. 1 (2008): 5–39.

———. "Craft Guild Legislation and Woollen Production: The Florentine Arte della Lana in the Fifteenth and Sixteenth Centuries." In *Innovation and Creativity in Late Medieval and Early Modern European Cities*, edited by Karol Davids and Bert De Munck, 55–79. Farnham: Ashgate 2014.

———. "Florentine Woolen Manufacture in the Sixteenth Century: Crisis and New Entrepreneurial Strategies." *Business and Economic History On-Line*, 7 (2009): 1–9.

———. "Francesco di Marco Datini's Wool Workshops." In *Francesco di Marco Datini: The Man, the Merchant*, edited by Giampero Nigro, 489–514. Florence: Firenze University Press, 2010.

———. "Production et productivité du travail dans les ateliers laniers florentins du XVIe siècle." In *Les temps du travail: Normes, pratiques, évolutions (XIVe-XIXe siècle)*, edited by Corine Maitte and Didier Terrier, 225–49. Rennes: Presses Universitaires de Rennes, 2014.

———. " 'Se non piace loro l'arte, mutinla in una altra': I 'lavoranti' dell'Arte della lana fiorentina tra XIV e XVI secolo." *Annali di Storia di Firenze* 7 (2012): 5–33.

Ammannati, Francesco, Davide De Franco and Matteo Di Tullio. "Misurare la diseguaglianza economica nell'età preindustriale: Un confronto fra realtà dell'Italia centro-settentrionale." No. 65. Dondena Working Paper (2014). ftp://ftp.dondena.unibocconi.it/WorkingPapers/Dondena_WP065.pdf.

Ammirato, Scipione. *Istorie fiorentine di Scipione Ammirato*, vol. 4. Edited by Luciano Scarabelli. Torino: Cugini Pomba, 1853.

Anderson, Siwan. "Why Dowry Payments Declined with Modernization in Europe but Are Rising in India." *Journal of Political Economy* 111, no. 2 (2003): 269–310.

Andrews, D., and A. Caldera Sánchez. "Drivers of Homeownership Rates in Selected OECD Countries." Working paper. *OECD Economics Department* (2011).

Anonymous. "An Editorial Comment to Richard Goldthwaite's 'The Economy of Renaissance Italy'." *I Tatti Studies* 2 (1987): 11–13.

Arrow, Kenneth Joseph. "The Theory of Risk Aversion." In *Essays in the Theory of Risk-Bearing*, 90–120. Chicago: Markham, 1971.

Ashenfelter, Orley, and James Heckman. "The Estimation of Income and Substitution Effects in a Model of Family Labor Supply." *Econometrica* (1974): 73–85.

Atack, Jeremy, and Fred Bateman. "Egalitarianism, Inequality, and Age: The Rural North in 1860." *Journal of Economic History* 41, no. 1 (1981): 85–93.

Atkinson, Anthony B., Thomas Piketty and Emmanuel Saez, "Top Incomes in the Long Run of History," *Journal of Economic Literature* 49, no. 1 (2011): 3–71.

Babbage, Charles. *On the Economy of Machinery and Manufactures*, 4th ed. 1835; New York: A. M. Kelly, 1971.

Bairoch, Paul. *Cities and Economic Development. From the Dawn of History to the Present*. Chicago: University of Chicago Press, 1988.

Balchin, Paul N. *Urban Development in Renaissance Italy*. Chichester, UK: Wiley, 2008.

Barbadoro, Bernardino. *Le finanze della Repubblica fiorentina: Imposta diretta e debito pubblico fino all'istituzione del Monte*. Biblioteca storica toscana, no. 5. Florence: Olschki, 1929.

Barbot, Michela. "Gli estimi, una fonte di valore." In *Ricchezza, valore, proprietà in età preindustriale 1400–1850*, edited by Guido Alfani and Michela Barbot, 23–27. Venice: Marsilio, 2009.

Barducci, Roberto. "Cum parva difficultate civium predictorum … Spunti introduttivi per un regesto della legislazione finanziaria fiorentina del Trecento (1345–1358)." In *Renaissance Studies in Honor of Craig Hugh Smyth*, edited by Andrew Morrogh, Fiorella Superbi Gioffredi, Piero Morselli and Eve Borsook, 1: 3–15. Florence: Giunta Barbèra, 1985.

————. "Politica e speculazione finanziaria a Firenze dopo la crisi del primo Trecento (1343–1358)." *Archivio storico Italiano* 137, no. 2 (1979): 177–219.

————. "Le riforme finanziarie nel tumulto dei Ciompi." In *Il tumulto dei Ciompi: Un momento di storia fiorentina ed europea*, 95–102. Florence: Olschki, 1981.

Baron, Hans. *From Petrarch to Leonardo Bruni: Studies in Humanistic and Political Literature*. Chicago: University of Chicago Press, 1968.

Barreiros, Maria Helena. "Urban Landscapes: Houses, Streets and Squares of 18th Century Lisbon." *Journal of Early Modern History* 12, no. 3 (2008): 205–32.

Bartoli Langeli, Attilio. "Parole introduttive." In *Margini di libertà: Testamenti femminili nel medioevo*, edited by Maria Clara Rossi, 9–19. Verona: Cierre, 2010.

Battara, Pietro. *La popolazione di Firenze alla metà del '500*. Florence: Rinascimento del Libro, 1935.

Baumann, Wolf-Rüdiger. *The Merchants Adventurers and the Continental Cloth-trade (1560s-1620s)*. Berlin: Walter de Gruyter, 1990.

Baumol, William J. "The Transactions Demand for Cash: An Inventory Theoretic Approach." *Quarterly Journal of Economics* 66, no. 4 (1951): 545–56.

Baxandall, Michael. *Painting and Experience in Fifteenth-Century Italy: A Primer in the Social History of Pictorial Style*. Oxford, UK: Oxford University Press, 1972.

Becker, Gary S. *Human Capital: A Theoretical and Empirical Analysis, with Special Reference to Education*, 3rd ed. Chicago: University of Chicago Press, 1993.

————. "A Theory of Marriage." In *The Economic Approach to Human Behavior*, 205–50. Chicago: University of Chicago Press, 1976.

————. "A Theory of the Allocation of Time." *Economic Journal* 75, no. 299 (1965): 493–517.

————. *A Treatise on the Family*. Cambridge, MA: Harvard University Press, 1981.

Becker, Gary S., and Kevin M. Murphy. "Sorting by Marriage." In *Social Economics: Market Behavior in a Social Environment*, 29–46. Chicago: University of Chicago Press, 2000.

Becker, Gary S., Kevin M. Murphy and Robert Tamura. "Human Capital, Fertility, and Economic Growth." *Journal of Political Economy* 98, no. 5, pt. 2 (1990): S12–37.

Becker, Marvin B. *Florence in Transition*. Vol. 1, *The Decline of the Commune*. Baltimore: Johns Hopkins University Press, 1967.

————. *Florence in Transition*. Vol. 2, *Studies in the Rise of the Territorial State*. Baltimore: Johns Hopkins University Press, 1968.

Belfani, Carlo Marco. "A Chain of Skills: The Production Cycle of Firearms Manufacture in the Brescia Area from the Sixteenth to the Eighteenth Centuries." In *Guilds, Markets and Work Regulations in Italy, 16th–19th Centuries*, edited by Alberto Guenzi, Paola Massa and Fausto Piola Caselli, 266–83. Brookfield, VT: Ashgate Publishing Company, 1998.

Bellavitis, Anna. "Apprendiste e maestre a Venezia tra Cinque e Seicento." Special issue, *"Donne, lavoro, economia a Venezia e in Terraferma tra medioevo ed età moderna." Archivio veneto* 143 (2012): 127–44.

Bellavitis, Anna, and Linda Guzzetti, eds. Special issue, *"Donne, lavoro, economia a Venezia e in Terraferma tra medioevo ed età moderna." Archivio veneto* 143 (2012).

————. "Introduzione." Special issue, *"Donne, lavoro, economia a Venezia e in Terraferma tra medioevo ed età moderna". Archivio veneto* 143 (2012): 5–17.

Bellomo, Manlio. "Dote (Diritto Intermedio)." In *Enciclopedia del diritto*, 14: 8–32. Milan: Giuffrè, 1965.

Bennett, Judith M. "The Village Ale-Wife: Women and Brewing in Fourteenth-Century England." In *Women and Work in Preindustrial Europe*, edited by Barbara A. Hanawalt, 20–37. Bloomington: Indiana University Press, 1986.

Bernocchi, Mario. *Le monete della Repubblica fiorentina*. Vol. 4, *Valute del Fiorino d'Oro 1389–1432*. Florence: Olschki, 1978.

Bertoni, Laura. "Investire per la famiglia, investire per sé: La partecipazione delle donne ai circuiti creditizi a Pavia nella seconda metà del XIII secolo." In *Dare credito alle donne. Presenze femminili nell'economia tra medioevo ed età moderna*, edited by Giovanna Petti Balbi and Paola Guglielmotti, 51–73. Asti, Italy: Centro studi Renato Bordone sui Lombardi, sul credito e sulla banca, 2012.

Black, Robert. *Education and Society in Florentine Tuscany: Teachers, Pupils, and Schools, c. 1250–1500*, vol. 1. Leiden, Netherlands: Brill, 2007.

Blau, Peter M. *Inequality and Heterogeneity: A Primitive Theory of Social Structure*. New York: Free Press, 1977.

Blau, Peter M., and Otis Dudley Duncan. *The American Occupational Structure*. New York: Free Press, 1967.

Bloch, Marc. *French Rural History: An Essay on Its Basic Characteristics*. Translated by Janet Sondheimer. Berkeley: University of California Press, 1966.

Boccaccio, Giovanni. *The Decameron*, 2nd ed. Translated by G. H. McWilliams. 1995; New York: Penguin, 2003.

Booth, G. Geoffrey, and Umit G. Gurun. "Volatility Clustering and the Bid-Ask Spread: Exchange Rate Behavior in Early Renaissance Florence." *Journal of Empirical Finance* 15 (2008): 131–44.

Borelli, Giorgio. "A Reading of the Relationship between Cities, Manufacturing Crafts and Guilds in Early Modern Italy." In *Guilds, Markets and Work Regulations in Italy, 16th–19th Centuries*, edited by Alberto Guenzi, Paola Massa and Fausto Piola Caselli, 19–31. Brookfield, VT: Ashgate Publishing Company, 1998.

Bornstein, Daniel E. *The Bianchi of 1399: Popular Devotion in Late Medieval Italy*. Ithaca, NY: Cornell University Press, 1993.

Bos, Kirsten I., Verena J. Schuenemann, G. Brian Golding, Hernán A. Burbano, Nicholas Waglechner, Brian K. Coombes, Joseph B. McPhee et al. "A Draft Genome of *Yersinia pestis* from Victims of the Black Death." *Nature* 478, no. 7370 (2011): 506–10.

Botticini, Maristella. "A Loveless Economy? Intergenerational Altruism and the Marriage Market in a Tuscan Town, 1415–1436." *Journal of Economic History* 59, no. 1 (1999): 104–21.

Botticini, Maristella, and Aloysius Siow. "Why Dowries?" *American Economic Review* 93, no. 4 (2003): 1385–98.

———— "Why Dowries?" Working paper. Boston University and University of Toronto (2002).

Braude, Benjamin. "International Competition and Domestic Cloth in the Ottoman Empire, 1500–1650: A Study in Undevelopment." *Review (Fernand Braudel Center): Research Foundation of SUNY* 2, no. 3 (1979): 437–51.

Braudel, Fernand. *The Mediterranean and the Mediterranean World in the Age of Philip II*. 2 vols. New York: Harper Colophon Books, 1976.

————. *Perspectives of the World*. Vol. 3 of *Civilization and Capitalism 15th–18th Century*. New York: Harper and Row, 1984.

————. *The Structures of Everyday Life*. Vol. 1 of *Civilization and Capitalism 15th–18th Century*. New York: Harper and Row, 1981.

————. *The Wheels of Commerce*. Vol. 2 of *Civilization and Capitalism 15th–18th Century*. New York: Harper and Row, 1982.

Braun, Rudolf. *Industrialisation and Everyday Life*. Translated by Sarah Hanbury Tenison. Cambridge, UK: Cambridge University Press, 1990.

Brealey, Richard A., and Stewart C. Myers. *Principles of Corporate Finance*, 7th ed. Boston: McGraw Hill Irwin, 2003.

Brinton, Mary C., and Victor Nee, eds. *The New Institutionalism in Sociology*. Stanford, CA: Stanford University Press, 1998.

Brittain, John. *Inheritance and the Inequality of Material Wealth*. Washington, DC: Brookings Institution, 1978.

Brown, Alison. *Bartolomeo Scala, 1430–1497, Chancellor of Florence: The Humanist as Bureaucrat*. Princeton, NJ: Princeton University Press, 1979.

Brown, Judith C. "Prosperity or Hard Times in Renaissance Italy?" *Renaissance Quarterly* 142, no. 4 (1989): 761–80.

————. "A Woman's Place Was in the Home: Women's Work in Renaissance Tuscany." In *Rewriting the Renaissance: The Discourses of Sexual Difference in Early Modern Europe*, edited by Margaret W.

Ferguson, Maureen Quilligan and Nancy J. Vickers, 206–24. Chicago: University of Chicago Press 1986.

Brown, Judith C., and Robert C. Davis. *Gender and Society in Renaissance Italy*. London: Longman, 1998.

Brown, Judith, and Jonathan Goodman. "Women and Industry in Florence." *Journal of Economic History* 40, no. 1 (1980): 79–80.

Brucker, Gene A. *The Civic World of Early-Renaissance Florence*. Princeton, NJ: Princeton University Press, 1977.

———. "Un documento fiorentino sulla guerra, sulla finanza e sull'amministrazione pubblica." *Archivio storico Italiano* 115, no. 2 (1957): 165–87.

———. "The Economic Foundations of Renaissance Florence." In *Lorenzo il Magnifico e il suo mondo*, edited by Gian Carlo Garfagnini, 3–15. Florence: Olschki, 1994.

———. *Florence: The Golden Age, 1138–1737*. Berkeley: University of California Press, 1998.

———. *Florentine Politics and Society, 1343–1378*. Princeton, NJ: Princeton University Press, 1962.

———. *Giovanni and Lusanna: Love and Marriage in Renaissance Florence*. Berkeley, CA: University of California Press, 1986.

———. *Living on the Edge in Leonardo's Florence: Selected Essays*. Berkeley: University of California Press, 2005.

———. *Renaissance Florence*. 1959; Huntington, NY: Krieger, 1975.

———, ed. *The Society of Renaissance Florence: A Documentary Study*. New York: Harper and Row, 1971.

Burckhardt, Jacob. *The Civilization of the Renaissance in Italy*. 2 vols. New York: Harper Colophon Books, 1973.

Burgess, Ernest W. "The Growth of the City: An Introduction to a Research Project." In *The City: Suggestions for Investigation of Human Behavior in the Urban Environment*, edited by Robert E. Park and Ernest W. Burgess, 47–62. 1925; Chicago: University of Chicago Press, 1966.

Caferro, William. "The Silk Business of Tommaso Spinelli, Fifteenth-Century Florentine Merchant and Papal Banker." *Renaissance Studies* 10, no. 4 (1996): 417–39.

Canestrini, Giuseppe. *La scienza e l'arte di stato desunta dagli atti ufficiali della Repubblica fiorentina e dei Medici*. Florence: Le Monnier, 1862.

Cantini, Lorenzo. *Legislazione toscana raccolta e illustrata (1532–1775)*. 32 vols. Florence: Fantosini, 1800–1808.

Cappelli, Adriano. *Dizionario di Abbreviature Latine ed Italiane*. Milan: Hoepli, Milan, 1979.

Carlos, Ann M., and Stephen Nicholas. "Theory and History: Seventeenth-Century Joint-Stock Chartered Trading Companies." *Journal of Economic History* 56, no. 4 (1996): 916–24.

Carlton, Dennis W., and Jeffrey M. Perloff. *Modern Industrial Organization*, 4th ed. Boston: Addison Wesley, 2005.

Carmichael, Ann G. *Plague and the Poor in Renaissance Florence*. Cambridge, UK: Cambridge University Press, 1986.

Carmona, Maurice. "La Toscane face à la crise de l'industrie lainière: Techniques et mentalités économiques aux XVIe et XVIIe siècles'." In *Produzione, commercio e consumo de panni di lana nei secoli XII-XVII, Istituto internazionale di storia economica 'F. Datini'Prato, Series II: Atti delle 'Settimane di Studio'e altri convegni*, edited by Marco Spallanzani, 151–68. Florence: Leo S. Olschki, 1976.

Carocci, Guido. "Il Centro di Firenze (Mercato Vecchio) nel 1427, Studio di Guido Carocci, Ispettore degli Scavi e dei Monumeni." In *Studi Storici sul Centro di Firenze Pubblicati di Occasione del IV Congresso Storico Italiano*. Florence: Arnaldo Forni, 1889, after p. 15.

———. "Il Centro di Firenze nel 1427." In *Studi Storici sul Centro di Firenze Pubblicati di Occasione del IV Congresso Storico Italiano*, 17–75. Florence: Arnaldo Forni, 1889.

———, ed. *L'illustratore fiorentino: Calendario storico per l'anno 1909*. Florence: Tipografia Pozienicana, 1908.

Carus-Wilson, E. M. *Medieval Merchant Venturers*, 2nd ed. London: Methuen, 1967.

Casson, Mark, and Mary B. Rose, eds. *Institutions and the Evolution of Modern Business* (London: Frank Cass), 1998.

Castelnuovo, Guido. "Offices and Officials." In *The Italian Renaissance State*, edited by Andrea Gamberini and Isabella Lazzarini, 368–84. Cambridge, UK: Cambridge University Press, 2012.

Cavaciocchi, Simonetta, ed. *La donna nell'economia, secc. XIII–XVIII*. Prato: Le Monnier, 1990.

Chabot, Isabelle. *Le dette des familles: Femmes, lignage et patrimonie à Florence au XIVe et XVe siècles*. Rome: École Française de Rome, 2011.

———. "Lineage Strategies and the Control of Women in Renaissance Florence." In *Widowhood in Medieval and Early Modern Europe*, edited by Sandra Cavallo and Lyndan Warner, 127–44. Harlow, Essex, UK: Longman, 1999.

———. "La réconnaissance du travail des femmes dans la Florence du bas Moyen Âge: Contexte idéologique et réalité." In *La donna nell'economia, secc. XIII–XVIII*, edited by Simonetta Cavaciocchi, 563–76. Prato: Le Monnier, 1990.

———. *Ricostruzione di una famiglia: I Ciurianni di Firenze tra XII e XV secolo: Con l'edizione critica del "Libro propio" di Lapo di Valore Ciuranni e successor (1326-1429*. Florence: Le Lettere, 2012.

———. "Risorse e diritti patrimoniali." In *Il lavoro delle donne*, edited by Angela Groppi, 47–70 Rome: Laterza, 1996.

Chabot, Isabelle, Jérôme Hayez, and Didier Lett. *La famille, les femmes et le quotidien (XIVe-XVIIIe siècle)*. Paris: Publications de la Sorbonne, 2006.

Chandler, Alfred D., Jr. *The Visible Hand: The Managerial Revolution in American Business*. Cambridge, MA: Harvard University Press, 1977.

Chojnacki, Stanley. "Getting Back the Dowry, Venice c. 1360–1530." In *Time, Space, and Women's Lives in Early Modern Europe*, edited by Anne Jacobson Schutte, Thomas Kuehn and Silvana Seidel Menchi, 77–115. Kirksville, MO: Truman State University Press, 2001.

Chorley, Patrick. "The Evolution of the Woollen, 1300–1700." In *The New Draperies in the Low Countries and England, 1300–1800*, edited by N. B. Harte, 7–33. Oxford, UK: Oxford University Press, 1997.

———. "*Rascie* and the Florentine Cloth Industry during the Sixteenth Century: A Case Study." *Journal of European Economic History* 32, no. 3 (2003): 487–526.

———. "The Volume of Cloth Production in Florence, 1500–1650: An Assessment of the Evidence." In *Wool Products and Markets (13th–20th Century)*, edited by Giovanni Luigi Fontana and Gérard Gayot, 551–71. Padua: Coop. Libraria Editrice Università di Padova, 2004.

Ciabani, Roberto. *Firenze di gonfalone in gonfalone*. Florence: Meridiana, 1998.

Ciappelli, Giovanni. *Fisco e società a Firenze nel Rinascimento*. Rome: Istituto Nazionale di Studi di Rinascimento, Edizioni di Storia e Letteratura, 2009.

———. "Il mercato dei titoli del debito pubblico a Firenze nel Tre-Quattrocento." In *Actes: Colloqui corona, municipis i fiscalitat a la Baixa Edat Mitjana*, edited by Manuel Sánchez and Antonio Furió, 623–41. Lleida: Institut d'Estudis Ilerdencs, 1997.

Cipolla, Carlo M. *Before the Industrial Revolution: European Society and Economy 1000–1700*. 2nd ed. New York: Norton, 1980.

———. "The Decline of Italy: The Case of a Fully Matured Economy." *Economic History Review* ser. 2, 5 (1952): 178–87.

———. "The Economic Decline of Italy." In *Crisis and Change in the Venetian Economy in the Sixteenth and Seventeenth Centuries*, edited by Brian Pullan, 127–45. London: Methuen and Co. Ltd., 1968.

———. "The Economic Depression of the Renaissance?" *Economic History Review* ser. 2, 16, no. 3 (1964): 518–24.

———. *Faith, Reason, and the Plague in Seventeenth-Century Tuscany*. New York: Norton, 1979.

———. *The Monetary Policy of Fourteenth-Century Florence*. Berkeley: University of California Press, 1982.

———. *Money in Sixteenth-Century Florence*. Berkeley: University of California Press, 1989.

Clark, Alice. *Working Life of Women in the Seventeenth Century*. 1919; Abingdon, UK: Frank Cass, 1968.

Clark, Gregory. "The Condition of the Working Class in England, 1209–2004." *Journal of Political Economy* 113, no. 6 (2005): 1307–40.

———. *A Farewell to Alms: A Brief Economic History of the World*. Princeton, NJ: Princeton University Press, 2007.

———. "Human Capital, Fertility, and the Industrial Revolution." *Journal of the European Economic Association* 3, nos. 2/3 (2005): 505–15.

Cleveland, William S. *The Elements of Graphing Data*. Monterey, CA: Wadsworth, 1985.

Coase, R. H. "The Nature of the Firm." In *The Firm, the Market, and the Law*, 33–56. Chicago: University of Chicago Press, 1988.

Cochrane, John H. *Asset Pricing*, rev. ed. Princeton, NJ: Princeton University Press, 2005.

Cogné, Albane. "Distribuzione della proprietà a Milano a metà Settecento: La realizzazione di un GIS a partire dal catasto teresiano (1758)." In *Ricchezza, valore, proprietà in età preindustriale 1400–1850*, edited by Guido Alfani and Michela Barbot, 101–25. Venice: Marsilio, 2009.

Cohn, Samuel K., Jr. "The Black Death: End of a Paradigm." *American Historical Review* 107, no. 3 (2002): 703–38.

———. *The Black Death Transformed: Disease and Culture in Early Renaissance Europe*. New York: Oxford University Press, 2002.

———. "Burckhardt Revisited from Social History." In *Language and Images of Renaissance Italy*, edited by Alison Brown, 217–34. Oxford, UK: Clarendon Press, 1995.

———. "Corrispondenza." *Rivista storica Italiana* 98, no. 3 (1986): 919–21.

———. *Death and Property in Siena: 1205–1800*. Baltimore: Johns Hopkins University Press, 1988.

———. *The Laboring Classes in Renaissance Florence*. New York: Academic Press, 1978.

———. *Women in the Streets: Essays on Sex and Power in Renaissance Italy*. Baltimore: Johns Hopkins University Press, 1996.

Coleman, James S. *Foundations of Social Theory*. Cambridge, MA: Harvard University Press, 1990.

Consiglio comunale di Firenze. *Stradario storico e amministrativo della città e del commune di Firenze*. 2nd ed. Florence: Enrico Ariani, 1929.

Conti, Elio. *I catasti agrari della Repubblica fiorentina e il catasto particellare toscano (secoli XIV–XIX)*. Rome: Palazzo Borromini, 1966.

———. *L'imposta diretta a Firenze nel Quattrocento (1427–1494)*. Rome: Palazzo Borromini, 1984.

———, ed. *Matteo Palmieri ricordi fiscali (1427–1474) con due appendici relative al 1474–1495*. Rome: Palazzo Borromini, 1983.

Conzen, Michael P. "Historical Geography: Changing Spatial Structure and Social Patterns of Western Cities." *Progress in Human Geography* 7 (1983): 88–107.

Corti, Gino, and J-Gentil Da Silva. "Note sur la production de la soie à Florence, au XVe siècle." *Annales. Histoire, Sciences Sociales* 20, no. 2 (1965): 309–11. EHESS, 1965.

Costantini, Massimo. "Arti e stato in area veneta nel tardomedioevo; spunti di analisi comparativa." In *Dalla corporazione alla società di mutuo soccorso*, edited by Paola Massa and Angelo Moioli, 87–106. Milan: Franco Angeli 2004.

Cox, Gary W. "Was the Glorious Revolution a Constitutional Watershed?" *Journal of Economic History* 72, no. 3 (2012): 567–600.

Cox, Lawanda S. "Tenancy in the United States, 1865–1900: A Consideration of the Validity of the Agricultural Ladder Hypothesis." *Agricultural History* 18 (1944): 97–105.

Crossick, Geoffrey. *The Artisan and the European Town, 1500–1900*. Hants, UK: Scolar Press, 1997.

Dahl, Gunnar. *Trade, Trust, and Networks: Commercial Culture in Late Medieval Italy*. Lund, Sweden: Nordic Academic Press, 1998.

Dale, Marian K. "The London Silkwomen of the Fifteenth Century." *Economic History Review* 24, no. 3 (1933): 324–35.

Davids, Karol, and Bert De Munck, eds. *Innovation and Creativity in Late Medieval and Early Modern European Cities*. Farnham, UK: Ashgate, 2014.

Davis, Natalie Zemon. "Women in the Crafts in Sixteenth-Century Lyons." In *Women and Work in Preindustrial Europe*, edited by Barbara A. Hanawalt, 167–97. Bloomington: Indiana University Press, 1986.

De Divitiis, Gigliola Pagano. *English Merchants in Seventeenth-Century Italy*. Translated by Stephen Parkin. Cambridge, UK: Cambridge University Press, 1997

De Roover, Raymond. *The Bruges Money Market around 1400*. Brussels: Paleis der Academiën, 1968.

———. "Cambium ad Venetias: Contribution to the History of Foreign Exchange." In *Business, Banking, and Economic Thought in Late Medieval and Early Modern Europe*, edited by Julius Kirshner, 239–59. 1957; Chicago: University of Chicago Press, 1974.

———. "The Development of Accounting Prior to Luca Pacioli According to the Account Books of the Medieval Merchants." In *Business, Banking, and Economic Thought in Late Medieval and Early Modern Europe*, edited by Julius Kirshner, 119–80. 1955; Chicago: University of Chicago Press, 1974.

———. "A Florentine Firm of Cloth Manufacturers." In *Business, Banking, and Economic Thought in Late Medieval and Early Modern Europe*, edited by Julius Kirshner, 85–118. 1938; Chicago: University of Chicago Press, 1974.

———. "A Florentine Firm of Cloth Manufacturers." *Speculum* 16, no. 1 (1941): 3–33.

———. "Labour Conditions in Florence around 1400: Theory, Policy, and Reality." In *Florentine Studies: Politics and Society in Renaissance Florence*, edited by Nicolai Rubinstein, 277–313. Evanston, IL: Northwestern University Press, 1968.

———. "Monopoly Theory Prior to Adam Smith: A Revision." In *Business, Banking, and Economic Thought in Late Medieval and Early Modern Europe*, edited by Julius Kirshner, 273–305. 1951; Chicago: University of Chicago Press, 1974.

———. *The Rise and Decline of the Medici Bank, 1397–1494*. Cambridge, MA: Harvard University Press, 1963.

———. "The Story of the Alberti Company of Florence, 1302–1348." In *Business, Banking, and Economic Thought in Late Medieval and Early Modern Europe*, edited by Julius Kirshner, 39–84. Chicago: University of Chicago Press, 1974.

de Vries, Jan. *European Urbanization 1500–1800*. Cambridge, MA: Harvard University Press, 1984.

———. *The Industrious Revolution: Consumer Behavior and the Household Economy, 1650 to the Present*. Cambridge, UK: Cambridge University Press, 2008.

———. "Renaissance Cities." *Renaissance Quarterly* 142, no. 4 (1989): 781–93.

de Vries, Jan, and A. van der Woude. *The First Modern Economy: Success, Failure, and Perseverance of the Dutch Economy, 1500–1815*. Cambridge, UK: Cambridge University Press, 1997.

Dear, Michael J., ed. *From Chicago to L.A.: Making Sense of Urban Theory*. Thousand Oaks, CA: Sage, 2002.

Dei, Benedetto. *La cronica*. Eited by Roberto Barducci. Florence: Papafava, 1984.

Della Valentina, Marcello. " 'Parone': Donne alla guida di una bottega artigiana a Venezia nel '700.' " In *Donne, lavoro, economia a Venezia e in Terrafirma tra medioevo ed età moderna*, edited by Anna Bellavitis and Linda Guzzetti, *Archivio veneto* 143 (2012): 145–64.

Demo, Edoardo. "L'industria tessile nel Veneto tra XV e XVI secolo: Tecnologie e innovazione dei prodotti." In *Dalla corporazione alla società di mutuo soccorso*, edited by Paola Massa and Angelo Moioli, 329–41. Milan: Franco Angeli 2004.

Dini, Bruno. "L'industria serica in Italia. Secc. XIII–XV." In *Filaseta in Europa, Secc. XIII–XX*, edited by Simonetta Cavaciocchi, 91–123. Florence: Le Monnier 1993.

———. *Manifattura, commercio e banca nella Firenze medievali*. Florence: Nardini, 2001.

Dixon, E. "Craftswomen in the *Livre des Métiers*." *Economic History Review* 5, no. 18 (1895): 209–28.

Dondorp, Harry, and Eltjo J. H. Schrage. "The Sources of Medieval Learned Law." In *The Creation of the "Ius Commune": From "Casus" to "Regula,"* edited by John W. Cairns and Paul J. du Plessis, 7–56. Edinburgh: Edinburgh University Press, 2010.

Dören, Alfred. *Studien aus der Florentiner Wirtschaftgeschichte*. Vol. 1, *Die Florentiner Wollentuchsindustrie vom Vierzehnten bis zum Sechzehnten Jahrhundert*. Stuttgart: J. G. Cotta'sche Buchhandlung Nachfolger, 1901.

———. *Studien aus der Florentiner Wirtschaftgeschichte*. Vol. 2, *Das Florentiner Zunftwesen vom 14 bis zum 16 Jahrhundert*. Stuttgart: J. G. Cotta'sche Buchhandlung Nachfolger, 1908.

Dougherty, Ann, and Robert Van Order. "Inflation, Housing Costs, and the Consumer Price Index." *American Economic Review* 72, no. 1 (1982): 154–64.

Douglas, Paul H. *Real Wages in the United States: 1890 to 1926*. Boston: Houghton Mifflin Co. 1930.

Drancourt, M., G. Aboudharam, M. Signoli, O. Dutour and D. Raoult. "Detection of 400-Year-Old *Yersinia pestis* DNA in Human Dental Pulp: An Approach to the Diagnosis of Ancient Septicemia." *Proceedings of the National Academy of Sciences* 95 (1998): 12637–40.

Droback, John N., and John V. C. Nye, eds., *The Frontiers of the New Institutional Economics*. San Diego: Academic Press, 1997.

Duncan, Otis Dudley, "A Socioeconomic Index for All Occupations." In *Class: Critical Concepts*, vol. 1, edited by John Scott, 388–426, London: Routledge, 1996.

Earenfight, Theresa, ed. *Women and Wealth in Late Medieval Europe*. New York: Palgrave MacMillan, 2010.

Eckert, Edward A. "Seasonality of Plague in Early Modern Europe: Swiss Epidemic of 1628–1630." *Clinical Infectious Diseases* 2, no. 6 (1980): 952–59.

Eckstein, Nicholas A. "Addressing Wealth in Renaissance Florence: Some New Soundings from the Catasto of 1427." *Journal of Urban History* 32, no. 5 (2006): 711–28.

———. *The District of the Green Dragon: Neighbourhood Life and Social Change in Renaissance Florence*. Florence: Olschki, 1995.

———. "The Neighborhood as Microcosm of the Social Order." In *Renaissance Florence: A Social History*, edited by Roger J. Crum and John T. Paoletti, 219–39. New York: Cambridge University Press, 2006.

Edler, Florence. *Glossary of Medieval Terms of Business: Italian Series, 1200–1600*. Medieval Academy of America. 1934; New York: Kraus Reprint Co., 1970.

———. *The Silk Trade of Lucca during the Thirteenth and Fourteenth Centuries*. PhD diss., University of Chicago, 1930.

Edler de Roover, Florence. "Andrea Banchi, Florentine Silk Manufacturer and Merchant of the Fifteenth Century." *Studies in Medieval and Renaissance History* 3 (1966): 225–83.

———. *L'arte della seta a Firenze nei secoli XIV e XV*. Florence: Olschki, 1999.

Eggertsson, Thráinn. *Economic Behavior and Institutions*. Cambridge, UK: Cambridge University Press, 1990.

Ehmer, Josef. "Artisans Journeymen, Guilds and Labor Markets: Thinking about European Comparative Practices." In *Dalla corporazione alla società di mutuo soccorso*, edited by Paola Massa and Angelo Moioli, 57–69. Milan: Franco Angeli 2004.

Ekelund, Robert B. Jr., and Robert D. Tollison. *Mercantilism as a Rent-Seeking Society: Economic Regulation in Historical Perspective*. College Station: Texas A&M University Press, 1981.

———. "Mercantilist Origins of the Corporation." *Bell Journal of Economics* 11, no. 2 (1980): 715–20.

Elam, Carolyn. "Lorenzo de' Medici and the Urban Development of Renaissance Florence." *Art History* 1 (1978): 43–66.

Ell, S. R. "Some Evidence for the Interhuman Transmission of the Medieval Plague." *Review of Infectious Diseases* 1 (1979): 563–66.

Emigh, Rebecca Jean. "Loans and Livestock: Comparing Landlords and Tenants Declarations from the Catasto of 1427." *Journal of European Economic History* 25, no. 2 (1996): 705–23.

———. "Traces of Certainty: Recording Death and Taxes in Fifteenth-Century Tuscany." *Journal of Interdisciplinary History* 30 (1999): 181–98.

———. *The Undevelopment of Capitalism: Sectors and Markets in Fifteenth-Century Tuscany*. Philadelphia: Temple University Press, 2009.

———. "What Influences Official Information? Exploring Aggregate Microhistories of the Catasto of 1427." In *Small Worlds: Method, Meaning, and Narrative in Microhistory*, edited by James F. Brooks, Christopher R. N. DeCorse and John Walton, 199–223. Santa Fe: School for Advanced Research Press, 2008.

Endrei, Walter. "Manufacturing a Piece of Woollen Cloth in Medieval Flanders: How Many Work Hours?". In *Textiles of the Low Countries in European Economic History. Proceedings Tenth International*

Economic History Congress, Leuven, August, 1990, vol. 19. Edited by Erik Aerts, 14–23. Louvain, Belgium: Leuven University Press, 1990.

Ennen, Edith. *Die europäische Stadt des Mittelalters*. Göttingen: Vandenhoeck and Ruprecht, 1979.

———. *Frühgeschichte der europäischen stadt*. Bonn: Ludwig Röhrscheid, 1953.

———. *The Medieval Town*. New York: North-Holland, 1979.

Epstein, Mordecai. *The Early History of the Levant Company: Its Foundation and Its History to 1640*. New York: Burt Franklin, 1968; London: Routledge and Sons, 1908.

Epstein, Stephan R. "Craft Guilds, Apprenticeship, and Technological Change in Pre-Modern Europe." *Journal of Economic History* 53, no. 3 (1998): 684–713.

———. "Craft Guilds in the Pre-Modern Economy: A Discussion." *Economic History Review* 61, no. 1 (2008): 155–74.

———. *Freedom and Growth: The Rise of States and Markets in Europe, 1300–1750*. London: Routledge, 2000.

———. "The Late Medieval Crisis as an 'Integration Crisis.'" In *Early Modern Capitalism: Economic and Social Change in Europe, 1400–1800*, edited by Maarten Prak, 25–50. London: Routledge, 2001.

———. "Property Rights to Technical Knowledge in Pre-Modern Europe, 1300–1800." *American Economic Review* 94, no. 2 (2004): 382–87.

———, ed. *Town and Country in Europe, 1300–1800*. Cambridge, UK: Cambridge University Press, 2001.

Epstein, Stephan R., and Maarten Prak, eds. *Guilds, Innovation, and the European Economy, 1400–1800*. Cambridge, UK: Cambridge University Press, 2008.

———. Introduction to *Guilds, Innovation, and the European Economy, 1400–1800*, edited by Stephan R. Epstein and Maarten Prak, 4–24. Cambridge, UK: Cambridge University Press, 2008.

Epstein, Steven A. "The Family." In *Italy in the Central Middle Ages, 1000–1300*. Oxford, UK: Oxford University Press, 2004.

———. "Labour in Thirteenth-Century Genoa." *Mediterranean Historical Review* 3 (1988): 114–40.

———. *Wage Labor and Guilds in Medieval Europe*. Chapel Hill: University of North Carolina Press, 1991.

———. *Wills and Wealth in Medieval Genoa: 1150–1250*. Cambridge, MA: Harvard University Press, 1984.

Esposito, Anna. "Perle e coralli: Credito e investimenti delle donne a Roma (XV–inizio XVI secolo)." In *Dare credito alle donne. Presenze femminili nell'economia tra medioevo ed età moderna*, edited by Giovanna Petti Balbi and Paola Guglielmotti, 247–57. Asti, Italy: Centro studi Renato Bordone sui Lombardi, sul credito e sulla banca, 2012.

Fanelli, Giovanni. *Le città nella storia d'Italia: Firenze*. Rome: Laterza, 1981.

Fanfani, Amintore. "Effimera la ripresa economica di Firenze sul finire del secolo XVI?" *Economia e storia* 12 (1965): 344–51.

Fanfani, Tommaso. "The Guilds in Italian Economic Development in the Early Modern Era: Guilty or Innocent?." In *Guilds, Markets and Work Regulations in Italy, 16th–19th Centuries*, edited by Alberto Guenzi, Paola Massa and Fausto Piola Caselli, 409–22. Brookfield, VT: Ashgate Publishing Company, 1998.

Farr, James R. *Artisans in Europe, 1300–1914*. Cambridge, UK: Cambridge University Press, 2000.

Favrier, Jean, ed. *Les contribuables Parisiens a la fin de la guerre de cent ans: Les roles d'impôt de 1421, 1423, et 1438*. Geneva: Libraire Droz, 1970.

Federal Reserve Bank of Minneapolis. "A Widget Example of the Herfindahl-Hirschman Index." *FedGazette*, January 2000. http://research.mpls.frb.fed.us/publications_papers/pub_display.cfm?id=2389.

Felloni, G. "Structural Changes in Urban Industry in Italy from the Late Middle Ages to the Beginning of the Industrial Revolution: A Synthesis." In *The Rise and Decline of Urban Industries in Italy and in the Low Countries*, edited by Herman Van der Wee, 153–60. Louvain, Belgium: Leuven University Press, 1988.

Ferguson, Margaret W., Maureen Quilligan and Nancy J. Vickers, eds. *Rewriting the Renaissance: The Discourses of Sexual Difference in Early Modern Europe* Chicago: University of Chicago Press, 1986.

Ferrie, Joseph P. "The Wealth Accumulation of Antebellum European Immigrants to the U.S., 1840–60." *Journal of Economic History* 54, no. 1 (1994): 1–33.

Fischel, William A. "Property Taxation and the Tiebout Model: Evidence for the Benefit View from Zoning and Voting." *Journal of Economic Literature* 30, no. 1 (1992): 171–77.

Fishback, Price, Jonathan Rose and Kenneth Snowden. *How the New Deal Safeguarded Home Ownership.* Chicago: University of Chicago Press, 2013.

Fisher, F. J. "Some Experiments in Company Organization in the Early Seventeenth Century." *Economic History Review* 4, no. 2 (1933): 177–94.

Fisher, Irving. *The Nature of Capital and Income.* New York: Macmillan, 1906.

Fisher, J. "Income, Spending, and Saving Patterns of Consumer Units in Different Age Groups." In *Studies in Income and Wealth*, vol. 15. New York: National Bureau of Economic Research, 1952.

Fiumi, Enrico. "Fioritura e decadenza dell'economia fiorentina." *Archivio storico Italiano* 115 (1957): 385–439; 116 (1958): 443–510; 117 (1959): 427–502.

———. "L'imposta diretta nei comuni medioevali della Toscana." In *Studi in onore di A. Sapori*, 327–53. Milan: Cisalpino, 1957.

Floud, Roderick, Robert W. Fogel, Bernard Harris and Sok Chul Hong. *The Changing Body: Health, Nutrition, and Human Development in the Western World since 1700.* Cambridge, UK: Cambridge University Press, 2011.

Fogel, Robert W. "The Specification Problem in Economic History." *Journal of Economic History* 27, no. 3 (1967): 283–308.

Fogel, Robert W. and G. R. Elton, *Which Road to the Past: Two Views of History*. New Haven, CT: Yale University Press, 1983.

Fontaine, Laurence. *History of Pedlars in Europe.* Translated by Vicki Whittaker. Durham, NC: Duke University Press, 1996.

Fontana, Giovanni Luigi, and Gérard Gayot, eds. *Wool: Products and Markets (13th–20th Century).* Padua: CLEUP, 2004.

Franceschi, Franco. *Oltre il "Tumulto": I lavoratori fiorentini dell'Arte della Lana fra Tre e Quattrocento.* Florence: Olschki, 1993.

Franceschi, Francesco, and Luca Mola. "Regional States and Economic Development." In *The Italian Renaissance State*, edited by Andrea Gamberini and Isabella Lazzarini, 444–66. Cambridge, UK: Cambridge University Press, 2012.

Franchetti-Pardo, Vittorio. "Cultura brunelleschiana e trasformazioni urbanistiche nella Firenze del Quattrocento." In *Storia dell'urbanistica: Dal Trecento al Quattrocento*, edited by P. Ruschi, G. C. Romby and M. Tarassi, 87–98. Florence: Vallecchi, 1979.

———. *Storia dell; urbanistica: Dal Trecento al Quattrocento* (Bari, Italy: Laterza, 1994.

Furubotn, Eirik G., and Rudolf Richter. *Institutions and Economic Theory: The Contribution of the New Institutional Economics.* Ann Arbor: University of Michigan Press, 2000.

Fuss, D., and D. McFadden. *Production Economics: A Dual Approach to Theory and Applications.* Amsterdam: North-Holland, 1978.

Galenson, David W. "Economic Opportunity on the Urban Frontier: Nativity, Work, and Wealth in Early Chicago." *Journal of Economic History* 51, no. 3 (1991): 581–603.

Galenson, David W., and Clayne L. Pope. "Economic and Geographic Mobility on the Farming Frontier: Evidence from Appanoose County, Iowa, 1850–1870." *Journal of Economic History* 49, no. 4 (1989): 635–55.

———. "Precedence and Wealth: Evidence from Nineteenth-Century Utah." In *Strategic Factors in Nineteenth-Century American Economic History: A Volume to Honor Robert W. Fogel*, edited by Claudia Goldin and Hugh Rockoff, 225–42. Chicago: University of Chicago Press, 1993.

Gamberini, Andrea, and Isabella Lazzarini. Introduction to *The Italian Renaissance State*, edited by Andrea Gamberini and Isabella Lazzarini, 1–6. Cambridge, UK: Cambridge University Press, 2012.

————, eds. *The Italian Renaissance State*. Cambridge, UK: Cambridge University Press, 2012.

Gargiolli, Girolamo. *L'arte della seta a Firenze Trattato del secolo XV*. Florence: G. Barbera, 1868.

Gaye, Giovanni. *Carteggio inedito d'artisti dei secoli XIV, XV, XV. Vol. 1, 1326–1500*. Florence: Giuseppe Molini, 1839.

Gerard, Hercule, ed. *Paris sous Philippe le Bel*. 1837; Tübingen, Germany: Max Niemeyer, 1991.

Geremek, Bronislaw. *Le Salariat dans L'artisanat Parisien aux XIIIᵉ–XVᵉ Siècles*. Paris: Mouton, 1968.

Glezen, W. Paul, Robert B. Couch and Howard R. Six. "The Influenza Herald Wave." *American Journal of Epidemiology* 116, no. 4 (1982): 589–98.

Goldberg, P. J. P. *Women, Work, and Life Cycle in a Medieval Economy: Women in York and Yorkshire, ca. 1300–1520*. Oxford, UK: Clarendon Press, 1992.

Goldin, Claudia. "A Grand Gender Convergence: Its Last Chapter." *American Economic Review* 104, no. 4 (2014): 1091–119.

————. "The U-Shaped Female Labor Force Function in Economic Development and Economic History." In *Investment in Women's Human Capital*, edited by T. Paul Schultz, 61–90. Chicago: University of Chicago Press, 1995.

Goldin, Claudia, and Lawrence Katz. *The Race Between Education and Technology*, (Cambridge, MA: Harvard University Press, 2008).

Goldthwaite, Richard A. *The Building of Renaissance Florence*. Baltimore: Johns Hopkins University Press, 1980.

————. *The Economy of Renaissance Florence*. Baltimore: Johns Hopkins University Press, 2009.

————. "The Economy of Renaissance Italy: The Preconditions for Luxury Consumption." *I Tatti Studies* 2 (1987): 15–39.

————. "An Entrepreneurial Silk Weaver in Renaissance Florence." *I Tatti Studies* 10 (2005): 69–126.

————. "The Florentine Palace as Domestic Architecture." *American Historical Review* 77, no. 4 (1972): 977–1012.

————. "The Florentine Wool Industry in the Late Sixteenth Century: A Case Study." *Journal of European Economic History* 32, no. 3 (2003): 527–54.

————. "L'interno del Palazzo e il consume dei beni." In *Palazzo Strozzi metà millennio, 1489–1989: Atti del convegno di studi, Firenze, 3–6 luglio 1989*. Rome: Istituto della Enciclopedia Italiana, 1991, 159–66.

————. *Private Wealth in Renaissance Florence: A Study of Four Families*. Princeton, NJ: Princeton University Press, 1968.

————. *Wealth and the Demand for Art in Italy, 1300–1600*. Baltimore: Johns Hopkins University Press, 1993.

Goldthwaite, Richard A., Enzo Settesoldi and Marco Spallanzani, eds. *Due Libri Mastri degli Alberti: Una grande compagnia di Calimala 1348–1358*. 2 vols. Florence: Cassa di Risparmio di Firenze, 1995.

Gombrich, H. M. "The Early Medici as Patrons of Art." In *Italian Renaissance Studies*, edited by Ernest Fraser Jacob, 279–311. London: Faber and Faber, 1960.

Goodman, Jordan. "Financing Pre-modern European Industry: An Example from Florence 1580–1660." *Journal of European Economic History* 10, no. 2 (1981): 415–36.

————. "Tuscan Commercial Relations with Europe, 1550–1620: Florence and the European Textile Market." In *Firenze e la Toscana dei Medici nell'Europa del'500*. Vol. 1, *Strumenti e veicoli della cultura relazioni politiche ed economiche*, 327–41. Florence: Leo S. Olschki, 1983.

Goodnight, James H., and T. D. Wallace. "Weaker Criteria and Tests of Linear Restrictions in Regressions." *Econometrica* 42, no. 4 (1972): 699–709.

Goody, Jack. "The Evolution of the Family." In *Household and Family in Past Time*, edited by Peter Laslett and Richard Wall, 103–24. Cambridge, UK: Cambridge University Press, 1972.

Gottardi, Giovanni. "Ruoli della corporazioni artigiane nella promozione dell'innovazione tecnologica." In *Dalla corporazione alla società di mutuo soccorso*, edited by Paola Massa and Angelo Moioli, 275–85. Milan: Franco Angeli 2004.

Greci, Roberto. "Donne e corporazioni: La fluidità di un rapporto." In *Il lavoro delle donne*, edited by Angela Groppi, 71–91. Rome: Laterza, 1996.

Greif, Avner. *Institutions and the Path to the Modern Economy: Lessons from Medieval Trade*. Cambridge, UK: Cambridge University Press, 2005.

Grendler, Paul F. *Schooling in Renaissance Italy: Literacy and Learning, 1300–1600*. Baltimore: Johns Hopkins University Press, 1989.

Groppi, Angela. "Introduzione." In *Il lavoro delle donne*, edited by Angela Groppi, v–xvi. Rome: Laterza, 1996.

———, ed. *Il lavoro delle donne*. Rome: Laterza, 1996.

Guenzi, Alberto, and Paola Massa. "Introduction." In *Guilds, Markets and Work Regulations in Italy, 16th–19th Centuries*, edited by Alberto Guenzi, Paola Massa and Fausto Piola Caselli, 1–15. Brookfield, VT: Ashgate Publishing Company, 1998.

Guenzi, Alberto, Paola Massa and Fausto Piola Caselli, eds. *Guilds, Markets and Work Regulations in Italy, 16th–19th Centuries*. Brookfield, VT: Ashgate Publishing Company, 1998.

Guidi, Guidubaldo. *Il Governo della città-repubblica di Firenze del primo Quattrocento*. 3 vols. Florence: Leo S. Olschki, 1981.

Gurrieri, Francesco, and Patrizia Fabbri. *Palaces of Florence*. New York: Rizzoli, 1996.

Gustafsson, Bo. "The Rise and Economic Behaviour of Medieval Craft Guilds." In *Power and Economic Institutions*, edited by Bo Gustafsson, 69–106. Aldershot, UK: Edward Elgar, 1991.

Guzzetti, Linda. "Gli investimenti delle donne veneziane nel medioevo." In *Donne, lavoro, economia a Venezia e in Terraferma tra medioevo ed età moderna*, edited by Anna Bellavitis and Linda Guzzetti, *Archivio veneto* 143 (2012): 41–66.

Hajnal, J. "European Marriage Patterns in Perspective." In *Population in History: Essays in Historical Demography*, edited by D. V. Glass and D.E.C. Eversley, 101–43. London: E. Arnold, 1965.

Hamilton, James D. *Time Series Analysis*. Princeton, NJ: Princeton University Press, 1994.

Hanawalt, Barbara A. Introduction to *Women and Work in Preindustrial Europe*, edited by Barbara A. Hanawalt, vii–xviii. Bloomington: Indiana University Press, 1986.

———. "Peasant Women's Contribution to the Home Economy in Late Medieval England." In *Women and Work in Preindustrial Europe*, edited by Barbara A. Hanawalt, 3–19. Bloomington: Indiana University Press, 1986.

———. *The Wealth of Wives: Women, Law, and Economy in Late Medieval London*. Oxford, UK: Oxford University Press, 2007.

———, ed. *Women and Work in Preindustrial Europe*. Bloomington: Indiana University Press, 1986.

Hao, Lingxin. "Wealth of Immigrant and Native-Born Americans." *International Migration Review* 38, no. 2 (2004): 518–46.

Hardy, Charles Oscar. *Risk and Risk Bearing*, 2nd ed. Chicago: University of Chicago Press, 1931.

Harris, Chauncy D., and Edward L. Ullman. "The Nature of Cities." *Annals of the American Academy of Political and Social Science* 242, no. 1 (1945): 7–17.

Harte, N. B., ed. *The New Draperies in the Low Countries and England, 1300–1800*. Oxford, UK: Oxford University Press, 1997.

Hayami, Yujiro. "Induced Innovation, Green Revolution, and Income Distribution: Comment." *Economic Development and Cultural Change* 30, no. 1 (1981): 169–76.

Heckman, James J. "A Life Cycle Model of Earnings, Learning, and Consumption." *Journal of Political Economy* 84, no. 4, pt. 2 (1976): S11–44.

Henderson, John. "The Black Death in Florence: Medical and Communal Responses." In *Death in Towns: Urban Responses to the Dying and the Dead, 100–1600*, edited by Stephen Bassett, 136–50. London: Leicester University Press, 1992.

———. "Historians and Plagues in Pre-Industrial Italy over the 'longue durée.'" *History and Philosophy of the Life Sciences* 25, no. 4 (2003): 481–99.

———. "The Parish and the Poor in Florence at the time of the Black Death: The Case of S. Frediano." *Continuity and Change* 3, no. 2 (1988): 247–72.

Herlihy, David. *The Black Death and the Transformation of the West*, edited by Samuel K. Cohn Jr. Cambridge, MA: Harvard University Press, 1997.

———. "Deaths, Marriages, Births, and the Tuscan Economy." In *Population Patterns in the Past*, edited by R. D. Lee, 135–64. Cambridge, UK: Cambridge University Press, 1977.

———. "Did Women Have a Renaissance?" In *Women, Family, and Society in Medieval Europe: Historical Essays, 1978–1991*, edited by Anthony Molho, 33–56. Providence, RI: Berghahn Books, 1995.

———. "Marriage at Pistoia in the Fifteenth Century." In *Cities and Society in Medieval Italy*. London: Variorum, 1980, sec. 6.

———. *Opera Muliebria: Women and Work in Medieval Europe*. Philadelphia: Temple University Press, 1990.

———. "Quantification and the Middle Ages." In *The Dimensions of the Past. Materials, Problems, and Opportunities for Quantitative Work in History*, edited by Val Lorwin and J. M. Price, 13–51. New Haven, CT: Yale University Press, 1972.

———. "Women and Sources of Medieval History: The Towns of Northern Italy." In *Women, Family, and Society in Medieval Europe: Historical Essays, 1978–1991*, edited by Anthony Molho, 13–32. Providence, RI: Berghahn Books, 1995.

———. *Women, Family and Society in Medieval Europe: Historical Essays, 1978–1991*, edited by Anthony Molho. Providence, RI: Berghahn Books, 1995.

Herlihy, David, and Christiane Klapisch-Zuber. *Census and Property Survey of Florentine Domains and the City of Verona in Fifteenth-Century Italy* [machine-readable data file]. Cambridge, MA: David Herlihy, Harvard University, Department of History and Paris, France: Christiane Klapisch-Zuber, Ecole Pratique des Hautes Etudes [producers], 1977. Madison: University of Wisconsin, Data and Program Library Service [distributor], 1981.

———. *Les Toscans et leurs familles: Une étude du Catasto Florentine de 1427*. Paris: Fondation nationale des sciences politiques, 1978.

———. *The Tuscans and Their Families*. New Haven, CT: Yale University Press, 1985.

Hicks, John R. "Liquidity." *Economic Journal* 72, no. 288 (1962): 787–802.

Hickson C. R., and E. A. Thompson. "A New Theory of Guilds and European Economic Development." *Explorations in Economic History* 28, no. 1 (1991): 127–68.

Hirshleifer, J. *Investment, Interest, and Capital*. Englewood Cliffs, NJ: Prentice-Hall, 1970.

Hocquet, Jean-Claude. "À Venise, dette publique et speculations privées." In *L'impôt dans les villes de l'Occident méditerranéen XIIIe–XVe siècle, Colloque tenu à Bercy les 3, 4, et 5 octobre 2001*, edited by Denis Menjot, Albert Rigaudière and Manuel Sánchez Martínez, 15–37. Paris: Comité pour l'Histoire Économique et Financière de la France, 2005.

Hoffman, Philip T., and Kathryn Norberg, eds. *Fiscal Crises, Liberty, and Representative Government, 1450–1789*. Stanford, CA: Stanford University Press, 1993.

Homer, Sidney. *A History of Interest Rates*. New Brunswick, NJ: Rutgers University Press, 1963.

Homer, Sidney, and Richard Sylla. *A History of Interest Rates*, 4th ed. Hoboken, NJ: Wiley, 2005.

Honeyman, Katrina, and Jordan Goodman. "Women's Work, Gender Conflict, and Labour Markets in Europe, 1500–1900." *Economic History Review* 44, no. 4 (1991): 608–28.

Horrell, Sara, Jane Humphries and Ken Sneath. "Consumption Conundrums Unravelled." *Economic History Review* 68, no. 3 (2015): 830–57.

Hoshino, Hidetoshi. *L'arte della lana nel basso medioevo in commercio della lana e il mercato dei panni fiorentini nei secoli XIII–XV*. Florence: Olschki, 1980.

———. *Industria tessile e commercio internazionale nella Firenze del tardo medioevo*. Florence: Leo S. Olschki, 2001.

———. "The Rise of the Florentine Woollen Industry in the Fourteenth Century." In *Cloth and Clothing in Medieval Europe. Essays in Memory of E. M. Carus-Wilson*, edited by N. B. Harte and K. G. Ponting, 1852–04. London: Heineman Educational Books, 1983.

Howard, Peter. "Preaching Magnificence in Renaissance Florence." *Renaissance Quarterly* 61, no. 2 (2008): 325–69.

Howell, Martha C. *Commerce before Capitalism in Europe, 1300–1600*. Cambridge, UK: Cambridge University Press, 2010.

———. *Women, Production, and Patriarchy in Late Medieval Cities*. Chicago: University of Chicago Press, 1986.

———., "Women, the Family Economy, and the Structures of Market Production in Cities of Northern Europe during the Late Medieval Ages." In *Women and Work in Preindustrial Europe*, edited by Barbara A. Hanawalt, 198–222. Bloomington: Indiana University Press, 1986

Hoyt, Homer. *The Structure and Growth of Residential Neighborhoods in American Cities*. Washington, DC: Federal Housing Administration, 1939.

Huang, Angela Ling, and Carsten Jahnke, eds. *Textiles and the Medieval Economy: Production, Trade and Consumption of Textiles 8th–16th Centuries*. Oxford, UK: Oxbow Books, 2015.

Hughes, Diane Owen. "La famiglia e le donne nel Rinascimento fiorentino." *Quaderni storici* 24 (1989): 629–34.

———. "Urban Growth and Family Structure in Medieval Genoa." *Past and Present* no. 66 (1975): 3–28.

Hutaserani, Suganya, and James Roumasset. "Institutional Change and the Demographic Transition in Rural Thailand." *Economic Development and Cultural Change* 40, no. 1 (1991): 75–100.

Hyman, Isabelle. *Fifteenth-Century Florentine Studies: The Palazzo Medici and a Ledger for the Church of San Lorenzo*. New York: Garland, 1977.

Ildefonso il San Luigi. *Delizie degli eruditi toscani*. Vol. 16, *Stefani Marchionne di Coppo, Istoria fiorentina*. Florence: Gaetano Cambiagi, 1783.

Isenberg, Sasha. *The Victory Lab: The Secret Science of Winning Campaigns*. New York: Crown Publishers, 2012.

Jacob, Margaret C. *The First Knowledge Economy: Human Capital and the European Economy, 1750–1850*. Cambridge, UK: Cambridge University Press, 2014.

Jardine, Lisa. *Worldly Goods: A New History of the Renaissance*. New York: W. W. Norton, 1996.

Jehel, Georges. "'Le rôle des femmes et du milieu familial a Gênes dans les activités commercials." *Revue de l'histoire économique et sociale* 53 (1975): 193–215.

Jenks, Stuart. "The Missing Link: The Distribution Revolution of the 15th Century." In *Textiles and the Medieval Economy: Production, Trade and Consumption of Textiles 8th–16th Centuries*, edited by Angela Ling Huang and Carsten Jahnke, 230–52 Oxford, UK: Oxbow Books, 2015.

Jones, Alice Hanson. *Wealth of a Nation to Be: The American Colonies on the Eve of the Revolution*. New York: Columbia University Press, 1980.

Jones, Philip J. "Communes and Despots: The City-State in Late Medieval Italy." *Transactions of the Royal Historical Society*, 5th series, 15 (1965): 71–96.

———. "From Manor to Mezzadria: A Tuscan Case Study in the Medieval Origins of Modern Agrarian Society." In *Florentine Studies, Politics, and Society in Renaissance Florence*, edited by Nicolai Rubinstein, 193–241. London: Faber and Faber, 1968.

Jones, S. R. H., and Simon P. Ville. "Efficient Transactors or Rent-Seeking Monopolists? The Rationale for Early Chartered Trading Companies." *Journal of Economic History* 56, no. 4 (1996): 898–916.

Judge, George G., W. E. Griffiths, R. Carter Hill, Helmut Lütkepohl and Tsoung-Chao Lee. *The Theory and Practice of Econometrics*, 2nd ed. New York: Wiley, 1985.

Karmin, Otto. *La legge del Catasto fiorentino del 1427 (Testo, introduzione, e note)*. Florence: Bernardo Seeber, 1906.

Kearl, J. R., and Clayne L. Pope. "Choices, Rents, and Luck: Economic Mobility of Nineteenth-Century Utah Households." In *Long-Term Factors in American Economic Growth*, edited by Stanley L. Engerman and Robert E. Gallman, 215–60. Chicago: University of Chicago Press, 1986.

Kearl, J. R., Clayne L. Pope and Larry T. Wimmer. "Household Wealth in a Settlement Community." *Journal of Economic History* 40, no. 3 (1980): 477–96.

Kedar, Benjamin Z. "The Genoese Notaries of 1382: The Anatomy of an Urban Occupational Group." In *The Medieval City*, edited by Harry D. Miskimin, David Herlihy and A. L. Udovitch, 73–94. New Haven, CT: Yale University Press, 1977.

Keene, Derek. "The Early History of English Guilds: Their Role in Social and Economic Organisation." In *Dalla corporazione alla società di mutuo soccorso*, edited by Paola Massa and Angelo Moioli, 71–85. Milan: Franco Angeli 2004.

Keister, Lisa A. *Wealth in America: Trends in Wealth Inequality*. Cambridge, UK: Cambridge University Press, 2000.

Kelly-Gadol, Joan. "Did Women Have a Renaissance?" In *Becoming Visible: Women in European History*, edited by Renate Bridenthal and Claudia Koonz, 137–64. Boston: Houghton Mifflin, 1977.

Kent, Dale V. *Cosimo de' Medici and the Florentine Renaissance: The Patron's Oeuvre*. New Haven, CT: Yale University Press, 2000.

———— "The Florentine *Reggimento* in the Fifteenth Century." *Renaissance Quarterly* 28 (1975): 624–32.

Kent, Dale V., and Francis William Kent. *Neighbours and Neighbourhood in Renaissance Florence: The District of the Red Lion in the Fifteenth Century*. Locust Valley, NY: J. J. Augustin, 1982.

Kent, Francis W. *Bartolomeo Cederini and His Friends: Letters to an Obscure Florentine*. Florence: Olschki, 1991.

————. "La famiglia patrizia fiorentina nel Quattrocento: Nuovi orientamenti nella storiografia recente." In *Palazzo Strozzi metà millennio, 1489–1989: Atti del convegno di studi, Firenze, 3–6 luglio 1989*. Rome: Istituto della Enciclopedia Italiana, 1991, 70–91.

————. *Household and Lineage in Renaissance Florence*. Princeton, NJ: Princeton University Press, 1977.

————. "Palaces, Politics, and Society in Fifteenth-Century Florence." *I Tatti Studies* 2 (1987): 41–70.

King, M. A., and L-D. L. Dicks-Mireaux. "Asset Holding and the Life-Cycle." *Economic Journal* 92 (1982): 247–67.

Kirshner, Julius. "Angelo degli Ubaldi and Bartolomeo Saliceto." *Rivista Internazionale di Diritto Comune* 14 (2003): 83–117.

————. "Authority, Reason, and Conscience in Gregory of Rimini's *Questio prestitorum communis Venetiarum*." In *Reichtum im späten Mittelalter. Politische Theorie, ethische Norm und soziale Akzeptanz (voraussichtlich: Vierteljahrschrift für Sozial- und Wirtschaftsgeschichte. Beihefte)*, edited by Petra Schulte and Peter Hesse, 115–43. Stuttgart: Franz Steiner, 2015.

————. "Custom, Customary Law, and Ius Commune in Francesco Guicciardini." *Bologna nell'età di Carlo V e Guicciardini* (2002): 163–76.

————. "Encumbering Private Claims to Public Debt in Renaissance Florence." In *The Growth of the Bank as Institution and the Development of Money-Business Laws*, edited by V. Piergiovanni, 19–75. Berlin: Duncker & Humblot, 1993.

————. "Introduction: The State Is 'Back in.'" *Journal of Modern History, Supplement: The Origins of the State in Italy, 1300–1600* 67 (1995): S1–10.

————. *Marriage, Dowry, and Citizenship in Late Medieval and Renaissance Italy*. Toronto: University of Toronto Press, 2015.

————. "The Morning After: Collecting Monte Dowries in Renaissance Florence." In *From Florence to the Mediterranean and Beyond: Essays in Honor of Anthony Molho*, edited by Diogo Ramada Curto, Eric R. Dusteler, Julius Kirshner and Francesca Trivellato, 1: 29–61. Florence: Olschki, 2009.

————. "Review of *Industry and Decline in Seventeenth-Century Venice*, by Richard Tilden Rapp." *Journal of Modern History* 49, no. 2 (1977): 319–21.

————. "Review of *Plague and the Poor in Renaissance Florence*, by Ann G. Carmichael." *Journal of Modern History* 59, no. 4 (1987): 870–73.

————. "States of Debt." Paper presented at *Mellon Sawyer Seminar on Debt, Sovereignty, and Power*, University of Cambridge, 2006.

————. "'Ubi est ille?' Franco Sacchetti and the Monte Comune of Florence." *Speculum* 59, no. 3 (1984): 556–84.

————. "Women Married Elsewhere: Gender and Citizenship in Italy." In *Time, Space, and Women's Lives in Early Modern Europe*, edited by Anne Jacobson Schutte, Thomas Kuehn and Silvana Seidel Menchi, 117–49. Kirksville, MO: Truman State University Press, 2001.

Kirshner, Julius, and Jacob Klerman. "The Seven Percent Fund of Renaissance Florence." In *Banchi pubblici, banchi private e monti di pieta nell'Europa preindustriale: Amministrazione, tecniche operative e ruoli economici: Atti del convegno internazionale*, Genova, 1–6 ottobre 1990, 1: 367–98. Genova: Società Ligure di Storia Patria, 1991.

Kirshner, Julius, and Anthony Molho. "The Dowry Fund and the Marriage Market in Early *Quattrocento* Florence." *Journal of Modern History* 50 (1978): 403–38.

Kirshner, Julius, and Suzanne F. Wemple, eds. *Women of the Medieval World: Essays in Honor of John H. Mundy*. Oxford, UK: Basil Blackwell, 1985.

Kisch, Herbert. *From Domestic Manufacture to Industrial Revolution: The Case of the Rhineland Textile Districts*. New York: Oxford University Press, 1989.

Klapisch-Zuber Christiane. "Le Catasto florentin et le modele europeen du marriage et de la famille." In *Les cadastres anciens des villes et leur traitement par l'informatique*, edited by J. L. Bbiget, J. C. Herve and Y. Tachert, 21–31. Rome: Collection de Ecole Francaise de Romes, 1989.

———. "The 'Cruel Mother': Maternity, Widowhood, and Dowry in Florence in the Fourteenth and Fifteenth Centuries." In *Women, Family, and Ritual in Renaissance Italy*. Translated by Lydia G. Cochrane, 117–31. Chicago: University of Chicago Press, 1985.

———. "Household and Family in Tuscany in 1427." In *Household and Family in Past Time*, edited by Peter Laslett and Richard Wall, 267–81. Cambridge, UK: Cambridge University Press, 1972.

———. "State and Family in a Renaissance Society: The Florentine *Catasto* of 1427–30." In *Women, Family, and Ritual in Renaissance Italy*. Translated by Lydia G. Cochrane, 1–22. Chicago: University of Chicago Press, 1985.

———. *Women, Family, and Ritual in Renaissance Italy*. Translated by Lydia G. Cochrane. Chicago: University of Chicago Press, 1985.

———. "Women Servants in Florence during the Fourteenth and Fifteenth Centuries." In *Women and Work in Preindustrial Europe*, edited by Barbara A. Hanawalt, 56–80. Bloomington: Indiana University Press, 1986.

Klein, Julius. *The Mesta: A Study in Spanish Economic History, 1273–1836*. Cambridge, MA: Harvard University Press, 1920

Knapp, Michael. "The Next Generation of Genetic Investigations into the Black Death." *Proceedings of the National Academy of Sciences* 108, no. 38 (2011): 15669–70.

Knight, Frank H. *Risk, Uncertainty, and Profit*, 4th ed. 1921; 1957; Mineola, NY: Dover, 2006.

Kowaleski, Maryanne. "Women's Work in a Market Town: Exeter in the Late Fourteenth Century." In *Women and Work in Preindustrial Europe*, edited by Barbara A. Hanawalt, 145–64. Bloomington: Indiana University Press, 1986.

Kriedte, Peter, Hans Medick and Jürgen Schlumbohm. *Industrialization before Industrialization*. Translated by Beate Schempp. Cambridge, UK: Cambridge University Press, 1981; orig. German, 1977.

Kuehn, Thomas. "Daughters, Mothers, Wives, and Widows: Women as Legal Persons." In *Time, Space, and Women's Lives in Early Modern Europe*, edited by Anne Jacobson Schutte, Thomas Kuehn and Silvana Seidel Menchi, 97–115. Kirksville, MO: Truman State University Press, 2001.

———. *Heirs, Kin, and Creditors in Renaissance Florence*. Cambridge, UK: Cambridge University Press, 2008.

———. *Law, Family, and Women: Toward a Legal Anthropology of Renaissance Italy*. Chicago: University of Chicago Press, 1991.

Kuznets, Simon. "Economic Growth and Income Inequality," *American Economic Review* 45, no. 1 (1955): 1–28.

La Roncière, Charles M. de. *Un changeur florentin du Trecento: Lippo di Fede di Sega (1285 env.–1363 env.)*. Paris: S.E.V.P.E.N., 1973.

———. *Florence centre économique regional au XIVe siècle*. Vol. 1, *Le marché des denrées de première nécessité à Florence et dans sa champagne et les conditions de vie des salariés (1320–1380)*. Aix-en-Provence: S.O.D.E.B., 1976.

———. *Florence centre économique regional au XIVe siècle*. Vol. 2, *Formation des prix et des salaires a Florence: Les éléments de la conjoncture locale*. Aix-en-Provence: S.O.D.E.B., 1976.

————. *Florence centre économique regional au XIVe siècle.* Vol. 3, *Florence centre d'animation régionale structures et conditions du commerce dans le Contado.* Aix-en-Provence: S.O.D.E.B., 1976.

————. *Florence centre économique regional au XIVe siècle.* Vol. 4, *Notes et documents.* Aix-en-Provence: S.O.D.E.B., 1976.

————. *Florence centre économique regional au XIVe siècle.* Vol. 5, *Sources et bibliography.* Aix-en-Provence: S.O.D.E.B., 1976.

————. "Indirect Taxes or 'Gabelles' at Florence in the Fourteenth Century." In *Florentine Studies: Politics and Society in Renaissance Florence,* edited by Nicolai Rubinstein, 140–92. Evanston, IL: Northwestern University Press, 1968.

————. *Prix et salaires à Florence au 14e siècles: 1280–1380.* Rome: Ecole Française de Rome, 1982.

La Sorsa, Saverio. *L'organizzazione dei cambiatori fiorentini nel Medio Evo.* Cerignola, Italy: Scienza e Diletto, 1904.

Laderman, Elizabeth S. "Changes in the Structure of Urban Banking Markets in the West." *Economic Review Federal Reserve Bank of San Francisco* 1 (1995): 21–34.

LaFontaine, Francine, and Margaret Slade. "Vertical Integration and Firm Boundaries: The Evidence." *Journal of Economic Literature* 45, no. 3 (2007): 629–85.

Laitinen, Riitta, and Dag Lindström. "Urban Order and Street Regulation in Seventeenth-Century Sweden." *Journal of Early Modern History* 12, no. 3 (2008): 257–87.

Lanaro, Paola. "Guild Statutes in the Early Modern Age: Norms and Practices. Preliminary Results in the Veneto Area." In *Guilds, Markets and Work Regulations in Italy, 16th–19th Centuries,* edited by Alberto Guenzi, Paola Massa and Fausto Piola Caselli, 191–207. Brookfield, VT: Ashgate Publishing Company, 1998.

Lancaster, Kelvin J. "A New Approach to Consumer Theory." *Journal of Political Economy* (1966): 132–57.

Landsberger, M. "The Life-Cycle Hypothesis: A Reinterpretation and Empirical Test." *American Economic Review* 60 (1970): 175–84.

Lane, Frederic C., and Reinhold C. Mueller. *Money and Banking in Medieval and Renaissance Venice.* Vol. 1, *Coins and Moneys of Account.* Baltimore: Johns Hopkins University Press, 1985.

Langton, John. "Late Medieval Gloucester: Some Data from a Rental of 1455." *Transactions of the Institute of British Geographers,* new ser. 2 (1977): 259–77.

————. "Residential Patterns in Pre-Industrial Cities: Some Case Studies from Seventeenth-Century Britain." *Transactions of the Institute of British Geographers* 65 (1975): 1–27.

Lansing, John B., and John Sonquist. "A Cohort Analysis of Changes in the Distribution of Wealth." In *Six Papers on the Size Distribution of Income and Wealth,* edited by Lee Soltow, 31–74. New York: National Bureau of Economic Research, 1969.

Laudani, Simona. "Mestieri di donne, mestieri di uomini: Le corporazioni in età moderna." In *Il lavoro delle donne,* edited by Angela Groppi, 183–205. Rome: Laterza, 1996.

Layard, P. R. G., and A. A. Walters. *Microeconomic Theory.* New York: McGraw Hill, 1978.

Leboutte, Rene, ed. *Proto Industrialization: Recent Research and New Perspectives. In Memory of Franklin Mendels.* Geneva: Librarie Droz, 1996.

Levine, David. *Family Formation in an Age of Nascent Capitalism.* New York: Academic Press, 1977.

Lewis, Robert. "The Segregated City: Class Residential Patterns and the Development of Industrial Districts in Montreal, 1861 and 1901." *Journal of Urban History* 17, no. 2 (1991): 123–52.

Lindholm, Richard T. "Studies of the Renaissance Florentine Woolen Industry." PhD diss., University of Chicago, 1993.

Lindert, Peter H., and Jeffrey G. Wiliamson. *Unequal Gains: American Growth and Inequality Since 1700.* Princeton, NJ: Princeton University Press, 2016.

Lindow, James R. *The Renaissance Palace in Florence: Magnificence and Splendour in Fifteenth-Century Italy.* Aldershot, UK: Ashgate, 2007.

Lisci, Leonardo Ginori. *I Palazzi di Firenze nella storia e nell'arte,* 2 vols. Florence: Giunti, 1972.

Litchfield, R. Burr. *Emergence of a Bureaucracy: The Florentine Patricians, 1530–1790*. Princeton, NJ: Princeton University Press, 1986.

———. *Florence Ducal Capital, 1530–1630*. New York: ACLS Humanities E-Book, 2008. http://quod.lib.umich.edu/cgi/t/text/text-idx?c=acls;idno=heb90034.

Little, Lester, *Religious Poverty and the Profit Economy in Medieval Europe*. Ithaca, NY: Cornell University Press, 1978.

Ljungberg, Jonas, and Jan-Pieter Smits, eds. *Technology and Human Capital in Historical Perspective*. Houndmills, UK: Palgrave Macmillan, 2004.

Lopez, Robert S. "Concerning Surnames and Places of Origin." *Medievalia et Humanistica* 8 (1954): 6–16.

———. "Hard Times and Investment in Culture." In *The Renaissance, Medieval or Modern*, edited by Karl H. Dannenfeldt, 50–63. Boston: D. C. Heath, 1959.

Lowder, Stella. *The Geography of Third-World Cities*. Totowa, NJ: Barnes and Noble, 1986.

Lucas, Robert E. Jr. *Lectures on Economic Growth*. Cambridge, MA: Harvard University Press, 2006.

Lucassen, Jan, Piet Lourens and Bert de Munck. "The Distribution of Guilds in the Low Countries, 1000–1800." In *Dalla corporazione alla società di mutuo soccorso*, edited by Paola Massa and Angelo Moioli, 33–56. Milan: Franco Angeli 2004.

Luenberger, David G. *Optimization by Vector Space Methods*. New York: Wiley, 1969.

Lydall, Harold. "The Life Cycle in Income, Saving, and Asset Ownership." *Econometrica* 23, no. 2 (1955): 131–50.

MacDonald, James. *A Free Nation Deep in Debt: The Financial Roots of Democracy*. Princeton, NJ: Princeton University Press, 2003.

Machiavelli, Niccolò. *Florentine History*. Translated by W. K. Marriott. 1909; London: Dent, 1976.

Maclean, Ian. *The Renaissance Notion of Women: A Study of the Fortunes of Scholasticism and Medical Science in European Intellectual Life*. Cambridge, UK: Cambridge University Press, 1980.

Maitte, Corine, and Didier Terrier, eds. *Les temps du travail: Normes, pratiques, évolutions (XIVe–XIXe siècle)*.Rennes: Presses Universitaires de Rennes, 2014.

Malanima, Paolo. *La decadenza di un'economia cittadina: L'industria di Firenze nei secoli XVI–XVIII*. Bologna: Il Mulino, 1982.

———. "An Example of Industrial Reconversion: Tuscany in the Sixteenth and Seventeenth Centuries." In *The Rise and Decline of Urban Industries in Italy and in the Low Countries*, edited by Herman Van der Wee, 63–72. Louvain, Belgium: Leuven University Press, 1988.

———. "L'industria fiorentina in declino fra Cinque e Seicento: Linee per un'analisi comparata." In *Firenze e la Toscana dei Medici nell'Europa del'500*. Vol. 1, *Strumenti e veicoli della cultura relazioni politiche ed economiche*, 295–308. Florence: Leo S. Olschki, 1983.

Markowitz, Harry. "Portfolio Selection." *Journal of Finance* 7 (1952): 77–91.

Marks, L. "The Financial Oligarchy under Lorenzo." In *Italian Renaissance Studies*, edited by Ernest Fraser Jacob, 123–47. London: Faber and Faber, 1960.

Marri, Giulia Camerani, ed. *Statuti dell'arte del cambio di Firenze (1299–1316) con aggiunte e correzioni fino al 1320*. Florence: Olschki, 1955.

Martin, Ian. "On the Valuation of Long-Dated Assets." *Journal of Political Economy* 120, no. 2 (2012): 346–58.

Martin, John L. "The Impact of AIDS on Gay Male Sexual Behavior Patterns in New York City." *American Journal of Public Health* 77 (1987): 578–81.

Martines, Lauro. *Social World of the Florentine Humanists, 1390–1460*. Princeton, NJ: Princeton University Press, 1963.

———. "A Way of Looking at Women in Renaissance Florence." *Journal of Medieval and Renaissance Studies* 4 (1976): 15–28.

Massa, Paola. "The Genoese Guilds in the Sixteenth to the Eighteenth Centuries. The Food Administration Offices and the Food Sector Guilds in Genoa: Organisation and Conflict." In

Guilds, Markets and Work Regulations in Italy, 16th–19th Centuries, edited by Alberto Guenzi, Paola Massa and Fausto Piola Caselli, 246–65. Brookfield, VT: Ashgate Publishing Company, 1998.

———. "Presentazione." In *Dalla corporazione alla società di mutuo soccorso*, edited by Paola Massa and Angelo Moioli, 9–11. Milan: Franco Angeli 2004.

Massa, Paola, and Angelo Moioli, eds. *Dalla corporazione alla società di mutuo soccorso*. Milan: Franco Angeli 2004.

Mazzaoui, Maureen Fennell. *The Italian Cotton Industry in the Later Middle Ages, 1100–1600*. Oxford, UK: Oxford University Press, 1983.

McCloskey, Donald N. "The Open Fields of England: Rent, Risk, and the Rate of Interest, 1300–1815." In *Markets in History: Economic Studies of the Past*, edited by David W. Galenson, 5–51. Cambridge, UK: Cambridge University Press 1989.

McElroy, Marjorie. "Weaker MSE Criteria and Tests for Linear Restriction in Regression Models with Non-Spherical Disturbances." *Journal of Econometrics* 6, no. 3 (1977): 389–94.

McGee, T. G. *The Southeast Asian City*. New York: Praeger, 1967.

McLean, Paul D., and John F. Padgett. "Was Florence a Perfectly Competitive Market? Transactional Evidence from the Renaissance." *Theory and Society* 26, nos. 2/3 (1997): 209–44.

Meese, Richard, and Ken Rogoff. "Empirical Exchange Rate Models of the Seventies: Do They Fit Out of Sample?" *Journal of International Economics* 14 (1983): 3–24.

———. "The Out-of-Sample Failure of Empirical Exchange Rate Models: Sampling Error or Misspecification?" In *Exchange Rates and International Macroeconomics*, edited by Jacob A. Frenkel, 67–112. Chicago: University of Chicago Press, 1983.

———. "Was It Real? The Exchange Rate–Interest Rate Differential Relation over the Modern Floating-Rate Period." *Journal of Finance* 43, no. 4 (1988): 933–48.

Melis, Federigo. *Aspetti della vita economica medievale: Studi nell'Archivio Datini di Prato*. Siena, Italy: Monte dei Paschi di Siena, 1962.

———. *L'azienda nel Medievo*. Florence: Le Monnier, 1991.

———. *Documenti per la storia economica dei secoli XIII–XVI*. Florence: Leo S. Olschki, 1972.

———. *L'economia fiorentina del Rinascimento*. Florence: Le Monnier, 1984.

———. "La formazione dei costi sull'industria laniera alla fine del Trecento." In *Industria e commercio sulla Toscana medieval*, edited by Bruno Dini (Florence: Datini, 1989).

———. *Industria e commercio nella Toscana medievale*. Florence: Le Monnier, 1989.

———. *I mercanti italiani nell'Europa medievale e rinascimentale*. Florence: Le Monnier, 1990.

———. *Storia della ragioneria*. (Bologna: Il Mulino, 1950).

———. *I trasporti e le comunicazioni nel Medioevo*. Florence: Le Monnier, 1985.

Michaelsson, Karl, ed. *Le Livre de la Taille de Paris: L'an 1297*. Göteborg: Elanders Bokriyckeri Aktiebolag, 1962.

———. *Le Livre de la Taille de Paris: L'an 1313*. Göteborg: Werner and Kerbers, 1951.

Mickwitz, G. *Die Kartellfunktionen der Zünfte und ihre Bedeutung bei der Enstehung des Zunftwesens*. Helsinki: Societas scientiarum Fennica, 1936.

Milanovic, Branko, Peter H. Lindert and Jeffrey G. Williamson. "Pre-Industrial Inequality." *Economic Journal* 121, no. 551 (2011): 255–72.

Miller, Edward, and John Hatcher. *Medieval English Towns: Commerce and Crafts, 1086–1548*. London: Longman, 1995.

Mincer, Jacob. *Schooling, Experience, and Earnings*. Chicago: National Bureau of Economic Research, 1974.

Mirer, Thad W. "The Wealth-Age Relation among the Aged." *American Economic Review* 69, no. 3 (1979): 435–43.

Mishkin, Frederic S. *The Economics of Money, Banking, and Financial Markets*, 4th ed. New York: Harper Collins, 1995.

Mocarelli, Luca. "Guilds Reappraised: Italy in the Early Modern Period." *International Review of Social History* 53, no. S16 (2008): 159–78.

Modigliani, Franco, and A. K. Ando. "The 'Life-Cycle' Hypothesis of Saving: Aggregate Implications and Tests." *American Economic Review* 53, no. 1 (1963): 55–84.

Moioli, Angelo. "The Changing Role of the Guilds in the Reorganisation of the Milanese Economy throughout the Sixteenth to Eighteenth Centuries." In *Guilds, Markets and Work Regulations in Italy, 16th–19th Centuries*, edited by Alberto Guenzi, Paola Massa and Fausto Piola Caselli, 32–55. Brookfield, VT: Ashgate Publishing Company, 1998.

———. "I risultati di un'indagine sulle corporazione nell città italiane in età moderna." In *Dalla corporazione alla società di mutuo soccorso*, edited by Paola Massa and Angelo Moioli, 15–31. Milan: Franco Angeli 2004.

Molà, Luca. "Le donne nell'industria serica veneziana del Rinascimento." In *La seta in Italia dal Medioevo al Seicento: Dal baco al drappo*, edited by Luca Molà, Reinhold C. Mueller and Claudio Zanier, 423–60. Venice: Marsilio, 2000.

———. *The Silk Industry of Renaissance Venice*. Baltimore: Johns Hopkins University Press, 2000.

Molho, Anthony. "Créditeurs de Florence en 1347: Un aperçu statistique du quartier de Santo Spirito." In *Firenze nel Quattrocento*. Vol. 1, *Politica e Fiscalità*, 97–112. Rome: Edizioni di Storia Letteratura, 2006.

———. "Deception and Marriage Strategy in Renaissance Florence: The Case of Women's Ages." *Renaissance Quarterly* 41 (1988): 193–217.

———. *Florentine Public Finances in the Early Renaissance, 1400–1433*. Cambridge, MA: Harvard University Press, 1971.

———. *Marriage Alliance in Late Medieval Florence*. Cambridge, MA: Harvard University Press, 1994.

———. "Names, Memory, Public Identity in Late Medieval Florence." In *Firenze nel Quattrocento*. Vol. 2, *Famiglia e Società*, 85–103. Rome: Edizioni di Storia Letteratura, 2008.

———, ed. *Social and Economic Foundations of the Italian Renaissance*. New York: Wiley, 1969.

———. "The State and Public Finance: A Hypothesis Based on the History of Late Medieval Florence." In *Firenze nel Quattrocento*. Vol. 1, *Politica e Fiscalità*, 165–202. Rome: Edizioni di Storia Letteratura, 2006.

———. "The State and Public Finance: A Hypothesis Based on the History of Late Medieval Florence." *Journal of Modern History* 67 (1995): S97–135.

———. "Visions of the Florentine Family in the Renaissance." *Journal of Modern History* 50, no. 2 (1978): 304–11.

Montanari, Paolo, ed. *Documenti su la popolazione di Bologna alla fine dell' Trecento*. Bologna: Istituto per la Storia di Bologna, 1966.

Mori, Attilio, and Giuseppe Boffito. *Firenze nelle vedute e piante: Studio storico topografico cartografico*. Rome: Bonsignori, 1926.

Morrison, Alan S., Julius Kirshner and Anthony Molho. "Epidemics in Renaissance Florence." *American Journal of Public Health* 75, no. 5 (1985): 528–35.

Muellbauer, John. "Household Production Theory, Quality, and the 'Hedonic Technique'." *American Economic Review* 64, no. 6 (1974): 977–94.

Mueller, Reinhold C. *The Venetian Money Market: Banks, Panics, and the Public Debt, 1200–1500*. Baltimore: Johns Hopkins University Press, 1997.

Mumford, Lewis. *The City in History*. New York: Basic Books, 1961.

Munro, John H. "The Dual Crises of the Late-Medieval Florentine Cloth Industry, c. 1320–c. 1420." In *Textiles and the Medieval Economy: Production, Trade and Consumption of Textiles 8th–16th Centuries*, edited by Angela Ling Huang and Carsten Jahnke, 113–48 Oxford, UK: Oxbow Books, 2015.

———. "Industrial Protectionism in Medieval Flanders: Urban or National?". In *The Medieval City*, edited by Harry D. Miskimin, David Herlihy and A. L. Udovitch, 229–67. New Haven, CT: Yale University Press, 1977.

———. "The Medieval Origins of the Financial Revolution: Usury, *Rentes*, and Negotiability." *International History Review* 25, no. 3 (2003): 505–62.

————. "The 'New Institutional Economics' and the Changing Fortunes of Fairs in Medieval and Early Modern Europe: The Textile Trades, Warfare, and Transaction Costs." *VSWG: Vierteljahrschrift für Sozial-und Wirtschaftsgeschichte* 88, no. H. 1 (2001): 1–47.

————. "The Rise, Expansion, and Decline of the Italian Wool-Based Cloth Industries, 1100–1730: A Study in International Competition, Transaction Costs, and Comparative Advantage." *Studies in Medieval and Renaissance History* 9 (2012): 45–207.

————. "Urban Regulation and Monopolistic Competition in the Textile Industries of the Late-Medieval Low Countries." In *Textiles of the Low Countries in European Economic History: Proceedings Tenth International Economic History Congress, Leuven, August, 1990*, vol. 19, edited by Erik Aerts, 41–52. Louvain, Belgium: Leuven University Press, 1990.

Murphy, Kevin M., and Robert H. Topel. "Human Capital Investment, Inequality, and Economic Growth." *Journal of Labor Economics* 34, no. 2, pt. 2 (2016): S1–29.

Muth, Richard F. "Household Production and Consumer Demand Functions." *Econometrica* (1966): 699–708.

Muzzarelli, Maria Giuseppina, Paola Galetti and Bruno Andreolli. *Donne e lavoro nell'Italia medievale.* Turin: Rosenberg and Sellier, 1991.

Nagatani, K. "Life-Cycle Saving: Theory and Fact." *American Economic Review* 62 (1972): 344–53.

Najemy, John M. *Corporatism and Consensus in Florentine Electoral Politics, 1280–1400*. Chapel Hill: University of North Carolina Press, 1982.

————. *A History of Florence, 1200–1575*. Malden, MA: Blackwell, 2006.

————. "Linguaggi storiografici sulla Firenze rinascimentale." *Rivista storica Italiana* 97, no. 1 (1985): 102–59.

————. "Replica." *Rivista storica Italiana* 98, no. 3 (1986): 922–25.

Neal, Larry. *The Rise of Financial Capitalism: International Capital Markets in the Age of Reason*. Cambridge, UK: Cambridge University Press, 1990.

Nelson, Ralph L. *Concentration in the Manufacturing Industries of the United States*. New Haven, CT: Yale University Press, 1963.

Nigro, Giampiero, ed. *Francesco di Marco Datini: The Man the Merchant*. Florence: Firenze University Press, 2010.

Noonan, John T. Jr. *The Scholastic Analysis of Usury*. Cambridge, MA: Harvard University Press, 1957.

North, Douglass C. *Institutions, Institutional Change, and Economic Performance*. Cambridge, UK: Cambridge University Press, 1990.

————. *Structure and Change in Economic History*. New York: W. W. Norton and Co., 1981.

————. *Understanding the Process of Economic Change*. Princeton, NJ: Princeton University Press, 2005.

North, Douglass C., and Barry R. Weingast. "Constitutions and Commitment: The Evolution of Institutional Governing Public Choice in Seventeenth-Century England." *Journal of Economic History* 49, no. 4 (1989): 803–32.

North, Douglass C., and Robert Paul Thomas. *The Rise of the Western World. A New Economic History.* Cambridge, UK: Cambridge University Press, 1973.

North, Douglass C., John Joseph Wallis and Barry R. Weingast. *Violence and Social Orders: A Conceptual Framework for Interpreting Recorded Human History*. Cambridge, UK: Cambridge University Press, 2009.

O'Hara, Maureen. *Market Microstructure Theory*. Malden, MA: Blackwell, 1995.

Ogilvie, Sheilagh C. *A Bitter Living: Women, Markets, and Social Capital in Early Modern Germany*. Oxford, UK: Oxford University Press, 2003.

————. "The Economics of the Guild." *Journal of Economic Perspectives* 28, no. 4 (2014): 169–92.

————. "Guilds, Efficiency, and Social Capital: Evidence from German Proto-Industry." *Economic History Review*, 2nd ser., 57, no. 2 (2004): 286–333.

————. *Institutions and European Trade: Merchant Guilds, 1000–1800*. Cambridge, UK: Cambridge University Press, 2011.

————. "Rehabilitating the Guilds: A Reply." *Economic History Review* 61, no. 1 (2008): 175–82.

————. *State Corporatism and Proto Industry: The Wurttemberg Black Forest: 1580–1797.* Cambridge, UK: Cambridge University Press, 1997.

————. "'Whatever Is, Is Right'? Economic Institutions in Pre-Industrial Europe." *Economic History Review* 60, no. 4 (2007): 649–84.

Ogilvie, Sheilagh, C., and Markus Cerman, eds. *European Proto Industrialization.* Cambridge, UK: Cambridge University Press, 1996.

Olson, Mancur. *The Logic of Collective Action: Public Goods and the Theory of Groups.* Cambridge, MA: Harvard University Press, 1971.

Online *Tratte* of Office Holders, 1282–1532, Florence, Italy. Florentine Renaissance Resources, Online *Tratte* of Office Holders, 1282–1532 [machine-readable data file]. David Herlihy, R. Burr Litchfield, Anthony Molho and Roberto Barducci, eds. Florentine Renaissance Resources/STG: Brown University, Providence, Rhode Island, 2002.

Origo, Iris. *The Merchant of Prato: Francesco di Marco Datini 1335–1410.* New York: Alfred A. Knopf, 1957.

Otis, Leah L. "Municipal Wet Nurses in Fifteenth-Century Montpellier." In *Women and Work in Preindustrial Europe,* edited by Barbara A. Hanawalt, 83–93. Bloomington: Indiana University Press, 1986.

Padgett, John F. "Open Elite? Social Mobility, Marriage, and Family in Florence, 1282–1494." *Renaissance Quarterly* 63 (2010): 357–411.

Pamuk, Sevket. "The Black Death and the Origins of the 'Great Divergence' across Europe, 1300–1600." *European Review of Economic History* 11 (2007): 289–317.

Parsons, Talcott. *The Structure of Social Action: A Study in Social Theory with Special Reference to a Group of Recent European Writers,* vol. 1. 1937; New York: Free Press, 1968.

Persson, Karl Gunnar. *Pre-Industrial Economic Growth: Social Organization and Technological Progress in Europe.* Oxford, UK: Blackwell, 1988.

Pezzolo, Luciano. "Bonds and Government Debt in Italian City-States, 1250–1650." In *The Origins of Value: The Financial Innovations That Created Modern Capital Markets.* International Center for Finance at the Yale School of Management, edited by William N. Goetzman and K. Geert Rouwenhorst, 145–63. Oxford, UK: Oxford University Press, 2005.

————. *Una finanza d'Ancien Régime: La Repubblica veneta tra XV e XVIII secolo.* Vol. 8, Storia Finanziara: Collana di Studi, Atti e Documenti. Naples: Edizioni Scientifiche Italiane, 2006.

————. *Una finanza d'Ancien Régime: La Repubblica veneta tra XV e XVIII secolo.* Naples: Edizioni Scientifiche Italiane, 2009.

————. "Fiscal System and Finance in Northern Italy in the Early Modern Age." Unpublished paper. Università degli Studi di Venezia, 2003.

————. *Il fisco dei veneziani: Finanza pubblica ed economia tra XV e XVII secolo.* Verona: Cierre, 2003.

————. "Government Debts and Credit Markets in Renaissance Italy." In *Government Debts and Financial Markets in Europe,* edited by Fausto Piola Caselli, 17–32. London: Pickering and Chatto, 2008.

————. "Italian Monti: The Origins of Bonds and Government Debt." Paper presented at the Yale School of Management Conference on the "History of Financial Innovation," New Haven, CT, 2003.

————. "Republics and Principalities in Italy." In *The Rise of Fiscal States: A Global History, 1500–1914,* edited by Bartolomé Yun-Casalilla and Patrick K. O'Brien, 267–84. Cambridge, UK: Cambridge University Press, 2012.

————. "The Venetian Government Debt, 1350–1650." In *Urban Public Debts: Urban Government and the Market for Annuities in Western Europe (14th–18th Centuries).* Studies in European Urban History (1100–1800), vol. 3, 61–74. Tourhout, Belgium: Brepols, 2003.

Pfister, Ulrich. "Craft Guilds and Economic Development in Early Modern Europe." In *Dalla corporazione alla società di mutuo soccorso,* edited by Paola Massa and Angelo Moioli, 287–308. Milan: Franco Angeli, 2004.

————. "Craft Guilds, the Theory of the Firm, and Early Modern Proto Industry." In *Guilds, Innovation, and the European Economy, 1400–1800*, edited by Stephan R. Epstein and Maarten Prak, 25–51. Cambridge, UK: Cambridge University Press, 2008.

Piccinni, Gabriella. "Le donne nella vita economica, sociale e politica dell'Italia medievale." In *Il lavoro delle donne*, edited by Angela Groppi, 5–46. Rome: Laterza, 1996.

Piketty, Thomas. *Capital in the Twenty-First Century*. Translated by Arthur Goldhammer. Cambridge, MA: Harvard University Press, 2014.

Piketty, Thomas, and Emmanuel Saez. "Income Inequality in the United States, 1913–1998." *Quarterly Journal of Economics* 118, no. 1 (2003): 1–39.

Pistarino, Geo. "La donna d' affari a Genova nel secolo XIII." In *Miscellanea di storia Italiana e mediterranea per Nino Lamboglia*, edited by G. Pistarino, 155–69. Genoa: Università di Genova, 1978.

Plesner, Johann. *L'émigration de la campagne à la ville libre de Florence au 13e siècle*. Copenhagen: Gylendal, 1934.

Pollak, Robert A., and Michael L. Wachter. "The Relevance of the Household Production Function and Its Implications for the Allocation of Time." *Journal of Political Economy* 83, no. 2 (1975): 255–78.

Posner, Richard A. *The Economics of Justice*. Cambridge, MA: Harvard University Press, 1983.

Prak, Maarten, ed. *Early Modern Capitalism: Economic and Social Change in Europe, 1400–1800*. London: Routledge, 2001.

Prak, Maarten, Catharina Lis, Jan Lucassen and Hugo Soly, eds. *Craft Guilds in the Early Modern Low Countries: Work, Power, and Representation*. Aldershot, UK: Ashgate Publishing, 2006.

Pratt, John W. "Risk Aversion in the Small and in the Large." *Econometrica* 32, no. 1/2 (1964): 122–36.

Preyer, Brenda. "I documenti sulle fondamenta di Palazzo Strozzi." In *Palazzo Strozzi metà millennio, 1489–1989: Atti del convegno di studi, Firenze, 3–6 luglio 1989*, 195–213. Rome: Istituto della Enciclopedia Italiana, 1991.

Pullan, Brian, ed. *Crisis and Change in the Venetian Economy in the Sixteenth and Seventeenth Centuries*. London: Methuen and Co. Ltd., 1968.

Repetti, Emanuele. *Dizionario geografico fisico storico della Toscana: I-VI*. Florence: A. Tofani, 1833–36.

Reyerson, Kathryn L. "Women in Business in Medieval Montpelier." In *Women and Work in Preindustrial Europe*, edited by Barbara Hanawalt, 117–44. Bloomington: Indiana University Press, 1986.

Richards, Gertrude. *Florentine Merchants in the Age of the Medici: Letters and Documents from the Selfridge Collection of Medici Manuscripts*. Cambridge, MA: Harvard University Press, 1932.

Richardson, Gary. "Brand Names before the Industrial Revolution." *National Bureau of Economic Research Working Paper*, no. 13930, April 2008.

————. "Guilds, Laws, and Markets for Manufactured Merchandise in Late-Medieval England." *Explorations in Economic History* 41, no. 1 (2004): 1–25.

————. "A Tale of Two Theories: Monopolies and Craft Guilds in Medieval England and Modern Imagination." *Journal of the History of Economic Thought* 23, no. 2 (2001): 217–42.

Riemer, Eleanor S. "'Women, Dowries, and Capital Investment in Thirteenth-Century Siena." In *The Marriage Bargain: Women and Dowries in European History*, edited by Marion A. Kaplan, 59–79. New York: Institute for Research in History, 1985.

Rivera, Milagros. "'Modelos de participación de las mujeres en la vida económica bajomedieval: 'Le livre des Trois Vertus' de Christine de Pizan (1364–1430)." In *La Donna nell'Economia Secc. XIII–XVIII*, edited by Simonetta Cavaciocchi, 605–11. Prato: Le Monnier, 1990.

Rodolico, Niccolò. *I Ciompi: Una pagina di storia del proletario operaio*. Florence: Sansoni, 1971.

————. "Il sistema monetario e le classi sociali nel Medio Evo." *Rivista Italiana di sociologia* 8 (1904): 462–69.

Roff, Shelley R. "'Appropriate to Her Sex'? Women's Participation on the Construction Site in Medieval and Early Modern Europe." In *Women and Wealth in Late Medieval Europe*, edited by Theresa Earenfight, 109–34. New York: Palgrave MacMillan, 2010.

Rolova, Aleksandra, "La Manifattura nell'industria tessile di Firenze del Cinquecento," In *Firenze e la Toscana dei Medici nell'Europa del'500. Vol. 1, Strumenti e veicoli della cultura relazioni politiche ed economiche*, 309–25. Florence: Leo S. Olschki, 1983.

Romano, Ruggiero. "A Florence au XVIIe siècle: Industries textiles et conjoncture." *Annales. Histoire, Sciences Sociales* 7, no. 4 (1952): 508–12.

Rosen, Harvey S., Kenneth T. Rosen and Douglas Holtz-Eakin. "Housing Tenure, Uncertainty, and Taxation." *Review of Economics and Statistics* 66 (1984): 405–46.

Ross, Edward A. "Uncertainty as a Factor in Production." *Annals of the American Academy of Political and Social Sciences* 8 (1896): 92–119.

Rossi, Barbara. "Exchange Rate Predictability." *Journal of Economic Literature* 53, no. 4 (2013): 1063–119.

Rothschild, Nan A. *New York City Neighborhoods: The 18th Century*. San Diego: Academic Press, 1990.

Rugolo, Carmela Maria. "Donna e lavoro nella Sicilia del basso Medioevo." In *Donne e lavoro nell'Italia medievale*, edited by Bruno Andreoli, Paola Galetti and Maria Giuseppina Muzzarelli, 67–82. Turin: Rosenberg & Sellier, 1991.

Ruiz Martín, Felipe. *Lettres marchandes échanges entre Florence et Medina del Campo*. Paris: Armand Colin, 1965.

Sabbatini, Renzo, and Antonella Moriani. "Corporazioni e vita cittadina nella 'Toscana minore': Alcuni considerazioni su Lucca, Arezzo e Siena." In *Dalla corporazione alla società di mutuo soccorso*, edited by Paola Massa and Angelo Moioli, 107–36. Milan: Franco Angeli 2004.

Safley, Thomas Max, and Leonard N. Rosenband. *The Workplace before the Factory: Artisans and Proletarians, 1500–1800*. Ithaca, NY: Cornell University Press, 1993.

Sahlins, Marshall D. *Stone Age Economics*. London: Routledge, 1978.

Salutati, Coluccio. *Epistolario di Coluccio Salutati*, edited by Francesco Novati, vol. 2. Rome: Istituto Storico Italiano, 1891–1911.

Sapori, Armando, ed. *Una compagnia di Calimala ai primi del Trecento*. Florence: Leo S. Olschki, 1932.

———. *The Italian Merchant in the Middle Ages*. Translated by Patricia Ann Kennen. New York: Norton, 1970.

———. *I Libri degli Alberti del Giudice*. Milan: Garzanti, 1952.

———, ed., *I Libri di Commercio dei Peruzzi*. Milan: Fratelli Treves, 1934.

———, ed., *Libro Giallo della Compagnia dei Covoni*. Milan: Cisalpino, 1970.

Sargent, Thomas J., and François R. Velde. *The Big Problem of Small Change*. Princeton, NJ: Princeton University Press, 2002.

Scargill, D. I. *The Forms of Cities*. New York: St. Martin's, 1979.

Schaefer, Donald F. "A Model of Migration and Wealth Accumulation: Farmers at the Antebellum Southern Frontier." *Explorations in Economic History* 24 (1987): 130–57.

Scherman, Matthieu. "La distribuzione della ricchezza in una città: Treviso e I suoi estimi (1434–1499)." In *Ricchezza, valore, proprietà in età preindustriale 1400–1850*, edited by Guido Alfani and Michela Barbot, 169–84. Venice: Marsilio, 2009.

Schmarzo, Bill. *Big Data MBA: Driving Business Success with Data Science*. Indianapolis: Wiley, 2015.

Schmid, Boris V., Ulf Büntgen, W. Ryan Easterday, Christian Ginzler, Lars Walløe, Barbara Bramanti and Nils Chr Stenseth. "Climate-Driven Introduction of the Black Death and Successive Plague Reintroductions into Europe." *Proceedings of the National Academy of Sciences* 112, no. 10 (2015): 3020–25.

Schnore, Leo F., and Peter R. Knights. "Residence and Social Structure: Boston in the Ante-Bellum Period." In *Nineteenth-Century Cities*, edited by Stephan Thernstrom and Richard Sennett, 247–57. New Haven, CT: Yale University Press, 1969.

Schultz, Theodore W. "Nobel Lecture: The Economics of Being Poor." *Journal of Political Economy* 88, no. 4 (1980): 639–51.

Schumpeter, Joseph A. *The Theory of Economic Development: An Inquiry into Profits, Capital, Credit, Interest, and the Business Cycle*. Translated by Redvers Opie. 1934; New Brunswick, NJ: Transaction, 1983.

Scott, William Robert. *The Constitution and Finance of English, Scottish and Irish Joint-Stock Companies to 1720. Vol. 1 , The General Development of the Joint-Stock System to 1720.* Cambridge, UK: Cambridge University Press, 1912.

Segalen, Martine. "Review of *Women, Family, and Ritual in Renaissance Florence,* by Christiane Klapisch-Zuber." *American Journal of Sociology* 92 (1986): 203–5.

Sella, Domenico. "Industrial Production in Seventeenth-Century Italy: A Reappraisal." *Explorations in Entrepreneurial History,* ser. 2, 6 (1969): 235–53.

———. "Les Mouvements longs: L'industrie lainière à Venise aux XVIe et XVIIe siècles." *Annales: Économies, Sociétes, Civilisations* 12 (1957): 29–45.

———. "The Rise and Fall of the Venetian Woolen Industry." In *Crisis and Change in the Venetian Economy in the Sixteenth and Seventeenth Centuries,* edited by Brian Pullen, 106–26. London: Methuen, 1965.

Shannon, Claude E., and Warren Weaver. *The Mathematical Theory of Communication.* Urbana: University of Illinois Press, 1963.

Shevky, Eshref, and Wendell Bell. *Social Area Analysis: Theory, Illustrative Application and Computational Procedures.* Stanford, CA: Stanford University Press, 1955.

Shorrocks, A. F. "The Age-Wealth Relationship: A Cross-Section and Cohort Analysis." *Review of Economics and Statistics* 57, no. 2 (1975): 155–63.

Silva, José-Gentile da. "Aux XVIIe siècle: La strategié du capital florentin," *Annales E. S. C.* 19 (1964): 480–91.

Silvey, S. D. "The Lagrangian Multiplier Test." *Annals of Mathematical Statistics* 30, no. 2 (1959): 389–407a.

Simms, Anngert, "Medieval Dublin: A Topographical Analysis." *Irish Geography* 12 (1979): 25–41

Sjaastad, Larry A. "The Costs and Returns of Human Migration." *Journal of Political Economy* 70, no. 5, pt. 2 (1962): 80–93.

Sjoberg, Gideon. "The Preindustrial City." *American Journal of Sociology* 60, no. 5 (1955): 438–45.

———. *The Preindustrial City: Past and Present.* New York: Free Press, 1960.

Smith, Adam. *The Wealth of Nations.* Edited by Alan Krueger. 1776; New York: Bantam Dell, 2003.

Sogner, Solvi, and Hilde Sandvik. "Minors in Law, Partners in Work, Equals in Worth? Women in the Norwegian Economy in the 16th to the 18th Centuries." In *La Donna nell'Economia Secc. XIII–XVIII,* edited by Simonetta Cavaciocchi, 633–53. Prato: Le Monnier, 1990.

Solow, Robert M. "A Contribution to the Theory of Economic Growth." *Quarterly Journal of Economics* 70, no. 1 (1956): 65–94.

Soltow, Lee. *Men and Wealth in the United States, 1850–1870.* New Haven, CT: Yale University Press, 1973.

Soltow, Lee, and Jan Luiten Van Zanden. *Income and Wealth Inequality in the Netherlands 16th–20th Century.* Amsterdam: Het Spinhuis, 1998.

Sombart, Werner. *Der moderne Kapitalismus: Historisch-systematische Darstellung des gesamteuropäischen Wirtschaftslebens von seinen Anfängen bis zur Gegenwart,* 3 vols. Munich: Duncker & Humblot, 1924–27.

Spallanzani, Marco, ed. *Produzione, commercio e consumo de panni di lana nei secoli XII–XVII, Istituto internazionale di storia economica 'F. Datini'Prato, Series II: Atti delle 'Settimane di Studio'e altri convegni.* Florence: Leo S. Olschki, 1976.

Spence, A. Michael. *Market Signaling: Informational Transfer in Hiring and Related Screening Processes.* Cambridge, MA: Harvard University Press, 1974.

Spence, Craig. *London in the 1690s: A Social Atlas.* London: University of London, 2000.

Spillman, W. J. "The Agricultural Ladder." *American Economic Review: Papers and Proceedings* 9 (1919): 170–79.

Staley, Edgcumbe. *The Guilds of Florence: Illustrated after Miniatures in Illuminated Manuscripts and Florentine Woodcuts.* 1906; New York: Benjamin Blom, 1967.

Stark, Rodney. *The Rise of Christianity: How the Obscure, Marginal Jesus Movement Became the Dominant Religious Force in the Western World in a Few Centuries.* San Francisco: HarperSanFrancisco, 1996.

Stasavage, David. *Public Debt and the Birth of the Democratic State: France and Great Britain, 1688–1789*. Cambridge, UK: Cambridge University Press, 2003.

——. *States of Credit: Size, Power, and the Development of European Politics*. Princeton, NJ: Princeton University Press, 2011.

Steckel, Richard H. "Poverty and Prosperity: A Longitudinal Study of Wealth Accumulation, 1850–1860." *Review of Economics and Statistics* 72, no. 2 (1990): 275–85.

Stefani, Marchionne di Coppo. *Cronaca fiorentina*. Edited by Niccolò Rodolico. 1913; Florence: Reggello, 2008.

Stella, Alessandro. *La révolte des Ciompi: Les hommes, les lieux, le travail*. Paris: Editions de l'Ecole des Hautes Etudes en Sciences Sociales, 1993.

Stifel, Laurence. "Patterns of Land Ownership in Central Thailand during the Twentieth Century." *Journal of Siam Society* (1976): 237–74.

Stigler, George J. "Competition." In *The Organization of Industry*, 5–22. Chicago: University of Chicago Press, 1968.

——. "The Division of Labor Is Limited by the Extent of the Market." *Journal of Political Economy* 59, no. 3 (1951): 185–93.

——. "The Economies of Scale." *Journal of Law and Economics* 1 (1958): 54–71.

——. "Measurement of Concentration." In *The Organization of Industry*. Chicago: University of Chicago Press, 1968, 29–38.

Stigler, George J., and Gary S. Becker. "De Gustibus Non Est Disputandum." *American Economic Review* 67, no. 2 (1977): 76–90.

Stone, Lewi, Ronen Olinky and Amit Huppert. "Seasonal Dynamics of Recurrent Epidemics." *Nature* 446 (2007): 533–36.

Strocchia, Sharon T. "Death Rites and the Ritual Family in Renaissance Florence." In *Life and Death in Fifteenth-Century Florence*, edited by Marcel Tetel, Ronald G. Witt and Rona Goffen, 120–45. Durham, NC: Duke University Press, 1989.

Stuard, Susan Mosher. "Dowry and Other Marriage Gifts." In *Women and Gender in Medieval Europe: An Encyclopedia*, edited by Margaret Schaus, 229–31. London: Routledge, 2006.

——. "To Town to Serve: Urban Domestic Slavery in Medieval Ragusa." In *Women and Work in Preindustrial Europe*, edited by Barbara A. Hanawalt, 39–55. Bloomington: Indiana University Press, 1986.

Tanzini, Lorenzo. "Tuscan States: Florence and Siena." In *The Italian Renaissance State*, edited by Andrea Gamberini and Isabella Lazzarini, 90–111. Cambridge, UK: Cambridge University Press, 2012.

Tien, Joseph H., Hendrik N. Poinar, David N. Fisman and David J. D. Earn. "Herald Waves of Cholera in Nineteenth-Century London." *Journal of the Royal Society Interface* 8, no. 58 (2011): 756–60.

Tilly, Charles. *Coercion, Capital, and European States, A.D. 990–1992*. Cambridge, MA: Blackwell, 1992.

Timms, Duncan W. G. *The Urban Mosaic: Towards a Theory of Residential Differentiation*. Cambridge, UK: Cambridge University Press, 1971.

Tinbergen, Jan. "Substitution of Graduate by Other Labour." *Kyklos* 27, no. 2 (1974): 217–26

Tobin, James. "The Interest-Elasticity of Transactions Demand for Cash." *Review of Economics and Statistics* 38, no. 3 (1956): 241–47.

——. "Liquidity Preference as Behavior Towards Risk." *Review of Economic Studies* 25 (1958): 65–86.

Tognetti, Sergio. *Il Banco Cambini: Affari e mercati di una compagnia mercantile-bancaria nella Firenze del XV secolo*. Florence: Olschki, 1999.

——. "The Development of the Florentine Silk Industry: A Positive Response to the Crisis of the Fourteenth Century." *Journal of Medieval History* 31, no. 1 (2005): 55–69.

——. *Un'industria di lusso al servizio del grande commercio: Il mercato dei drappi serici e della seta nella Firenze del Quattrocento*. Florence: Leo S. Olschki, 2002.

Tomas, Natalie R. *The Medici Women: Gender and Power in Renaissance Florence*. Aldershot, UK: Ashgate, 2003.

Topel, Robert, and Sherwin Rosen. "Housing Investment in the United States." *Journal of Political Economy* (1988): 718–40.

Trachtenberg, Marvin. *Dominion of the Eye: Urbanism, Art, and Power in Early Modern Florence.* Cambridge, UK: Cambridge University Press, 1997.

Trexler, Richard C. "La prostitution florentine au 15e siècle." *Annales E.S.C.*, 1981, 983–1015.

———. *Public Life in Renaissance Florence.* New York: Academic Press, 1980.

Tufte, Edward R. *The Visual Display of Quantitative Information.* Cheshire, CT: Graphics Press, 1983.

Unwin, George. *Industrial Organization in the Sixteenth and Seventeenth Centuries.* Oxford, UK: Clarendon Press, 1904.

US Bureau of the Census. *Household Wealth and Asset Ownership: 1984.* Washington, DC: US Government Printing Office, 1986.

US Department of Justice and the Federal Trade Commission. "Market Concentration in Horizontal Merger Guidelines, Issued August 19, 2010." http://www.justice.gov/atr/public/guidelines/hmg-2010.html#5c.

Van Zanden, Jan Luiten. *The Long Road to the Industrial Revolution: The European Economy in a Global Perspective, 1000–1800.* Leiden: Brill, 2009.

———. "The Skill Premium and the 'Great Divergence.'" *European Review of Economic History* 13 (2009): 121–53.

———. "Tracing the Beginning of the Kuznets Curve: Western Europe during the Early Modern Period." *Economic History Review* 48, no. 4 (1995): 643–64.

Vance, James E. "Land Assignment in the Precapitalist, Capitalist, and Postcapitalist City." *Economic Geography* 47, no. 2 (1971): 101–20.

Varian, Hal R. *Microeconomic Analysis*, 3rd ed. New York: Norton, 1992.

Veblen, Thorstein. *The Theory of the Leisure Class*, unabridged. 1899; New York: Dover, 1994.

Veseth, Michael. *Mountains of Debt: Crisis and Change in Renaissance Florence, Victorian Britain, and Postwar America.* New York: Oxford University Press, 1990.

Voigtländer, Nico and Hans-Joachim Voth, "Malthusian Dynamism and the Rise of Europe: Make War, Not Love, Urbanization, Mortality, and Fertility in Malthusian England, Disease and Development: Historical and Contemporary Perspectives." *American Economic Review: Papers and Proceedings* 99, no. 2 (2009): 248–54.

Weber, Max. *The City.* Translated by Don Martindale and Gertrud Neuwirth. New York: Free Press, 1958.

———. *The Protestant Ethic and the Spirit of Capitalism and Other Writings*, edited and translated by Peter Baehr and Gordon C. Wells. New York: Penguin, 2002.

Weissman, Ronald F. E. *Ritual Brotherhood in Renaissance Florence.* New York: Academic Press, 1982.

Welch, Finis, ed. *The Causes and Consequences of Increasing Inequality.* Chicago: University of Chicago Press, 2001.

Wheatley, Paul. "What the Greatness of a City Is Said to Be: Reflections on Sjoberg's 'Preindustrial City.'" *Pacific Viewpoint* 4 (1963): 163–88.

White, Eugene N., Kenneth Snowden and Price Fishback, eds. *Housing and Mortgage Markets in Historical Perspective.* Chicago: University of Chicago Press, 2014.

Whittle, Peter. *Prediction and Regulation by Linear Least Square Methods.* 2nd ed. rev. Minneapolis: University of Minnesota Press, 1983.

Wiesner, Merry E. "Early Modern Midwifery: A Case Study." In *Women and Work in Preindustrial Europe*, edited by Barbara A. Hanawalt, 94–114. Bloomington: Indiana University Press, 1986.

———. "Guilds, Male Bonding, and Women's Work in Early Modern Germany." In *La Donna nell'Economia Secc. XIII–XVIII*, edited by Simonetta Cavaciocchi, 655–69. Prato: Le Monnier, 1990.

———. *Working Women in Renaissance Germany.* New Brunswick, NJ: Rutgers University Press, 1986.

Williamson, Oliver E. *The Economic Institutions of Capitalism.* New York: Free Press, 1985.

———. *Markets and Hierarchies: Analysis and Antitrust Implications.* New York: Free Press, 1975.

Witt, Ronald G. *Hercules at the Crossroads: The Life, Works, and Thought of Coluccio Salutati.* Durham, NC: Duke University Press, 1983.

Wolff, Edward N. "The Accumulation of Household Wealth over the Life-Cycle: A Microdata Analysis." *Review of Income and Wealth* 27, no. 1 (1981): 75–79.

———. *Inheriting Wealth in America: Future Boom or Bust?* Oxford, UK: Oxford University Press, 2015.

Wood, Alfred Cecil. *A History of the Levant Company.* London: Frank Cass and Co., 1964.

Yunus, Muhammad. *Banker to the Poor: Micro-lending and the Battle against World Poverty.* 1999; New York: Perseus, 2007.

Zell, Michael. *Industry in the Countryside: Wealden Society in the Sixteenth Century, Cambridge Studies in Population, Economy, and Society in Past Time.* Cambridge, UK: Cambridge University Press, 1994.

Zellner, Arnold. "An Efficient Method of Estimating Seemingly Unrelated Regressions and Tests for Aggregation Bias." *Journal of the American Statistical Association* 57, no. 298 (1962): 348–68.

Zhang, Junsen, and William Chan. "Dowry and Wife's Welfare: A Theoretical and Empirical Analysis." *Journal of Political Economy* 107, no. 4 (1999): 786–808.

Ziliak, Stephan T., and Deirdre N. McCloskey. *The Cult of Statistical Significance: How the Standard Error Costs Us Jobs, Justice, and Lives.* Ann Arbor: University of Michigan Press, 2008.

Zucca Micheletto, Beatrice. "À quoi sert la dot? Aliénations dotales, économie familiale et stratégies des couples à Turin au XVIIIe siècle." *Annales de Démographie Historique* 121 (2011): 161–86.

———. "Reconsidering the Southern Europe Model: Dowry, Women's Work, and Marriage Patterns in Pre-industrial Urban Italy (Turin, Second Half of the 18th Century)." *History of the Family* 16 (2011): 354–70.

.

INDEX